WYTHE COUNTY CHAPTERS:

A GATHERING OF MATERIALS FROM SCARCE, RARE OR OUT-OF-PRINT SOURCES ABOUT WYTHE COUNTY, VIRGINIA

James S. Presgraves

HERITAGE BOOKS
2008

HERITAGE BOOKS
AN IMPRINT OF HERITAGE BOOKS, INC.

Books, CDs, and more—Worldwide

For our listing of thousands of titles see our website at
www.HeritageBooks.com

Published 2008 by
HERITAGE BOOKS, INC.
Publishing Division
100 Railroad Ave. #104
Westminster, Maryland 21157

Copyright © 1972 James S. Presgraves

All rights reserved. No part of this book may be reproduced or transmitted in any form or by any means, electronic or mechanical, including photocopying, recording or by any information storage and retrieval system without written permission from the author, except for the inclusion of brief quotations in a review.

International Standard Book Numbers
Paperbound: 978-0-7884-1379-7
Clothbound: 978-0-7884-7023-3

TABLE OF CONTENTS

Hardesty's Historical and Geographical Encyclopedia... Special Virginia Edition...Special Information in Regard to Wythe County	1
Boyd, Charles. *Resources of South-west Virginia Showing the Mineral Deposits*	23
Bruce, Thomas. *Southwest Virginia and Shenandoah Valley*	71
Whitman, James. *The Iron Industry of Wythe County From 1792*	79
Whitman, James. *Historical Facts About The Churches of Wythe County*	117
Chataigne's Virginia Gazetteer and Classified Business Directory 1893 - 1894	171
Heuser, H.M. *A Short Historical and Physical Description of Wythe County, Virginia*	185
Wytheville: Illustrated Prospectus of the "Mountain City"	199
Nye Lithia Springs	249
Map of Wytheville. *Gray's Atlas*, Ca. 1883	262
Hardesty's Historical and Geographical Encyclopedia... Special Virginia Edition...Personal Histories of Wythe County	267
Daniel, J.R.V. *Jack Jouett and Paul Revere in Petticoats. The Heroine of the Battle of Wytheville*	299
Coleman, Elizabeth D. *Showers of Shot* [Old Shot Tower]	303
Davis, Curtis C. *That Daring Young Man* [James Hays Piper]	306
Davis, Curtis C. *The Small Bang at Bangs* [Crockett-Wise Duel]	313
Index	321

Please note that the table of contents gives page references. Individual bibliographic details appear on the title pages of those volumes from which extracts have been made, while no bibliographic data was felt necessary for items reproduced completely.

Preface

In 1959, when I began teaching in Richmond, one of the chapters in the Virginia history text referred to the part Wythe County played in the War of 1812. Determined Wythe men marched north, participated in the Battle of Lake Erie, and brought home a trophy, a ship's bell. It is not remarkable that they succeeded in their capture; but bringing home the bell is remarkable when one remembers the difficult travel conditions they faced. In 1962, I was privileged, as President of the Secondary Teachers Association of Richmond, to be a delegate to the National Education Association's annual meeting in Denver, Colorado; the return trip brought me through Wytheville where wide streets and Otis Durham's hospitality made lasting and pleasant impressions. My wife and I moved to Wytheville in 1967 when I became Coordinator of the Learning Laboratory at the Community College. Today, July 1, 1972, marks the beginning of my sixth year here, and I have come to know and respect that same determination that characterized my first acquaintance over a decade ago.

One major difficulty in finding material about Wythe County is that, up to now, there has been no history, compact and available, of the county. To accomplish the self-imposed task of learning more about the area, I have had to search beyond the county boundaries—even beyond the state of Virginia—to acquire the materials contained herein. Indeed, one of the volumes used in this work came from a helpful bookdealer in California, another from Tennessee, and still others from closer home. The point is that no book currently brings these materials together in a readily available form.

This work, therefore, seeks to assemble the printed material I have collected, together with other items loaned by citizens of Wythe who likewise feel this need for a history. This collection is in no way complete, and I hope to encourage the development of another volume which will amplify and supplement from still other sources the lore and traditions of this county. Certain limitations are readily apparent in this compilation. For one thing, many authors borrowed freely and liberally from each other or from the same source, and they perpetuated errors in dating, names, locations and the like. For another, there should be at least as much material I have not found, particularly in periodicals, newspapers, attics, basements, and private hoards. Also, recording oral history will preserve a vast mine of information soon to disappear; and the primary sources in the record offices of Wythe and its parent counties also need to be compiled, edited, and made available. Another limitation to this effort is in terms of a cut-off date; the dates used here largely reflect availability rather than any arbitrary standard.

Elizabeth Barrett Browning once said, "How do I love thee? Let me count the ways." Who should I thank? Let me try to name those who helped: Mrs. Helen Grove, Ray O. Hummel, Jr., and Anna Ray Roberts for library assistance; the late James Blackford, Berkeley Franklin, F. M. Hill, Mary Clark Roane, and Bernard Way for making available scarce titles at reasonable prices; Reid Fulton for being an experience unto himself; the late F. B. Kegley for inspiration beyond the grave; Mrs. Mary B. Kegley for assistance, encouragement, and a host of valuable data; Mr. and Mrs. Garland Stephens, Paul Heuser, P. A. Early, and Mrs. Albert Shumate for sharing from their resources; James E. Crockett and Mrs. Eleanor Terry Noel for insight and suggestions; James A. Williams, Jr., for never saying no when I had a question; and all the citizens of Wythe county for hospitality, friendship, and their continued good graces.

A special note of thanks to Mrs. Genevieve Simmerman and her sister, Mrs. Marion Lambert, for permission to reproduce faithfully the two pamphlets of their father Mr. Whitman. It will be noted that there is no final note of thanks. I don't think the poetess had a final way to express her love; likewise, there is no final person to thank—Who knows now who will purchase the last copy of this book?

Jim Presgraves

Introduction

Not everyone can afford to buy out-of print rare books in order to have certain information in a library collection. Many books of this type cannot be circulated from any library and in many instances the books are not part of local collections.

Mr. James Presgraves has therefore performed a service to the community by gathering scarce books and pamphlets, and abstracting from them items pertaining to Wythe County. These hard-to-find items are now consolidated in one volume bringing together for the first time past writings concerning our County and some of its people. This volume will be a welcome addition to most personal and public libraries and will bring to their attention information they perhaps did not know existed.

The problem with such a collection appears to be the acceptance of its authenticity. Has there been new evidence found during research on Wythe County that would change or modify the materials presented here? The answer of course is yes, and every day can bring further enlightenment leading to still further changes. No doubt each author presented what he knew to the best of his ability at the time. With the collection representing a period of over 150 years, it should be pointed out that some errors do exist in the original material. As it goes to press still others may be found.

Some of these descrepancies have been brought to my attention over the years. It seems fair to pass this information on to the reading public, with the contribution in no sense to be considered critical to the author or to the compiler but rather constructive to the understanding of those who read from these pages. Specifically then, let me bring to the reader's attention some details that may need clarification.

On page 188 the date of 1750 for the discovery of lead is probably too early. Most authorities state this took place in 1756, and the mineral company celebrated its 200th anniversary in 1956 commemorating this event in Austinville. Although Colonel Chiswell did discover the lead, he did not establish Fort Chiswell; rather it was his good friend William Byrd who is generally given credit for its establishment, and it was Byrd who chose to name it for his friend, Chiswell. The date of 1756 is too early for its establishment, the army being there in the fall of 1760 and the name first being used early in 1761.

A picture on page 197 is designated as part of Old Fort Chiswell erected in 1755, a date which does not correspond with the statement on page 188, nor to the date suggested above. The question has also been raised concerning the ownership of this particular building. Was it a Courthouse as so often mentioned in local accounts, or was it a jail as suggested by Howe in his book. Was it constructed by the armies who passed this way during the French and Indian War, at the same time as the Fort was established? To date no document has been found to answer this question, but perhaps a future archeological salvage operation will assist in this respect.

On page 194 Cornwallis should read Cornstalk. General Smyth did not defeat the British on Lake Erie but was relieved of his command as a consequence of his inaction against the British.

Page 88 mentions Poplar Camp furnace as possibly being established about 1790, but it may have been there as early as 1778, for a stone bearing that date was found and identified with the furnace. (James Swank's Iron Mfg. 1891, p. 268.)

Page 91 states, quoting Watson, that the Grahams operated the Cedar Run Furnace from 1800 till the coming of the coke furnaces. The reader should also see the commentary on pps. 103 and 104 in which Mr. Whitman substantiates the status of the Crocketts, Andrew and James, as the initial operators of the Furnace. Likewise on page 189 a date of 1832 is given for the Cedar Run Furnace; but both the furnace and the forge were purchased by David Graham in 1826, and from that time since were operated under Graham ownership. (Deed Book 10-361.)

Page 48 mentions a Mount Airy which was then a town in western Wythe County, and it should not be confused with the town of same name in North Carolina.

The shot tower mentioned on page 54 should not be confused with the one near Jackson's Ferry on the New River which was abandoned many years before.

Finally the reader is cautioned that names were sometimes inaccurately spelled through oral or written errors. Cassel sometimes was transcribed as Kapel (page 131). Sometimes translations such as Braun — Brown were made. Also pronunciation shifts sometimes resulted in Bruner — Pruner or Geckley — Kegley. These errors should not be taken as a reflection on the work of those who recorded them, but rather they should be noted so that all phonetic possibilities can be explored.

Mary Kegley

HISTORY OF
WYTHE COUNTY

Taken from *Hardesty's Historical and Geographical Encyclopedia, Special Supplement* by R. A. Brock - New York, 1884. pps. 404-409.

ITS ORIGIN.

In 1634, twenty-seven years after the landing at Jamestown, Virginia was divided into eight counties or shires, similar to the minor civil divisions of England; these, the first counties formed in the New World, were named as follows: James City, Henrico, Charles City, Elizabeth City, Warwick River, Warrosquoyacke (changed in 1637 to Isle of Wight), Charles River and Accomack. The population rapidly increased, and settlements were extended in every direction. Virginia ever tried to keep civil government abreast with her most adventurous pioneers. To accomplish this her house of burgesses continued to make provision for the formation of new counties. An hundred years passed away, and at the close there were no less than thirty-one counties checkered upon the map of her eastern domain. After the eight original ones came the others in the order named: Northampton and Gloucester, in 1642; Northumberland, in 1648; Surry and Lancaster, in 1652; Westmoreland, in 1653; Sussex and New Kent, in 1654; Stafford and Middlesex, in 1675; Norfolk, Princess Anne, and King and Queen, in 1691; Richmond, in 1692; King William, in 1701; Prince George, in 1702; Spotsylvania, King George, Hanover, and Brunswick, in 1720, and Goochland and Caroline, in 1727.

In 1716, under the leadership of Alexander Spotswood, then lieutenant-governor of Virginia, the Blue Ridge was crossed, and the illimitable wilderness west of it was opened to settlement. In 1734, Orange county was formed, all Virginia's vast western domains included in its boundaries. In 1738, this county was divided, the portion west of the Blue Ridge becoming the district of West Augusta. The years passed on, settlement pushed steadily west and southwest, the pioneers of the Old Dominion founding homes south of the James, on the Roanoke and over on the waters of the Holston. Civilization was reducing the wilds of West Augusta, and in 1769 Botetourt county was formed, for the convenience of the settlers in the southwest part of the colony. In 1772, Fincastle county was formed, and in 1776 the title was extinguished and three distinct counties formed from its territory,

Kentuckie, Washington and Montgomery. Nearly 12,000 square miles were included in what was then Montgomery county; since then, twenty-five counties have been taken, wholly or in part, from it. These are: Greenbrier, in 1778; Kanawha, in 1789; Wythe, 1790; Grayson, 1793; Monroe, 1799; Mason, 1804; Giles, 1806; Cabell, 1809; Logan, 1824; Floyd, 1831; Mercer, 1837; Pulaski, 1839; Tazewell, 1799; Raleigh, 1848; Wayne, 1842; Fayette, 1831; Putnam, 1848; Roanoke, 1838; Summers, 1867; Lincoln, 1867; Craig, 1848; Boone, 1849; McDowell, 1866; Wyoming, 1865; and Bland, 1847. Wythe county was named in honor of George Wythe, the eminent chancellor of Virginia, and one of the signers of the Declaration of Independence. A sketch of his life is elsewhere given in these pages.

ITS BOUNDERIES, TOPOGRAPHY, PRODUCTIONS, RESOURCES, POPULATION.

Wythe county is bounded on the north by Bland and Pulaski counties, on the east by Pulaski and Carroll counties, on the south by Grayson county, on the west by Smyth county. New river flows across the southeastern part of the county, and its tributaries are the creeks that water the county. A spur of mountains separate Grayson and Carroll from Wythe, New river entering the county from Carroll between the hills. Small grain of all kinds is easily and profitably raised in the county, and the cereals are grown with facility. Grazing and the raising of fine stock occupies the attention of the farmers more and more in the years that have succeeded the war. The mineral wealth of the county is the resource whose future development should bring wealth into the county. Gypsum is found in the the county, there are large undeveloped beds of coal, iron is abundant everywhere, lead is found all along the river, and in working the lead mines, copper and silver specimens have been found. The Wythe valley is an elevated table-land, and the mean elevation of the county is 1,600 feet above sea level. The area of the county is 520 square miles.

In 1810 the population of Wythe county was 8,356; in 1820, 9,692; in 1830, about 10,000; in 1880 the census showed a population of 14,318. The following total of taxation in the county in 1834 has some curious features: On lots, $112.12; on land, $985.74; on 1,040 slaves, $260.00; on 4,326 horses, $259.56; on 26 studs, $223.00: on 11 coaches, $28.50; on 31 carryalls, $32.00; on 1 gig, 50 cents; total, $1,901.42. With over 4,000 horses, and less that 50 vehicles of all kinds, it is evident that horse-back riding was the fashionable method of travel in 1834.

Wytheville, the countyseat, had a population of 1,885 at the census enumeration of 1880, and is the principal station in the county of the Norfolk & Western Railroad, which passes through the very center of the county. The postoffices of the county are: Black Lick, Crockett Depot, Grahams Forge, Ivanhoe Furnace, Jacksons Ferry, Kents Mills, McTeer, Max Meadows, Red Bluff,

Reed Island, Rural Retreat, Speedwell, Wytheville. The lead mines are about thirteen miles east of the court house, on New river, opposite the mouth of Cripple creek. About nine miles east of Wytheville, within the present century stood Fort Chiswell, erected and occupied by British troops during Braddock's war. On the same spot was once the countyseat of Montgomery county. As late as 1840 a log hut was standing which had been used as a jail for the now almost forgotten countyseat of a county whose area was 12,000 square miles.

WYTHE COUNTY IN THE WAR BETWEEN THE STATES.

No section of Virginia, in proportion to its population, has furnished so many soldiers to uphold the honor of Virginia on the battlefields where her flag has been unfurled as that in which Wythe is now embraced. Ever since the first pioneers gained a foothold upon the highlands of Southwest Virginia, they or their descendants have been wherever the cause of suffering humanity, liberty and the rights of Virginia called them. For an hundred years they withstood the shock of savage warfare and witnessed the indiscriminate slaughter of men, women and children by a barbarous and relentless foe. But they came to conquer, not only the savage, but the wilderness in which they had sought a home for themselves and an inheritance for their posterity, and well they did their work. Scarcely a battlefield on this continent on which the blood of Virginians has not mingled with that of the sons of her sister colonies or states. They were at Fort Necessity and Braddock's defeat; at Point Pleasant and Donnelly's Fort; at Germantown, Brandywine, Kings Mountain, Guilford and Yorktown; at Fallen Timbers and Tippecanoe; at Fort Meigs and Norfolk; at Beuna Vista, Monterey, Vera Cruz and Mexico; at Bull Run, Seven Pines, Malvern Hill, Fredericksburg, Chancellorsville, Sharpsburg, South Mountain, Gettysburg, in the Wilderness, a hundred other bloody fields, and at Appomattox. We append, with some regimental mention, as complete a roster as diligent research has enabled us to gather, of Wythe county soldiers in the service during the civil war.

ROLL OF HONOR OF THE SOLDIERS OF WYTHE COUNTY.

[In the following rosters, where no date of enlistment is given, it was during the first year of the war; where no date of death or discharge, the service was till the close of the war; where no rank is given, the enlistment was as private. In the miscellaneous service are rosters of men who reside in Wythe county, but enlisted in other counties.]

CO. A, FOURTH VIRGINIA INFANTRY—"WYTHE GREYS."

The Wythe Greys were enlisted April 17, 1861, reported to Colonel James F. Preston, at Christiansburg, and on April 24th, with other companies under his command, forming the basis of a regiment, was transferred to Richmond, camping on the old fair grounds. After drilling there ten days these volunteers moved to Harpers Ferry, where eight companies were organized into the Fourth Virginia Infantry. These companies were the Montgomery Invincibles, Montgomery Highlanders, Fort Lewis Guards, Wythe Greys, Smyth Blues, Rockbridge Greys, Grayson Dare Devils, Liberty Hall Company. The Wythe Greys become Company A of the regiment, and the regiment was included in the First Virginia Brigade, with the Second, Fifth, Twenty-Seventh and Thirty-Third, the organization destined to pass into enduring history as the "Stonewall Brigade." The first fighting of the regiment was at Haynesville, near Martinsburg. Then it fell back to Winchester, and on the 18th of July it was force-marched to Piedmont, and went thence by rail to Manassas Junction, where it arrived on the 19th; remained inactive on the 20th and took a gallant part in the terrible battle of the 21st. The brigade remained in the vicinity of Fairfax Court House and Centerville until November, 1861, when it was transferred to Winchester, where it lay until January 2, 1862, when it marched to Bath, in Morgan county; thence to Hancock, on the Potomac, to intercept the Federal forces under General Kelly. Thence it marched on what was known as the "Romney Campaign," and after the utmost suffering retired to Winchester, and went into winter quarters about the 1st of February. It remained at Winchester until the middle of March, when the place was evacuated and the troops marched up the valley as far as Mount Jackson, in Shenandoah county, and from there force-marched back to Kernstown, where it took part in the battle of that place March 23, 1862, and the regiment fell back to New Market, thence into Rockingham county. During the spring of 1862 it was engaged in the battles of McDowell, Franklin, Front Royal, Winchester, Harpers Ferry, Cross Keys, Port Republic and numerous skirmishes.

In the latter part of June it was transferred to Richmond, marching on foot by way of Rockfish Gap and Charlottesville to Gordonsville, thence by rail on the Chesapeake & Ohio railroad to Beaver dam, and from there on foot to Cold Harbor, where it was engaged June 28, 1862, and on the 30th at White Oak Swamp, and later on in the desperate battles of Fraziers Farm and Malvern Hill. After the pursuit of the enemy as far as Westover, it returned to Gordonsville, took part in the battle of Cedar Run, the second battle of Manassas, shared the fortunes of Lee's army in the invasion of Maryland, was at the surrender of Harper's Ferry, the battles of South Mountain and Sharpsburg, and returned to Virginia and participated in the battle of Fredericksburg, December 13, 1862. It spent the winter at Guinea Station, and in May,

1863, was actively engaged in the sanguinary battle of Chancellorsville, where their idolized leader—Jackson—fell, after which it accompanied Lee in his invasion of Pennsylvania, was hotly engaged for three days at Gettysburg, and returned with the retreating army. The winter of 1863-64 was passed on the banks of the Rapidan river. During the summer of 1864 it took part in the battles of the Wilderness, and was in front of Grant's advance all the way from Spotsylvania Court House to Cold Harbor; was then transferred to the Valley, where it was with General Early in his advance upon Washington City, took part in the battles of Monocacy, Winchester, Fishers Hill, Cedar Creek, then served in the defenses around Petersburg until the fall of that city, and finally surrendered with the Army of Northern Virginia at Appomattox April 9, 1865. The following is the original muster roll of this company from Wythe county:

William Terry, captain, promoted general.
John H. Fulton, first lieutenant.
John G. Sayers, second lieutenant.
Samuel C. Sanders, third lieutenant.
Jacob S. Chatwell, second sergeant.
William Stuart, sergeant.
Pelton Gallagher, sergeant.
Francis S. Spiller, corporal.
James B. Miller, corporal.
George M. Hanson, corporal.
William G. Baldwin, corporal.

Bailey, Robert K.
Bray, Lewis.
Bateman, Daniel.
Bowles, George W.
Crockett, Robert J.
Clemmons, John I.
Campbell, ——.
Crockett, Edward L.
Davidson, Erastus G.
Dix, Henry M.
Eversole, Leander, taken prisoner at Chancellorsville; sent to Elmira.
Furgerson, Samuel H.
Gose, William G.
Hallen, Edwin C.
Inman, William P.
Kent, George M.
King, George W.
Lampkin, Henry S.
McGavock, James H.
Meyers, Thomas I.
Neighbours, William H.
Newman, Thomas I.
Osteman, Eugene.
Oury, Alfred S.
Pattison, Thomas W.
Perkins, John E.
Rogers, John D.
Rider, James H.
Raper, William I.
Sexton, John M.
Snodgrass, Henderson.
Smith, William.
Sanders, Steven C.
Tate, William.
Taylor, Robert M.
Williams, Samuel B.
Williams, Henry.
Beville, James A.
Brown, John W.
Black, James A.
Bowles, William A.
Chatwell, Thomas.
Cook, Jacob C.
Calvin, Pelter J.
Crockett, Joseph.
Davis, Lewis.
Evans, James.
Fulton, Benjamin D.
Gruchs, Davidson.
Holbrook, Garland S.
Harrison, William H.
Johnson, George D.
Kuhners, George.
Lockett, Samuel D.
McClintock, George L.
McClintock, Charles.
Matthews, Harold I.
Neighbours, Charles W.
Oglesby, Albert M.
Oury, Henry C.
Paulett, Weslie S.
Pattison, Charles E.
Peirce, Joseph B.
Rider, James A.
Rider, Albert C.
Shepherd, James H.
St. Clair, James H.
Steptoe, John L.
Smith, John W.
Shaffer, Jacob.
Tate, James G.
Umberger, James L
Williams, James E.

FURTHER MENTION OF WYTHE SOLDIERS IN THE FOURTH.

Allison, David S., enlisted in Smyth county; Smyth Blues; wounded 1862 near Richmond; captured, May 12, 1864, at Spotsylvania C. H.; held at Elmira, N. Y., 15 months; battles, 25; service, 4 years.
Archer, Robert C., enlisted March, 1862; Co. A; wounded May 3, 1863, at Chancellorsville; captured at Spotsylvania C. H., May 12, 1864; held at Point Lookout 13 months; battles, 15; discharged from Point Lookout prison, June, 1865.
Brown, Robert C , Co. C; promoted sergeant.
Bourn, J. A., enlisted in Grayson county, Co. F; discharged and re-enlisted in 1862; Co. D, 4th Virginia Cavalry; captured at Front Royal, November 12, 1864; held in hospital one day and escaped; battles, 12; service, 4 years.
Bourn, A. P., Co. F; promoted lieutenant; wounded 1862 at Seven Pines, Sharpsburg; near Richmond, mortally; died in Richmond hospital, 1864.
Butner, Alexander H., enlisted April 10, 1862; Co. A; wounded at Mine Run, at Gettysburg; battles, 15; service, 3 years.

Chatwell, Jacob, Co. A, enlisted 1862; killed.
Crockett, Samuel F., Co. A; killed at 1st Manassas by shell, at the age of 16.
Crockett, Joseph M., enlisted at Manassas; Co. A; wounded at Gettysburg; again at Mine Run; captured at Cedar Mountain; held at Old Capitol 1 month; battles, 10; service, 3 years.
Cassell, M. B , enlisted March 1, 1862; Co. A; captured at Spotsylvania C. H.; held at Elmira, N. Y., 14 months; battles, 15; service, 3 years; discharged June 25, 1865, at Elmira, N. Y.
Crockett, James T., enlisted February, 1862; Co. A; transferred Jenkins' Cavalry, February, 1863; battles, 13; service, 3 years.
Eversole, Isaac, enlisted 1862; Co. A; wounded at Kernstown; battles, 3 service, 3 years.
Eversole, C. H., enlisted 1862; Co. A; taken prisoner in the Valley of Virginia; held at Elmira, N. Y.
Eversole, E. C., enlisted 1863; Wythe artillery; transferred October, 1863, to Co. E, 4th Virginia Reserves; promoted first sergeant, then first lieutenant; battles, 2 ; service, 2 years.
Fulhon, John H., enlisted at Richmond, Co. A; second lieutenant; promoted captain; wounded at 2d Manassas; lost left leg at Chancellorsville, then resigned.
Groseclose, Solomon, enlisted 1862; Co. A.
Gilman, Michael, enlisted 1862; Co. A; service, 3 years.
Gleaves, James T., Co. A; promoted sergeant; died December, 1861, at Winchester.
Henly, James, enlisted 1862; Co. A; killed during the 7 days battle around Richmond 1862.
Henly, Robert, enlisted 1862; Co. A; service, 3 years.
Holiday, Wiley, Co. A.
Henley, Lewis, enlisted 1862; Co. A.
Holbrook, G. J., Co. A; wounded October 4, 1864, at Bridgewater; most of the battles of Army of Northern Virginia; discharged at Augusta, Georgia, May, 1865.
Kent, Joseph F., Co. A; captain; promoted major, afterwards colonel of a regiment of local reserves; discharged at Wytheville.
La Hue, S. C., enlisted April 1, 1862; Co. A.
Mathews, Harold J., enlisted at Harpers Ferry; Co. A; promoted first sergeant ; wounded at 2d Manassas, and Gettysburg; captured at Fishers Hill; held at Fort Delaware 9 months; battles, 15; service, 4 years; discharged at Fort Delaware.
McGavock, James H., enlisted at Harpers Ferry; wounded at 2d Manassas; transferred to cavalry 1864; battles, 4.
Neighbors, H. W., Co. A; wounded in the left leg at Winchester, February 18, 1862; battles, 8 or 10; service, 4 years.
Neighbors, A. B., enlisted August 8, 1862, near Gordonsville; Wythe Grays.
Newman, T. J., Co. A; promoted quartermaster sergeant; captured at Moorefield, August, 1864; held at Camp Chase about 8 months; discharged at Camp Chase, April, 1865.

6

Oglesby, Nicholas P., Co. A; wounded at Spotsylvania.C. H., May 12, 1864; battles, most of regiment; service, 3 years, 6 months.
Oglesby, Albert M., Co. A; service, 2 years; discharged at Winchester.
Pierce, J. B., Co. A; promoted sergeant; re-enlisted in same company at New Market, March, 1862; wounded at Chancellorsville and at Monocacy; captured at Frederick City, Maryland; held 3 months at Fort McHenry; battles, most of the regiment.
Perkins, John E., Co. A; promoted corporal; wounded at 2d Manassas and at Gettysburg; captured at Spotsylvania C. H.; held at Point Lookout 15 months; battles, 15; service, 3 years.
Raper, William J., Co. A; battles, 4; service, 16 months; discharged 1862.
Rider, James A, Co. A; wounded at Chancellorsville May 3, 1863; battles, most of regiment.
Rider, James F., enlisted April, 1862; Co. A; lost right leg, June 3, 1863; discharged August 29, 1863.
Sexton, Joseph Campbell, Co. A; promoted captain September 11, 1861, major April 19, 1862; all the battles of Army of Northern Virginia.
Shepard, R. F., enlisted 1862; Co. A; wounded; died 1864 at Richmond hospital.
Sprecker, Jonas, enlisted 1862; Co. A; discharged in the Valley of Virginia, 1863; died 1863.
Smith, Richard, enlisted 1862; Co. A; discharged 1864 in the Valley of Virginia; died 1864 in Wythe county.
Tate, James G; Co. A; sergeant; wounded at Malvern Hill 1862, Chancellorsville 1863, and at Spotsylvania C. H., 1864; battles, 15; service, 3 years; killed near Shepardstown, August 25, 1864.
Thorn, William S., enlisted March, 1862; Co. A; detailed as clerk at lead mine.

COMPANY B, 29TH VIRGINIA INFANTRY,

Enlisted August 4, 1861; served to close of war unless otherwise stated.

W. R. B. Horn, captain, promoted major; discharged 1862.
George W. Mercer, first lieutenant, promoted captain; taken prisoner 1864 at Cold Harbor; sent to Johnsons Island.
H. B. Groseclose, second lieutenant, promoted first lieutenant.
Alex. Phillippe, third lieutenant, promoted chaplain.
R. A. Adkins, first sergeant, promoted hospital steward.
N. T. Vaught, second sergeant, promoted first sergeant and lieutenant.
Alex. Staley, sergeant, promoted wagon master.
George Davis, sergeant; taken prisoner 1865 at High Bridge.
Alex. Buchanan, sergeant; taken prisoner 1865 at High Bridge.
James A. Irvin, corporal; discharged 1864.
E. J. Steffey, corporal.
J. Z. Vaught, corporal; wounded 1865 at Hatchers Run.
L. Steffey, corporal; killed 1864 at Cold Harbor.
Anders, Henry.
Arny, John, transferred 1863 to 63d Virginia Infantry.
Buchanan, William A.   Buchanan, William N.
Bennington, Madison, taken prisoner 1864 at Drurys Bluff; sent to Elmira.
Burkett, Mitchell, taken prisoner 1864 at Cold Harbor; sent to Elmira.
Blackard, Austin, died 1864.   Burkett, George.
Copenhaver, Daniel.
Clark, H. C., taken prisoner 1864 at City Point; sent to Elmira and died.
Chadwell, Strolter, killed 1864 at Drurys Bluff.
Copenhaver, Pierson, wounded 1864 at Drurys Bluff.
Copenhaver, Isaac, wounded 1864 at Drurys Bluff.
Crigger, Eli, promoted first sergeant.
Crigger, Franklin, wounded 1864 at Drurys Bluff, and died.
Crigger, James, taken prisoner 1865 at Five Forks; sent to Harts Island.
Catron, Peter.   Coley, James N.

7

Catron, Joseph, killed 1864 at Drurys Bluff.
Catron, John, died 1862. Coley, C. K., promoted corporal.
Coley, Isaac, killed 1864 at Drurys Bluff.
Coley, Jeff., wounded 1864 at Drurys Bluff, and 1865 at Five Forks.
Derting, J. F.
Derting, David, killed 1864 at Drurys Bluff.
Deckerd, George, killed 1864 at Drurys Bluff.
Derting, Thomas E. Deckerd, Peter.
Derting, Thomas, died November 27, 1862.
Davis, William, discharged 1862. Davis, James.
Davis, Henry, died 1863. Etter, Ephraim, died 1862.
Evans, John, killed 1864 at Drurys Bluff.
Foglesong, Crockett, taken prisoner 1865 at Five Forks; sent to Elmira.
Foglesong, Thomas, wounded 1864, at Drurys Bluff.
Flannagin, William. Flannagin, A. C.
Flannagin, Madison, accidentally wounded 1861 at Abingdon.
Freeman, George, wounded 1864 at Drurys Bluff.
Fuller, J. W., wounded 1865 at Five Forks.
Gray, E. C. Groseclose, John.
Groseclose, Stephen, taken prisoner 1865 at Five Forks; sent to Harts Island.
Grubb, Harvey, wounded 1864 at Drurys Bluff.
Grubb, Wesley, discharged 1862.
Grubb, Emory, taken prisoner 1865 at Five Forks; sent to Harts Island.
Houdashall, Andrew.
Huddle, B. J., wounded 1861 at Middle Creek, Ky., and 1864 at Drurys Bluff.
Hillenbury, Eli. Huddle, Emory.
Hillenbury, Austin.
Horn, Isaac, transferred to 63d Virginia Infantry, July, 1863.
Horn, John, died 1863. Hughes, John.
Johnson, Augustus. Johnson, Thomas.
Jonas, Peter. Litz, John.
Lindsay, William, died 1862.
Lambert, Riley, taken prisoner 1864 at City Point; sent to Elmira.
Litz, John J., died 1863 at Richmond.
Mitchell, George D., wounded 1864 at Drurys Bluff.
Mercer, W. W.
Mercer, Walter, taken prisoner 1865 at High Bridge; sent to Elmira.
Mercer, Albert, died 1863.
Mercer, Sanders, wounded 1864 at Drurys Bluff.
Mercer, Madison, taken prisoner 1864 at Cold Harbor, sent to Elmira.
Miller, Michael, transferred from 45th Virginia Infantry in 1862.
Miller, Winton. Miller, John.
Miller, Felix, taken prisoner 1864 at Drurys Bluff.
Newman, David, taken prisoner 1865 at High Bridge; sent to Point Lookout.
Newman, Alex., taken prisoner 1865 at Five Forks; sent to Elmira.
Neff, Jacob, wounded 1864 at Suffolk. Neff, Pearson.
Phelps, George. Painter, Thomas.
Painter, Ezra. Painter, James.
Painter, Sidney, promoted lieutenant and captain, quartermaster.
Phillippe, L. K., wounded 1864 at Drurys Bluff; taken prisoner 1865 at Five Forks; sent to Harts Island.
Phillippe, Andrew, wounded 1864 at Cold Harbor.
Phillippe, E. W., taken prisoner 1865 at Five Forks; sent to Harts Island and died.
Phillippe, William H., wounded at Drurys Bluff 1864.
Phillippe, E. M.
Phillippe, Daniel, died 1864 in Wythe county.
Phillippe, Christ. Steffey, Peter.
Scott, A. P., wounded 1864 at Cold Harbor.
Sutphin, Elkanet. Sprecker, Jacob.
Turner, Marshall.
Tobler, Stephen, wounded 1864 at Cold Harbor.
Vaught, J. M., taken prisoner 1865 at High Bridge; sent to New York.
Vaught, Ephraim.
Vaught, D. B., taken prisoner 1865 at Five Forks; sent to Harts Island.

Vaught, William F.
Vaught, Christ, killed 1864 at Drurys Bluff.
Vaught, George W.
Vaught, Stephen, wounded 1864 at Drurys Bluff.
Wetherly, Hosea, died 1862.
Wood, James, wounded 1864 at Drurys Bluff.
Williams, John.
Winn, Henry H.
Vaught, Franklin, promoted sergeant.
Wilkerson, Samuel.

THE FORTY-FIFTH VIRGINIA INFANTRY

Was enlisted in the early months of 1861, Companies B, C and D largely recruited in Wythe county. The most active field service of this regiment was in 1864, when it was almost constantly engaged in the last effort to save the beautiful valley of Virginia from the spoilation of invading vandals. It was engaged against the Federal army of West Virginia, May 9 and 10, 1864, at Cloyd Mountain and New River Bridge, where nearly a thousand soldiers of the Confederacy gave up life or liberty; again at Piedmont, or Mount Crawford, against the same enemy, where many of the Forty-Fifth fell, and many more were captured, and the enemy were driven at a frightful cost. In Early's last campaign, the regiment was commanded by Major Alex. M. Davis, and served in Wharton's (old) brigade, Wharton's division. Opequan, Fishers Hill, Cedar Creek were the great battles of this campaign, the two former usually spoken of as the "Winchester battles." In these the Forty-Fifth maintained its reputation for gallantry, and at Early's last stand, at Waynesboro, its loss in captured was heavy.

The following muster by companies shows the principal enlistments in Wythe county. Where no date of enlistment is given it was at the organization of the company, in the early months of 1861; where no date of discharge is given the service was till the close of the war, or until a subsequent release from imprisonment; where no place of enlistment is given it was in Wythe county; where no rank is given the service was as private.

COMPANY B.

John Buchanan, captain; discharged November, 1863.
James Buchanan, first lieutenant; promoted captain.
Charles Baumgardner, second lieutenant; promoted captain; discharged June 17, 1865; taken prisoner September 19, 1864, at Winchester; held at Fort Delaware.
R. D. L. Steptoe, second lieutenant; promoted first lieutenant.
James M. Snaveley, promoted second lieutenant; wounded June 5, 1862, at Williamsburg; taken prisoner May, 1864, at Port Republic; held at Point Lookout.
Akers, Vachael, died 1862.
Baumgardner, M. L.
Baumgardner, Ephraim.
Brown, J. B., killed May 9, 1864, at Cloyd Mountain.
Buck, Franklin, killed May 9, 1864, at Cloyd Mountain.
Buckley, John, killed May 9, 1864, at Cloyd Mountain.
Buchanan, Robert, killed May 9, 1864, at Cloyd Mountain.

Buchanan, Harvey, died 1863. Buckley, Joel S.
Buckley, R. J. Buckley, Wm. A.
Brown, Andy: Brown, M. D.
Buck, Felix. Buck, James H.
Blessing, Peter F., wounded August, 1863, at Dry Run.
Blessing, Granville; taken prisoner June 5th, 1864, in the valley of Virginia; held at Indianapolis; discharged March 15, 1865.
Berry, Wm. J., died 1862. Burress, James.
Barrett Nelson. Bailey, G. W.
Blackwell, Wm. P., died December 7, 1861.
Cooley, J. M. Cassell, Franklin, died 1863.
Cline, Ephraim, Cline, Jackson, died 1862.
Crigger, Austin. Crigger, H. A.
Crigger, Wm. R. Chadwell, Henry.
Chadwell, Wm. S. Crigger, Amandreth.
Collins, W. D. Davis, H. H.
Doak, H T.
Deyerle, Charles, died at Princeton, West Virginia, 1862.
Deyerle, John B.
Earhart, David, killed May 9, 1864, at Cloyd Mountain.
Earhart, A. C. M., died 1863.
Etter, James A. Etter, Ephraim, died 1862.
Etter, John J. Groseclose, Simon.
Groseclose, Alex. Goodman, N. W., died 1862.
Groseclose, Andrew. Gold, R. D.
Goodman, J. E. Gillman, Richard.
Gold, C. A. Harkrider, John.
Harkrider, B. D. Holston, Harvey.
Huddle, James, killed May 9, 1864, at Cloyd Mountain.
Huddle, Eli. Hildreth, James T.
Hildreth, John J. Hoffman, E. H.
Hubble, James. Hoffman, George W.
Hatton, W. G. Harden, Andrew.
Hillenburg, A. W., died 1863.
Harsh, John C., taken prisoner May 9, 1864, at Cloyd Mountain; held at Camp Chase; discharged July 1, 1865.
Harsh, J. F., taken prisoner July, 1864, at Fredericksburg; held at Fort Delaware; died February 22, 1865.
Hounshell, Jeff.
Hounshell, Robert, killed May 9, 1864, at Cloyd Mountain.
Hutchinson, H. H., wounded May 9, 1864, at Cloyd Mountain.
Hudson, Wm. Harmon, J. B.
Hurst, A., killed May 9, 1864, at Cloyd Mountain.
Johnson, J. H., died October 11, 1861, at Lewisburg, West Virginia.
Jones, John. Jones, Jacob.
Kinder, John G., killed May 9, 1864, at Cloyd Mountain.
Kinder, Joseph M. King, J. J.
Kinder, Isaac. King, John S., died 1862.
Leslie, J. W. Leggon, Samuel, died May, 1863.
Meadows, John, while a prisoner crippled on cars.
Mathews, Joseph, died August, 1864.
Mize, E. C. Miller, Joseph M.
Musser, Franklin. Musser, J. J.
Miller, D. K., died at Princeton, November 21, 1864; wounded May 9, 1864, at Cloyd Mountain. Nye, A. B.
Nye, W. H. Neff, Henry.
Oury, Stephen. Oury, James.
Painter, Stewart, wounded 1861 at Hawks Nest.
Pauley, J. B. Reese, J. N.
Repass, Walter, killed 1861 at Lewisburg.
Repass, Alfred Stiffey, W. A.
Stiffey, I. J., killed May 9, 1864, at Cloyd Mountain.
Smith, John W.
Sittle, W. R., wounded 1864 in East Tennessee.

Silcox, R. J.
Snaveley, Thomas S.
Thornburg, W. J.
Umberger, Wm.
Umberger, James.
Umberger, Harvey.
Vaught, John W., wounded 1861 at Hawks Nest.
Vaught, Stephen D., killed 1862 at Lewisburg.
Williams, James M.
Williams, John.
Williams, Jacob, killed 1864 at Richmond.
Williams, James M.
Wilson, George W.
Wilson, A. S.
Wyatt, Henry, wounded 1861 at Hawks Nest.
Wampler, Isaac A.
Wampler, A. A.
Wiseley, James P.
Wiseley, Isaac N.
Wiseley, Michael.
Yonce, James A., died 1862.

COMPANY D.

Robert H. Gleaves, captain; discharged 1862; afterwards captain of cavalry.
Allen C. Burns, first lieutenant, promoted adjutant; taken prisoner 1864 at Cloyd Farm; sent to Elmira.
William C. Sanders, second lieutenant, promoted captain; wounded 1864 at Piedmont.
William O. Moore, third lieutenant, promoted adjutant 29th Virginia Infantry; afterwards captain Co. G, 22d Virginia Cavalry.
H. H. Lockett, lieutenant; transferred July, 1861; killed 1864 at Cloyd Farm.
Thomas M. Garaway, first sergeant; discharged October, 1861.
Andrew Davis, sergeant.
John Porter, sergeant.

Henry Davis, corporal; died 1861.
Wm. Davis, sergeant, died 1861.
Stephen Sanders, corporal; killed September 11, 1862, at Fayette C. H.
Joseph Clemens, corporal.
Thomas Robertson, corporal; killed 1864 at Cloyd Farm.
Aker, Joseph, prisoner 1864 at Cloyd Farm; sent to Camp Chase.
Allison, David, transferred to 51st Virginia Infantry; promoted lieutenant; killed September 1864 in the Valley.
Allison, James, transferred to 51st Virginia Infantry.
Arnburn, John, captured 1865 at Waynesboro; sent to Fort Delaware, died.
Adkins, Freal, taken prisoner 1864 at Piedmont; sent to Fort Delaware.
Archer, Thomas, taken prisoner 1865 at Waynesboro; sent to Fort Delaware.
Blair, Thomas, died September, 1861, at Lewisburg.
Blair, Andrew, wounded 1864 at Cloyds Farm.
Bolling, David, died 1862.
Blair, Daniel, enlisted 1862; wounded at Fayette C. H., 1862.
Boothe, William, died 1862.
Bralley, G. W. J. M., transferred from 51st Virginia Infantry 1862; killed September 19, 1864, at Winchester.
Bralley, Mitchell, enlisted 1863; taken prisoner 1864 at Piedmont; sent to Camp Morton.
Bralley, Samuel, enlisted May, 1862; promoted first lieutenant; discharged January, 1865.
Bralley, Stephen C., wounded 1864 at Cloyd Farm and Piedmont; prisoner 1864 at Piedmont and paroled.
Bralley, Jeff, discharged 1863.
Caldwell, William.
Cassel, Charles, taken prisoner 1864 at Piedmont and paroled.
Catlett, Dabney, died September, 1861, at Blue Sulphur.
Cooley, Felix, taken prisoner 1864 at Piedmont; sent to Camp Morton.
Crigger, Ephraim, enlisted 1862; killed 1864 at Cloyd Farm.
Crigger, John, wounded 1863 at Salt Works and discharged.
Crockett, John, taken prisoner 1864 at Piedmont; sent to Camp Morton.
Crockett, James.

Dallihide, Andrew, taken prisoner 1864 at Piedmont; sent to Camp Morton.
Davis, James, died 1861.   Davis, Marion, enlisted 1864.
Davis, John C., discharged 1861.
Davis, Melville, enlisted 1863; taken prisoner 1864 at Cloyd Farm; sent to Camp Chase and died.
Dunford, William, wounded 1862 at Fayette C. H.
Earhart, Alfred, enlisted 1862; killed 1864 at Cloyd Farm.
Fisher, Lewis, enlisted 1864; taken prisoner 1865 at Wayesboro; sent to Fort Delaware.
Fisher, Joseph, taken prisoner 1865 at Waynesboro; sent to Fort Delaware.
Fisher, Jason L, taken prisoner 1864 at Piedmont; sent to Camp Morton.
Fisher, Melville, wounded 1864 at Winchester; taken prisoner 1864 at Waynesboro; sent to Fort Delaware.
Foster, John, enlisted 1862; captured 1864 at Waynesboro; sent to Ft. Delaware.
Foster, William B, enlisted 1863; discharged 1863.
Goodson, Elijah, discharged 1862.
Gose, Stephen, enlisted 1863; died 1863 at Red Sulphur.
Grubb, Curtis A, discharged 1861.   Hancock, William, died 1861.
Highley, Jason, discharged 1862; re-enlisted in Co. G, 22d Virginia Cavalry.
Hilton, Joseph, discharged 1861.
Hines, William, taken prisoner 1864 at Piedmont; sent to Camp Morton.
Holliday, Robert, taken prisoner 1864 at Piedmont; sent to Camp Morton.
Hoytman, Charles, discharged 1861.
Hoback, Clifton, taken prisoner 1862 at Dry Creek; sent to Camp Morton, died.
Hounshell Pearson, died 1861.
Hufford, James, taken prisoner 1864 at Piedmont; sent to Camp Morton.
Hudson, Robert, transferred to 51st Virginia Infantry; taken prisoner 1861 at Carnifex Ferry.
Irvin, Jacob, died 1861.
Jackson, Thomas, promoted sergeant; taken prisoner 1864 at Piedmont; sent to Camp Morton.
Jackson, William, promoted lieutenant; taken prisoner 1864 at Piedmont; sent to Johnsons Island.
Jackson, Robert, wounded 1862 at Fayette C. H.
Jackson, Calhoun, enlisted 1863; taken prisoner 1864 at Piedmont; sent to Camp Morton.
Jackson, Burton, died June 5, 1861, at Wytheville.
Jones Henderson, taken prisoner 1864 at Piedmont and escaped.
Jones, Calvin, died 1861.   Kelley, James.
Kelley, John, enlisted 1862; wounded 1864 at Cloyd Farm; taken prisoner 1864 at Waynesboro; sent to Fort Delaware.
King, Stephen R., taken prisoner 1864 at Piedmont; sent to Camp Morton.
Liddle, William, detailed 1862 to Lead Mine.
Leslie, James W., discharged 1863.   Leedy, Martin, died 1861.
Lockett, David, wounded 1861 at Fayette C. H.; taken prisoner 1864 at Cloyd Farm; sent to Camp Chase.
Louthien, John.
Mallory, Robert, died 1861 at Blue Sulphur.
Mallory, Thomas.
Mathews, Marion, transferred from Co. C to Co. D in 1861.
Manuel, Sampson, taken prisoner at Waynesboro; sent to Fort Delaware.
McGuire, Elijah, died 1861.   Myers, David, discharged 1863.
Morris William, taken prisoner 1864 at Piedmont; sent to Camp Morton.
Nichols, William C., died 1865.
Patterson, James, wounded 1862 at Fayette C. H.
Painter, George, discharged 1861.
Painter, Leicester, taken prisoner 1864 at Piedmont; sent to Camp Morton.
Parmer, James.
Pope, Lafayette, taken prisoner 1864 at Piedmont; sent to Camp Morton.
Porter, David, discharged 1862.
Porter, Kenney, taken prisoner at Piedmont; sent to Camp Morton.
Porter, Stephen S., enlisted 1863; taken prisoner 1864 at Piedmont; sent to Camp Morton.

Porter, Calvin, promoted lieutenant; killed 1864 at Cloyd Farm.
Ratcliff Joseph, wounded 1861 at Sewell Mountain and died.
Rhoter, William. Sailor, Alfred, discharged 1863.
Rosenbaum, Peter, enlisted 1862.
Rosenbaum, Stephen, enlisted 1864. Rosenbaum, Frank, enlisted 1864.
Sanders, George, enlisted 1864.
Seagle, John, enlisted 1863; killed 1864 at Cloyd Farm.
Shupe, John, died 1862.
Slagle, George, taken prisoner 1865 at Rockfish Gap; sent to Fort Delaware.
Scott, James R., taken prisoner in 1864 at Piedmont; sent to Camp Morton.
Shrader, William, taken prisoner 1864 at Cloyd Farm; sent to Camp Chase.
Shrader, Archibald, taken prisoner 1864 at Piedmont; sent to Camp Morton.
Smith, William.
Smith, Calvin, taken prisoner 1864 at Piedmont; sent to Camp Morton.

Sprecker, Alexander, enlisted 1862; discharged 1863.
Sprecker, Stephen, enlisted 1863.
Spense, Wiley. Spense, Henry.
Sarett, James H., taken prisoner 1864 at Cloyd Farm; sent to Camp Chase.
Smeltzer, Ferrell. Tucker, ——— enlisted 1862.
Umbarger, Michael, taken prisoner 1864 at Piedmont; sent to Camp Morton.
Umbarger, Edley, taken prisoner 1864 at Piedmont; sent to Camp Morton.
Umbarger, James. Vaughan William A.
Vaughan Daniel, taken prisoner 1864 at Piedmont; sent to Camp Morton.
Wallace, James, discharged 1863 and died.
Ward, John D., transferred to another company in 1864.
Ward, James E., taken prisoner 1864 at Piedmont; sent to Camp Morton.
Ward, E. Rush, enlisted 1862; captured 1864 at Piedmont; sent to Camp Morton.
Winskell, John, enlisted 1862; transferred to cavalry in 1863.
Wolford, Henry, taken prisoner 1861 at Carnifex Ferry; sent to Camp Chase.
Wolford, Charles.
Whitman, A. C., wounded 1862 at Fayette C, H.; taken prisoner 1864 at Waynesboro; sent to Fort Delaware.
Whitman, James W., enlisted 1863; transferred 1863 to Co. G, 22d Virginia Cavalry.

FURTHER MENTION OF WYTHE SOLDIERS IN THE FORTY-FIFTH.

Brown, Nicholas C., Co. C; promoted sergeant; captured at Winchester; held at Elmira, N. Y., about 7 months; battles, 12; service, nearly 4 years.
Brown, Robert A., Co. C; captured at Winchester; held at Point Lookout about 7 months; battles, 12; service, nearly 4 years.
Catterson, John, Co. B; captured at Cloyd Mountain; held at Camp Chase; died November 8, 1864.
Catterson, William, Co. B; captured at Cloyd Mountain; held at Camp Chase.
Crockett, John F., Co. D; captured at Winchester; battles, 10; service, 4 years.
Cassell, Charles W., Co. D; sergeant; detailed wagonmaster; wounded June 5, 1864, at Piedmont; battles, 7; service, 4 years.
Eversole, E., enlisted at Richmond 1863; Co. D; transferred. Wythe County Reserves; service, 1 year; discharged 1864.
Etter, S. S., enlisted December, 1862, at Red Sulphur Springs; Co. B; captured at Piedmont: held 12 months at Indianapolis, Indiana; battles, 2; service, 3 years; discharged at Camp Morton July 12, 1865.
Fisher, Joseph S., Co. D; captured at Waynesboro; held at Fort Delaware 4 months; battles, 25; service, 4 years.
Gleaves, Robert H., Co. D; captain; transferred to Co. E, 21st Virginia Cavalry, Wythe county, 1863; service, 3 years; discharged October, 1864.
Hillenburg, Austin, Co. B; discharged 1862; re-enlisted 1862; Co. B, 29th Virginia Infantry; service, 3 years, 6 months.
Harsh, J. B., enlisted October 3, 1863; Co. B.
Jackson, Wm. J., Co. D; captured at Piedmont; held at Johnsons Island 12 months; battles, 10; service, 4 years.
Jackson, Thomas M., Co. D; captured at Piedmont; battles, 6; service, 4 years.
King, Wm. R., enlisted April 10, 1863; Co. G.

Leslie, James W., Co. D; promoted first sergeant, sergeant-major; captured and paroled at Wytheville October, 1862; battles, 12; service, 4 years.
Lindamood, Joseph L., enlisted January 28, 1863; Co. H; wounded and captured at Winchester; held at Baltimore.
Leedy, Martin, Co. B; died in October, 1861.
Leslie, H. W., enlisted at Pearisburg, April 1, 1863; Co. D.
Morehead, James W., enlisted at Pearisburg March, 1862; Co. B; captured at Piedmont Valley, June 5, 1864; held at Camp Morton 9 months; battles, 6; service, 3 years; discharged at Camp Morton March 25, 1865.
Morehead, John C., enlisted March 1, 1862, at Pearisburg; Co. B; captured at Piedmont Valley June 5, 1864; held at Camp Morton 9 months; battles 6; service, 3 years; discharged at Camp Morton March 12, 1865; died in Richmond March 20, 1865.
Neff, Jacob M., enlisted May, 1861; Co. B; discharged May, 1862, in Giles county; re-enlisted May, 1862, in Tazewell; Co. B, 29th Virginia Infantry; wounded April, 1863, at Suffolk; transferred 1864, at Wytheville, to Co. G, 22d Virginia Cavalry; service, 4 years; discharged in Wythe county.
Porter, John M., Co. D; detailed wagonmaster; battles, 15; service, 4 years.
Porter, David H., enlisted at Sweet Springs, Monroe county; Co. D; served about 2 years; discharged March, 1862, at home.
Porter, S. S., enlisted April, 1863, in Monroe county, West Virginia; Co. D; captured at Piedmont, held at Camp Morton about 4 months; wounded at Camp Morton, Indiana; battles, 2; service, about 2 years; discharged at Camp Morton March 20, 1865.
Painter, Leicester E., Co. D; captured at Piedmont; held at Camp Morton 9 months; battles, 10; service, 4 years.
Rosenbaum, Peter, enlisted April 1, 1862; Co. D; service, 3 years.
Slagle, George W., Co. D; captured at Waynesboro; held at Fort Delaware 3 months, 21 days; battles, 25; service, 4 years.
Seagle, J. B., enlisted November, 1863; Co. D; battles, 5; service, 2 years; discharged at Christiansburg.
Seagle, John A., enlisted April 1, 1862; Co. D; battles, 12; service, 2 years; killed at Cloyd Mountain May 9, 1864.
Troster, Wm. B., enlisted at Red Sulphur Springs, Monroe county, 1862; Co. D; wounded 1864 at Cloyd Farm; battles, 2; service, about 15 months; discharged after battle at Cloyd Farm.
Vaughan, Wm. A., Co. D; wounded at Cold Harbor 1863 and at Five Forks 1865; transferred 1862 into Co. E, 24th Virginia Infantry; battles, 20; service, 4 years.
Vaught, Peter, enlisted December, 1862; Co. B; wounded at Cloyd Mountain; service, 2 years, 4 months.
Wampler, Austin, enlisted 1862 at Red Sulphur Springs, Monroe county; Co. B; wounded at Cloyd Mountain; captured at Piedmont; held at Camp Morton 10 months.
Ward, James E., Co. D., promoted color sergeant; captured at Piedmont Valley; held at Camp Morton about 9 months; battles, 15; service nearly 4 years.

THE FIFTY-FIRST VIRGINIA INFANTRY

Was enlisted early in 1861, and was assigned to Floyd's brigade marching into West Virginia and in Loring's division taking part in the Kanawha Valley campaign, which included the fighting at Cross Lanes, in Nicholas county, and the battles of Gauley and Cotton mountains. Returning into Virginia, it accompanied General Floyd into Kentucky, was embarked on transports on the Cumberland river, debarked at Dover and on February 13, 1862, entered the fortifications at Fort Donelson. Here it was under heavy bombardment until the morning of the 15th, when, with the charging battalions it marched out and took part in the most desperate fighting that had yet occurred on the banks of the Cumberland. The next day the fort surrendered, but during the night the Virginians of Floyd's brigade were landed on the west bank of the river, whence they marched to Murfreesboro, which they reached in about a week. Returning to their native State via Chattanooga and Knoxville, Tennessee, the men of Floyd's command almost immediately plunged into the West Virginia campaign again. In 1863 and 1864, the Fifty-First saw constant field service with the Army of Northern Virginia and fighting Sheridan in the Shenandoah Valley. In the last battle of the Shenandoah Valley, Waynesboro, March 2, 1865, very many of the regiment were captured and sent to Fort Delaware and to Elmira, New York, where they were held until after the close of the war. The flag of the Fifty-First was borne and defended on the battle-fields of Fayettesville, Cotton Mountain, Fort Donelson, Carnifax Ferry, Princeton, Frederick City, Winchester, Kernstown, Bull Gap, Casslemans Ferry, New Market, Leetown, Newtown, Waynesboro.

The following Roll of Honor is the enlistments in this regiment of Wythe county soldiers, giving companies. Where no date of enlistment is given, it was at the organization of the company, or in the first year of the war; where no date of death or discharge is given, the service was until the surrender of the Army of Northern Virginia; where no rank is given the service was as private.

Anderson, G. W., Co. B; promoted first sergeant; wounded at Fort Donelson and Winchester; captured at Waynesboro; held at Fort Delaware; battles, 15; service, 4 years.
Allen, Samuel, Co. B; battles, 10; service, 3 years; killed July, 1864, at Casslemans Ferry.
Allen, Carr, Co. B; captured at Waynesboro; held at Fort Delaware; battles, 15; service, 4 years.
Allen, William, Co. B; wounded July, 1864, at Casslemans Ferry; battles, 10; service, 4 years.
Allison, Leander S., Co. B; first sergeant: promoted ordnance sergeant; captured at Waynesboro; held at Fort Delaware 4 months; battles, 15; service, 4 years.
Bralley, G. S., enlisted at Wytheville April, 1862; Co. B; promoted sergeant; battles, 20; service, 3 years.
Brown, J. C , enlisted December, 1862; Co. C.
Carter, R. M., Co. C; battles, 15; service, 4 years.
Clark, David G., Co. B; wounded at New Market; captured August, 1864, at Leetown; held at Camp Chase 10 months; battles, 10; service, 4 years.
Davis, Joseph S , enlisted April, 1862; Co. C; wounded August 25, 1864, at Lee Town; battles, 10; service, 3 years.
Dunford, George W., enlisted at Glade Springs, 1863; Co. B; wounded at New Market, 1864; service, 2 years.
Fuller, James, Co. B; wounded August, 1864, at Leetown; battles, 10; service, 4 years.
Felts, Raleigh, Co. B; died October, 1861, at Lewisburg.
Fisher, Thomas, enlisted 1862 at Wytheville; Co. C.
Findly, George D., Co. E; wounded at Bull Gap, 1864; at Carnifax Ferry; transferred to Co. A, 1st Engineer Regiment, Army of Tennessee; battles, 7: service. 4 years.

Fuller, Daniel, Co. B; died December, 1861, at Princeton.
Filtey, Jacob, Co. E; service, about 1 year.
Graham, David P., Co. B; captain; promoted major; battles, 5; service, 3 years; discharged 1864 at Dublin.
Grosseclose, William, Co. C.
Hill, John, Co. B; corporal; wounded July, 1864, at Winchester; battles, 10; service, 3 years.
Hudson, John, Co. B; service, 9 months; discharged at Wytheville 1861.
Inman, Jesse, Co. B; mortally wounded at Fort Donelson; died at Nashville, Tennessee, March, 1862.
Inman, John, Co. B.
Johnson, Gustavus, Co. B; sergeant; wounded February 15, 1862, at Fort Donelson; battles, 10; service, 3 years; killed July, 1864, at Casslemans Ferry.
Kisling, Harry, Co. B; service, 4 years.
Kisling, E., Co. B; service, 8 months; died February, 1862, at Fort Donelson.
Kisling, G. M. P., service, 1 year; discharged at Wytheville 1862.
Kisling, Joseph, Co. B; battles, 10; service, 3 years; killed at Leetown, August, 1864.
Lawson, Joseph, enlisted January, 1862, Co. B; died at Nashville, Tennessee, March, 1862.
Lloyd, William F., enlisted January 26, 1863; Co. C.
McMillian, William, Co. B; corporal; service, 2 years; discharged 1862 at Narrows, New River.
Mabybe, Pleasant, Co. B; died in Pulaski county, February, 1863.
McGee, J. P., enlisted in Patrick county; Co. D; captured March, 1865; held at Point Lookout 3 months; battles, 20; service, 4 years.
Morris, William, Co. B; sergeant; captured at Waynesboro; held at Fort Delaware; battles, 15; service, 4 years.
McMillian, Samuel B., Co. B; corporal; wounded August, 1864, at Leetown; captured September, 1864, at Winchester; battles, 12; service, 4 years.
Murry, Ransom, enlisted spring of 1862; Co. C; service, 3 years.
Nixon, Robert P., Co. B; wounded and captured at Winchester, September 19, 1864; battles, 12.
Puck, William M., Co. E, captured at Waynesboro; held in prison about 3 months; battles, 8; service, 4 years.
Porks, W. M., enlisted 1864 in Giles county; Co. I; captured at Waynesboro; held at Fort Delaware 4 months; battles, 7; service, 15 months.
Peck, John A., enlisted May 1, 1862; Co. C; captured at Waynesboro; held at Fort Delaware; battles, 8; service, 3 years; discharged at Fort Delaware June 21, 1865.
Painter, William, Co. H; third lieutenant; promoted captain; wounded at Fort Donelson, Princeton, and Winchester; battles, 20; service, 4 years.

Repass, Newlon H., enlisted 1862; Co. C; promoted lieutenant; captured at Winchester; held at Fort Delaware 9 months; battles, 20; service, 3 years; discharged June 19, 1865, from Fort Delaware.
Repass, William G., enlisted in Bland county; Co. K; promoted sergeant, lieutenant, captain and major; slightly wounded five times, 1862, 1863 and 1864; captured in Kentucky in 1862; held at Camp Chase 2 months; transferred 1862 to 7th Confederate Battalion Cavalry; battles, 28; service, during the war; discharged at Christiansburg.
Stone, Riley, Co. B; battles, 15; service, 4 years.
Swecker, Robert E., Co. B; promoted captain; captured at Leetown; held at Camp Chase; battles, 20; service, 4 years.
Sayers, David H., enlisted June, 1862; Co. B; captured at Waynesboro; held at Fort Delaware 4 months; battles, 20; service, 3 years.
Smart, David, Co. B; wounded at Fort Donelson; battles 10; service, 4 years.
Smart, William P., Co. B; service, 4 years.
Shenall, Calvin, enlisted July, 1862; Co. B.
Saul, Edmund, Co. B; wounded at Fayettesville; service, 18 months; discharged December, 1862, at Narrows, New River.
Stone, Samuel, Co. B; promoted sergeant and lieutenant; wounded at Winchester; battles 12; service, 4 years.
Sayers, James A., enlisted in Patrick county; Co. B; wounded at Winchester; captured at Waynesboro; held at Fort Delaware 4 months; battles, 10; service, 4 years.

Sayers, Thomas, Co. B; transferred April, 1864, to 8th Virginia Cavalry; battles, 5; service, 4 years.
Sheffey, D. W., enlisted March, 1865; Co. B; service, 3 weeks.
Shafer, Cloyd, Co. B; wounded at Frederick City; transferred 1864 to Captain Moore's Co., Bowen's Regiment; battles 15; service, 3 years, 6 months.
Tate, Robert C., enlisted May, 1863; Co. B; quartermaster's department; service, 2 years
Tate, William H., Co. B; first lieutenant, promoted captain; battles, 15; service, 3 years; killed at New Market.
Thompson, James, Co. B; promoted sergeant; wounded at Newton; battles, 10; service, 4 years.
Umberger, W. A., Co. C; corporal; promoted first sergeant; captured at Waynesboro; held at Fort McHenry 3 months; battles, 25; service, 4 years; discharged at Fort McHenry June 20, 1865.
Umberger, Charles W., Co. C; promoted sergeant; captured at Waynesboro; held at Fort Delaware about 4 months; battles, 10; service, 4 years; discharged at Fort Delaware, June 21, 1865.
Umberger, Isaac M., enlisted July, 1862; Co. C; battles, 12; service, 3 years.
Umberger, E. H., enlisted March, 1863, at Narrows, Giles county; Co. C; wounded September 19, 1864, at Kernstown; captured at Waynesboro; held at Fort Delaware 4 months; battles, 10; service, 2 years; discharged at Fort Delaware June 25, 1865.
Wheeler, William R., Co. B; promoted quartermaster sergeant; battles, 7; service, 4 years.
Wheeler, Samuel B., Co. B; promoted commissary sergeant; captured at Waynesboro; held at Fort Delaware 4 months; battles, 8; service, 4 years.

COMPANY H, SIXTY-THIRD VIRGINIA INFANTRY.

Reynold's Brigade, Loring's Division ; enlisted May, 1861.

G. W. Keasling, captain; discharged 1863.
Sylvester Phillippe, first lieutenant; promoted captain.
Joseph Wassum, second lieutenant.
William L. Huddle, third lieutenant; wounded 1863 at Columbia, Tennessee.
David Gray, first sergeant; taken prisoner 1864 at Atlanta; sent to Camp Chase.
B F. Phillippe, sergeant. James F. Painter, sergeant.
John S. Derting, sergeant; taken prisoner 1864 in Georgia and died in prison.
G. W. Gray, corporal.
Michael Neff, corporal, promoted sergeant.
—— Anderson, corporal.
Anderson, John. Arnold, William.
Avery, Franklin. Avery, John.
Alford, ——
Bumgardner, Jacob, wounded 1864 at Zions Church.
Bumgardner, Silvester. Buck, Ephraim.
Buck, Lafayettee.
Catron, Ephraim, wounded 1864 at Zions Church.
Crigger, Ephraim. Crigger, James.
Crigger, John. Collins, William.
Collins, Weyman. Fisher, Harvey J.
Grubb, Jackson. Hedrick, Joseph.
Hall, Alexander, wounded 1863 at Chickamauga.
Horn, Isaac, transferred to Co. B, 29th Virginia Infantry.
Kegley, James, taken prisoner 1865 in South Carolina.
Kegley, Lee. Kegley, Alexander.
Keesler, Gordon.
Lindsay, Calvin, taken prisoner at Zions Church.
Musser, Michael. Matting, Henry.
Nelson, Isham.
Neff, William, wounded at Zions Church, Georgia, June, 1864.

Patton, Russel.
Painter, Gus, died 1863.
Prim, David.
Simmerman, Christopher.
Soultien, J. W.
Thomas, Jacob.
Weaver, Joseph, wounded 1863 at Chickamauga.
Walters, John B.
Wampler, George.
Wyrick, William.
Patton, John.
Parks, Whelan.
Steffey, Franklin.
Simmerman, Andrew.
Swecker, Isaac N.
Tartar, James.
Walters, James.
Williams, Charles.

FURTHER MENTION OF WYTHE COUNTY SOLDIERS.

[Where date of enlistment is not given it was in 1861; where place is not given it was in Wythe county; where no date of death or discharge is given, the service was till the close of the war. Where no rank is given the service was as private.]

Armbrist, George W., enlisted 1863; Co. G, 22d Virginia Cavalry; battles, 20; service, 2 years.
Arnold, George, enlisted 1863; Co. G, 8th Virginia Infantry Reserves; service, 2 years.
Baker, R. P., enlisted April 20, 1864; Co. B, 38th Virginia Infantry.
Bramblett, W. H., M. D., enlisted in Grayson county; Co. C, 8th Virginia Cavalry; captain; appointed surgeon in 1862, in 2d army brigade, West Virginia, and army of Tennessee, and finally hospital duty; battles, 6; service, 4 years.
Bourne, H. G., enlisted at Sharpsburg, Bath county, Kentucky; Co. I, 8th Kentucky Cavalry; captured on Morgan's raid July 26, 1863; held at Camp Chase and Camp Douglas 19 months, 24 days; battles, 20; service, 3 years.
Bowen, H. S., enlisted in Tazewell county; Marshall's staff; cavalry; staff officer; promoted colonel; battles, 20 or more; service, through the war.
Brown, Montgomery P., enlisted in May, 1862; Co. D, 4th Virginia Infantry; died June 25, 1862.
Cornett, W. H., enlisted 1863 in Grayson county; Co. C, 8th Virginia Infantry Reserves; service, 2 years.
Carter, Franklin, enlisted May, 1863; Co. K, 54th Virginia Infantry; wounded in Georgia; battles, 10; service, 2 years.
Collins, William P., enlisted April 1, 1862; Co. H, 54th Virginia Infantry.
Colfre, R. A., enlisted April, 1863; Co. E, 67th Virginia Infantry; service, about 6 months.
Criggar, J. M., enlisted April 1, 1862; Co. H, 63d Virginia Infantry.
Calfee, William B., enlisted at Christiansburg; Co. F, 54th Virginia Infantry; wounded June 22, 1864, at Mount Zion, Ga.; battles, 10; service, 4 years.
Corvin, Stephen, enlisted April 13, 1862; Co. D, 23d Virginia Infantry.
Campbell, Dr. C. C., enlisted in 1864; 4th Georgia Battalion Engineers; surgeon; battles, 2; service, 11 months.
Caterson, E. D., enlisted April 10, 1862; Co. H, 63d Virginia Infantry; wounded at New Hope.
Cassell, S. H., Co. E, 23d Battalion Infantry; promoted third lieutenant; service, 4 years.
Doak, K. D., first sergeant; Co. B. 24th Virginia Infantry; promoted second lieutenant; wounded near Richmond, August, 1864.
Doak, N. S, enlisted October 1, 1862; Co, I, 12th Virginia Cavalry; captured at Dry Creek, January, 1864; held at Point Lookout.
Dutton, Jonas, 63d Virginia Infantry; captured 1864; held at Fort Delaware; died 1865 on way from prison.
Fisher, H. J., enlisted 1862; Co H, 63d Virginia Infantry.
Fisher, James W., enlisted February, 1864; Co. G, 8th Virginia Infantry Reserves; promoted sergeant; service. 14 months.

Felts, John W., enlisted August, 1862; Co. G, 22d Virginia Cavalry; battles, 20; service, 3 years.

Gleaves, G. Wythe, enlisted in 1863; Home Guards; promoted major; battles, 3; service, 2 years.

Gleaves, Samuel C, infantry; surgeon; promoted division surgeon and medical director; battles, 20; service, 3 years; discharged 1864 on account of sickness.

Graham, Wirt B., enlisted in Greenbrier county, West Virginia; Co. A, 8th Virginia Cavalry; promoted sergeant-major, first lieutenant; wounded at Bunkers Hill, September 4, 1864; battles, 35; service, 4 years.

Hukrader, I. R., enlisted May 15, 1862, at Camp Jackson; Co. D, 23d Battalion Infantry; detailed wagonmaster; service, 3 years.

Howe, W. G., enlisted August 1, 1864; Co. F, 14th Virginia Cavalry.

Hancock, J. M., enlisted June, 1864; Co. B, 1st Virginia Reserves; service, 1 year.

Hillenburg, Eli, enlisted April, 1862; Co. B, 29th Virginia Infantry; battles, 23; service, 3 years.

Huddle, B J., enlisted at Camp Fulkerson; Co. B, 29th Virginia Infantry; wounded January 10, 1862, at Prestonburg, Kentucky; April 1, 1865, at Five Forks; battles, 12; service, 3 years, 8 months.

Henly, William, enlisted 1864; Co. K, 1st Virginia Reserves; service, 1 year.

Hancock, J. A., Co. E, 50th Virginia Infantry; second sergeant; captured at at Fort Donelson February 16, 1862; captured again, at Spotsylvania C. H., May 5, 1864; held at Point Lookout, then Elmira, N. Y.; battles, 5; service, 4 years, 2 months; discharged at Elmira, N. Y., June 3, 1865.

Jones, B. F., Co. B, 29th Virginia Infantry; battles, 6; service, 3 years, 6 months

Kitchens, B. F., enlisted 1864; Co. G, 8th V. I. Reserves; service, 1 year.

Kesner, George P., enlisted in Smyth county; Co. A, 8th Virginia Cavalry; wounded at Carnifex Ferry 1861, at Kernstown 1864; battles, 22; service 4 years.

Landreth, Robert, enlisted 1863, Co. G, 22d Virginia Cavalry; battles, 13; service, 2 years.

Lindamood, Stephen, enlisted April 1, 1862; Co H, 65th Virginia Infantry.

Lindamood, Robert A., Co. I, 60th Virginia Infantry; first sergeant; promoted captain; killed at Missionary Ridge.

Mercer, W. W., enlisted at Abingdon; Co. B, 29th Virginia Infantry; battles, 18; service, about 4 years.

Miller, T. K., enlisted April, 1864; Co. A, 14th Battalion Virginia Reserves.

Mitchell, George D., Co B, 29th Virginia Infantry; wounded May 12, 1864, between Richmond and Petersburg; service, 4 years.

Mize, J. M., enlisted at Richmond; Co. F, 16th Georgia Infantry; captured near Fredericksburg 1863; battles,.16; service, 4 years.

Myers, W. A., enlisted at Salisbury, North Carolina; 6th North Carolina Infantry; orderly; promoted first lieutenant; acting adjutant; wounded May 31, 1862, at Seven Pines; at Plymouth, N. C., May, 1863; captured near Winchester March, 1865; held at Governors Island 3 months; battles, 25; service, 4 years.

Morlick, James M., enlisted in Botetourt county; Co. I, 28th Virginia Infantry; captured at Port Gibson 1863; held at Alton, Illinois, 2 months; transferred to Anderson's Battalion 1861; battles, 6; service, 4 years.

Malory, Thomas, Co. D, 22d Virginia Cavalry; wounded at Cedar Mountain, 1863; battles, 10; service, 4 years.

Matuny, William H, enlisted 1863; Co. H, 63d Virginia Infantry; service, 2 years.

Neese, G. J., enlisted May 1, 1862; Co. A, 63d Virginia Infantry; detailed blacksmith; captured and paroled at Franklin, Tennessee; battles, 3; service, 3 years.

Neff, Michael, enlisted May, 1862; Co. H, 63d Virginia Infantry; promoted sergeant; service, 3 years; discharged at Greensboro, N. C.

Poff, Harvey S., Co. B, 29th Virginia Infantry; battles, 16; service, 4 years.

Pendleton, M. M., enlisted at Abingdon; Co. D, 1st Virginia Cavalry; promoted first sergeant; battles, 15 or 20; service, 4 years.

Porter, A. S., enlisted 1864, at Bull Gap, Tennessee; Co. A, 1st Tennessee Cavalry Battalion: battles, 4; service, 1 year.

Peirce, David S., enlisted October, 1862, at Cadet Military Institute at Lexington; Co. B, corps of cadet, artillery; sergeant; wounded at battle of New Market, by shell; went into active service at the age of 16; battles, New Market and others.
Phillippe, John M., Co. H, 63d Virginia Infantry; promoted color corporal; wounded at Bentonville, N. C., 1865; battles, 9.
Quisenbury, James G., enlisted 1862; Co. G, 21st Virginia Cavalry.
Quisenbury, William, enlisted 1863; Co. G, 8th Virginia Infantry Reserves; service, 2 years.
Rosenbaum, A. J., enlisted in Smyth county; Co. A, 8th Virginia Cavalry; detailed blacksmith; captured at Five Forks; held 2½ months at Point Lookout; battles, 12; service, 3 years, 9 months; discharged at Point Lookout June 12, 1865.
Robinson, J. M., enlisted at Bristol, Tennessee, 1864; Co. A, 1st Tennesee Battalion Infantry; first lieutenant; captured near Bristol, December 4, 1864; held at Camp Chase 6 months.
Rowen, H. S., enlisted in Tazewell county; 22d Virginia Cavalry; major; promoted colonel; battles, about 20; service, 4 years.
Rodgers, Thomas H., enlisted at Bowling Green, Kentucky; Co. I, 11th Tennessee Cavalry; promoted sergeant and lieutenant; wounded near Nashville, Tennessee; captured at Fort Donelson, and at Missionary Ridge; held at Camp Douglas, and at Rock Island, Ill., 11 months; battles, 25; service, 4 years.
Sharetz, John P., enlisted October 1, 1864; Co. K, 1st Virginia Infantry; captured at Farmville; held at Point Lookout.
Staley, William R., enlisted 1863; Co. K, 21st Virginia Cavalry; battles, 6; service, 2 years.
Slagle, T. G., enlisted February, 1864; Co. G, 8th Virginia Infantry Reserves; service, 14 months.
Smith, John, Alleghany Artillery; wounded 1862 at Winchester.
South, James F., enlisted at Laurel Springs, N. C.; Co. A, 34th North Carolina Infantry; promoted sergeant; wounded at Malvern Hill and at Chancellorsville; battles, 10; service, 3 years, 8 months.
Spangler, William H., enlisted at Dublin, 1864; Co. G, 36th Virginia Infantry; wounded at Cedar Creek, October 19, 1864; battles, 5; service, 1 year.
Sutherland, John, enlisted 1864; Co. A, 17th Virginia Infantry; battles, 4; service, 1 year.
Tarter, James H., enlisted April 8, 1862; Co. H, 63d Virginia Infantry; battles, 8; service, 3 years; discharged near Petersburg, March 25, 1865.
Taylor, Jonathan, enlisted at Kinston, N. C.; Co. C, 29th Virginia Infantry; battles, 25; service, 4 years.
Terry, William, Co. A, 4th Virginia Infantry; enlisted April 1, 1861; discharged April, 1862; re-enlisted Co. C, 4th Virginia Cavalry, April 20, 1862; first lieutenant; promoted captain, major, colonel, and brigadier general; wounded at second Manassas, Mine Run, twice at Spotsylvania C. H., and at Petersburg; battles, about 20.
Vaught, N. T., Co. B, 29th Virginia Infantry; second sergeant, promoted first lieutenant; battles, 24.
Wilson, J. J. M., enlisted April, 1862; Co. A, 63d Virginia Infantry; promoted sergeant; service, 3 years.
Wisley, Albert, enlisted at Abingdon; Co. A, 63d Virginia Infantry; promoted first lieutenant; battles, 10; service, 3 years; discharged at Salisbury, N. C.
Welsh, Nicholas S., enlisted 1864; Co. G, 8th Virginia Infantry Reserves; battles, 2; service, 2 years.
Walters, William, enlisted at Camp Lee, October 30, 1864; Co. I, 29th Virginia Infantry; service, 9 months.
Walker, James A., enlisted at Richmond; Co. C, 4th Virginia Infantry; captain; promoted lieutenant-colonel in June, 1861, and transferred to 18th Virginia Infantry; colonel in April, 1862; brigadier general, "Stonewall Brigade," May, 1863; major-general, Early's division, March, 1865; wounded at Sharpsburg, and at Spotsylvania C. H.

Wohlford, George M., enlisted 1863; Co. K, 21st Virginia Cavalry; promoted sergeant; captured 1864 at Moorefield; held at Camp Chase 8 months; battles, 12; service, 2 years.

Williams, Andy F., enlisted 1864; Co. E; service, 1 year.

Wood, R. Raper, enlisted April, 1863; Co. H, 8th Virginia Cavalry; battles, 20; service, 22 months.

Ward, S. R., enlisted in 1863; Wythe Home Guards; captain; service, 2 years.

Ward, Chester, enlisted 1862 in Lee county; Co. I, 37th Virginia Cavalry; promoted first sergeant; wounded and captured at Frederick City, Maryland, 1863; held at Baltimore 6 months; battles, 10; service, 3 years.

Ward, D. J., Co. H, 61st Virginia Infantry; wounded at Fort Donelson, February, 1862; battles, 2; service, 1 year.

Yates, J. A., enlisted at Charlestown, West Virginia, 1862; Co. B, 12th Virginia Cavalry; captured at Brandy Station; escaped near Berryville same year; captured again near Berryville; held at McHenry about 6 weeks; service, about 2 years.

RESOURCES

OF

SOUTH-WEST VIRGINIA

SHOWING THE

MINERAL DEPOSITS OF IRON, COAL, ZINC, COPPER AND LEAD.

ALSO,

THE STAPLES OF THE VARIOUS COUNTIES, METHODS OF TRANSPORTATION, ACCESS, ETC.

ILLUSTRATED BY NUMEROUS PLATES AND LARGE COLORED MAP REPRESENTING THE GEOGRAPHY, GEOLOGY AND TOPOGRAPHY OF THE COUNTRY.

BY

C. R. BOYD, E. M.,

MEMBER OF AM. SOC. OF CIVIL ENGINEERS, AND OF THE INSTITUTE OF MINING ENGINEERS.

THIRD EDITION.

Pps. 47 - 90 are reproduced herewith.

NEW YORK:
JOHN WILEY & SONS,
15 ASTOR PLACE.
1881.

WYTHE COUNTY.

To open the chapter on Wythe County in a manner worthy of the high claims it has upon the consideration of the public, will be quite as difficult as it will be to close it with the consciousness of having done justice to the subject.

Every endeavor has been made to treat all the territory described in this volume with the utmost impartiality; and it is not to be supposed, because development has been pushed to a much greater extent in Wythe than in any other county, that an impartial description of it, as it presents itself, is intended in the least to detract from the just merits of the other fine counties composing Southwestern Virginia.

On the contrary, an apology is due to the patient friends, who have so kindly awaited the appearance of this book, for the imperfect manner in which this great county, with its varied resources of a superior character, is treated. But it is due, also, to the reader to say that much that is interesting with regard to Wythe would have been omitted had the book made its appearance twelve months ago.

In the development of its different ore fields the county is making rapid strides toward a position of commercial importance, well calculated to excite the just pride of her citizens, as well as to encourage the friends of the State in the hope that so progressive a spirit, showing in other counties of the section as well, will tend far toward the early solution of those financial difficulties which have well nigh compromised her honor, and which, without the active development of the lately-hidden resources of the State, would find but a tardy settlement.

That Wythe is nobly doing its duty in increasing the tax-paying power of its own and neighboring communities, no one can doubt who will look at the different FURNACES and mines recently put in operation in the county. And these works, it may be submitted, supplying extensive home markets, besides employing the industrious labor of the country at remunerative wages, are making the burdens of the State much easier to be borne than formerly; not only releasing old residents from embarrassment, but bringing in new men, wealthy, and, at the same time, willing to help the country out of its troubles.

It is in no wise intended in such an introduction to underrate the importance of the agricultural interests of the county, nor of the manufacturing enterprises which are struggling through a healthy infancy to a mature age of great usefulness and importance.

If conditions of transportation could once be made to assume a correct relation to the different interests of agriculture, mines, and manufactures, Wythe would not be long in taking a leading position among the counties most noted for high commercial prosperity; and this comparison might very safely be extended to the most favored localities throughout the whole country.

HOW BOUNDED.

Wythe is separated from Bland County, on the north, by Big Walker's Mountain, except six miles of the northeastern end of the line, which leaves Big Walker's Mountain, and cuts over south to the top of Little Walker's, or Cloyd's Mountain.

On the south it is divided from the counties of Grayson, to the southwest, and Carroll, to the southeast, by Iron Mountain and its extension, known as Poplar Camp Mountain. On the east is Pulaski County, and on the west is the county of Smyth.

Within these boundaries may be considered to lie an extent and variety of mineral and agricultural lands which, taken together, are unsurpassed by the same area anywhere else in the United States.

Alternating with each other, in the south side of the county, are wonderful veins and deposits of Iron ores, Manganese ores, and Lead and Zinc ores of extraordinary purity. While in the northern half of the county fine magnetic and brown ores lie close to good workable veins of semi-bituminous and semi-anthracite coal. Lying between these great mineral belts, and interlaced with them, are fine blue-grass and farming lands of a high order, mineral springs not being uncommon.

HOW WATERED.

The county is well watered by New River (which flows through the southeastern portion of the county), and some of its principal tributaries, such as Cripple Creek and Reed Creek. These streams, with their many minor tributaries, leave but a small space of the whole area which is not thoroughly well watered, and, like all mountain streams of the section, are unfailing.

New River yields, at the Wythe Lead Mines, about 1,500 cubic feet per second. Reed Creek, watering the central and northern portions of the county, passes, at different points, from 30 up to 180 cubic feet per second; while Cripple Creek, watering the southwestern portion of the county, yields nearly as much, presenting much excellent water power throughout the county, as the descent is sufficient to give, on every two miles' length of the smaller streams, a fall of over twelve feet average; while New River, except the twelve feet at Pearce's Falls, shows an average fall per mile of about eight feet.

GEOLOGICAL.

Beginning on the south side of the county, and proceeding north in the description, Wythe County holds the rocks of nearly all the epochs, and their subdivisions between the

Huronian and Cambrian on the south, and the Proto-Carboniferous toward the north side of the county, and in nearly all the eras represented by these rocks nature seems to have expanded herself to the full in a lavish deposition of some of the best and most useful ores.

As will be seen by examining the accompanying sections, the Potsdam sandstones, and subjacent hydro-mica slates and conglomerates, compose the Iron Mountain mainly. Only here and there do the felspars, which are so common in Grayson, to the south, assume any importance. This Iron Mountain is then flanked on the north by the red Calciferous slates, the Potsdam and Calciferous being usually separated by an extraordinary band of brown iron ore and manganese ores of great thickness and persistency. Next to the north of the red slates are the great bands of variegated limestones, holding dolomites (sometimes bedded on bands of silicious limestones), which are the gangue of the unsurpassed lead and zinc deposits now being so well developed in the New River section.

In these rocks are also the deposits of iron sulphurets, which, decomposing, have left such vast deposits of pure brown iron ore.

Passing north of this line, crossing the line of Cripple Creek and New River, there are found the upturned edges of these same rocks again, but now dipping southwardly, as on the south side they dipped northwardly for the most part, or were so overturned as to dip southwardly in reverse order; altogether making of the south side of the county a great trough-like basin, flanked on the south by Iron Mountain, and on the north by Lick Mountain, and its continuation, Draper's Mountain.

In Lick Mountain, in the center of the county, the Potsdam rocks, with their peculiar fossil—the Scolithus—form a great broken anticlinal, giving way on the north side to the band of red Calciferous slates and shales, from which they are separated by the usual bands of iron and manganese ores. On the north of this is the great band of Lower Silurian or upper Calciferous limestones, with steep dips flanked on the north of Wytheville by the brown sandstones and black slates of Pine Ridge for the west half of the county, but by a repetition of the same limestones further east in the direction of Max Meadows. To the north of these the conditions materially change, the persistency of strata from northeast to southwest being broken by the influence of the great cross flexures and compressions common to the range of mountains just north of this line—in the north boundary of the county. Thus, passing north of Wytheville and west of Queen's Knob, you encounter the upturned edges of Lower Silurian limestones—here and there showing magnetic and brown iron ores and variegated marble—until you reach a great fault at the south base of Little Walker's Mountain; there you are suddenly brought into contact with the rocks of the Proto-Carboniferous, holding good coal veins. But when you pass east of Queen's Knob, for nearly the whole of that portion of the county there has been no bringing up, on so large a scale, of the Lower Silurian limestones. On the contrary, very valuable areas of the Lower Coal Measures still remain, as those north of Clark's Summit and Max Meadows. To the north of these, as in the Cove, is a band of the lower limestones again, running up into the Hudson River and Clinton series in the Cove Mountain, but flanked on the north by the great fault just mentioned, at the south foot of Little Walker's Mountain, bringing in the Proto-Carboniferous dipping southwardly.

These measures are underlaid in the heart of Little Walker's Mountain, by Devonian rocks, including the representative of the Olean conglomerate, and these again are underlaid in regular order by the slates and shales of the Marcellus, Ham-

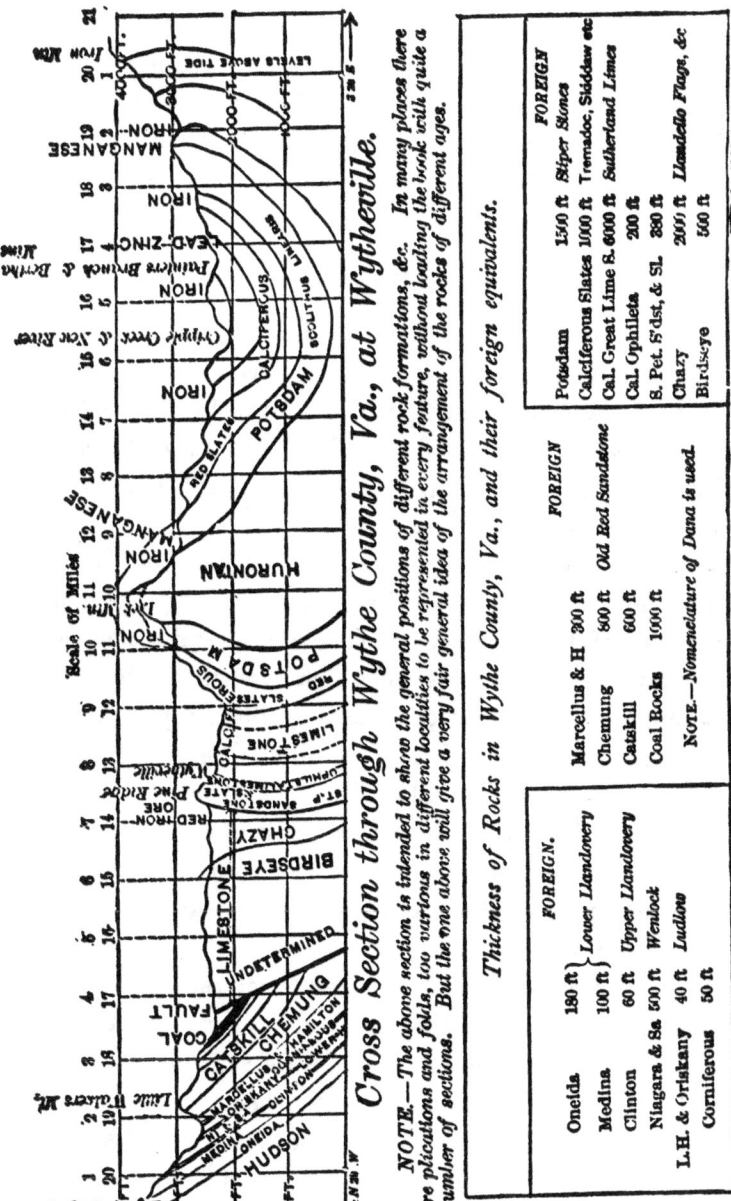

Cross Section through Wythe County, Va., at Wytheville.

NOTE.—The above section is intended to show the general positions of different rock formations, &c. In many places there are plications and folds, too various in different localities to be represented in every feature, without loading the book with quite a number of sections. But the one above will give a very fair general idea of the arrangement of the rocks of different ages.

Thickness of Rocks in Wythe County, Va., and their foreign equivalents.

		FOREIGN			FOREIGN
Oneida	180 ft		Marcellus & H	300 ft	
Medina	100 ft	} Lower Llandovery	Chemung	800 ft	Old Red Sandstone
Clinton	60 ft	Upper Llandovery	Catskill	600 ft	
Niagara & Sa.	500 ft	Wenlock	Coal Rocks	1000 ft	
L.H. & Oriskany	40 ft	Ludlow	NOTE.—Nomenclature of Dana is used.		
Corniferous	50 ft				

		FOREIGN
Potsdam	1500 ft	Skper Stones
Calciferous Slates	1000 ft	Tremadoc, Siddaw etc
Cal. Great Lime S.	6000 ft	Sutherland Limes
Cal. Ophileta	200 ft	
S. Pet. S'dst, & Sl.	380 ft	
Chazy	2000 ft	Llandeilo Flags, &c
Birdseye	500 ft	

ilton, Corniferous, and Oriskany series, to get to them passing through the American equivalent of the Old Red Sandstone. Next to the north of these, in regular order, dipping southwardly, are the rocks of the Upper Silurian Age, including the Dyestone iron ore series, taking us to the Oneida grit in the heart of Big Walker's Mountain—our north boundary line for Wythe County.

COAL.

Wythe holds a very respectable area of the upper New River series of coal measures. This coal is usually assigned to the Proto-Carboniferous Epoch. It shows thirteen distinct veins, and many of the fossils developed would lead one as readily to place this coal in one epoch as another, except, perhaps, the upper measures.

As may be seen in the accompanying map, the coal is confined to the northern side of the county, running along the south base of Little Walker's Mountain, except a considerable area in the northeast side, which spreads southwardly, extending to and just over the Atlantic, Mississippi and Ohio Railroad; this condition being observable near to, as well as about four miles east of Max Meadows Depot.

The veins of coal in the south flank of Little Walker's Mountain run, almost continuously for twenty-four miles, through that part of the county, with a general average dip of 30 , trend north, 70° east.

These outcrops are then separated from those nearer the Atlantic, Mississippi and Ohio Railroad by an uprising of lower rocks, as in Cove Mountain and the little ridge just south of it. Thus the area in which the openings have been made near Max Meadows may be said to be about six miles long, east and west, and two miles wide from north to south, at its widest.

The veins in Little Walker's Mountain have been opened

at several points along their length in the county, notably at Boyd's Mine, where the Stony Fork of Reed Creek cuts through the mountain; at Asa Brown's; at two or three places north of Rural Retreat Depot in the west end, and at Brown's Coal Bank, in the Cove.

As already remarked, these veins number thirteen so far as known. Beginning below is an eight-inch seam, bedded upon a thin stratum of quartzeous black slate overlying a heavy band of grindstone grit. Next above this seam are ten feet of black slate and hard sandstone, the sandstone being the foot wall of a three-feet vein of semi-bituminous coal of good quality; overlying this, are twenty feet of alternate bands of black and gray slates and shales; then twenty-one inches of really excellent flaming bituminous coal, of which the analysis appears below; then thirty feet of gray and black slates and shales and thin bedded sandstones, leading up to a fourteen-inch vein of good bituminous coal; then one hundred feet of alternations of gray slates and thin sandstones, holding nine veins of coal, no one of which is a foot thick. These measures are not constant, though the veins are continuous for great distances. The disturbances to which they have been subjected have caused them, in places (as at Stony Fork), to sometimes assume a thickness of eight feet for short distances. This may be owing to end compressions, as well as to folding from the opposite direction.

In the Max Meadows and Clark's Summit coal area, the most important openings are those made by Joseph Crockett, two and a half miles north of Max Meadows Depot, showing coal eight feet thick: and by Draper and others, one mile north of Clark's Summit, near the Pulaski line. This coal, for the greater part of the area, is of a semi-bituminous variety, nearly approaching an anthracite. At the Draper and Clark opening the coal dips southwardly, showing several good veins, the best of which is six feet thick. These veins occupy a basin, the southern rim of which is one quarter of a mile south of the Atlantic, Mississippi and Ohio Railroad, just east of Clark's Summit.

The analysis of the coal from Stony Fork is as follows, by THOMAS EGLESTON:

Water.................................... 0.34
Volatile combustible matter 21.30
Fixed carbon..............................70.32
Sulphur 1.61
Ash...................................... 6.43

The coal, the analysis of which is just shown, from Little Walker's Mountain, is much preferred by blacksmiths. It is also used to some extent in grates in the town of Wytheville, giving very general satisfaction.

The quantity so far taken from these veins does not exceed twelve hundred tons. From the excellent coke this coal makes, and its nearness to existing lines of through transportation, it should assume a much more important position than it now occupies.

IRON.

Brown Iron Ore.

It is difficult to know where to begin the description of what is commonly known as "brown hematite iron ore," there is so much of it, of a superior grade, in different parts of the county. The first great continuous horizon of it, mentioned in describing the geology, occupies a position in the north flank of Iron Mountain, near the division between the Potsdam and Calciferous sub-epochs. It is in the continuation of the same great belt described as existing in the north flank of Pilot Mountain, in Montgomery County, and in the Laurel Creek country in Pulaski County. In Wythe County, at nearly any point you choose to inspect along the range, you will find heavy masses of this brown ore, sometimes mixed with manganiferous iron ore, and sometimes giving way to pure manganese ore. This great vein often attains a thickness of more than one hundred feet, but does not yield as fine a quality of ore as the deposits which lie nearer to the lead and zinc horizon.

The quantity of ore which this immense vein will yield in the county, on the Iron Mountain spurs, is far greater than that of all other deposits combined; but, as a general rule, contains a few hundredths more of phosphorus than will admit it as a strictly Bessemer ore, as may be seen from an inspection of the analysis here given by Mr. BRITTON, of ore from this horizon:

ANALYSIS BY J. BLODGETT BRITTON.

Metallic iron	57.98
Insoluble silicious matter	.49
Sulphur	.19
Phosphorus	.29

This ore can be seen in large masses by following up Francis Mill Creek near to its head, upon which are now located the Sayers and Oglesby Furnace, and the Noble Furnace. These furnaces, however, as will be seen further on, derive their ores from the purer horizon nearer the lead and zinc lead. It has been remarked, in the description of Montgomery County, that this Iron Mountain or Pilot Mountain deposit of brown ore is derived from the decomposition of sulphurets; a decomposition, however, which seems to have been carried to great depths. Within the Calciferous rocks, and within nine hundred yards to the north of the vein just described, there are two more deposits, more or less continuous, rarely ever exceeding twenty feet in thickness, and very much the same kind of ore. This series of veins extends, almost continuously, the whole length of the south side of the county.

The Second Horizon of Brown Ores.

Going northwardly, the next great belt of brown ores, are those extending from near the mouth of Reed Island Creek up the New River (both sides) to the mouth of Cripple Creek; thence up that creek to its head, into Smyth County, whence they pass on to the southwest.

This truly great and valuable band of ores is the one lying about the Lead and Zinc Belt, and upon which are located the furnaces and forges chiefly. It is sometimes several miles in width, being governed in this by the gentleness or steepness of the dip of the great band of rocks holding the lead and zinc. This ore, as has been stated, is due to the decomposition of sulphureted ores; and the hills in which it is usually found, being from 80 to 200 feet above the neighboring water-courses, there is mining and stripping above the undecomposed ore for many years to come. This band of ore, as on the old furnace lands of David Graham, seems sometimes to occupy a fissure in the great limestone belt. This may very well be true. It is plain that there has been fissure action along that line. A close inspection of the Old Lead Mines shows that lead, zinc, and iron have all been so acted upon by the heat resulting from pressure as to have been fused and interjected into the gangue surrounding and above it.

Following the zone either way a short distance from the old lead mines, you see these same measures resume their original position as a stratification between well-defined ledges. On the Graham lands this fissure action is evident from the lode cutting across the trend of the strata. And it can be accounted for by recurring to the action of the forces engaged in folding the earth's crust thereabouts. The crumpling or folding action was evidently from southeast to northwest, and where fragments of the crust did not slide up upon each other in monoclinal shape, they proved " pieces of resistance " to each other, to such an extent that, in order to satisfy the general, conditions of the whole action, they were crushed and fused by the great pressure, bringing about fissure action in the attempt of fused matter, gases, etc., to break their way to the atmosphere above. In the extract quoted on page 59, Sir Robert Mallet gives a very good general formula deduced from his reasoning on the subject of Volcanic Force and Energy: but in this district these calculations would have to be based, perhaps, upon somewhat different data than those assumed by him. Not to be guilty of too great a diversion just here, it may be as well to say that the once-heated substance of the earth, in cooling, no doubt left a crust upon the outer surface, which, as the whole continued to cool inward, was left more or less unsustained, except by its own strength as a great arch. This arch or crust, not being able to sustain its own pressure, gave way in certain lines of fracture (some of which are represented by the trend of the Alleghanies and Blue Ridge Mountains), now represented by great fragments extruded and riding up upon each other, the force from the opposite direction (as the force of compression is supposed to have been equal in all directions upon the spherical arch) being compensated by cross flexures and the interlacing and intersliding of great fragments. Hence, though it may appear impracticable to apply the formula given—which was, no doubt, based upon equal resistance to a pressure exerted from all sides alike—still the study of it may lead to a determination of the problem as to the probable depth at which the fusing took place in this instance. To the general reader this departure may be of no interest whatever, but it is interesting to some individuals to inquire into many of these things which are puzzling the curious of our day and generation; and it may be appropriate to submit the conjecture, before dismissing the subject, that the great lines of fracture represented by the position of the Alleghanies, Blue Ridge, Rocky Mountains, and other mountains, have resulted from lines of vibration in the earth's crust, established in their direction by known forces, commencing, no doubt, with the first movements of the earth upon its axis, and gathering in intensity and definiteness, having been modified and somewhat controlled by the different forces of magnetism and gravitation which were exerted, from time to time, by other heavenly bodies.

SIR ROBT. MALLET ON VOLCANIC ENERGY.

In treating the subject of the immense geological formation holding the iron, lead, and zinc in Wythe and adjacent counties, it is thought wise to introduce the following interesting exposition regarding the probable history of the veins, as illustrated by a quotation from the elaborate paper of SIR ROBERT MALLET, F.R.S., upon kindred subjects.

In an excellent treatise on Volcanic Energy, by SIR ROBERT MALLET, F.R.S., etc., kindly loaned the author by Professor Francis Smith, of the University of Virginia, are found, not only the formula mentioned on the preceding page, but a remarkably clear and able exposition of the origin of volcanic force and energy. SIR ROBERT MALLET employs his trained mathematical reasoning and elaborate experiments with wonderful tact; and not only the writer, but numerous others would be delighted to see him engage in an investigation, to show whether the expansive force of the heat of the still-heated nucleus of the earth has anything to do in counteracting the pressure of the arched crust upon itself, which, without any such check, would at once, by its own gravitation, begin to be exerted with destructive effect; this expansive force itself being held in equilibrium by the nicely-proportioned weight of the superincumbent dome, having such a thickness and weight as would be required to suppress a dangerous excess of expansive energy from below. Such an investigation, in such able hands, might lead to a clear and incontrovertible showing of the thickness of the earth's crust, within a few thousand feet of the truth.

The author will present the formula, with the theorem upon which it is based, leaving to the reader to investigate the *whole* subject in SIR ROBERT'S paper.

"If a curved surface (of the nature of a hollow shell or membrane) be in equilibrium when exposed to forces acting normally to the surface everywhere, then the normal pressure at any point is equal to the force in the direction of the surface (or shell) at that point multiplied into the sum of the reciprocals of the principal radii of curvature.

* * * * * * * *

"83. Let P (Fig. 7) be the normal pressure upon the unit of surface (square inch or mile) cut from a pair of intersecting ribbons of the curved surface, as a, b, and c, d, at right angles to each other, and of unit breadth; T the tangential thrust on any of the faces of the unit square, respectively opposite (which, as being small in relation to the radii of curvature, may be considered as plane).

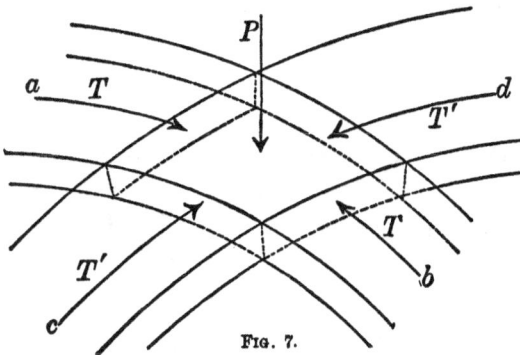

FIG. 7.

"Let the two radii of principal curvature (in a, b, and c, d,) be g_1 and g_2, then, as expressed in the theorem,

$$P = T\left(\frac{1}{g_1} + \frac{1}{g_2}\right). \quad \ldots \ldots \ldots \text{I.}$$

"T^1 having the same value.

"As regards the present application of the theorem, as the differences of g_1 and g_2 for our globe are very small (comparable with the difference between the polar and equatorial radii), and scarcely sensibly affect the curvature of the surface within limited areas, we may consider our globe as spherical, and $g_1 = g_2$, whence Equation I. becomes

$$P = \frac{2T}{g}, \quad \ldots \ldots \ldots \ldots \text{II.}$$

And

$$T = P \times \frac{g}{2}, \quad \ldots \ldots \ldots \text{III."}$$

With this formula, which is sustained by such eminent authority as "Lagrange" and "PROFESSOR R. S. BALL," of

Dublin, Sir Robert calculates the thrust or pressure near the earth's surface, represented by T, to be 952,666 tons per square foot, basing the calculation upon the density and resistance of granite, which pressure is 472 times greater than is necessary to crush granite or porphyry.

For a continuation of the subject, the reader is referred to the paper by SIR ROBERT MALLET, recorded in the "Philosophical Transactions of the Royal Society," June 20th, 1872.

To return to the subject of the brown iron ore of the great belt of Wythe, it is of such importance, both from its purity and quantity, that it can very truthfully be declared worthy of a full discussion, both as to its origin and the accidents to which it has been subjected; but brief space renders it necessary to give all the information obtained in relation to it in as few words as possible.

Perhaps the largest development of these ores near the eastern, or Pulaski side of the county, will be found at Rich Hill, the property of Forney, and on Little Reed Island Creek, a mile or more south. No exact measure of these deposits is possible to be taken. That they are very extensive the wide surface showings amply prove; and at the beds in Little Reed Island Creek, the ores show for hundreds of feet in width, in terrace shape, about 60 feet above the present level of the creek—the only probable evidence of the terrace epoch in this section of the country. These ores have resulted, in all probability, not only from the decomposition of adjacent sulphurets, but the creek at a remote day has no doubt brought them down in solution from the great decomposing sulphureted beds and veins of iron and copper in the county of Carroll above. That they are in surprising masses, and in the position indicated, the most casual examination will show.

From these latter beds the "Boom Furnace" will derive the most of its ores when completed. The next good showing is at Graham's new furnace, south bank of New River. The next great outcrop then is at the old Peirce ore bank, about two-thirds of a mile south of Peirce's Falls on New River. A quantity of this ore was at one time used at the Old Poplar Camp Forge, now not in existence. This ore is evidently bedded on a limestone foot wall, which has a dip toward southwest of about 45°, and is distant from the uprising hard Potsdam sandstone in Roaring Falls Mountain about one-fourth of a mile to the southwest. It appears to be over 40 feet thick at this point, trending east and west.

Then again, near the new furnace of the Wythe County Mining and Manufacturing Co., near Peirce's Falls, is a new opening in the ore of great richness and value. From both these places the furnace last mentioned will derive its ore.

A section taken north and south, across the general direction of this series in the neighborhood, determines the ore field to be not less than two and three-quarter miles broad, which is divided nearly equally by New River at Peirce's Falls. Thus, on the north side of the river, nearly opposite the last-named furnace, is that part of this rich ore belt in which one of the first iron-masters of the section, Mr. David Graham, located his first furnace and the forge, rolling-mill and nail works, now known as Graham's Forge. Although a great deal of ore has been both stripped and mined in this neighborhood, it is highly probable that the great body of the ore still remains intact. A most cursory examination will show the great limestones, which accompany the lead and zinc veins, outcropping throughout this part of the ore belt. Their dip is usually southwardly through the Graham lands, but this is by no means constant. Holding as they do large quantities of sulphurets, their decomposition (sometimes *in situ*) has left large quantities of a pure brown iron ore. It is in this immediate section, near the residence of D. P. Graham, that twelve feet thickness of sulphuret may be noticed, just below water level, in a fissure between great masses of the limestone. This is a part of the fissure referred to on page 58. It is also alluded to in a paper on this section, reported in the "Transactions of the American Institute of Mining Engineers," vol. v., page 85, also in a report on the "Minerals of New River," made by the author to Col. Wm. P. Craighill of the U. S. Engineers, Exec. Doc., Nov. 25th, Third Session, 45th Congress, U. S.

Then, again, as you proceed southwest, in a section taken across this series of ores, near the old Wythe lead and zinc mines, the same broad exhibit of surface showing is to be found. Over the Lead Mine's Hill, south of New River, and in the vicinity of Walton Furnace, about two miles north of the river, these excellent brown ores have been mined and their intrinsic value fully tested.

It is possible that these ores make a metal that has no superior for car-wheels and all other purposes requiring an iron of uniform strength.

Then, again, going southwest, this series shows other great deposits in the vicinity of Brown Hill Furnace, Cripple Creek, the ores now mined there being taken from the great lead and zinc band near Abraham Painters, the deposits of iron ore being within 150 feet of the zinc ores.

In fact the original sulphureted veins are now known to alternate with the veins of lead and zinc, though generally distinct. This ore, which has been in use for some time at Brown Hill Furnace, assays as follows for Mr. JOHN M. SHERRARD, analyst:

Metallic iron	55.702
Silica	4.590
Phosphorus	0.0745

Then, one-half mile north of Brown Hill Furnace, the same

band of rocks outcrop, yielding very much the same kind of ore.

A few miles west of the last-named vicinity the old forge lands of the late Alexander Peirce present the same general features, showing this brown iron ore in masses sufficient to warrant the belief of its existence in very large quantities, such as would be required to carry on operations of some magnitude. In some places the mass of strata, which, by decomposing, has given such immense surface quantities of this ore, is fully 180 feet thick, as found in position almost undisturbed.

Then, again, at the old Eagle Furnace, for miles on both sides of Cripple Creek, these same conditions are observable.

The old Lockett and Huddle Forges, now out of use, have sent some of the finest blooms to market, made from these ores, that perhaps were ever made. Except for small quantities of impurities, other than sulphur and phosphorus, the blooms were chemically pure.

A few miles farther west this series makes surface showings more southwardly. The Ravenscliff Furnace, the furnace of Sayers & Oglesby, the new furnaces on and near Francis Mill Creek, and the Noble and Beverly furnaces derive and expect to obtain their ores from beds of this series, which are well nigh thrust up within the area covered by the Iron Mountain ores proper; but still they are decidedly distinct, the accompanying variegated limestones peculiar to the lead and zinc measures at once betraying their origin.

Here these ores form a body which will yield not less than one million of tons, together with its immediately neighboring deposits of the same series.

A close analysis rendered by Mr. JAMES AUMANN and others gives nearly the following results:

BROWN HILL FURNACE, WYTHE CO., VA.

No. 1.—*Air Dry.*

Metallic iron 58.149	Powder a deep reddish brown.
Water 12.90	
Alumina 2.32	
Silica 1.09	The roasted ore gave 67.235 per cent. of metallic iron.
Magnesia .... Trace.	
Phosphorus .... None.	

No. 2.—*Air Dry.*

Metallic iron 55.54	
Water 11.72	
Alumina 5.89	Roasted, the ore gave 68.04 per cent. of metallic iron.
Silica 2.78	
Magnesia .... Trace.	
Phosphorus .... None.	

No. 3.—*Air Dry.*

Metallic iron 47.82	
Alumina 11.58	
Water 10.83	Roasted, the ore gave 53.28 per cent. of metallic iron.
Silica 9.87	
Magnesia 0.06	
Phosphorus .... None.	

Next to the southwest in this series occur the ores used by the old Porter Forge—of excellent character. Then, again, near to and just south of the Speedwell Furnace, these ores outcrop, across their general direction, for more than a mile. Their excellence and purity still remain a chief feature.

Then, again and again, as you proceed southwest, toward Smyth County, the same peculiar brown iron ore, either compact or honeycombed, makes its appearance, staining the soil red all along with a color peculiar to the ore.

It will be impossible to give any approximate idea of the quantity this great lead of iron ore will yield. That it will go high into the millions developments will no doubt amply prove.

The Brown Iron Ores and Manganiferous Ores of Lick and Draper's Mountains.

The ores of this series belong to the same horizon as those in the north spurs of the Iron Mountain and Pilot Mountain, and their general character is nearly the same, though they occasionally yield an ore of high purity.

Some of these veins and deposits are exceedingly massive, often running for great distances, preserving a thickness measuring sometimes one hundred and fifty feet, but usually not over twenty-eight or thirty feet, the fine manganiferous ore of the Glade Ore Bank not being over ten feet thick.

Both in Lick Mountain, on either side, and in Draper's Mountain, these ores are persistent, and give the following results by analysis:

No. 1.—Taken from a deposit of Kent & Stuart's, near A. Hoilman's, south of Wytheville; analyzed by Dr. J. W. Mallet, gave the following results:

Ferric oxide.................................77.46—Metallic iron, 54.43.
Manganese oxide.............................. 0.64
Alumina...................................... 1.07
Lime... .82
Magnesia..................................... .45
Silica and insoluble silicious matter.......10.60
Phosphorus protoxide......................... 0.27
Organic matter..............................Trace.
Water.. 8.72

No. 2, by the same chemist.........................46.62 p. ct. met. iron.
No. 3,   "   "   from the Sun Rocks.........55.61   "   "
No. 4,   "   "   Stroup's Branch............46.85   "   "
No. 5,   "   "   6¼ miles south of Wytheville, 46.32 "   "
No. 6,   "   "   above Hudson's.............59.16   "   "

These ores are all of the horizon in the lowest part of the Calciferous beds, and lower than the lead and zinc zone.

They may be said to extend in lines, not so persistent from the Wythe-Pulaski line, just south of Clark's Summit, through Draper's and Lick Mountains, in the direction of the White Rock or Panic Furnace, but dying out with Lick Mountain, before reaching the Wythe-Smyth boundary line. They again come up in the series of ridges making up Glade and White Rock Mountains in Smyth County, and are fully described in detail in the chapters on Smyth County.

Going northwardly, passing over some minor deposits in the Coal Measures, in the eastern end of the county, and a band of Oriskany brown ores in the south of Cove Mountain and Queen's Knob, the next deposit of magnitude is in a line of ores extending through Crockett's Cove, and found in position between the Black River and Trenton limestones, from six to eighteen feet in thickness. This range of ores extends from the western termination of Queen's Knob, through the above cove, nearly to the northeast corner of the county, yielding an ore generally regarded as being of good quality.

The Cove ore, just mentioned, together with the band of ores lying near the Coal Measures in Little Walker's Mountain, and the Oriskany brown ores and others in Big Walker's Mountain, make up quite a respectable aggregate for the north side of the county.

The Coal Measure ores seem to present two distinct bands: one lying just south of the measures throughout the whole length of the county, giving masses frequently 10 feet thick, and the other a vein 30 feet above the upper coal vein, about 18 inches, and, likewise, persistent. The analysis of the first by THOMAS EGLESTON, of Columbia College, is as follows:

```
Metallic iron...............................57.7
Silica...................................... 1.56
Sulphur..................................... 0.085
Phosphorus.................................. 0.850
```

The analysis of the Coal Measure brown ore taken from Stony Fork Gap, is as follows, by the same chemist:

Metallic iron..............................54.00
Silica...................................... 8.71
Sulphur.................................... 0.104
Phosphorus................................ 0.205

After this, and last of any consequence, is the Oriskany brown ore in the south slope of Big Walker's Mountain. This measure is often 18 to 20 feet thick, sometimes perfectly free from silica, but usually well mixed with it; sometimes highly manganiferous, and occasionally replaced by manganese. Fragments of this ore taken from near where the Tazewell Turnpike crosses this ore series, give the following analysis by THOMAS EGLESTON:

Metallic iron...............................43.5
Silica......................................27.60
Sulphur.................................... 0.158
Phosphorus................................ 0.082

This band of ore is generally persistent, and frequently along its length in Wythe County yields fine bodies of ore of both iron and manganese.

To conclude the chapter on brown iron ores, it might be appropriate to give some idea of the quantity the county of Wythe is likely to yield. An impartial examination into this question of quantity will leave any one at a loss to approximate the great array of figures necessary to determine it. Could these brown ores, the magnetic ores, and the red iron ores of the county be brought together, such would be the quantity, and such the general character, that it would be difficult to find anywhere else all the conditions so favorable for the production of a high grade of metal on a large scale.

Red Iron Ores.

Occasionally in the great New River and Cripple Creek series of brown ores, the ores will assume the character of a red or true hematite, but these instances are only local.

No doubt there are valuable bands of specular ore in Iron Mountain, but they have not been sufficiently explored yet to determine their exact position, measures, quality, etc.

But Wythe County, like Washington, and the west end of Smyth County, possesses a valuable band of semi-magnetic red iron ores, which sometimes attains a thickness of 15 feet, and rarely measures less than 9 feet.

What is known as the Yost, or Blair ore bank, found two miles northwest from Wytheville, is in this series. It yields as follows, by the analysis of THOMAS EGLESTON of Columbia College:

Metallic iron 61.7
Silica 4.21
Sulphur 0.096
Phosphorus 0.075

Much of the ore in this band will do better than the above in every respect; and, as to quantity, so unusual has it been to attribute any large quantity of ore to the northern side of the county, by the old iron workers on the south side, that it would be difficult to convince the general public of the fine prospect that a good yield of ore may be expected from the beds under discussion. An examination of this line of ores, extending over a period of several years, shows that the ore near Wytheville is not an accidental deposit, but belongs to a series, composed sometimes of more than one vein, which belongs geologically to a system of rocks near what are known as the St. Peter sandstones, sometimes next to them, and again separated from them by a broad band of black slates and dark ferruginous sandstones. In Washington County this condition is amply shown at the Gollaher ore bank, four miles east of Abingdon, as well as at other points.

It is on the north side of Pine Ridge, in Wythe County, that the best exhibits of this ore are found, and a farther and closer examination, in the thirteen miles length on the west side of the county, is expected to show several valuable deposits.

The only other band of red iron ore in the county yet explored is the dyestone, or fossil band on the south flank of Big Walker's Mountain, near the north boundary line of the county. This ore is in two distinct measures—one, the fossil ore, 18 inches thick, made up of aggregations of fossils and pebbles, yielding rarely over 45 per cent. of iron. The other is an ore of compact slaty structure, which will yield more iron no doubt, and would be a fine ore to mix with other varieties. This latter is found three feet thick on the road leading from Mount Airy to Rich Valley.

Magnetic Iron Ore.

Except in the red ores, two miles northwest from Wytheville, magnetic ore is not positively located in Wythe County in any appreciable quantities. In the Iron Mountain a vein of this ore is reported. This report is credited by a great many iron men, but as yet it is not positively ascertained.

Sulphureted Iron Ores.

It is the belief of the author that all the ores enumerated, except the dyestone ores, and the stratum of ore nearest the coal measures, are derived from the decomposition of sulphureted ores. This opinion has been adopted after a long and close study of all the deposits and their extensions at many different points. But the quantity of iron sulphuret, known as such, in the county, is great.

In the lead and zinc veins, and in strata lying near to them, are large quantities of iron pyrites. This taken in connection with the quantity of sulphuret below water level, underlying the great iron veins mentioned, must aggregate so vast a quantity as to be without limit.

MANGANESE.

The localities in which manganese is found in any quantity are Iron Mountain, the Reed Island country, Lick and Draper's Mountains, the Glade, and Big Walker's Mountain.

The manganese ores in the north spurs of Iron Mountain are sometimes quite pure and abundant; usually as black oxide, but occasionally a handsome crystalline ore of high purity. The ores near New River, above the mouth of Reed Island Creek, belong to the variety known as Manganese Cream, and seem to be abundant.

At the Glade ore bank, four miles southwest from Max Meadows Depot, the manganese is found both combined with and entirely distinct from the iron ore. It appears to be in quantities.

In Lick and Draper's Mountains there are occasional deposits, the extent of which is not yet fully known. The ores found in Big Walker's Mountain are those mentioned as running with the Oriskany Rocks. They are now and then very pure and handsome.

LEAD AND ZINC.

It would be a pleasure to give a very thorough and complete description of the lead and zinc deposits of Wythe; their geological position, the kind of rocks in which they occur, and their exact thickness; together with a complete history of their discovery and utilization. But it is feared that many interesting points will be overlooked; not through any disposition to slight one of the most important and interesting subjects mentioned in the book, but want of space compels brevity.

Geological.—The lower rocks of No. 2, in which occur the great lead and zinc series of Southwestern Virginia, pass almost continuously through the whole length of the southern section of Wythe County; not always presenting the strata of like richness in ore throughout, but over considerable areas, developing the veins in thick and massive measures. Here and there, the strata next in order beneath have been thrust up so prominently across the direction of the series, as to cause the extrusion and consequent loss of some of the lead and zinc ores.

The rocks in which the ores occur are usually mentioned as dolomites, but this statement cannot be fully accepted, as much of the material accompanying the ore strata is a highly crystalline limestone, sometimes silicious. It would be difficult to say precisely how far above the last of the Scolithus-marked sandstones the lead and zinc zone lies. The two are separated by alternations of red Calciferous slates, and blue and white limestones, in some places nearly 900 yards thick, with the immediate ore-bearing ledges generally, but not always, resting upon silicious limestone. The ore-bearing strata is marked all the way through by a wavy white and blue spotted limestone, looking as though it was once full of what now appears an indistinct fossil; or, perhaps, owing its appearance to gentle wave action in a shallow, chopping sea. The ore strata along the continuation of the series in a direction north 70° east, and south 70° west, dips at various angles. At the old Wythe Lead and Zinc Mines, at Austinville, New River, the measures and dips are as follows: The principal vein was found 40 feet thick, dipping south 20° east, at an angle of about 70°, reached by a tunnel 1,600 feet long, the shaft from the top of the hill down to water level being about 245 feet in depth. The walls of the vein here are the so-called dolomite—highly crystalline. It is highly probable that this immediate portion of the series has been so acted upon by heat resulting from pressure that the original character of the walls has been greatly changed; but at Hendrick's, formerly Kitchen & Painters', the original conditions are preserved. Thus, according to the measures taken there, a true reading is as follows: Beginning on the floor or southeast wall of the main measure, we have 144 feet of heavy zinc blende-bearing strata dipping northwest at an angle of 30°; then 36 feet of dolomite with occasional spots of zinc and lead; 36 feet of iron sulphuret and oxide; 90 feet dolomite rock, containing large veins and deposits of zinc and lead sulphuret, one of which is 18 feet thick; 180 feet of iron, zinc, and barytes heavily disseminated in the rock; then toward the northern side or hanging wall, an indefinite amount of crystalline limestone more or less charged with barytes.

At the Bertha Zinc Mine, in the eastern or lower end of the county, and at Forney's Mine, next west of the Bertha, the mining has not extended below the decomposed surface ores, hence no exact measures have been taken there. At Sayers, on Little Reed Island Creek, lead sulphuret in some masses has been mined; and toward the west end of the series, on Upper Cripple Creek, on land of D. C. James and others, west of that point, lead sulphuret and fragments of zinc ore are occasionally found.

The kinds of zinc ores of the whole series are oxides, sulphides, and large quantities of a silico-carbonate—both at the old Wythe Mines, at Austinville, and at the Bertha and Forney's Mines. About 15,000 tons of zinc silicates and carbonates have been taken from surface mines at the Wythe Lead and Zinc Mines, and from the Bertha Mines about 2,100 tons of a very handsome silicate and carbonate, mixed with oxide, and smelted at the new zinc works at Martin's Station, Pulaski County, Virginia, yielding 30 per cent. of metal.

In the deep workings of the Wythe Lead and Zinc Mines the zinc ore is a blende principally, as well as at the Crusenberry & Kitchen Mine. At the latter two the ores of zinc and lead are sometimes alternately stratified. The great mass of these ores in the county is far above the power of computation, as they are not only thick, but extend over much ground. The kinds of lead ore are, galena, carbonate, oxide, arseniate, phosphate, and occasionally molybdate; galena being the most abundant ore, the carbonate is nearly exhausted, and the others exceedingly rare.

THE FURNACE AND WORKS OF THE WYTHE LEAD AND ZINC MINES COMPANY.

The first work done at these mines was about the year 1756, the lead being reduced from the ore in the most primitive manner; but it was not until the mines fell into the hands of Raper, Sr., and his associates, about 1830, that the old Scotch system was introduced. This, with some modifications, is still in use.* The power used to crush and separate the ores and gangue is derived from New River, upon the south bank of which the works are situated, and they now employ in the mines, furnaces and separators about 150 men.

In the last three years the company has constructed four round buddles, twelve jigs, and a new roasting reverberatory furnace; having, also, introduced a fine air compressor to ventilate the mines with, and to run a Burleigh drill, the air being forced through a four-inch wrought-iron pipe.

The company sells its zinc ores, only reducing the lead.

* Up to 1881, the old plant with some changes was in use; but the Superintendent, MR. RAPER, has adopted the excellent plant made by BECKETT and McDOWELL, Cortlandt St., New York, planned by MR. GYBBON SPILLSBURY. and now being erected by MR. BRAWLEY

WYTHE LEAD AND ZINC MINES.

The product of the mines is now three tons of metal daily. As the markets seem to justify it, this product is made into pig lead or shot, sometimes both. The shot tower in use is a shaft 242 feet deep, situated nearly at the farther extremity of the 1,600 feet tunnel. The shot is then loaded into a car on a tramway and run out to the shot-house at surface, where they are put through the process of separation, sizing, and glazing. The shot tower is, perhaps, one of the best in the world; and, owing to the nature of the lead, the shot made is looked upon in the markets as the equal, if not the superior, of the best shot made anywhere else.

It may be as well to say, before closing the subject, that the capital stock of this company is $400,000, divided into shares of twenty dollars each.

COPPER.

Many of the most valuable ores being so lavishly distributed in different parts of the county, it would seem that it had already enough without attempting to enumerate others; but so far as copper ore is known in Wythe, the quantity ascertained is small.

Beautiful specimens have been taken from ground near Abraham Painter's, by Gallimore, an experienced miner. They comprise both carbonates and sulphides, the former apparently resulting from the decomposition of the latter. It is not probable that the vein is a thick one. It occurs near the middle of an eighteen-feet measure of lead and zinc, mentioned in the description of the Lead and Zinc Zone.

The slates of the Calciferous sub-epoch sometimes yield small quantities of Copper ore, but the only other deposit worthy of mention is a body of ore yielding nine per cent. of copper, lying one mile northwest from Max Meadows Depot, which is supposed by many persons to have resulted from glacial action. It is a sulphuret in course of decomposition, and may really be a larger deposit, and nearer its parent vein than is generally supposed; for a long and patient examination of the line of Lower Silurian limestones on the north side of the Lick Mountain range, shows the baryta beds, which pass through the greater part of Wythe and Smyth counties, to be a copper-bearing series as well. Occasionally, this series shows very handsome bodies of copper ore; and it may be taken with almost absolute certainty, that the Max Meadow copper ores, as well as those showing in Smyth County, near Mount Airy, result from the disintegration of this series of rocks.

GYPSUM.

Hydrous sulphate of lime is found in beautiful crystals at Stoner's, on Cripple Creek, near where the Grayson turnpike crosses. The amount so far brought to the surface does not warrant a conjecture as to the probable quantity. Future developments may show much more than is now suspected.

MARBLE.

The different varieties of variegated marble and onyx-like limestone in the county are very great. Handsome varieties of brown and red variegated ledges are found in heavy masses on the lands of Abraham Umbarger, three miles northwest from Wytheville, supposed to be Bird's Eye and Black River series. The fossils contained in them are, however, very indistinct, rendering it premature as yet to declare the exact age of the rocks. From these quarries stones of any size may be obtained. This series of rocks extends for many miles through the county, being thrown out east, by Queen's Knob, and passing westward into Smyth County, but not always presenting the same beautiful appearance.

In Black Lick Township, near the residence of Mr. Davis, both the brown and nearly white varieties are found.

At Frye's Hill, five miles southwest from Wytheville, the variety resembling onyx is found in masses about a large cave, no doubt derived from the decomposition of the soluble limestones of which the hill is composed. Many of these blocks are like alabaster in purity, translucent, and much of it tinged with amber coloring.

This material is found at places northeast and southwest of Frye's, and at various places on Cripple Creek.

BARYTES.

Sulphate of baryta is found near Frye's marble quarry, not in very large quantities, but very pure. This is nearly in the true lead and zinc zone; but on that side of Lick Mountain the series is barren of both lead and zinc.

Barytes is found in very large masses on the north side of the great lead and zinc deposits. On a hill near Painter's Store, Brown Hill P. O., the quantity of this mineral is very great, extending along with the lead and zinc for miles. Other localities in the county require more development to be worthy of notice.

KAOLIN.

In Lick Mountain, as well as with the coal measures of Wythe, there are large quantities of kaolin. That accompanying the coal veins doesn't vitrify under great heat as does the Lick Mountain clay.

The kaolin of Lick Mountain shows to best advantage toward the head of Stroup's Branch, about five miles south of Wytheville. This deposit is in the Potsdam series, and is nearly 50 yards in thickness, showing a length of two miles.

TIMBER AND CHARCOAL.

Very few of the great timber boundaries, once so plentiful on the south side of the county, still remain intact. The great demand for charcoal for furnace purposes has thinned out the timber on that side of the county very much; but on the north side and in the middle section there are large boundaries of very good timber. The predominant kinds are white oak, chestnut oak, black oak, red oak, spanish oak, hickory, poplar, walnut, sugar-maple, chestnut, white pine, yellow pine, butternut, and all other trees and shrubs native to the climate. The most numerous is the white oak; white pine has been greatly decimated for shingling; but there remains a great deal of chestnut oak, good for tanning purposes.

AGRICULTURE.

In Wythe County agriculture has been carried to its highest perfection only in the department of grazing. The inexhaustible fertility of some of its soil, together with the care and economy habitual to many whose lands were not originally so fertile, enables the county to make an exhibit alike flattering to the land-owners, and worthy of the widest publicity.

It would be an invidious task to attempt to mention those whose labors have contributed most to place the county in the fine position it is esteemed to hold among the best grazing and farming counties in the State. The result of their efficient labors is shown in the fine herds of the best improved cattle and flocks of sheep, and the intelligent use by them of fertilizers in improving their wheat and corn lands is a compliment which is well earned.

That the whole state of agriculture in the county is making fine progress under all the discouragements it has had to contend with, no impartial observer can doubt. It is plain that the great improvement in this direction, together with the rapid development of the different massive bands of ores, is fast raising the county to a position among the foremost in point of wealth and importance. The cattle-men of the county have been all the time abreast with the leading men in like pursuits in others of the best grass countries in Southwestern Virginia. And this is saying a great deal, for the herds and herd books throughout the section named, when once inspected, will show an advanced interest and results achieved, that would astonish both the English and those Americans of other sections, who arrogate to themselves the name of being first in such pursuits. It would be a pleasant task indeed to follow this subject through all its details, bringing in a description of the fine localities whose high state of improvement lends such interest to the beautiful landscapes, in which different parts of the county abound; but a regard for time and space compels the abandonment of a subject of the highest interest.

MANUFACTURES.

Beside the iron furnaces and forges and the lead works, the different manufacturing enterprises of the county are few in number, but seem to be directed by men who are determined to win success.

At Wytheville, and in that vicinity, the plow works, foundries, machine shops, wagon and carriage-making establishments, and tanneries seem to be running to their utmost capacity, some of them even finding it necessary to increase their facilities for manufacturing. Thus, the best grades and most improved patterns of plows, saw-mills, cane-mills, castings, wagons, buggies, carriages, leather, harness, and other articles are made there and distributed over a large extent of country.

At Kent's Mills the fine water-power of Reed Creek is utilized to run a good flouring-mill, besides a first-class woolen mill, which turns out cassimeres, linseys, jeans, blankets, etc.

At Max Meadows is a tobacco factory, engaged principally in the manufacture of chewing tobacco. At Crockett's, beside at Wytheville and other places in the county, plaster is ground for use as a fertilizer. Flouring-mills, saw-mills, and ordinary grist-mills abound throughout the county. Perhaps the greatest power in the State unused is that at Peirce's Falls, on New River.

SCENERY, ETC.

The mountain ranges, divided by valleys, which are threaded by numerous streams of widely different volume, flowing awhile through beautiful green meadows, and then under lofty cliffs of massive limestone, render the scenery very attractive.

There can be nothing more beautiful than that part of New River near the lead mines, or the fine stretch of river at Jackson's Ferry. At the latter, the southern bank rises abruptly into a cliff, which is crowned by an old tower covered with ivy; while the northern bank slopes away gently for several hundred yards to an eminence, upon which is an elegant country residence, built in a style of architecture in perfect keeping with the noble scenery around it.

At Wytheville, the north side of Lick Mountain, in summer afternoons, while the slanting rays of the sun bring out in fine relief the prominent ridges and deep hollows with their marvelous alternations of light and shade, presents a picture of incomparable beauty.

At Max Meadows, the broad fields, whether decked in the fresh colors of leafy June, or crowned with the golden yellow of the fall season, contribute many rare views, to which the streams and neighboring mountains lend a character vivid and animating in a high degree.

SCENERY, MINERAL SPRINGS, ETC.

There are many such views, which the feeble power shown in this volume could but faintly portray.

The Chimney Rocks, near Wytheville, have been for many years a resort of the young people in search of the commanding views, cool shades, and the fine limpid spring near that elevated place.

The great body of the valleys of the county being composed of heavy bands of limestone, their unequal solubility has caused many caves in the county, some of which, if thoroughly explored, would rival the Luray Cave in extent and beauty of adornment. The section of the county known as The Cove, among many other localities in the county, seems to have some of great beauty, besides being of easy accessibility.

The mineral springs of the county are confined principally to the line of the coal rocks and the adjacent strata, except the fine alum-chalybeate, which is now brought into Wytheville through pipes. The spring from which this water is derived, like several others near it, is in the black slates of Pine Ridge, whose position is near the St. Peter sandstones. There are few except alum-chalybeate springs in the county, of a strictly mineral character; and these, while of high medicinal virtue, are numerous.

WYTHEVILLE.

Wytheville, the county seat, which, by the last census, contains about 2,300 inhabitants, is situated near the center of the county, on the Atlantic, Mississippi and Ohio Railroad. The high improvement of its streets, the air of neatness and cleanliness, and its elevation of 2,300 feet above the sea, combine to render it a very attractive place in the summer season.

It out-rivals a great many of the lesser watering-places in the number of visitors, in search of health, it entertains during the summer and fall. Beside several well-kept hotels and boarding-houses, usually dispensing well-cooked and wholesome fare, the fine alum and chalybeate water, now flowing from hydrants on the streets, adds an attractive and valuable feature.

It is hardly necessary to say that all denominations of Christians, common to other parts of Virginia, have churches in the town or its vicinity. The schools, though unpretentious, are among the best in the State. Beside well-regulated public schools, there are private boarding-schools, of a select order, for young ladies.

In addition to flourishing manufactories and machine shops, for the making of anything from an engine to a plow point, there are numerous stores which are supplied with a more than usually select list of goods. Thus, everything is found for sale in ordinary merchandise, millinery, fancy goods, notions, groceries, hardware, leather supplies, and tinware.

Though sewing machines, reapers, and mowers, and the like are not made there, several companies are represented by handsome displays. The carriages, buggies, and wagons made at its factories, and proportioned, in strength of make, to the roads over which they are expected to run, out-rival any others for use in the adjacent country.

The two newspapers, *The Enterprise* and *Dispatch*, published at the place, always occupying an advanced position in advocacy of progress and improvement, give full information of the proceedings of all the courts, including the Supreme Court of Appeals of the State, which sits there annually, beginning about the 10th of July.

Wytheville is healthy, and the scenery around it is of a high order.

Max Meadows, a name now commonly applied to the depot of that name on the Atlantic, Mississippi and Ohio Railroad, was originally used to designate the wide-spreading meadows of great fertility in which the depot was built. The place has several excellent stores, and a tobacco factory. Max Meadows is one of the great shipping depots for pig iron, lead, and zinc.

Rural Retreat, in the west of the county, besides being a depot on the Atlantic, Mississippi and Ohio Railroad, is a growing place, having an advanced school, good stores, shops, etc.

Crockett's, is a depot on the Atlantic, Mississippi and Ohio Railroad, seven miles west of Wytheville, and is now the shipping point for much of the pig metal made in that end of the county. It has a good steam mill for grinding plaster, besides other improvements, stores, etc.

There are quite a number of other noted places in the county, but their description is now impracticable for want of space.

LINES OF TRANSPORTATION.

The ATLANTIC, MISSISSIPPI AND OHIO RAILROAD, running through from Norfolk, west and southwest, to all points south and west, passes through the heart of the county. This great line is of ample carrying capacity, being of five-feet gauge, and, once out of its financial embarrassments, may do much more than formerly to develop the material resources of the section through which it runs.

There are proposed lines of transportation, organized for the purpose of developing the great ore belts; prominent among which are the southern extension of the New River Railroad, the Virginia and Statesville Railroad, and the road of the Lobdell Car Wheel Company.

FISH CULTURE.

Since the adoption by the Fish Commissioner of a site near Wytheville for a hatchery, fish culture is assuming some importance. At a fine large spring, of proper temperature, near the Atlantic, Mississippi and Ohio Railroad, three and a half miles west of Wytheville, all the necessary buildings for this interesting business were completed in 1879, and the young fish of many improved varieties have been shipped to various streams in this and other parts of the State. The whole matter has been a success, under the intelligent management of PROFESSOR McDONALD, and now that the hatchery is in successful operation, only a short time must elapse before all the streams of the county and the section will be stocked with varieties suitable to them.

PRODUCTION OF CATTLE, SHEEP, WHEAT, PIG METAL, LEAD, AND ZINC ORE.

Fat cattle, annually shipped............	1,800.
Stock cattle " "	2,600.
Sheep, " "	5,000.
Wheat, " "	180,000 bushels.
Pig metal (chiefly for car-wheels)	8,000 tons of late, which will be increased hereafter.
Lead from Wythe Lead and Zinc Mines.	1,000 tons annually.
Zinc ore " " " "	50,000 tons have been mined up to date.
Zinc ore from the Bertha Mine..........	2,100 tons to date.

QUOTATION FROM HOWARD SHRIVER, A.M., OF WYTHEVILLE, ON THE FLORA AND CLIMATE OF WYTHE COUNTY.

"Owing to the altitude of Southwest Virginia, averaging half a mile above sea level, the climate resembles that of the Middle States, many of our plants belonging to Pennsylvania and New York. Whereas, in the same latitude, east of us, near the seashore, the fig ripens its two crops, and plants common to North Carolina are found.

"Hence, it is less necessary to enumerate the prevailing plants, and we shall confine our list to a few that may be regarded characteristic of the Flora. Among the first and most attractive, is the splendid Rhododendron Catawbiense, Michena, which abound on the hillsides and often extend to their summits, being sometimes intermixed with R. maximum L. and Kalmia Latifolia—common farther north.

"Along the streams are Clethra Acuminata and Alnifolia, Andromeda Floribunda Purch. and Magnolia Fraseri, Walt., Umbrella Lam. and Acuminata L. The mountain roads are lined in the early spring with the fragrant white flowers of Leucothæ Recurva Buck.

"Among a large number of Vaccinia are found V. Erythrocarpon Michx. and Macrocarpon. Of the Azaleas, there are A. arborescens, Purch., Viscosa L., Nudiflora L., and the most splendid Calendarlacea, Michx. in every conceivable variety of coloring. Galax Aphyllea beautifies the woods in winter, with Chimaphila and several Pyrolas. In summer the Monotropa, and sweet-scented Schweinitzia Odorata, Ell. Ilea is well represented, including I. Monticola, Gray., Halesia Tetraptera is found in the water-courses. The Labiatæ are well represented, including the somewhat rare Cedronella Cardata, Benth., Scutellaria Versicolor, Pelosa, Servosa, etc. Stachys Cordata, Ridd. Ascarum Canadense, L., Virginicum L., and Arifolium Michx. are common with Aristolochia Sipho, L'Her. and Serpentana, L. Pyrularia Oleifera, Gray., Euphorbiæ of various species, including Commulata, Eng., Unularia Grandiflora, and Lessifolia, L. are common, as also Prosartes Lanuginosa, Don. and Clintonia Borealis, Raf., Umbellata Torr., Convellaria Majalis prevails on the mountains, even to their summits. Of the Carices, some twenty-five or thirty are common, while Carea Fraseriana, Linn's is rare.

"The ferns are quite numerous, and, at times, grow in great luxuriance. The whole ground is often covered with a dense growth of Cystopteris Bulbifera, Bernh., the fronds from a foot to a foot and a half in height. In the same abundance are found Aspidium Goldianum, Hook. and Clintonianum; while the open woods are carpeted with A. Pedatum Phegopteris, and A. Marginale, Sw., and Acrostichoide, Sw., with occasionally Adiantum Capillus Veneris. The rock crevices exhibit Asplenium Montanum, Willd., A. Ruta Muraria L., Cheilanthes Vertita, Sw., Perlaca Atropurpurea, Link., and Polypodium Vulgaro and Incarium, Sw., A. Tricomanes L., Camptosorus Rhozophyllus, Link. In all some thirty species."

RAIN-FALL; AND AVERAGES FOR MONTH AND YEAR.

BY HOWARD SHRIVER, A.M., WYTHEVILLE, WYTHE CO., VA.

	Jan.	Feb.	Mch	April	May	June	July	Aug.	Sept.	Oct.	Nov.	Dec.	Avge.
1860	3.1	3.6	3.3	3.6	3.4	3.1	4.1	3.7	2.6	9.4	4.3	4.4	47.0
1861	6.3	5.3	2.3	3.6	3.6	3.2	8.1	3.1	5.3	5.8	4.3	0.2	51.1
1862	4.6	8.0	4.0	6.5	3.2	5.9	4.6	3.2	0.3	2.8	0.5	1.1	44.7
1868	3.1	1.7	2.3	3.3	3.8	2.5	6.6	3.4	4.3	2.6	1.3	3.2	38.2
1869	2.2	2.8	3.2	1.9	4.4	2.0	2.8	2.6	4.2	2.7	1.6	4.1	34.4
1870	2.3	3.0	4.3	2.8	2.3	5.8	2.5	7.6	1.3	2.8	1.5	1.4	37.6
1871	2.3	2.8	4.0	3.3	4.7	3.2	1.7	3.4	3.4	1.7	1.6	6.0	38.1
1872	1.5	2.1	3.3	4.0	5.7	4.9	2.3	2.5	2.4	1.0	1.5	2.9	34.8
1873	3.8	5.4	3.0	3.4	7.3	2.8	2.2	5.3	2.5	2.2	2.5	3.1	43.5
1874	2.7	3.9	2.7	6.2	1.1	3.8	5.6	2.7	5.7	1.1	3.2	1.2	39.9
1875	3.8	4.0	6.5	4.0	0.5	9.1	7.8	4.6	2.4	0.5	3.8	2.7	49.0
1876	2.1	3.0	2.0	0.8	3.4	4.0	4.5	2.6	4.5	1.9	5.4	1.0	38.1
1877	4.0	0.8	5.7	5.4	3.0	4.0	4.1	1.9	3.3	3.9	7.1	4.1	46.8
1878	5.7	2.7	3.2	4.3	5.0	2.9	6.4	8.8	8.8	3.2	3.8	3.2	52.5
1879	4.4	2.4	1.5	2.6	5.1	2.0	2.8	4.5	1.8	5.2	1.1	5.4	38.9

MONTHLY AVERAGE FOR WHOLE PERIOD.

3.4 3.4 3.6 3.8 3.7 3.8 4.5 3.7 3.3 3.0 2.9 2.9   41.9

MONTHLY AVERAGE TEMPERATURE AND GENERAL AVERAGES FOR MONTH AND YEAR.

BY HOWARD SHRIVER, A.M., WYTHEVILLE, VIRGINIA.

	Jan.	Fb.	Mh.	Ap.	My	Ju.	Jy.	Au.	Sep	Oct	No.	Dec	Av. Yr.
1860		41	45	52	65	68		71	62	55	43	38	54
1861	57	40	41	51	60	72	67	74	65	55	43	40	54
1862	41	34	42	56	61	68	75		67	56	44	37	55
1866	33					64	74						
1868		31	45	49	50	65	74	69	64	53	40	29	53
1869	38	37	40	51	59	68	72	74	61	47	36	34	50
1870	37	37	37	52	57	68	74	72	64	53	41	31	53
1871	36	35	35	52	61	71	74	73	60	55	41	34	53
1872	36	40	40	55	62	67	74	73	60	53	37	30	54
1873	30	34	37	55	64	69	71	73	64	53	37	38	53
1874	34	37	47	52	61	70	74	69	64	50	38	39	53
1875	37	39	44	50	58	72	73	68	61	53	39	41	54
1876	34	38	44	49	63	73	72	72	60	49	44	26	52
1877	41	40	41	50	62	68	73	70	64	51	43	41	52
1878	33	39	41	52	63	68	74	71	63	55	43	41	53
1879	31	37	37	53	60	64	74	71	62	51	43	28	53
1879	31	31	45	50	62	67	72	76	60	59	44	42	53

MONTHLY AVERAGE FOR WHOLE PERIOD OF FOURTEEN YEARS.

36 37 43 52 60 69 73 71 63 53 41 35

MAXIMA AND MINIMA OF THERMOMETER.

BY HOWARD SHRIVER, A.M., WYTHEVILLE, VA.

	Jan.	Febr.	March	April	May	June	July	August	Sept.	Oct.	Nov.	Dec.
1861	48 25	56 25	63 27	70 38	75 44	80 43	80 61	81 62	73 49	67 44	57 31	56 26
1862	63 29	52 29	56 25	66 35	74 50	74 56			73 59	69 40	63 32	59 20
1866	63 8	62 3	72 17	81 31	83 40	89 48	96 54	88 56	84 36	76 26	68 21	50 10
1868		56 8	72 10	83 28	81 44	82 48	92 61	82 58 47	82 36	68 25	65 18	53 13
1869	50 15	65 14	76 1	78 28	84 40	90 53	88 52	92 47	80 45	71 34	66 20	60 4
1870	60 6	54 5	60 10	80 36	84 40	86 56	86 57	84 62	83 37	79 31	68 22	68 8
1871	62 17	60 14	72 28	82 38	84 43	86 59	88 51	89 56	88 42	79 31	57 6	58 0
1872	59 6	63 6	70 10	80 33	88 42	86 56	87 65	87 59	85 39	74 21	64 2	64 2
1873	61 11	63 3	69 1	81 33	83 46	85 51	86 59	88 52	84 49	74 28	70 17	69 21
1874	64 3	74 20	70 21	74 31	90 44	92 56	89 57	89 56	84 36	75 30	65 21	66 7
1875	60 4	63 5	70 24	75 20	86 40	88 55	88 65	85 58	84 36	77 27	75 23	51 0
1876	70 13	69 8	73 15	78 32	84 37	87 54	90 50	88 56	85 50	80 33	69 12	73 13
1877	65 3	61 18	72 11	78 33	90 38	87 48	91 58	89 57	88 44	83 12	70 23	52 5
1878	54 4	62 9	74 23	83 31	83 32	85 44	91 54	88 54	81 41	77 22	70 23	64 10
1879	60 6	65 6	74 20	79 22	84 32	86 45	91 55	87 47	82 32	86 22	83 8	

Average Temperature for Month for a period of thirteen to fourteen Years, Observations taken at or near 7 A.M.,

2 P.M. and 9 P.M., until Oct. 1st, '78, subsequently

by Self-registering Max. and Min. Instruments.

RANGE OF BAROMETER.

Reduced to 32° F. and corrected for Capillarity, Temperature, and Variation in level of mercury in cistern. Instrument (No. 1560 by J. GREEN, N. Y.: except from Nov. 1, '65 to Apl. 1, '69; and Sept. 1, '69, to Sept. 1, '72, during which time an ordinary instrument was used). Observations previous to Nov. 1, 1876, are reduced by the constant—.145 to correspond to current observations at present station. Add 27. to the thousandths in Table.

BY HOWARD SHRIVER, A.M., WYTHEVILLE, WYTHE CO., VA.

	Jan.	Feb.	Mch.	April	May	June	July	Aug.	Sept.	Oct.	Nov.	Dec.	Avg.
1865											569	588	
1866	649	649	921	579	512	597	648						
1870	631	473	520	574	571	608	659	654	697	686	685	591	608
1872	597	518	562	641	631	639	666	669	646	624	597	632	618
1869	537	490	567	570	470	634	647	694	749	591	582	675	600
1870	631	473	520	574	571	608	659	654	697	686	635	691	617
1871	711	604	580	539	604	604	638	630	717	726	596	646	633
1873	548	504	558	478	545	619	693	666	676	628	512	671	591
1874	664	620	568	552	578	627	665	632	678	680	692	676	635
1875	536	568	553	514	569	645	645	615	652	602	590	526	584
1876	687	618	522	572	626	605	685	675	576	575	642	526	609
1877	631	610	504	495	500	610	620	600	639	624	600	688	593
1878	540	459	521	408	541	568	627	570	700	683	546	518	552
1879	579	547	600	502	624	616	622	598	697	742	678	635	620

MONTHLY AVERAGES.

Jan.	Feb.	March	April	May	June	July	Aug.	Sept.	Oct.	Nov.	Dec.	Avg.
612	549	548	541	559	614	654	642	675	641	600	619	604

FURNACES AND FORGES IN WYTHE COUNTY, VIRGINIA—ALL COLD-BLAST CHARCOAL.

Cedar Run Furnace, Graham & Robinson, near Graham's Forge (Graham's old furnace), built by David Graham. One stack 32x9. 1832. Water power. Capacity 6 tons.

Barren Springs Furnace, J. Williamson M'Gavock, near Carter's Ferry, New River (Graham's new furnace), built by David Graham in 1853 and rebuilt by Graham & Robinson, 1873. One stack 35x8, cold blast. Capacity 5 tons.

Eagle Furnace, or Gray Eagle Furnace, built in 1863 by Buford, Stuart & Co., now owned by Graham & Robinson. One stack 33x9. Cold blast, water power. Capacity 5 tons.

Brown Hill Furnace, built by Abraham Painter & Sons, 1870, now owned by the Lobdell Car Wheel Company, Wilmington, Delaware. One stack 32x9. Cold blast, steam power. Capacity 8 tons.

Walton Furnace, built by Howard & Saunders, 1872, now owned by Lobdell Car Wheel Company, Wilmington, Delaware. One stack 33x9. Capacity 8 tons.

Ravenscliffe Furnace, Crockett & Co., one old stack 29x9, built in 1810, rebuilt 1876, and a new stack 33x9. Water power. Capacity 14 tons.

Speedwell Furnace, D. E. James & Son, built 1873. One stack 32x9. Water power. Capacity 6 tons.

Wythe Furnace, Sayers, Oglesby & Co., built in 1873. One stack 33x9. Steam power. Capacity 5 tons.

Irondale Furnace, Noble, Allen & Co., built 1880–81. P. O., Crockett's Depot. Capacity 10 tons.

Beverly Furnace, Crockett & Co., built in 1880. Water power. P. O., Crockett's Depot, 36x10. Capacity 12 tons.

Furnace of the New River Iron Co., at Pierce's Falls, New River, built in 1881. P. O., Jackson's Ferry, 34x10. Capacity 12 tons.

Furnace of the Hendricks' Bros., of New York, 1881. New River Mineral Co., now building at mouth of Painters' Branch, New River, two miles above Wythe Lead Mines. One stack 10½x40. Capacity 20 tons. P. O., Brown Hill.

Forges.—Of the numerous forges once existing only one remains, Graham's Forge Rolling Mills and Nail Works, built by David Graham, on Reed Creek, 1828. Three heating furnaces, four trains of rolls, five nail machines, and one hammer.

Southwest Virginia

AND

Shenandoah Valley.

AN INQUIRY INTO THE CAUSES OF THE RAPID GROWTH AND WONDERFUL DEVELOPMENT OF SOUTHWEST VIRGINIA AND SHENANDOAH VALLEY, WITH A HISTORY OF THE NORFOLK AND WESTERN AND SHENANDOAH VALLEY RAILROADS; AND SKETCHES OF THE PRINCIPAL CITIES AND TOWNS INSTRUMENTAL IN THE PROGRESS OF THESE SECTIONS.

BY

THOMAS BRUCE,

Author of "Cupid and Duty," "Historical Sketch of Roanoke," "Sketch of Radford," "That Bruisin' Lad o' Greystone Lodge."

COPYRIGHT SECURED.

Pps. 179 - 184 are reproduced herewith.

RICHMOND:
J. L. HILL PUBLISHING COMPANY.
1891.

CHAPTER XIII.

Wythe County—Max Meadows—Wytheville—Crockett and Rural Retreat—Washington county—Glade Springs—Saltville—Future of the cities and towns of Southwest Virginia.

LEAVING Pulaski City, in going westward we soon come into Wythe county, whose name is synonymous with agricultural resources and mineral wealth. This county plays an important part in the make-up of the New river-Cripple creek mineral region, as we have seen, and is noted for the fine stock raised within its borders. Some of its lands have been long celebrated for their productiveness, while years ago iron was made from its charcoal furnaces, and lead manufactured at Austinville. We know of no country which has a finer mineral territory, and why its towns have played so small a part in the recent development we cannot imagine for a moment. But this section is fast progressing now, and the day is not far distant when Wytheville will redeem itself for past errors in this respect and take its proper place as the county-seat of one of the wealthiest counties in Southwest Virginia.

Max Meadows a year or two ago was a station on the Norfolk and Western railroad, at which point iron from the furnaces on the Cripple creek region was hauled in wagons for a distance of ten miles. Capitalists, recognizing the vast mineral deposits near this place, purchased these ore banks and, forming a land company, bought the ground around the station, and now it has become quite a village, with every mark of improvement. A large furnace is in course of construction, built by the "Max Meadows Iron Company," with a capacity of one hundred and thirty-five tons *per diem*. This furnace draws its ores from lands of the company, some four miles away, or less. The company also constructed a handsome inn, which is now open to the public, and is a model of elegance and comfort. This place, for many reasons, has a future before it, two of which we need only mention—its natural advantages in reference to climate and agricultural resources, and the further fact that it is supported and controlled by the Virginia Development Company. The capital stock of the Max Meadows Iron Company is $400,000, and the shares owned by the Virginia Development Company in this amount to $75,000. In the Max Meadows Land and Improvement Company it owns $75,000 of its stock, and practically controls it. These facts lead us to naturally suppose that the place which in the last few months has developed so rapidly will grow into a town, or perhaps a city—who knows? The position of Max Meadows is a central one for its supply of coke and ores, as well as for the shipment of manufactured products to the northern and northwestern and eastern markets. The section around is one of the finest live-stock countries we know, and Fort Chiswell stock farm is but a short distance off. Throughout this whole productive country there will be a home demand in a few years for the supplies raised which will place the farming community upon a much sounder basis. Max Meadows is three hundred and twenty-nine miles from Norfolk and seventy-nine miles from Bristol. Its development and improvement is mainly due to the efforts of the Virginia Development Company, which is playing such an important part in the progress of the extreme Southwest that at this point in our work it deserves some notice.

On October 1, 1887, the Virginia Steel Company was organized under a broad and liberal charter of the Legislature of Virginia, and until 1889 confined itself to operations in the mining of ore. In May, 1889, desiring to extend the operations of the company by building blast furnaces, rolling mills, foundries, and other enterprises, and to develop in particular the resources of Southwest Virginia and Shenandoah Valley, the company increased its capital stock from $100,000 to $5,000,000, and the name was changed to that of the Virginia Development Company, with the following officers: President,

Richard S. Brock; First Vice-President and Treasurer, Clarence M. Clark; Second Vice-President, S. E. Chauvenet; Secretary, E. J. Collins. This company has a cumulative, full-paid, preferred stock of $1,000,000, and $4,000,000 of common stock, 20 per cent. of which is paid with provisions that not more than 15 per cent. can be called in any one calendar year. By liberal subscriptions on the part of this company industries and enterprises, by way of furnaces, land improvement companies, and other operations, have been put on foot and brought to completion in Radford, Max Meadows, Graham, Salem, and Pocahontas, in Southwest Virginia, giving an almost invaluable assistance to this section in developing its resources and utilizing them. Mr. Edmund C. Pechin, whom we have quoted frequently on the subject of ores, is general manager, and a gentleman eminently qualified to fill the onerous and important duties of this post. It has done more than any other joint-stock company that we know of for Southwest Virginia, and on that account is entitled to the thanks and gratitude of the people. As an engine of development it has struck telling blows, and wherever it touches progress comes as if by some magic hand. So we may well understand that when Max Meadows was centred upon as one of the points of investment for this company, it was but natural that it should make rapid strides materially.

Wytheville, the county-seat of Wythe, is situated on a beautiful plateau, slightly depressed, on the summit of the Alleghany mountains, 133 miles west of Lynchburg and 71 miles east of Bristol, the western terminus of the Norfolk and Western Railroad Company. Owing to its position in a country of unexcelled productiveness and charming scenery, and with a climate that is almost perfect, this place for many years has been a noted summer resort for people from many other States in the Union, particularly the Southern States. The place is 2,300 feet above the level of the sea. There is always a refreshing breeze, which not only relieves depression and debility, but gives an invigorating, healthy buoyancy to the system so pleasant to wearied humanity. The climate compares favorably with that of Turin and Geneva, in Europe, as can be seen from the following comparative temperature for some years:

	Spring.	Summer.	Autumn.	Winter.	Year.
Turin	52.2	70.3	54.2	34.0	52.07
Geneva	53.7	71.5	53.8	33.5	53.1
Wytheville	52	70.6	53	32.3	53

The thermometer is rarely above ninety degrees in summer or below zero in winter, and in the warm months of July and August the evenings are delightful, and the nights so cool that a blanket becomes comfortable.

This place is one of the oldest towns in Southwest Virginia, being over a century in years, and is very conservative in all its ideas and views. The place is one of the yearly circuits of the Court of Appeals of Virginia, which sits there every June for this section of Virginia. The town is well laid off, with broad streets, the main one being the old macadamized road which ran from Seven-mile Ford, in Smyth county, to Staunton, in Augusta county, Virginia. Standing at the upper end of Main street and looking down through the place, a beautiful vista is presented between the sidewalks, which becomes almost sublime when seen at night under the rays of the electric-lights, which the town has the good fortune to possess. From the earliest years of this century Wytheville has been a trading centre for the counties adjoining Wythe, and from this source principally it drew a support, and a handsome one, too. The past days of covered wagons, loaded with produce of every description, coming in from the country to get their supplies, are still within the memory of some of the inhabitants of the place, who deem railroads an invasion and regard the continued triumphs of science as a sign of the demoralization of these days in which we live.

Wytheville, owing to the demands of this trade of which we have just spoken, has always been something of a manufacturing place in order to supply them as far as profitable and practicable. A furniture establishment, carriage and wagon manufactory, a machine shop and foundry, a flouring mill, several cigar factories, a canning establishment, are in operation, all of which add materially to the welfare of the place. But now Wytheville is throwing off her lethargy and recognizing her vast agricultural and mineral resources, and is determined to take advantage of them. Capitalists are seizing hold of these; a development company has been organized, and new hotels are to be erected and a general improvement inaugurated. The construction of Jackson Park Hotel in the beautiful woodland west of the place will result in the erection of a building which will eclipse any other we know of in the way of natural scenery and beauty of situation. There is no reason that can be possibly assigned to show why this place should not become a great manufacturing centre and still retain its prestige as a summer resort and an educational point of celebrity.

Wytheville is certainly a seat of learning, if the number and good reputation of its schools constitute it. A great many institutions of learning are here, both male and female, among which may be mentioned Wytheville Male Academy, A. A. Campbell principal; Plummer Memorial Female College, Rev. S. R. Preston principal; Wytheville Seminary, Mrs. Thomas R. Drew principal. All of these schools are conducted upon the best possible educational principles, while moral and physical training are strictly attended to, and the comforts and pleasures of the students considered. These establishments have developed the minds of many a man and woman who have played no small part in the development of Southwest Virginia. Co-existing with these fine scholastic advantages are the best possible religious privileges, which have a material influence upon the place. The Roman Catholic, Episcopal, Presbyterian, Methodist, Christian, Lutheran, and Baptist denominations are here, all of which have churches, and divine worship is held every Sabbath; and Sunday-schools are in a flourishing condition. These educational facilities and Christian observances have not only a salient effect upon the residents of the place, but impress the minds of the visitors more or less.

The result is a state of society which is admirable and charming in every way, and which gives the place the reputation of being the most elegant and refined one in this section of country. Amusements are plentiful, and the German club, organized by the young men of the place, and which meets once a week at each of the hotels, is a distinctive feature in the make-up of the pleasures of the town.

While Wytheville has grown slowly, there has been an increase all the time in its population, for in the year 1860 there were only fifteen hundred people in the place, while now there are three thousand; and with the many natural advantages it possesses in the way of agricultural resources and mineral wealth almost at its doors, it should continue to increase—only more rapidly—than it has done hitherto. It is surrounded with the best type of ores, and a soil on which nature has expended her utmost force to render it rich and productive. The United States fish hatchery is near this town, and is an object of no small amount of curiosity.

Passing westward from Wytheville some thirteen miles, we arrive at Rural Retreat, which is 2,500 feet above the level of the sea, being the most elevated place on the line of the Norfolk and Western Railroad Company. Near this place is Crockett, which has been, and is now, a shipping point for the iron manufactured at the charcoal furnaces near by. Both this place and Rural Retreat are the centre of a section of country which is growing financially well off from the production and sale of cabbage. Large quantities of this succulent vegetable of the finest quality are produced and shipped South annually from these places. The cultivation of fruits, vegetables, poultry, and eggs is always a sign of prosperity among the farming community, and with a home demand, which they are fast gaining, to consume their supplies, they must necessarily become a rich and independent class.

THE IRON INDUSTRY

OF

WYTHE COUNTY

FROM

1792

BY J. A. WHITMAN
WYTHEVILLE, VA.

(Original Printing 1935)

REVISED EDITION 1942

Printed by
Southwest Virginia Enterprise
Wytheville, Va.

Reproduced for *Wythe County Chapters* by special permission of the Whitman family.

INTRODUCTION

Possibly but few of the present generation realize the enormous amount of iron ores and iron Wythe County has produced, since about 1790 and extending down to the early part of 1900. This is particularly true in the Cripple Creek valley, where the values of these products ran into millions of dollars.

The names of many of the individuals and families who assisted in this development, thus making history of the county, are no longer to be found. They have been replaced in later generations by new people to whom their story reads like ancient history.

Forges in the beginning of the iron industry were located near the ores to be used and also on some stream which would furnish power for operation.

Along with the furnaces were saw mills, used for cutting timber into lumber for building purposes; also grist mills for grinding grain; used at the various operations, and by the farmers in surrounding communities.

In the early days there was an abundance of lump ore scattered on top of the ground, which could be utilized without mining or washing.

At the same time as the forges, came what was known as the charcoal furnace.

In a number of instances a forge and a furnace were located at the same place and some of them were operated as long as 100 years or until the scarcity of wood made the charcoal furnace too expensive. Iron produced from the old type furnace (charcoal) sold at a premium. Notwithstanding this, hot blast or coke furnaces made their appearance and conditions in iron making changed.

The old furnaces were usually located on a stream that would furnish sufficient power for running the bellows and also near a deposit of ore and limestone which could be utilized. For the purpose of transporting the charcoal the furnace owners would use heavy wagons with large flare top beds which were drawn by four horses or mules driven by a single line, the driver riding what in those days was called the saddle horse or mule. Sometimes as many as 50 or more horses or mules were used at one of these furnaces, as well as 8 or 10 yoke of oxen in the coaling grounds.

These forges and furnaces manufactured all implements used on the farm and in the factories of those days. Among the articles were: cane mills, plows, stoves, bakers, wagon tires, horse shoes, blooms, kettles of all kinds—some of those used at Saltville, as will be noted later. The blooms were shipped to eastern markets and worked into all kinds of tools.

Before the coming of railroad transportation, the surplus iron was hauled to Lynchburg by wagon and shipped from there by water to eastern markets.

When the activities of the charcoal furnaces began to wane on account of the scarcity of timber and the long hauls of charcoal, then came the modern furnace and the modern method of mining. Steam power supplanted the use of the horse. Hauls from the ore banks to the washers would be by locomotive and the washed ore dumped into railroad cars for transportation to the furnaces. The steam shovel, hydraulic pump and the sluice trough played important parts in these changes. Millions of tons of ore were mined and shipped from Wythe County to Pulaski, Radford and Roanoke to be worked in the large furnaces that would produce one hundred tons of iron per day, while the old type furnaces had only produced from three to twelve tons in twenty-four hours.

Within the present limits of Wythe County, there have been 10 forges, 15 charcoal or cold blast furnaces, ranging from one to three tuyeres, 2 hot blast or coke furnaces, 1 nail factory, 1 pipe works, 1 rolling mill, 1 stove factory, etc. There was also one more furnace in the Cripple Creek Valley, which was in Smyth County, about one mile west of the Wythe-Smyth line.

Of all the Furnaces, Forges and Iron Mine operations in Wythe County not a single one is in operation to-day. There are still a number of deposits of iron ore, together with large quantities of zinc, which will doubtless be worked when the prices justify. The Bertha Mineral Company at Austinville is the only plant in operation in the county at this time (1935).

PEAK PRODUCTION

The peak production of charcoal iron in Wythe County was reached during the eighties, when about twelve or more of these furnaces were in blast. Among them were: Raven Cliff, Speedwell, Cedar Run, Little Wythe, Fosters Falls, Gray Eagle, Walton, Irondale, Cave Hill, Beverly, and White Rock. The latter was in the Cripple Creek valley in Smyth County, about a mile from the Wythe-Smyth line.

The operation of all of these plants gave employment to a large number of men and boys. It took many teams to do the hauling of coal, ore, and goods from the railway station and the pig iron to the station.

The price for the delivery of the iron to the station varied according to the distance, ranging from $2.50 to $3.00 per ton of 2240 lbs. This gave many farmers when not busy with farm work an opportunity to keep their teams employed and, in some cases, afforded all-time work.

One of the farmers we remember was Ephraim Catron, who resided west of Wytheville on the Old Stage road. He hauled from Irondale, driving four or six horses. The wagon used was of the old high-wheel road type with axle-skeins, and tar was used for lubrication. Mr. Catron's childrn relate that when Noble, Allen & Company failed, the company owed Ephraim Catron $400.00. A number of the other creditors brought suit and only received a small per cent. of the amount due them. Not so with Mr. Catron who did not institute any legal proceedings to collect. He received a message to come to the furnace and was very much surprised when he was paid in full with gold.

When the oldest son, Mr. C. D. Catron who now resides on the headwaters of Peak Creek in Pulaski County, was a youngster, he helped his father. He recently related to the writer that after he was grown he went to Fairfax, Missouri. One day he was called on to assist in digging a grave. He inquired for whom, and one can imagine his surprise when informed that it was for Mrs. Noble of Wythe County, Virginia,

Speedwell Furnace, which is the oldest of all the forges or furnaces in Wythe County. A colorful history is connected with this furnace.

SPEEDWELL FURNACE

We have been unable to find the origin of the name Speedwell, which has been used in the Cripple Creek Valley for a furnace, a church, a post office and a town. Some think it came from the wild flower by that name which grows in abundance in that locality. The first mention of Speedwell we have been able to find in the record is a court order of December 10th, 1799, establishing a road from Speedwell to the top of Lick Mountain.

There have been three Speedwell Furnaces in the United States: one in North Carolina, one in Wythe County and one in Roanoke County.

Of all the forges and furnaces that have been in Wythe County, Speedwell is the oldest and has the most colorful history.

The following is from Wythe County records:

AGREEMENT

Article of agreement made this the 24th day of November, 1792, between William Love, a blacksmith and James Byrne "to build a Bloomery at the south end of Love's mill dam on the waters of 'Creeple Creeke' and that said Love and Byrne is to pay equal parts each of them in building said Iron Works.

"Love agrees to grind grain for Byrne and family while said works a-building. Further agreed that 752 acres of land lying north of Jehu Stephens' land and 450 acres south of Peter Spanglors' land, Byrne to have privilege to cut cole wood and fire wood. It was further agreed that should either party pay more than his proportionate part in building said works, that he is to be repaid in six months after said works make iron." Witnesses to contract were: S. Sanders, Jehu Stephens and Mangus McDonald.

From the wording of the above contract it would indicate that the first Iron Works was a forge. The word Bloomery would not be used in connection with a furnace. The blooms were large blocks of iron hammered into shape by heavy trip hammers. The products from the furnaces were molded into "pigs", as they were called. It took a forge or mill to produce the finished products, such as wagon tires, etc. A number of the furnaces had forges near-by.

On September the 13th, 1808, William Love, by attorney, sold to Jehu Stephens several tracts of land containing 560 acres.

On the 8th day of December, 1808, Henry Stephens bargained and sold to King and Morgan, or Morgan, King and Trigg, "the privilege of mining and hauling away ore on the lands that I hold title to. Further agree to furnish good wagon road for the purpose of hauling said ore for the sum of $50.00."

On October the 21st, 1808, Jehu Stephens and wife Bethiah sold to the heirs of William King of Washington County, 6 tracts of land, 560 acres, in Wythe County on Cripple Creek.

"I further agree that if I shall sell my part of Furnace and Furnace Seat, lands and belongings attached to said Furnace that I call Kingsville, then the said $50.00 shall be deducted. Signed, Henry Stephens."

Henry Stephens may have been a son of Jehu Stephens. He married Catherine Pinkley or Binkley, a sister of Mrs. Alexander Smith. He moved to Blount County, Tennessee, and William Stephens was appointed guardian for Henry Stephens' children on December the 4th, 1832, at Blountville, Tenn. Recorded in Deed Book 13, page 275 Wythe County.

On December the 30th, 1816, the William King heirs sold 560 acres of land on Cripple Creek to Manassas Friel.

On May the 3rd, 1817, Manassas Friel sold the 560 tract of land to Francis Smith, of Washington County, Virginia.

On August the 17th, 1820 Francis Smith and wife, Mary, of Washington sold the 560-acre tract to Alexander Smyth. The tract of land was inherited by his daughter, Frances Smyth, who married Col. James H. Piper. Col. Piper was born in Rockbridge County, Va., May the first, 1800. He died at Grayson Sulphur Springs September the 8th, 1854 and was buried in Speedwell cemetery near the site of the Old Speedwell Furnace. Col. Piper was a surveyor and made the first map of the Town of Wytheville in 1839.

After the death of Col. Piper, his widow married Rev. John M. McTeer. Mrs. McTeer is buried in Wytheville.

The 260 acres of land was owned by Mrs. Piper for a number of years, as on May the 8, 1855, she gave a deed of trust on this, the property called the "Speedwell Tract," to Robert Gibboney of Wytheville.

The first Furnace erected at Speedwell, and which changed ownership a number of times, became obsolete and fell into disuse. We recently talked to a man by the name of George W. Chapman, who was born July the 1st, 1851 within a mile of Speedwell Furnace, who stated that when a boy he played around the old Furnace Stack and remembered distinctly when the second Furnace was erected and put into operation.

In 1873 the Providence Iron Company was organized by R. G. Baker, William Pyrus, and Robert Delham, and was merged into the Speedwell Iron Company the latter part of 1873 by David E. James, William C. Aumann, Robert Densham, R. G. Baker and others for the purpose of manufacturing Iron at the old Speedwell furnace site. The furnace was operated until it was sold to Crockett and Company in 1881.

In 1886 the name was changed to the Wythe-Speedwell Mining and Manufacturing Company and continued in operation from 1886 to 1890, at which time the property was transferred to the Pulaski Development Company. In 1898 the property went into the Carter Coal and Iron Company and in 1899 went to the Virginia Iron, Coal and Coke Company. The last blast at Speedwell Furnace was in 1890.

There is a tradition around Speedwell that William Gannaway Brownlow erected the first Speedwell Furnace but this is not borne out by any records. William Gannaway Brownlow was born near Speedwell August 29, 1805. He was a son of Joseph A. Brownlow and Catherine Gannaway Brownlow. He moved to Tennessee in 1826 and became a preacher and was nicknamed "Parson Brownlow." After serving for ten years as a minister he entered politics and was elected Governor of Tennessee and later United States Senator. He died in 1882.

Possibly the only minister connected with the Speedwell works was the Rev. Robertson Gannaway, who was not a minister at the time he lived at Speedwell. From his Autobiography we find the following: Born in Cumberland County, Virginia, July 7, 1770. Came to Cripple Creek, Wythe County, the winter of 1801 and worked at the carpenter's trade in the winter of 1801, at an Iron Works called Speedwell, on Cripple Creek. He continued to work at Speedwell the ensuing year of 1802. He married his cousin, Sallie Gannaway, December 24, 1801.

KING, TRIGG, MORGAN

We have been unable to get much information about this firm except that William King, who came to America in 1784, settled in Saltville in 1792 and acquired the Saltworks as it was then called. He married Mary Trigg, a daughter of Daniel Trigg, of Montgomery County, Virginia. Later he moved to Abingdon and died there October 13, 1808 Some, if not all, of the kettles used at Saltville for boiling the salt water for the manufacture of salt were made at Speedwell Furnace. These kettles were transported to Saltville by wagon. According to George W. Chapman, heretofore quoted, his father John vouched for the correctness of the statement.

Some of the kettles cast at Speedwell are still in use in this county, being used at hog-killing time for scalding the hogs. One of these is at "Bellefield", the home of Mr. A. B. Newberry east of Wytheville.

Another is at Mr. M. H. Jackson's home at Jackson's Ferry and was taken from the bottom of the old Shot Tower when the railway was being built. It is logical to conclude that these kettles were cast at Speedwell, since those for Saltville were made there.

CEMETERY

About a mile northwest of the Speedwell Church on the top of a high hill there is a cemetery in which the Morgans and possibly some of the Triggs are buried, together with some of their slaves.

At one time it could be seen by the stones that fifteen or twenty persons had been buried there but the stones have been removed and the land farmed over. A recent visit to the spot revealed a stone with "D. S." and other inscription below which had been effaced by the weather and could not be deciphered. There is, however, one that has been there for over 125 years which neither time nor weather can affect. It is an iron plate, 22 inches wide, 4 feet long and ½ in. thick and the following inscription is thereon:

Mary Trigg King Morgan
Born Oct. 13, 1807
Died Sept. 17, 1808

There is no question but the marker was cast at the Speedwell Iron Works.

General Alexander Smyth, one of the owners of the Old Speedwell Furnace property, possibly never operated it but has an enviable record as a soldier and statesman. He was born in Ireland in 1765, came to America in 1770, practiced law in Abingdon and later moved to Wythe County where he was trustee of Wytheville in 1792. He served in the General Assembly of Virginia, in the Senate, and was a Brigadier General in the United States Army. He captured the bell that is in the Courthouse in the war of 1812 from the British on Lake Erie. He married Nancy Brinkley on January 19, 1791. While a member of Congress he died in Washington on April 17, 1830 and was buried in the Congressional cemetery, Washington, D. C.

POPLAR CAMP FURNACE

Poplar Camp, located in the southwest corner of Wythe County on Federal Route No. 52, is one of the historic sections of the county. Only a short distance from the Wythe-Carroll line, it was the scene of industrial activity beginning about 1790. William Ross patented the land and erected a grist mill. On October the 1st, 1798, the Popular Camp land was sold to Greenburg G. McKinsie and Caleb Bobbett of Grayson County and Thomas Blair who formed a partnership for the erection of an Iron Furnace on the property with Thomas Blair as manager.

The next owners of the property were William and Thomas Herbert who, on August the 7th, 1807, sold a half interest in the Poplar Camp Furnace to David Peirce.

David Peirce, on September the 12th, 1815, sold to Jesse Evans, Sr., a saw mill and grist mill on Poplar Camp Creek.

It is known that there was a Forge at Poplar Camp but, we have been unable to find the date of erection. It was possibly erected about the time of the Furnace, or shortly afterwards, as a Forge was often erected near a Furnace to assist in working the iron product.

A service station stands on the site of the Old Furnace and a mill on the site of the Ross Mill.

A block of limestone with the inscription D. Peirce 1810 was taken from the site of the Old Furnace by Alexander Chaffin and it remained in his yard for a number of years.

RAVEN CLIFF FURNACE

From the best information obtainable the first Forge and Furnace were built at this place in 1810 by Joseph Bell and Andrew Kincannon. Recorded deeds reveal these interesting facts:—

On January 7, 1809, William Gleaves and wife, Peggy, deeded to Joseph Bell and Andrew Kincannon 420 acres of land on Cripple Creek.

On October 25, 1817, Andrew Kincannon sold to Joseph Bell, on Cripple Creek, 430 acres of land which came from William Gleaves, Jr., and 28 acres of land from Francis Smith, Agents of the Loyal Company, wherein stands the iron works built by said Bell and Kincannon and also 90 acres from Richard Hobbes.

Joseph Bell's estate appraised December 24, 1825.

J. A. Sanders, J. T. Gleaves and Andrew Porter, on July —1826 laid off the widow's dower, to Sarah Bell, widow of the late Joseph Bell, no dower right included in the Forge or Furnace tract.

Leonard Straw purchased the Joseph Bell land under a deed of trust sale.

On June 10, 1835, Leonard Straw sold to Andrew S. Fulton, a 28 acre tract on which stood the Forge and Furnace owned by Joseph Bell, deceased. On November 8, 1841, Stephen Sanders, commissioner, sold by a decree of court the 28 acre Forge tract, to James T. Gleaves, to satisfy a judgement of Isaac T. Leftwich, against Leonard Straw.

On December the 20th, 1857, James T. Gleaves sold to William Wilkinson 28 acres of land on both sides of Cripple Creek, Bell's Forge and Furnace tract.

Deed to Richard W. Sanders, John W. Green, J. P. M. Sanders, James N. Kincannon, A. K. Fulton, F. E. Kincannon, date November 4, 1861, land formerly owned by James T. Gleaves, Sr., on which there was a Furnace and Forge.

On January the 13th, 1866, James Wilkinson and William Wilkinson sold tract No. 5 to Andrew K. Fulton and John Green on which there was a Forge and Furnace formerly owned by James T. Gleaves, Sr.

On December the 10th, 1867, James H. Piper sold John W. Green, Andrew K. Fulton, J. P. M. Sanders, James E. Kincannon and Francis E. Kincannon a 72 acre tract of land.

On March 4, 1879, Crockett, Sanders and Company, purchased from C. B. Thomas, commissioner, a number of tracts of land on Cripple Creek; this was the Raven Cliff property. The firm of Crockett, Sanders and Company, was composed of James S. Crockett, John P. M. Sanders, John W. Robinson, M. B. Tate. Captain C. R. Boyd in his history of Southwest Virginia states the second furnace was built by Crockett, Sanders and Company in 1876.

The firm afterwards changed to Crockett and Company, when John P. M. Sanders sold his interests to David P. Graham.

Crockett and Company owned Raven Cliff until 1886, when the firm was changed to Wythe-Speedwell Mining and Manufacturing Company. The Furnace was not operated after having been purchased by the Wythe-Speedwell Mining and Manufacturing Company. The property was taken over by the Pulaski Development Company, then passed to the Carter Coal and Iron Company and in 1899 went to the Virginia Iron, Coal and Coke Company, the present owners.

For a number of years a grist mill and saw mill were operated at Raven Cliff in connection with the Furnace.

CEDAR RUN FURNACE

From Watson's Genealogy of Virginia, page 452:— "Cedar Run (Parry Mount) furnace with three successive stacks was operated by the Grahams from 1800 till the coming of coke furnaces."

A map made by James Madison and found in Washington by Daniel Cannaday, of Radford State Teachers College, gives an iron operation at Cedar Run prior to 1807, the date of the map. On Boyd's map of Southwest Virginia it is designated as "Old Furnace", also "Cedar Run Furnace."

A Memorandum of Iron

"Received of James and Andrew Crockett the part of a bond given to David McGavock for one ton. Received by Hugh and James McGavock, May 1800." The memorandum does not state whether the iron was from Cedar Run or the Forge. From old papers now in possession of Mr. Jacob C. McGavock, of Max Meadows. Found in the papers of Hugh McGavock.

From the foregoing facts we think it reasonable to conclude that the first Cedar Run furnace was erected possibly prior to 1800, not by the Grahams but by the Crocketts. The name James Crockett appears in the deed dated July the 19th, 1828. James Crockett was one of the owners of a Forge or iron works on Reed Creek as early as 1801, which was called Crockett's, now Graham's Forge. The records of Nov. 2, 1801 state that Andrew and James Crockett entered 10 acres of land on both sides of Reed Creek to include their iron works. The Crockett iron works were erected on Reed Creek prior to 1801.

Evidently the first Cedar Run furnace and the first Forge

or iron works on Reed Creek were owned and operated by the same persons. The furnace being three or more miles distant from the forge, in all probability the iron made at Cedar Run was transported to Crockett's Forge where it was worked into the finished product.

From the 1935 edition:

Cedar Run is a small stream in the eastern portion of Wythe County, flowing into Reed Creek a short distance from the point where the creek flows into New River.

There were two furnaces on this small stream, both using water power for operation. We have been unable to ascertain the date of the erection of the first. However, it was prior to 1826. On July the 19th, 1826, Lysander McGavock, of the County of Davidson, State of Tennessee, and William D. Crockett and James E. Brown, of the County of Wythe, sold to David Graham 12 certain tracts or parcels of land with the exception of (140 acres part thereof devised by James Crockett to Samuel and John Crockett) which said land have thereon a Furnace and other buildings necessary for the making of iron.

This furnace stood on the site where what is known as the Graham home now stands. The home was erected by the late Major David Peirce Graham, son of David Graham.

The plant was operated by David Graham for several years but in 1832 he erected a larger plant further down the stream which was operated until his death in 1870.

The property then passed into the hands of his son Maj. D. P. Graham, who operated it for a number of years and rebuilt it in 1888.

After the plant was rebuilt it was only operated one blast by the firm of Graham and Robinson. From that time on all of the iron ore in that vicinity was shipped to the Dora Furnace in Pulaski. The pipe for the first water system in Wytheville was made at Cedar Run Furnace. A half mile of the pipe is still in use, conveying water from a spring near St. John's Lutheran Church to the Ice Factory in Wytheville. From the Minutes of the Town of Wythe-

The third Cedar Run Furnace stack. After it was discontinued for making iron it was used to burn lime. The roof was put on to protect the lime from the weather.

ville, July 15, 1839. Wytheville Watering Co. was instructed to put in 7 fire plugs in addition to the one opposite the courthouse. This water system was put in about 1835. The minute book of the Wytheville Watering Co. was burned in the fire of March, 1924.

LITTLE WYTHE FURNACE

Built by Samuel E. and Daniel Porter in 1818. Water power. Rebuilt by Sayers, Oglesby and Company. Steam plant. Afterwards operated by Crockett and Oglesby. Later by Col. Robert Sayers. Sold at public auction and purchased by Crockett and Company, who were the last operators.

The Little Wythe Furnaces were located on Francis Mill Creek, which flows into Cripple Creek at Cripple Creek station. Some of the lands where the plant was located were owned at one time by Jehu Stephens, David Peirce and others. This was a very rich mineral section and after the furnace ceased operation thousands of tons of ore were mined and shipped to other points to be converted into iron. Ore was mined in this locality by the Virginia Iron, Coal and Coke Company and the Pulaski Iron Company:

BARREN SPRINGS FURNACE

Barren Springs Furnace was located on New River, down the river below Fosters Falls. The furnace was erected by David Graham in 1853 and rebuilt by Graham and Robinson in 1873. The latter firm purchased it from Mrs. J. Williamson McGavock, who was a Miss Graham, and who had inherited it from her father's estate.

The property was later purchased by Philadelphia capitalists, who mined it extensively.

GRAY EAGLE FURNACE

Gray Eagle Furnace, located on Cripple Creek about a mile below Raven Cliff, was built in 1863 by Stuart and

Tuttle, who operated it for some years. The property was sold to Mrs. Preston who operated the furnace. It was later sold to David McConnell together with a Forge, which was located on the north side of the creek nearby. Benj. Gallup operated both Furnace and Forge. Later David Huddle operated both plants. Later the property was purchased by Crockett and Company, who made the last blast at this plant.

In 1886 Crockett and Company was changed to the Wythe-Speedwell Mining and Manufacturing Company. In 1890 the property was transferred to the Pulaski Development Company, thence to the Carter Coal and Iron Company and in 1899 to the Virginia Iron, Coal and Coke Company, the present owners.

Both Furnace and Forge, as well as the mill for grinding grain were operated from the same dam.

FOSTERS FALLS FURNACE

Fosters Falls Furnace or Roaring Falls Furnace, as it was called at one time, was located on the east side of New River below Jackson's Ferry. It was erected by the Fosters Falls Mining and Manufacturing Company in 1880-1881, operated by water power from New River.

After erection, this plant was operated for many blasts until 1890 when the ownership passed to the Pulaski Development Company. Like Speedwell and Beverly in 1899 the property was purchased by the Virginia Iron, Coal and Coke Company. From 1890 to 1914 the plant was in operation the greater part of the time, except when out of blast for repairs. The last blast was made in 1914, this being the last of the charcoal furnaces to be operated in Wythe County. After this, large quantities of ore were mined on the property and shipped to Pulaski for working.

Fosters Falls Furnace where the last blast was Made In 1914.

WALTON FURNACE

Walton Furnace, located in the east central portion of Wythe County, was named for George Walton, one of the large land owners in that section years ago.

At the time of erection the furnace was on land owned by Jerome Blair. It was leased to Milton Howard and Dr. Richard Walton Sanders, who erected the furance.

Howard and Sanders operated the furnace for a number of years. In December, 1879, it was leased to the Lobdell Car Wheel Company, Wilmington, Delaware, and was operated by that Company more or less regularly until September, 1888. It has not been operated since that time. The furnace was operated by steam. The Lobdell Car Wheel Company was the first operating iron plant in this section to establish the monthly pay roll.

BROWN HILL FURNACE

Brown Hill Furnace was located on Cripple Creek, about one mile down the creek from the Peirce Forge site. The Brown Hill Iron Company was organized in 1872 and was composed of Abram Painter, William M. Painter, James Painter, John Walters and Benjamin Rowe. The furnace was operated for several years and later in 1880 was purchased by the Lobdell Car Wheel Company, of Wilmington, Delaware. It was not operated by the Lobdell company until 1883 and then for only one blast, with rather disastrous results on account of the low grade of ore. Although Brown Hill Furnace was located on Cripple Creek, it was operated by a steam plant and not water power.

Brown Hill Furnace Located On Cripple Creek

BEVERLY FURNACE

Beverly Furnace was located on Cripple Creek, a short distance east of where Francis Mill Creek empties into Cripple Creek. It was built by Crockett and Company about 1880 and operated until 1890. At that time the property passed to the Pulaski Development Company and was never again operated. It was acquired by the Carter Coal and Iron Company in 1898. In 1899 the property was taken over by the Virginia Iron, Coal and Coke Company, the present owners.

The plant was run by water power and was a successful operation. The dam which was built to operate the furnace is now used for power for a large roller mill, which was erected on the opposite side of the creek.

IRONDALE FURNACE

Irondale Furnace, known as the Noble Furnace, was located on Francis Mill Creek, a few hundred yards down the creek from the Little Wythe. The plant was operated by steam and was erected by Noble, Allen and Company 1880-1881. It was operated possibly for two or three blasts by that company but not successfully. It was sold to Crockett and Company and operated by this company for one or two blasts. It was among the largest of the charcoal type of furnaces in the county, but the engines installed were too small to produce sufficient air to run it to capacity.

IVANHOE FURNACE

The first Furnace at Ivanhoe was the charcoal type and was erected in 1880 by Hendrick Brothers, of New York. It was operated for a number of years and sold in 1890 to a firm of New York capitalists, operating under the name of the New River Mineral Company. The Charcoal furnace was dismantled and a hot blast or coke furnace erected on the same site. This plant continued to function for twenty-five or more years. The iron manufactured sold at a premium, bringing $3.00 per ton more than iron manufactured in the same type of furnace other places. Although the plant has not been operated for a number of years, orders are received for the iron. The property is owned by the Ivanhoe Mining and Smelting Corporation.

A Foundry was operated at one time by the New River Mineral Company in connection with the furnace.

CAVE HILL FURNACE

Cave Hill Furnace was located near the present Town of Speedwell and was erected by Col. Robert Sayers and associates of Wytheville in the early eighties. It was only operated for a few blasts. The plant was run by steam.

Large quantities of ore were mined on the property in recent years by the Virginia Iron, Coal and Coke Company.

MAX MEADOWS FURNACE

The Max Meadows Furnace was located on the Norfolk and Western Railway at Max Meadows and was one of the two hot blast furnaces erected in Wythe County. The furnace was built by Philadelphia Capitalists in 1890-1891, who operated the plant for several blasts. It was sold to the Virginia Iron, Coal and Coke Company in 1902, which company operated it for a few blasts. It was dismantled and sold for junk in 1934.

The Crescent Horseshoe and Iron Works built at the same place in 1892, was sold to the Virginia Iron, Coal and Coke Company, and moved to Bristol in 1907.

WHITE ROCK FURNACE
(In Smyth County)

White Rock Furnace was located in Smyth County about one mile from the Wythe line but was in the Cripple Creek Valley. It was erected in 1873 by Peter Gallagher, David S. Peirce and Gen. William Terry, all of Wytheville.

It was operated for several blasts and sold to the Lobdell Car Wheel Company, Wilmington, Delaware, January, 1880, who continued more or less regularly from date of purchase until August, 1904. The plant was operated by steam.

Irondale Furnace, located near Cripple Creek Station and the largest Furnace of this type ever built in the County.

BELL OR PEIRCE FORGE

The two oldest Forges in the county were at what are now Poplar Camp and Peirce's Mill. The latter was erected by Wm. Bell and Wm. Herbert on Cripple Creek about 2 miles from Ivanhoe. It is known as the Bell-Herbert Forge and was erected before July 1, 1794.

We have not been able to obtain the date of the Poplar Camp Forge.

The land was presumably patented by Charles Nuckolls who, according to record at Wythe County Court House, on April the 9th, 1793, sold to William Bell and William Herbert 500 acres of land on Cripple Creek.

On July 1, 1794, William Bell and William Herbert sold to Hugh Montgomery and Daniel Carlin 500 acres of land with Forges, Houses, Dam, etc., for operating the same. Thus it will be seen that the Bell or Peirce Forge was erected between April 1793 and July 1794.

On July 23, 1799, Hugh Montgomery and Robert Carlin sold to Robert Sanders 500 acres of land on Cripple Creek, with Houses, Forges, Barns, etc.

On December 9, 1800, Robert Sanders sold to David Peirce the 500-acre tract with the Forges, etc.

On March 11, 1806, David Peirce agreed to furnish Sampson King and Trigg $2,553.92 merchantable bar iron at $123.33 per ton of 2240 lbs.

On March 12, 1806, David Peirce gave to William King and John J. Trigg a mortgage on a 500-acre tract of land known as the Peirce Forge for the faithful performance of the above-mentioned contract.

On December the 10th, 1838, the 500-acre tract was partitioned among the David Peirce heirs.

A saw mill and grist mill was also operated at the Peirce Forge. The grist mill is still in existence.

Some of the later operators were: James Wilkinson, William Hiley and Robert P. Williams. The latter was probably the last person to operate the Forge. Mr. Williams lived to be nearly 94 years of age and died April 2, 1922.

HIGH ROCK FORGE

High Rock was located in the extreme east portion of Wythe County on Little Reed Island Creek and was quite a business center, dating back to the latter part of seventeen hundred. There was a postoffice called High Rock, which was later changed to Patterson; thus a place of historical interest lost its identity.

The history with the changes of ownership follows:—

On May the 8th, 1805, Thomas and William Herbert bought of Thomas Whitlock 340 acres of land on Reed Island Creek. On this tract a Forge was erected by said Herberts before 1811.

On October the 22nd, 1811, John Evans bought of Thomas Herbert 200 acres of land, on Reed Island Creek, known as the Forge tract.

On June the 10th, 1817, David Peirce purchased from John Evans 200 acres of land on Reed Island known as the High Rock Forge tract.

On March 19th, 1842, James Stephens purchased from David Peirce heirs 200 acres of land on Reed Island Creek, known as the High Rock Forge tract. The land remained in the Stephens family for many years and the mineral was sold to the Pulaski Iron Company, who mined a large quantity of iron ore, which was shipped to Pulaski where it was manufactured into pig iron.

At the site of the High Rock Forge, resided Samuel Wheeler, who later operated a grist mill, sawmill and furniture plant. Wheeler manufactured all kinds of furniture and specialized in coffins, that being the only plant of the kind in that section. The High Rock Roller Mills are in operation at this time at the site of the Wheeler activities and the High Rock Forge.

CROCKETT OR GRAHAM FORGE

A survey was made for James and Andrew Crockett of property at Reed Creek, February the second, 1796. The deed states that Purgatory branch flows through the property. This branch flows into Reed Creek a short distance below the Graham's Forge site. We think this indicates that James and Andrew Crockett were making preparations for the erection of the forge and iron works at that place in the 1790's.

From the Land Entry Book, Wythe County, Virginia, 1801, Nov. 2, Andrew and James Crockett by virtue of part of a land office treasury warrant of 20000 acres, enter ten acres of land on both sides of Reed Creek to include their iron works.

Andrew and James Crockett

Richmond State Archives, Vol. 17, pages 174; Jan. 2, 1805, Andrew and James Crockett of Reed Creek:— "Whereas it is represented to this present General Assembly that Andrew and James Crockett of the County of Wythe have erected a dam across Reed Creek, to the manifest injury to the inhabitants of the said county by obstructing the passage of fish up and down said creek. For remedy whereof be it therefore enacted that Stephen Sanders, James Newell and Thomas Whitlock gentlemen, be and they hereby are appointed commissioners whose duty it shall be to examine the said Creek and dam and to hear such evidence as may be offered them, either by the inhabitants residing on or near the said Creek and to report to the next General Assembly whether it will be of the most public utility to compel the said Andrew and James Crockett to make a slope to their dam for the passage of fish or to suffer the said dam to remain as at present erected, for the purpose of carrying on their iron works."

From 1935 edition: In D. B. 6, page 517, is recorded a court order, granting James Crockett a permit to build a dam and Forge on Reed Creek and appointing a commission to assess damages, if any, to property owners. Order dated March 5, 1815.

This Forge was located at what is now known as Graham's Forge and was purchased from Crockett by David Graham, who enlarged the plant and installed a number of iron working machines which were modern for that day (The purchase was prior to 1828, and at that time the plant consisted of Forge, Rolling Mills, Nail Works, three Heating Furnaces, five Nail Machines, one Hammer. The property is now owned by George L. Carter, who has a large grist mill and wood working plant on the site. This is possibly the only nail making machine ever operated in Wythe County (the other process in vogue at that time was the blacksmith shop.) W. R. Crockett, who resides south of Wytheville on Route 21 states he worked on one of the nail machines when a boy.

Another product at that time were wood heaters of a peculiar type. There was a draft at each end of the fire box and a large open space in the center. The writer remembers seeing two of these stoves with the name "David Graham, Graham's Forge," thereon. One was used a number of years ago in Old Fleming church on Cripple Creek and the other in Crowder's Tailor Shop, Wytheville.

TONCRAY FORGE

From information gleaned from old records and physical facts, recently obtained, there is no doubt that a forge was built and operated at what is known as Kent's Mill place on Reed Creek east of Wytheville the latter part of 1700 or early 1800.

In Entry Book 1, page 117 we find "Anthony Toncray had 200 acres, 50 of which was by part of a warrant assigned him by William King and dated December the 25th, 1785."

The Annals of Southwest Virginia by L. P. Summers, "Anthony Toncray was granted license Sept. 1, 1789, to keep an ordinary at his house at McCall's. An old map shows that McCalls was at what was afterwards called "Bellfield", the present home of Mr. A. B. Newberry. This property passed from the Toncray's to the Crockett's and from the Crockett's to the Kent family and thence to Newberry, the present owner.

In Deed Book 5, p. 428, Wythe County records we find that Robert Adams, commissioner, sold 300 acres of the Anthony Toncray land to James Toncray on February the 12th, 1812. The records would indicate that James Toncray borrowed money several times on the property, giving deeds of trust for various sums.

Book 14, p. 123: On June 12th, 1837 a deed of trust on 5 acres of land on Reed Creek was given to Robert Kent to secure certain sums to David Kent. This land was the tract on which James Toncray lived and on which were located a still house, mills, shops, etc. Sold at the courthouse on Sept. 10, 1838.

In Deed Book 16, p. 107: On April the 16th, 1842, James Toncray gave a deed of trust to Robert J. Crockett and Stephen S. Crockett on property on which there were valuable mills.

We have been unable to secure the date when the Forge was built. However, when a bridge was put across Reed Creek at this place a TRIP HAMMER, the type used in a forge, was covered up in the fill and remains there today.

A man by the name of George W. Jones, Sr., who was born in 1815 and who resided near the place, stated to his children and grandchildren, who are living near-by at this time, that he remembered the Forge. He died in 1896 at the age of 81 years. Mr. Newberry informs us that the hammer had been partly submerged in the mud ever since he owned the property but that he did not realize its significence or he would have rescued it. The hammer was the type used in forges in the early days of the iron industry in this county. We think it reasonable to conclude that the Forge was erected by Anthony Toncray. Anthony and son James Toncray are buried on land west of and in sight of their former operations.

Court records: "A tract of land 3 miles east of Wytheville known as Bellefield was purchased by Robert Emmet Kent from Stephen Crockett, April 16, 1842. Four hundred and twenty acres including mill on Reed Creek, which Stephen Crockett had purchased from James Toncray and his wife Mary."

KENT'S MILLS

After the property passed into the hands of the Kent family the operation was commonly known as Kent's Mills. A factory for the manufacture of various kinds of cloth, saddle blankets, etc., a grist mill and saw mill were all operated there at one time. During the War Between the States, during a raid through Southwest Virginia by Federal troops, a Federal officer by the name of Kent called at the Kent home and told Mrs. Kent that he would not allow the property to be burned because it belonged to the Kents. A guard was placed over the property and it was not burned.

There was also a Hat Factory operated there about the close of the war and afterwards, by Marion Sehorn, who lived in Wytheville and who came to this county from Rockbridge County. Mr. R. P. Johnson states that when a boy about fifteen years of age he worked in the hat factory and would walk back and forth, morning and night. The wool for the manufacture of the hats was imported from South Africa. The hat business was discontinued about 1870 and Mr. Sehorn moved to Tennessee and thence to California. The mill and factory were destroyed by fire March 5, 1893, and the only thing left today to mark the site of this once thriving business centre are some mud sills in the creek, showing where the dam was located.

CHATWELL FORGE

What was known as the Chatwell Forge was probably erected and operated by Henry Eller, as the land was called the Forge tract as far back as 1840.

On Sept. 11, 1792, Henry Eller purchased from John Ewing 250 acres of land on both sides of Cripple Creek, in the County of Montgomery, now Wythe County.

William Chatwell married Jane Eller, a daughter of Henry Eller, and the Forge tract came down to William Chatwell and Jane Eller Chatwell. William Chatwell operated the

Forge for a number of years. William Chatwell and wife sold the Forge tract to John P. M. Simmerman, Sept. 11, 1856.

Process for Making Steel

(Contributed)

The old Chatwell Forge was built prior to the year 1836 and was in operation as early as the year 1836, water from Cripple Creek, supplying the power. The equipment consisted of one 800-pound hammer and one furnace or forge fire. At this plant a semi-steel, called blister steel, was made by the following process: The iron bars or slabs, after forging, were placed in a charcoal fire which was allowed to burn very slowly until the coal was well ignited and the bars had attained a red heat. The whole was then covered with fine coal breeze and allowed to stand for several days. This permitted the iron to absorb carbon, thus converting it into a mild steel. This steel was used to form the cutting edge of axes made in quantity in a near-by blacksmith shop. Some of the older inhabitants of the neighborhood state that these axes were used by citizens of North Carolina, Kentucky and Virginia.

LOCKETT FORGE

On Oct. 3, 1866, James C. Halsey sold to David Huddle 369 acres of land on Cripple Creek, "except so much as was embraced in a Forge Seat, which had been sold to James W. Lockett."

James W. Lockett sold Forge to David Huddle Nov. 15, 1871. Huddle operated the Forge, together with a saw mill and corn mill until all were washed away in the freshet of September, 1878. Lockett built and operated the forge until sold to Huddle. James W. Lockett moved to Texas after selling the property.

PORTER FORGE

Porter's Forge was located on Cripple Creek, about three miles East of Speedwell and was erected in the early seventies by Stephen Porter and son, Andrew L. Porter. The plant was operated by water power. It was washed away in 1878 and was not rebuilt.

IRON ORE MINES

After the advent of the modern furnace and modern mining only a small portion of the ore mined in this county was worked in Wythe County Furnaces. The great majority was shipped elsewhere.

Among the mines operated were: Barren Springs, Bertha, Carter, Sanders, Walton, Morris, Hurst, Patterson, Crawford, Tipton, Fosters Falls, Hematite, Posey, Poplar Camp, Indian Camp, William Jackson, Gregory, Ivanhoe, Painter, Simmerman, Sisk, and Gray, Little Wythe, Porter, Norma. Gannaway, Percival, Andis, Clark's Summit, Locust Hill, Porter north side of Cripple Creek.

---o---

WYTHEVILLE FOUNDRYS

Barrett's Foundry

John B. Barrett came to Wytheville from Danville, Virginia, in 1858 and purchased from James K. Johnson land on Reed Creek, one mile south of Wytheville. Here he erected a dam to furnish power for a Foundry and Machine Shop, Grist Mill, Wool Carding Plant and Plaster Grinding Machine.

Cane Mills, Plows and farm machinery, together with all kinds of castings were turned out in the foundry and machine shop.

In 1861 the Confederate Government contracted with this foundry to furnish war materials. Small cannons, cannon balls and rifles were manufactured and repaired. The flint lock type of rifle was changed to the cap type of gun. The owner had patented what he called at that time a Gatling gun. The gun had a cylinder, with seven chambers and was operated by a crank. The plant continued in operation until sometime in the eighties, when the foundry and machine works were abandoned.

McDonald Foundry

E. H. McDonald purchased from Marion and Rebecca Sehorn a lot in Wytheville on June the 24th, 1868 on which he erected a small Foundry. The plant was operated by water power, secured from what is known as the "Town Branch." He manufactured all kinds of castings and did machine work. At one time his brother was associated with him, the firm name being McDonald Brothers. This plant continued until about 1900.

Wytheville Foundry

What was known as the Wytheville Foundry was located on Spring street, and was owned and operated by John Sexton, W. J. Keller (formerly of Salem, Virginia), and W. G. Bottimore, formerly of Philadelphia, Pennsylvania. The firm manufactured Threshers, Corn Shellers, Crushers, Iron Railings, Cast Window and Door Frames, together with all kinds of foundry work.

McWANE FOUNDRY

Charles P. McWane, a son of James McWane and Permelia Ryan, was born at Massie's Mill, Nelson County, Virginia, and came to Wytheville prior to "The War Between the States." From the Iron Worker published in Lynchburg: "During the War Between the States," Charles had been engaged in necessary industry behind the battle lines. The building and repairing of army wagons, the manufacture of gun stocks and the reconditioning of railroad rolling stock had kept him occupied at various times. After the close of the war, he had been employed in the foundry and machine shop operated in Wytheville by J. B. Barrett and Company. In this way he continued the training begun by his father and had added knowledge of the several trades in which he became adept."

James McWane, the father of Charles McWane, was an associate and co-worker of Cyrus McCormick and it is said that Charles, when a boy, played around the shop where the two worked.

In the year 1871 Charles McWane established a small iron foundry in Wytheville, Va. As his means were limited he made his own Cupola out of a discarded steam boiler. He made his own fan to furnish air to melt the iron in the Cupola, and bought a second hand horse power to operate the fan.

After he made his own plow patterns, he employed a moulder to make the castings, and only two casts a week were made.

While struggling on for several years, the McWane plow made its reputation, and the buildings were too small to take care of the increased business. As larger quarters were necessary, the little shop was abandoned for a new one on Fourth Avenue.

This was made possible by a partnership, formed in 1877, with Look & Lincoln Wagon manufacturers of Marion, Va. The new Iron foundry, under the firm name of C. P. McWane & Co., was a large one equipped with new and improved machinery that made it a modern up to date plant for those days. Not only plows were made, but many other agricultural implements, Corn shellers, Cane mills, Grist mills, Feed cutters, and Cider mills were included in the list. In addition, orders were solicited for all kinds of foundry and machine work. The firm name of C. P. McWane & Co. was afterwards changed to H. E. McWane & Co. This business was discontinued in the year 1891.

His sons followed in his footsteps, and made a wonderful record in the Iron business. H. E. McWane went to Lynchburg, Va., and organized the Lynchburg Foundry Co., and the Lynchburg Plow Works, two of the largest industries of its kind in the state. Charles W. McWane was associated

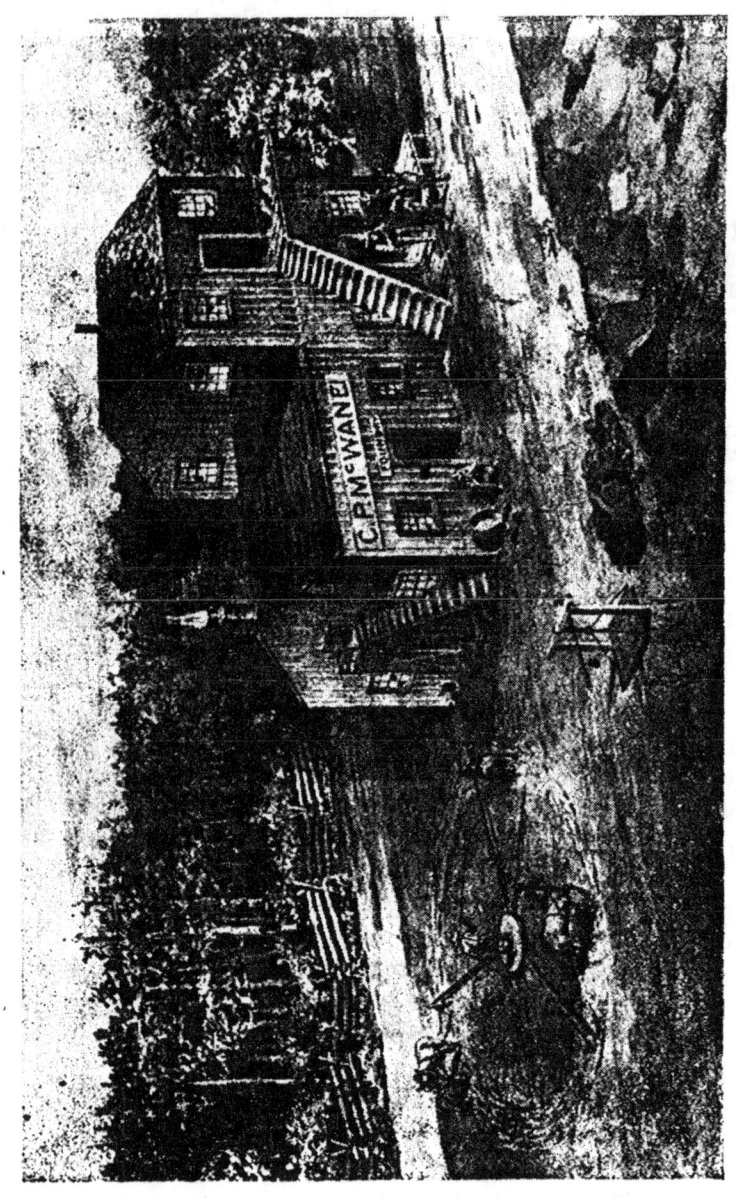

The above is an actual photo of the McWane Foundry at Wytheville in the year 1871, operated and owned by C. P. McWane. This photo was made a few months after the shop had been in operation.

with him in the plow business and through his inventive genius, their dream of a tremendous plow business was realized. One of his greatest achievements was the invention of the self-sharpening plow point which is nationally known, outwearing three to four of the old style points, and being a money saver to the farmer. J. R. McWane established a large Pipe foundry in Birmingham, Ala., and Prove, Utah. A. T. McWane is now connected with his company in Birmingham, Ala., the McWane Cast Iron Pipe Co.

Of the five sons, two are now living, Robert C., and Arthur T. McWane. It may be said that the little foundry Charles P. McWane started in 1871 is the birthplace of the largest plants in Virginia and Alabama.

Several years after its organization, the Lynchburg Foundry Company purchased the Radford Pipe and Foundry Co., of Radford, Va., and the plant is still in operation under the name of the Lynchburg Foundry Co. Robert C. McWane was the manager of this plant. He was later transferred to New York, as sales manager of the Lynchburg Foundry Company, in which capacity he served for a number of years.

Henry E. McWane, Jr., is now president of the Lynchburg Foundry Co., Lynchburg, Va.

William McWane, son of the late J. R. McWane, is president of the McWane Cast Iron Pipe Company, of Birmingham, Ala.

After the McWanes moved from Wytheville, the property was purchased by C. H. Calfee and Franklin Carter, of Wythe County.

The ownership afterwards passed to John B. Hurt.

The last operators were R. H. Crowgey, George R. Huffard and John Williams, who operated it from 1901 to 1903 or 1904. The site was sold to Humphreys-Davidson Hardware Company for building purposes.

Charles P. McWane, the founder of the McWane Foundry of Wytheville, from which sprang the other extensive McWane industries.

HOLLAND IRON WORKS

The Holland Iron Works was organized in 1872 by New York capitalists, who purchased 1200 acres of land in Wythe County on the south side of Reed Creek, extending to the top of Lick Mountain. A furnace stack was partially erected on Reed Creek east of Wytheville and the land prospected for iron. Iron was found but the erection of the furnace was abandoned.

HISTORICAL FACTS
ABOUT THE
CHURCHES
OF
WYTHE COUNTY

—BY—
J. A. WHITMAN
WYTHEVILLE, VA.

Printed by
Southwest Virginia Enterprise
Wytheville, Va.

1939

Reproduced for *Wythe County Chapters* by special permission of the Whitman family.

INTRODUCTION

The pioneers who settled Southwest Virginia in the section which is now Wythe County recognized the importance of religious organization and with that end in view proceeded to establish places where they could worship God according to the dictates of their conscience. Many of them, or their forefathers, had fled their native lands to escape religious persecution. In the wilderness country, which at that time was sparsely settled, the importance of a place of worship was early recognized.

All of the early buildings were crude log affairs but served the purpose. While services were conducted by itinerant ministers or layman in private residences, a definite movement for the establishment of permanent churches was started as early as 1770-71 when an organization was established at Fort Chiswell under the auspices of the Episcopal church.

In 1771 a movement was launched by Hanover Presbytery to establish Presbyterian organizations in this county. In about 1776, or earlier, it was followed by the Lutheran and Reformed Churches and permanent organizations soon followed these efforts.

Worship in those days was held, in many instances, under difficult circumstances. A number of historians record the fact that all the male members of the congregation would go to the place of worship with their trusty rifles which would be stacked at the door under the supervision of a sentinel whose duty it was to keep a sharp lookout for the approaching Indian.

On Sunday morning when the Parson was getting ready for service the last item of dress was the shot pouch and rifle.

We are not attempting to give a detailed history of the various churches, but merely give data gleaned from court and church records of the various denominations beginning with the Presbyterian, it being among the earliest.

PRESBYTERIAN CHURCHES
PERIOD OF CONGREGATIONAL ORGANIZATION: 1769-1785

The following is taken from an address made in Wytheville, in connection of the Diamond Jubilee Celebration, April 21, 1936.

"The period from 1769 to 1785 may, for convenience, be called the period of Congregational Organization, because within that period numerous Presbyterian congregations were formed, some independently and some under auspices of Hanover Presbytery. In 1785 Abingdon Presbytery was formed."

By 1768 the number of settlers in the far western part of Virginia had increased to such an extent that Hanover Presbytery in April of that year instructed the Rev. John Craig to make a tour of the western settlements, authorizing him to organize congregations. In the minutes of Hanover Presbytery as of April 13, 1769, it is recorded that in performance of this duty Mr. Craig organized eight congregations, three of which were in the present limits of Wythe County.

"The next notice of an organized congregation appears in the minutes of Hanover Presbytery as of April 10, 1771, when the Rev. Charles Cummings reported that he had carried out the instructions given him at the previous fall meeting of Presbytery to tour the western vacancies and to go as far as Royal Oak on Holston. On this tour he organized the Big Spring Congregation on the headwaters of Holston, with George Adams, Robert Buchanan, Richard Higgins and Alexander Neilly as elders. Robert Buchanan's house still stands beside a very large spring, one of the head springs of the Middle Form of Holston, in Smyth County, near the Wythe line, a few miles west of Rural Retreat, and it is a reasonable supposition that the Big Spring congregation was formed in his house and named for the spring. The name Big Spring does not appear again in the minutes, but shortly afterwards the name Salem Church on Reed Creek begins to appear and frequently occurs. The Doaks, who lived in Black Lick Valley, are named in connection of Salem on Reed Creek, and the Black Lick branch is a fork of Reed Creek. It is known that a very old log Presbyterian church stood along that branch for many years, from which I infer that the Big Spring congregation was organized in 1771 in the home of Robert Buchanan; that the congregation decided to build their meeting house some six or seven miles to the northeast on Black Lick, and changed the name to Salem. If so, this church was allowed to die, was later revived as Black Lick Church, and is now functioning as Rural Retreat Church."

"On October the 14, 1772, supplication to Hanover Presbytery for supply from Salem Church on Reed Creek."

In deed book A., Page 251 in the Christiansburg Clerk's Office, we find: "Patrick Campbell deeded to William Campbell 350 acres of land formerly owned by John Buchanan, deceased, called and known as the Salem tract, on the south fork of Reed Creek. March 5, 1782."

The name Salem on Reed Creek is also found in the records in the Wythe County Clerk's Office and will be fully explained later, as it figures in other places of worship.

Boiling Spring organization was made by Rev. John Craig on his western tour. This is one of the old land marks of Wythe County and mention of the name is found in Augusta records, when William Herbert was the owner of what is now Jackson's Ferry. The road ran from Herbert's Ferry to Boiling Spring. The Elders for this church were: Robert Montgomery, David Sayers, William Sayers, Nathaniel Welcher and William Herbert. Forty-two families.

Unity Church, on Reed Creek, had 45 families represented and the elders were: James Harris, James Davies, James Hollis, George Breckenridge, Samuel Montgomery. The exact location of this church is not known, but, is supposed to have been west of Max Meadows. It is reasonable to suppose that the Anchor of Hope Church was the outgrowth of Unity.

The records in Montgomery County, giving a number of land transfers, may give some light on the location of the people who figured in these early churches. "Deed from William Patton, Ex. to James Montgomery, Sept. 1 and 9, 1775."

"Deed of William Calhoun to Samuel Crockett on Reed Creek, on Dec. 2, 1772. Witnesses to deed were: John Montgomery, Samuel Montgomery and Joseph Montgomery."

"Montgomery to Quirk 500 acres of land on Reed Creek, joining Anchor of Hope on which they now dwell. Signed by Robert Montgomery, James Montgomery and William Montgomery. Sept. 26, 1782."

"Robert Doak to David Doak, a tract of land on Evans Creek, a branch of Reed Creek. Jan. 1773." Evans Creek is the branch of Reed Creek that flows by the Stuart farm.

"Henry Davies and Jane Davies to Thomas Davies, a tract of land. Aug. 31, 1872."

"Samuel Crockett to Samuel Montgomery, 125 acres, part of the original survey of Joseph and Easter Crockett of 1100 acres. Dec. 20, 1783."

ANCHOR OF HOPE

"Anchor of Hope" is one of the old Presbyterian Churches of Wythe County and was so called on account of the original royal grant of lands made by King George II in 1753 to John Buchanan. There have been three "Anchor of Hope" churches, all located on different sites but in the same locality.

The first, probably erected in 1792 near Max Meadows at Hager's Spring, was a log building and served as a schoolhouse and church. The first teacher was Rev. Thomas Erskine Birch, a clergyman of the Church-of-England, who doubtless served as pastor as well as teacher, from 1792 to 1810.

Rev. Samuel H. McNutt was called in 1815 as pastor and teacher and remained for 13 years or until 1828.

The next pastor, Rev. George Painter, assumed the duties as pastor and teacher at the new church built on the "Great Highway" near Fort Chiswell, "which leads southwestward to Tennessee and the cotton states."

The third Anchor of Hope church was erected in the town of Max Meadows and was used the first time on October 17, 1886. The Graham Memorial Building, an addition to the auditorium, containing rooms for Sunday School classes and other activities, was dedicated July 25, 1926 and was the gift of Miss Mary G. Graham, in memory of her parents, Mr. and Mrs. Wythe B. Graham and brother, Mr. Zeb V. Graham.

FROM THE MINUTES OF THE ANCHOR OF HOPE CHURCH

"The Anchor of Hope and Cove Churches secured Rev. William Sterling Lacy for a pastorate of four years (1869-73). He was installed October 17, 1869. He appointed a committee to correct the roster of church members.

"Galena, Sept. 18, 1870. Session met at the residence of Capt. Raper at ten a. m., and the meeting was constituted with prayer. Present, Rev. William S. Lacy, Moderator, Elders, Robert Raper, Samuel R. Crockett and Abraham Painter.

The committee of the session appointed April 3, 1870, to prepare a roll of the church submitted a report which, after recommendation, was adopted.—From a careful examination of the minutes of the Cove church since its organization in October, 1859, to the present, the following persons were enrolled belonging to the organization in Wytheville: Robert Raper, Mary C. Raper, Mary Ann Raper (now Mrs. William S. Thorn), John G. Crockett, Mary Ann Crockett, William G. Crockett, Joseph N. Crockett, Sallie F. Crockett, Maria Francis. The following from ———— Samuel R. Crockett, wife Mary H. Crockett, Mary Graham, wife of John Graham, Jane Graham, wife of John G. Graham. Robert Raper and Samuel R. Crockett were ordained Elders in October 1859."

Abraham Painter, formerly an elder in the Cripple Creek church, was elected elder June 12, 1869. The Cripple Creek Church was located at what is now Ivanhoe and was called Forest church, an interdenominational organization. The property was later acquired by the Southern Methodist.

The Anchor of Hope and Cove were united in one congregation July the 18, 1875, under the name of Anchor of Hope, which continued for a period of ten years.

November 21, 1885, those members residing near Galena, withdrew from the Anchor of Hope church and effected an organization. The Galena church is used today as a union church, both Presbyterian and Methodist conducting service.

MONKS CORNER

Monks Corner was located about two miles east of Max Meadows on land at one time owned by the late Samuel R. Crockett. When or by whom this Presbyterian church was organized seems to be unknown and its history may be forever lost. The name also seems to be a mystery. There is a Monk's Corner in South Carolina. General George Monk "Duke of Albemarle" figured in the early history of Albemarle Sound in North Carolina, was an American patriot, politician and an ardent Presbyterian. The church at Monk's Corner was in existence as late as October the 8, 1856, as on that date Capt. Robert Raper and wife Mary were dismissed from the Monk's Corner church to the Wytheville Presbyterian church. (From the Session records of the Wytheville Church.) The church was built by Samuel R. Crockett, Sr., and Crockett Graham, and was discontinued when the Anchor of Hope was moved to Max Meadows, the congregation uniting with the Max Meadows organization.

MOUNT TABOR PRESBYTERIAN CHURCH

From the minutes of the first book of records of the Wytheville Presbyterian Church, known as Mount Tabor, we find: "In the absence of any record of the first organization of the Presbyterian Church of Wytheville that in 1823 Rev. James McConnel, aided by Rev. Stephen Bovell, organized a church with the following members: Mrs. Jane L. Crockett, her daughter, Mrs. Maria M. Brown, the elder Mrs. Margaret Gibboney and Douglas Baker, who was elected Elder."

Rev. James McConnel did not remain over a year, after which there was no regular pastor until 1837, when Rev. Daniel Hoge took charge and reorganized. Douglas Baker was elected Elder and James Hall was made Clerk. The church applied to Abingdon Presbytery to take it under its care. Mr. Hoge was succeeded by the Rev. James Keen, his services being voluntary. Services were conducted by various ministers, among them Rev. George Painter and Rev. Robert Graham. Evidently the church had not been received by the Abingdon Presbytery for in 1844 Rev. James Naylor, an Evangelist of Montgomery Presbytery, took charge. By unanimous consent it was determined to join Montgomery Presbytery, and a complete organization effected and Elders elected. Mr. Naylor was succeeded by William Hickman, as stated supply, becoming regular pastor in 1848.

Rev. J. M. Wharey called 1862 and remained until 1863, when he was made a Chaplain in the Confederate Army.

This church was burned December the 16th, 1864, by order of the commanding officer of the U. S. troops during a raid. Ammunition had been stored in the church by order of the Confederate officer in charge of the local post.

PERIOD OF DIVISION—1837-1864

Rev. G. A. Wilson writes: "In the year 1837 the Presbyterian Church in America split into two distinct denominations, the Old School and the New School Presbyterian Churches, and Abingdon Presbytery passed out of existence. The line of cleavage ran straight through the Presbytery. Churches adhering to the Old School were: Beaver Creek, Green Spring, Rock Spring, Pleasant Grove (Rich Valley), Mt. Carmel, Kimberlin and Mt. Tabor (Wytheville).

Those adhering to the New School were: New Dublin, Harmony (Draper's Valley), Royal Oak, Anchor of Hope, Sharon, Glade Spring, Sinking Spring, Cold Spring and Paperville."

"The following churches were founded by New River Presbytery: Bristol First, Spring Creek in Washington County; South Fork in Smyth County; Hillsville and Bethesda in Carroll County; Jeffersonville and Thompson Valley in Tazewell; Lebanon in Russell; Black Lick and Wytheville in Wythe."

The records show that the Wytheville Presbyterian churches were under three Presbyteries: Montgomery, New River and Abingdon. Also under three Synods: United, Virginia and Appalachia.

PRESBYTERIAN CHURCH, WYTHEVILLE

"On October the 30th, 1867, Charles L. Crockett, Joseph F. Kent and Edward Walker, trustees of the Presbyterian Church of the first part; doth grant with the covenant of general warranty, unto William Zimmerman, Charles A. Haller, Albert H. Gibboney, trustees of the Evangelical Lutheran Church, in the Town of Wytheville, and their successors, a certain tract or parcel of land on the southeast side of Main Street, adjoining the lands of Isaac J. Leftwich and Anthony Lawson, for the sum of $380.00. The same lot was conveyed to the Presbyterian Church by A. S. Fulton and wife by deed May 16, 1854.

GALENA CHURCH

On October the 30th, 1879, William J. Raper and Sally V., his wife, and John C. Raper and Sally C., his wife, of the first part; William J. Raper, David Graham, J. P. M. Sanders, trustees of the Presbyterian Church, known as Galena, of the second part. Whereas, Captain Robert Raper in his life time laid off and set apart 2½ acres of land on which said church was built for use and benefit of said Christian denomination and intended to execute a deed therefor but negleced to do so. In carrying out the wishes of their father, the deed was made, for use of said Presbyerian Church and other Christian denominations, in the County of Wythe on the waters of New River.

The name Galena is derived from the sulphite of lead found most extensively in Illinois. A large number of the members of Galena congregation were interested in the Lead Mine, which was a few miles distant and large deposits of the lead being found at that place it was decided to name the church Galena.

NEW SCHOOL OR CHURCH STREET CHURCH

In October, 1863, in the Presbytery of New River, an organization of the new church was permanently made, the church having been dedicated on September 6, 1863. The sermon was preached by Rev. J. D. Mitchell, D. D. The pastor was Rev. J. T. Leftwich, of Alexandria, which place he left after the town was occupied by U. S. soldiers.

The following Elders were elected: Ed Watson, R. E. Grant, Robert Sayers, Dr. W. H. Ribble; Charles L. Fox was Clerk of the Session. Members were: Mrs. Susan Spiller, Mrs. Lucy Buford, Mrs. Nannie Stuart, Mrs. Kate Sayers, Mrs. Marcum Hammet, Mrs. Ellen Stuart, Mrs. Jane Carrington, Mrs. Malinda Haller, Mrs. M. Mathews, James W. Stuart, C. A. Fredeking, Mrs. J. A. Morrison, Mrs. C. A. Hanson.

The following is recorded:

"Received in the Wytheville Presbyterian Church from Monk's Corner Capt. Robert Raper and wife Mary, by letter from Rev. Robert Graham, October 8, 1856."

Later we find:

"On January 10, 1869, Mrs. Nannie M. Graham was dismissed from the Wytheville Presbyterian Church to Galena (known as the Cove Church)."

The church known as Cripple Creek was disbanded in August, 1871 and James P. Painter, a member, was received by the Wytheville church.

BRICK CHURCH

The records show that John Sanders and wife Hannah on August the 15th, 1837, deeded to the following trustees: Anderson Howard, Robert Raper, Adam Sanders and David Graham, land for a Union meeting house in which all denominations could worship. The first church was torn down and the material used for the erection of a new building near the site of the old one. At present, it is a Methodist church and is about two miles east of Galena church.

BRICK CHURCH

The Brick Church on Black Lick was erected in 1839.

SOME FACTS IN THE EARLY HISTORY OF THE MT. AIRY PRESBYTERIAN CHURCH

(Copied from a clipping from the Rural Retreat paper published at the time of the dedication of the Presbyterian Church at Rural Retreat.)

"Black Lick (now Mt. Airy) Presbyterian Church was organized the second Saturday in December, 1851, by a committee appointed by the New Presbytery consisting of Revs. Philip Wood, David P. Palmer and Lee C. Brown. The following persons were named for organization: Rebecca Doak, Polly Wauhop, Mrs. Janes Staley, Polly Brown, Polly Earhart, Mary Cregar, Perlina H. Brown, Frances Earhart, Frances Porter, Mrs. Vermillion, Mary C. Buchanan, D. T. Martin and Henry Earhart. Henry Earhart and D. T. Martin were elected Elders and ordained.

"At the next meeting of the Presbytery, which was in May, 1852, the church was received under the care of Presbytery by the name of the Black Lick Church, and Mr. Earhart being present, took his seat in the Presbytery. The church was supplied by Revs. David C. Palmer and Lee C. Brown for a number of years and then Black Lick Church had no pastor. It was reorganized September 17th, 1871, under a commission from Abingdon Presbytery by William V. Wilson. Dr. John D. Stuart and William S. Wilson were Elders and William A. Wilson and W. H. Rowe were elected Deacons and were installed by the Rev. William V. Wilson, who now became pastor of the church.

"The first session of the Mt. Airy Presbyterian Church was on the 24th day of November, 1872, by the Elders and Deacons of the Black Lick Church as the officers of said Mt. Airy Church. Rev. William V. Wilson supplied the church until 1874 when Rev. J. D. Thomas was pastor until 1877. In 1879 the Rev. J. O. Sullivan became pastor of Mt. Airy church and continued to supply it until August, 1884. In 1886 the Rev. William M. McPheeters became pastor of the church and supplied it until July 8th, 1888. The Rev. J. O. Sullivan again supplied the church from 1889 until sometime in 1891. The Rev. T. F. McFaden took charge of the flock about October, 1891 and is now the beloved pastor of Mt. Airy Church, consisting of 70 members with the following officers: L. K. Baumgardner, A. A. Gammon, Dr. T. C. P-pper and J. M. Hicks, Elders; Charles L. Baumgardner and Dr. E. C. Eversole, Deacons."

BRICK CHURCH IN THE COVE

On October the 13th, 1853, Mrs. Agnes Crockett, after making a number of bequests, willed the residue of her property for the purpose of erecting a Presbyterian Church on part of W. G. Crockett's land.

The church was organized by Rev. R. C. Graham and Rev. F. N. Lewis in October, 1859, with two elders, Robert Raper and Samuel R. Crockett, Sr. Robert Raper lived near Galena and Samuel R.

Crockett, Sr., lived near Max Meadows.

"Session met at the Cove Church, April 24, 1858. Received James Halsey, Mrs. Sarah Crockett, Miss Mary Anne Raper. Rev. J. W. Lewis, pastor of the Wytheville Church, presided. On April 24, 1858, Mrs. Mary Anne Crockett was received by the pastor."

LUTHERAN CHURCHES

There were many Lutherans among the early settlers of Wythe County when Rev. Paul Henkel visited this section in the nineties of the eighteenth century—however he was not the first minister. There were four churches organized before 1800, all being in the western portion of the county. There are no Lutheran churches in the eastern portion of Wythe County.

ST. PAUL

St. Paul, located a short distance south of the Lee Highway about three miles northeast of Rural Retreat, is the oldest Lutheran Church in Virginia west of New River and was organized in 1776. A record book was purchased in 1779 and the communion cloth, which is still in use, was made from home-grown flax upon which is embroidered the initials: C. A. D., R. I. N., N. A. K. and the name Mrs. Kregger, bearing the date 1784. The solid silver communion set is evidently of a very early date. The first minister of which there is a record was Rev. Paul Henkel.

The first church was a log structure and chestnut logs were used in the building. The next church was dedicated in 1829, Rev. Henry Graber preaching the sermon. A brick structure was erected in 1854 and, damaged by a storm in 1876, was rebuilt in 1877. This building was replaced by a modern brick church with Sunday School rooms attached in 1916 and is one of the best rural churches in this section of Virginia.

There is a tradition that the Sluss family residing at Ceres, Bland County, would walk to St. Paul for the eleven o'clock service and return that afternoon, crossing Walker's Mountain twice in one day.

"In the year of our Lord Jesus Christ, 1829, the last Sunday in April, this church was dedicated to the Triune God under the name of St. Paul Church. For the joint use of the Evangelical Lutheran and High German Reformed Church, by the Evangelical preachers. (Signed) Henry Graber, Daniel Scherer, Jacob Scherer."

Clerk's Office, Christiansburg, Va.
Record of Plats, Book B., Page 278.

Surveyed for Martin Kimberling, Michel Steffey, Michael Wampler and John Phillippi, Elders, etc. for the use of the congregation 100 acres of land by virtue of a certificate for 100 acres to them granted for the district of Washington and Montgomery Counties, and dated the 13th of September, 1782, lying in Montgomery County, on the waters of Reed Creek, a branch of New River and bounded as follows ...... Adjoining the lands of Henry Lambert and a tract known as the Paxton Glade ..... to Godfree Confree's land.

David McGavock, Asst. Sur.
John Preston, Sur. for Montgomery Co.
the 21st, March, 1783.

As above stated the foregoing deed, is on record in the Clerk's Office at Christiansburg and does not mention any denomination. The land was identified by those familiar with the neighborhood, knowing the location of the Henry Lambert land and the Paxton Glade.

From the minutes of the record of St. Paul's Lutheran Church, which were recently found on Black Lick. They were written in German and were translated in Richmond, Va.

ORDER OF AGREEMENT

WHEREAS, God is a God of order and all Christian regulations ordained and introduced by Him, and no christianity can either exist or be expected without discipline and order, and in all well ordered congregations such regulations have been observed and are still observed.

And as here in Wythe County of the Commonwealth of Virginia Christian churches and congregations have been erected and established under the joint name of the Protestant Church, therefore the Elders and Deacons of the congregations 1 (near the town); 2 (in the old church); 3 (in the new church) and 4 (the church on the Holston) unite themselves in name and as those authorized (to serve) by the subscription of their names to the following regulations.

1. These four congregations shall unite in one joint congregation and the Elders and Deacons of the same shall form a joint Church Council, together with the pastor or pastors then serving, to consider all matters of weighty character in the welfare of these congregations, and to this end no innovations in church matters are to be made by one congregation alone without the approval of the other three; in unimportant matters Elders and Deacons of each congregation may make the necessary arrangements according to their own pleasure, and yet in such manner that the Deacons will always rank under the Elders, and never exercise rights or powers without the advice or consent of the Elders.

2. To this end in each one of these congregations there shall be elected by a majority vote and duly installed a church Elder in addition

to the Deacons, in which (council) each Elder shall be elected to serve for three years and each Deacon for four years, and at the time of the election of the Elders, the older Deacons shall be installed as an Elder without an election, but another Deacon is not to be elected and installed without an election.

3. These congregations shall unite in a Christian union so that in the future no minister is to be received or dismissed unless three of the four congregations are satisfied; that is to say, that if a credited or even an uncredited minister comes, he is to preach once or twice or oftener in the congregations, and if three of the four congregations are willing to accept him, the fourth shall also agree, or be denied the benefits of his ministerial care, he on his part shall have the right to serve another fourth congregation that may be willing to unite with the others.

There were a number of other regulations governing the conduct of members, mode of Baptism, etc. * * * * *

Every one that accepts these regulations will not refuse to subscribe to the same; and in the future those of the masculine gender as they are confirmed wlil make it convenient to add their names.

·The names of the Deacons—
Jacob Brunner, John Peter Jantz, Casper Rather, George Armbrister, Jacob Kinzer, George Wampler, Henry Hoppes, George Wampler, Adam Dottinger, George Weber, John Schneberly, Philipp Aker.

Berned Willy, D. V. M.   May 30, 1798.
(Minister of the Word of God.)

Signatures—
Peter Wampler, Balzer Jansohn, Martin Neusang, Peter Steffey, Jacon Kinzer, George Kinzer, Joseph Wampler, John Ketring, John Steffey, Christopher Wampler, Michael Bach, Andrew Aker, George Mozer, Adam Mozer, John Wolf, John Moser, Leonard Stroh, Stephen Meiss, John Gutman, Peter Fuchs, Michael Wampler, Christian Bok, John David Jansohn, George Tany, Michael Wenrich, Philipp Kinder, Henry Steffey, Daniel Hildenberger, George Wampler, Martin Muller.

The church designated as No. 1 (near town) is St. John's, one mile north of Wytheville. No. 2 (in the old church) is St. Paul's and 3 (in the new church) is Kimberling on Black Lick. No. 4 (the church on the Holston) is St. Mark's in Smyth County, known as Pleasant Hill and is on a different location.

There have been five churches at St. Paul's, two were log buildings and three brick structures, the present one being modern in every respect.

When the church was organized at St. Paul's, there was also provision for a school, which continued until the public school system was established. In a number of instances there is mention of the school in the church records.

St. Paul has been under the jurisdiction of three Synods: Pennsylvania, North Carolina and Virginia.

ST. JOHN'S

St. John's Lutheran church, located about one mile north of Wytheville on the Lakes-to-Florida Highway, together with its cemetery is one of the historic spots of Wythe County. Judging from the dates on some of the stones in the cemetery, there was a cemetery there a number of years before the erection of the first church which was built by Lutheran and Reformed. The first church was built about 1800 or before. This church was replaced by the present building in 1855, which has been repaired several times but is still in a marvelous state of preservation. In 1816 a pipe organ was placed in this church, which was the first instrument of its kind west of New River. The writer has been told that the first organist was Andrew Whitman, his great grandfather. This congregation furnished a number of able men for the ministry and exerted a tremendous influence in the community and county, over a period of a century or more. The congregation was merged with Trinity in Wytheville in 1924, at which time an endowment was created for the upkeep of the cemetery and church property. Provision was also made for the holding of an occasional service and an annual "Home Coming" on the last Sunday in August of each year. Father Flohr was one of the first pastors and was instrumental in its organization. The organ cost $400.00 and $30.00 freight. It was installed the 1st and 2nd week in April, 1816 and was used the first time on Good Friday. Elders and Deacons for the Lutherans were: Elders, Casper Rother, Hohannes Herrcherother. Deacons: Andreas Braun, Henrich Brien. Reformed, Elders: Jacob Brunner; Deacons, George Michel Braun, Leonard Umberger. May 22, 1814. Nov. 1, 1840, Rufus Repass and Peter Yonce were appointed Elders and Joseph Brown and Anthony Ewald were appointed Deacons. On April 2, 1843, John A. Brown was elected Deacon of St. John's Church in the room of Anthony Ewald, resigned.

We have been informed that Anthony Ewald was one of the early Catholics, locating in Wytheville. Being a man of deep religious convictions and not having his church and desiring to be identified with a Christian organization, he made application for membership in St. John's Church, with the understanding that should a church of his denomination be organized, he would be allowed to withdraw and identify himself with his own church. The dates in the record substantiates this information. Doubtless he was a member at St. John's a number of years before becoming an officer. He served as Deacon from November 1, 1840, to April 2, 1843, at which time he resigned. Possibly this was about the time of the organization of St. Mary's Catholic Church in Wytheville, as it was dedicated on August 10, 1845.

Rev. George D. Flohr

Rev. George D. Flohr, a distinguished scholar and noted minister, who wielded a tremendous influence in Southwest Virginia, was born in Germany in 1759. Nothing is recorded of him, so far as we know, until 1793, when we find him in Paris studying medicine under an uncle. Here he witnessed the execution of Louis the XVI.

After a lapse of a few years we find him in Madison County, Virginia, studying for the ministry under the Rev. Mr. Carpenter. He also taught school in Culpeper County, before coming to Southwest Virginia. He was a member of the Pennsylvania Synod during his life as a minister. In 1799 he was called to pastoral charge of Evangelical Lutheran Congregation in Wythe County. Here he preached to five separate congregations, the following being his churches: St. John's and St. Paul's Churches, Wythe County; Collops Church, Smyth County; Evangelical Lutheran Church, Chilhowie; St. Peter's Church, Montgomery County.

He died in 1826 at his home near Wytheville and is buried in St. John's cemetery. His grave is marked in a most unusual manner. A stone, native to this section, has been hewn and chiseled in the form of a coffin and lies on Mr. Flohr's grave. This work was done by the late Mr. Crone, of Wythe County, a member of the German Reformed Church, at his private cost.

Deed

On November the 11, 1800, Daniel Etter and wife Mary made a deed for one acre of land for the erection of a church for the German-Lutheran and German-Reformed, neighborhood of Wythe Courthouse, Reformed or Presbyterian congregation. Elders and representatives of the German Lutheran Congregation, Casper Rader, George Armbrister; German Reformed or Presbyterian, Peter Yontz, Jacob Prooner. The deed states that there was a near-by spring, which the congregation could use.

Although, the above-mentioned deed is the first on record in the Wythe County Courthouse, there is proof of an active organization there a number of years before. In 1798 St. John's congregation, together with three others, formed a coalition to be governed as a single organization, which is fully explained in the records of St. Paul's Church.

List of Subscribers for the Building of St. John's Church, 1800

Casper Rader, Sr., George Armpriester, Philip Armpriester, John Hercherother, Christopher Braun, George Mayer, John Schoritz, Louis Hutzel, Michael Braun, Sr., Jacob Hercherother, Jacob Repas, Jr., Louis Wohlfart, Henry Umberger, Sr., Peter Bunckly, Erhart Zimmerman, Jacob Davies, Nicolaus Cassell, Carl Pfaff, Nicolaus Felty, John Jacob Repas, Sr., George Flohr, Adam Seftly, Henry Umberger, Jr., Joseph Davies, George Brunner, Bernhart Messerschmitt, Andrew Braun, Sr., Daniel Schoritz, Werner Knopp, John Repas, Andrew Syfer, Peter Wetzel, John Rader, Jacob Roder, John Schaffer, Frederick Lenhart, John Umberger, Daniel Etter, Jacob Mosser, John Schumacher, Henry Armpriester, Henry Buhn, Casper Rader, Jr., Christian Geckly, Daniel Weisly, Nicholaus Losser, Christopher Zimmerman, Michael Cassell, Louis Geckly, Martin Wayerich, Christian Vogelgesang, Carl Vogelgesang, Henry Riegel, Michael Braun, Jr., Edward Morphy, Henry Clemens, Widow Davies, Susanna Vogelgesang, Jacob Brunner.

List of subscribers for the organ of St. John's Church, installed first and second weeks of April, 1816, and was played the first time on Good Friday. The cost of organ $400.00, freight $30.00.

John Herkerother, Michael Cassel, John Baumgartner, G. Michael Brunner, Henry Fuchs, Lenhart Umberger, Christopher Brown, Jr., John Repass, Christian Keckly, Henry Buhn, Isaac Herkerather, Jacob Ziegel, Jacob Wohlfahrt, Sr., George Flohr, John Umberger, Jr., Jacob Davies, John Lindeberger, Jacob Wohlfahrt, Erhart Zimmerman Sr., Daniel Spantzler, Jacob Fischer, Henry, Umberger, Sr., John Brown, son of MB, Philip Umberger, Peter Knopp, Thos. Zimmermann, Philip Knopp, Jacob Haunschel, Christophen Zimmermann, George Jandler, Simon Riegel, John Etter, John Davies, John Wairick, Carl Pfaff, Michael Brown, Jr., David Herkerother, Joseph Mohler, Andrew Whittman, Henry Whittman, Richard Mathews, Daniel Sheffey, John Haller Dr., Richard Right, Michael Brunner, John Hutzel, John Ruth, Christopher Dilman, John Felty, Louis Wohlfahrt, John Keckly, Louis Keckly, Martin Keckly, Jacob Mosser, Michael Krieger, Sol. Herkerother, Henry Umberger, son JU, Henry Umberger, Sr., Michael Brown, son St. Br., Martin Wairick, Jr., William Repass, John Pfaff, Joseph Kent, Michael Brown, Sr., George Wetzel, Geo. Zimmermann, John Lindemuth, Jr., Anthony Blessing, Nicolas Wairick, Jacob Brown, John Brown, son A. Br., Andrew Kapel, David Kapel, Frederick Brunner, N. Wetzel, John Radick, Catherine Yantz, Michael Krieger, Jacob Felty, John Cahl, John Mies, George Lenart, John F. Ney, John Johnston, George Oury, Christopher Oury, James Tungry.

The above picture shows an improvised pulpit, where worship was held prior to the erection of the first church at Zion, in the Cripple Creek Valley. It was located in an oak grove and the locust bars were inserted in holes morticed in the trees. The locust bars are still in a perfect state of preservation, as shown in the picture, which was taken only a short time since. While it is impossible to get the date when worship was held, it is reasonable to conclude, it was possibly a number of years prior to 1790. We have been unable to locate a deed for the property, either in Wythe or Montgomery County. The deeds prior to 1790 are supposed to be in the Clerk's Office at Christiansburg. However, the indexing was badly done and the only way to locate old deeds is to read the records page by page. The deed for St. Paul's church was found in this way.

ZION

Zion is located in the Cripple Creek valley about five miles southwest of Crockett and is possibly the second oldest Lutheran church in Wythe County. The baptismal record shows Catherine Lits, baptised Jan., 1791, and Eva Huddle April, 1791. The first church building was a log structure, which was replaced in 1856 by a frame building, still in use. The first Zion church had two congregations, two sets of officers and two ministers, one being Lutheran and the other Reformed. The first church was dedicated in 1794 by the Rev. John Stanger, Lutheran, and the Rev. Daniel Repass, Reformed. At this time there were twenty-eight male members—sixteen Lutheran and twelve Reformed. Officers: Christophen Spraker and Henry Vaught, Lutheran, and Peter Spangler, Reformed.

KIMBERLIN

Kimberlin is in the western portion of the county and the first church building was a log structure and was dedicated in August, 1797. The land was deeded by Martin Kimberlin to George Weaver and Adam Dutton, trustees. The second church, a frame building, was built in 1854, and the third in 1913, is a modern and substantial structure. Among the early pastors were: the Rev. Leonard Willy and the Rev. George D. Flohr. Trustees: George Weaver and Adam Dutton and trustees of the two Dutch, Luhteran and Presbyterian Congregations. Deed signed Martin Kimberlin.

ST. PETER'S CHURCH

St. Peters, located near the present village on Cripple Creek, was organized in 1830 by the Rev. Scherer and the first church building, a frame structure, erected in 1839. The structure had a large gallery and an elevated pulpit as was the custom at that time.

A new church was erected in 1885 near the site of the old church, with a seating capacity of about 300.

LEBANON CHURCH

On the 10th day of January, 1853, Jefferson King and wife Cathrine, on the one part, and James L. Cassell and Andrew Lindamood trustees, acting for and in behalf of the Lutheran Evangelical Congregation, on the waters of Reed Creek, deed one acre of land, between the lands of Jefferson King and Rufus Wyrick. This church was located on Reed Creek some distance from where the present church stands, which is on the Lee Highway about five miles west of Wytheville. An organization was effected in 1851, by the Rev. Jacob Scherer. The present building was erected in 1882.

ST. LUKE

St. Luke, located in the west end of the Cove, was organized by the Rev. Alexander Phillippi, D. D. in 1894 and he served as pastor until his death in 1915.

HOLY ADVENT

Holy Advent was organized by Dr. Phillippi in 1912 and a neat frame building erected. It is served by the Rev. Raymond L. Booze, of Bland.

POPLAR GROVE

Poplar Grove, on Stony Fork, several miles north of Holy Advent, was organized by the Rev. D. S. Fox in 1897. It has been discontinued.

CORINTH

Corinth is located on Black Lick and was organized in 1892, largely from members of Kimberlin church, by the Rev. D. S. Fox, who resided in that community. Services were held for a number of years prior to its organization in the "Old Brick Church", which was owned by the Presbyterians.

In 1893 a commodious frame building with a number of rooms adjoining was erected, on land donated by Michael Cassell, purchased from the Presbyterians.

ST. MARK'S

St. Marks was organized by the Rev. Alexander Phillippi, D. D., in 1891 and was located about three miles east of Wytheville on Pepper's Ferry road. After about twenty years, services were discontinued, the property sold, and the members in the locality united with Holy Trinity in Wytheville.

HOLY TRINITY

Holy Trinity Lutheran church was organized in 1876 and shortly thereafter a Gothic brick building was erected at the corner of Main and Sixth streets in the Town of Wytheville. The organizer was the Rev. Alexander Phillippi, who used the rooms beneath the church for a boys' and girls' school, during the eighties and nineties. This school contributed to the growth and development of the church. In 1924 the Trinity and St. John's congregations were merged and Trinity became the successor of the historic mother church. The membership was materially increased by the merger.

GRACE LUTHERAN CHURCH

Grace Lutheran Church is located in the Town of Rural Retreat and is the outgrowth of services held by various pastors at school houses in that vicinity. A school house known as Oak Grove stood on the site of the church and was used for a number of years for holding services.

The first church was called Hawkins Chapel and steps toward organization were taken prior to 1868 but the church was not completed until 1872.

The present brick church was erected in 1910 and the Sunday School rooms added in 1913. A few years later a beautiful pipe organ was the gift of Mr. J. Stuart Etter. The church has a membership of over three hundred.

In 1889 one-fourth interest was secured in Fairview church, located about two miles south of Rural Retreat on the road to Cedar Springs. The church was served by the pastor from Rural Retreat, but it was abandoned and the members were transferred to the Rural Retreat church.

BETHANY LUTHERAN CHURCH

Bethany Lutheran Church, located near Henley's School House in the Cripple Creek valley, was organized by the Rev. K. Y. Umberger in 1904. A neat frame building was erected and dedicated in 1905. The building was enlarged and remodeled in 1926.

ROSENBAUM'S CHAPEL

Rosenbaum's Chapel, located in the Town of Crockett, was organized in 1875 by the Rev. J. A. Brown on land donated by Stephen Rosenbaum.

EPISCOPAL CHURCHES

WYTHE PARISH

The Wythe Parish is embraced in the limits of Wythe County. The first Episcopal service held in the county was doubtless at Fort Chiswell, possibly as far back as 1769-1770, by a British Chaplain. If there was a building at that place there does not seem to be any record of it. The salaries were paid in pounds, shillings and pence. From an account book of James McGavock now in the possession of Joseph G. Kent we find:

"April 8th, 1776, received of James McGavock, 8 pounds on account of Parish collection, to apply on account of Thomas Madison, due him from Parish account.

"Nov. 10, 1774, Received of James McGavock, 41 pounds, 9 shillings and 3 pence, part of the money due from the Vestry.

Thomas Madison.

"Ordered that the sum of £350 be levied for the building of a church in the parish.

"Ordered that the sum of £72 * * * be levyed for the Rev. Adam Smith for his services for 6 months past as Rector of this Parish."

Another entry: "To your Levys for 1769 and 1770", which included a number of names and amounts.

ST. JOHN'S CHURCH, WYTHEVILLE

Bishop Mead states: "At Wytheville the indefatigable efforts of a mother and daughter have raised a considerable sum of money for the erection of a church. A site has been obtained and progress made in the erection of a church. The mother, Mrs. Frances H. Williamson, of Elizabeth, N. J.; the daughter, Mrs. A. J. McGavock. Mrs. Susan Spiller, an ardent member of the Presbyterian church, was among the first who came to the assistance of Mrs. McGavock, with a substantial contribution. Hon. A. S. Fulton, a member of the Vestry, gave a lot on Main Street." This lot was later exchanged for the one on which the church now stands, while the Fulton lot was used by W. W. Rich to erect a furniture store.

On July 1, 1846, a paper was circulated for the purpose of securing funds for the erection of a church. Committee: E. McGavock, P. S. Buckingham, Thomas J. Boyd, R. T. Mathews, A. S. Fulton, and G. F. S. Trigg. Methodist, Presbyterians and Roman Catholics were among the contributors.

The Rev. James D. McCabe was Rector and the first Vestry was: James H. Piper, E. McGavock, P. S. Buckingham, A. S. Fulton, T. J. Boyd, R. T. Mathews. Mr. McCabe served until March 12, 1849.

The corner stone was laid in October, 1852 by the Wytheville Masonic Lodge and Hon. A. S. Fulton gave the address. The Rev. F. D. Goodwin accepted a call and took charge December 15, 1856. He held services in the basement until the church was completed. It was dedicated Sunday, June the 13th, 1858. Mr. Goodwin resigned the Rectorship on February 14, 1866, having served through the War Between the States, ministering to both Federal and Confederate soldiers who were wounded or died.

A number of Rectors served the Parish between 1866 and 1882, when the Rev. Mercer P. Logan accepted a call and served for over twenty years. He was followed by the Rev. W. H. K. Pendleton and the Rev. F. H. Craighill.

In 1901 a Parish House was erected in the rear of the church containing Sunday School rooms and serving as a community centre. In 1927 the church was renovated and greatly improved under the leadership of the present Rector D. L. Gwathmey, D. D., who has greatly endeared himself to the membership of his church and the community.

St. Andrew's Mission at Ivanhoe is served by the Rector from St. Johns.

HISTORY OF ASBURY CAMP GROUND AND ITS FOUNDERS

The Camp ground movement had its origin in Kentucky in 1799 and spread rapidly in this country and also in foreign lands. The first recorded movement of the activities of the Methodist Church in Wythe County was the establishment of Asbury Camp Ground on upper Cripple Creek.

Asbury Camp Ground was established in 1819, as shown by the following letter written in 1871:

"By request of your preacher, you desire me to tell you something of the origin of Cripple Creek Camp Ground. I did the first work that was done on the encampment fifty-three years ago next September. Taylor and Evis were the preachers in charge. Lewis Festic was the Presiding Elder. The meeting continued five days, commencing about the last of September. At that Camp Meeting there were 82 conversions.

"The next year, Samuel Kennerly, Morris and Rice were in charge. At that Camp Meeting there were over 100 conversions.

"The third year John Tivis was the Presiding Elder and the same preachers had charge of the Circuit. At that meeting there were 186 conversions and 8 sanctifications.

"Fourth year, _____ Green had charge of the Circuit, and J. Tivis, P. E., at which time there were over 100 conversions. I attended camp meetings on these grounds for ten years previous to leaving that section, and I witnessed over 1000 conversions.

"Yours in haste,

ANDREW VAUGHT."

John Newland and James Newland deeded the land, the first plot containing eleven acres, making the deed to Zachariah Mitchell, Casper Yost, David Horn, John Ganaway, Lewis S. Marshall, Peter Keesling, John Phillippi, William Scott and George Phillippi, on the 24th day of December, 1825, and recorded in Book No. 10, page 206.

Among the names of the promoters of Asbury Camp Meeting in the early days were: Phillippi, Keesling, Vaught, Newland, Mitchell, Ganaway, Yost, Horn, Fisher, Scott, Marshall, Whitman, Umbarger, Gray, Johnson, Swecker, Foster, Henley, Ward, Brawley, Seagle, Moore, Hedrick, Hale, Bryant, Stephens.

The above was taken from a short sketch of Asbury Camp Ground published by Rev. D. S. Gaines, in 1871.

In the first year that services were held at Asbury Camp Ground, about fifteen camps or houses were built. The first was erected by John Gannaway and the second by David Horn. A number of others followed shortly thereafter.

The last camp meeting held at Asbury Camp Ground was in September, 1884.

AN ACT TO INCORPORATE THE TOWN OF ASBURY PASSED MARCH 25TH, 1861

The thanks of the friends and of the church are due the Hon. Joseph T. Graham for using his influence in procuring a charter for Asbury Camp Ground, which was incorporated in the year 1861, and in form follows:

"Be it enacted by the General Assembly, that the place called Asbury Camp Ground in the county of Wythe, shall be and the same is hereby made a town corporate by the name of Asbury, and by the same shall exercise the powers conferred upon towns by, and be subject to the provisions of the 54th chapter of the Code of Virginia, so far as provisions of said chapter are not in conflict with the provisions of this act.

"The boundaries of said town shall be as follows: * * * * * * *

"The officers of said town shall consist of five trustees, three of whom shall form a quorum to transact business, and a sergeant, who shall hold their office, or until their successors are appointed.

"William Ward, J. G. Keesling, Wm. B. Buchanan, A. Vaught and Z. Mitchell are hereby appointed trustees of said town, to act as such until others may be elected, and they are authorized to act as commissioners in holding an election, at any time after giving twenty days notice, by advertising at said town and at the Court House of the county; and the parties thus named to appoint a sergeant to act as such in all matters of police, but not otherwise, in said town of Asbury, and for a distance of one mile in any direction, until his successor is elected.

"This act shall be in force from its passage and shall be subject to modifications or repeal at any time at the pleasure of the General Assembly.

"A copy from the rolls. Fee $1.00. Paid by Mr. Graham."

"Rules and Regulations of Asbury Camp Ground

"At a meeting of the Trustees of Asbury Camp Ground, held on the 20th day of April, 1871, the following rules and regulations were adopted:

"1st. No article of trade, merchandise or traffic will be allowed within the corporation, which is one mile in every direction.

"2nd. Gathering in groups, for the purpose of conversation, within the encampment, during hours of worship, is positively forbidden.

"3rd. It is expected that all persons, except one to keep charge of the sick, will leave the tents during hours of divine service.

"4th. The grounds for the retirement of ladies and gentlemen must be strictly observed, and no gentleman will be allowed to intrude upon the ladies' side of the right of the pulpit and from the centre, during public worship.

"5th. Any disturbance of the peace and quiet of the congregation, either by jesture or conversation, is positively prohibited, at the peril of the penalty of the law in such cases made and provided.

"6th. Galloping and racing horses within the corporate limits is forbidden.   Andrew Fisher, D. P. Windle, G. W. Vaught,
B. E. Ward, George Sanders."

The foregoing act gave the Methodist Church absolute control of Asbury Camp Ground but there were other camp grounds in Virginia, which did not enjoy this protection.

The General Assembly of Virginia, on the 28th of March, 1871, passed an act for the protection of camp meetings and other religious gatherings, which covered the entire State.

ASBURY CAMP GROUND

The following was contributed a number of years since by a former resident of the vicinity of Asbury Camp Ground.

"The Most Historical Spot of My Community

"One-half mile from my home and just across a creek from my great grandfather Fisher's old home is Asbury Camp Ground. This is a place, where for many years, the religious services known as camp meetings were held, but, by the older people of our community, it is always referred to as The Camp Ground. There are two or two and a half acres in The Camp Ground lot. It is a grassy plot of ground located at the foot of a large wooded hill. Cripple Creek flows by it, hence there was a bountiful water supply for the many horses used in bringing the people to the meeting. A clear, sparkling spring flowing from under the hill, known as The Camp Ground spring, furnished water for the thirsty people.

"The Camp Meetings were held in August at regular intervals and continued about a week. Thousands of people attended, some of which came for fifty or more miles. Great grandfather Fisher often accommodated for one night probably thirty or more people in the house, barn and other outbuildings. Many of the people brought tents, or built temporary buildings and stayed on the ground during the entire meeting.

"Although this was a religious gathering many people came to have a good time or transact business. Some of these 'loafers' secured their food by stealing chickens, eggs and other things that they could get from people who lived near. Others spent a great deal of time trading horses.

"Many of the best preachers of those days did the preaching. Hundreds of people were converted and much good was done at the regular service and at the sunrise prayer meetings which were conducted on the near by hill tops.

"One preacher who usually attended these meetings was the Rev. Robert Sayers Sheffey ('Uncle Bobby'). He was one of the most widely known preachers of that time. It is told that many things for which he prayed came to pass. For example, for a tree to blow on a still house that was about one mile from my home, and that some building for religious purposes might be erected. A Methodist parsonage now stands on that plot of ground.

"It has been many years since the last Camp Meeting. Old people of my community are very sorry that there are no more such meetings."

SALEM CAMP GROUND

The second Methodist Camp Ground is known as Salem Camp Ground and was located west of Wytheville on Reed Creek, as shown by the following deeds:

"On October the 31st, 1828, John Umberger, Jr., and Mary his wife, to William Newland, Solomon Harkrader, Leonard Umberger, John Umberger, Jr., and Mathias Darter, trustees in trust for the uses and purposes hereinafter mentioned, for and in consideration of the sum of $30.00 specie to them in hand, doth hereby acknowledge and hath given, granted, bargained, sold, released, confirmed and conveyed to said William Newland, et als, 1¼ acre of land, with all woods, houses, waterways, privileges and appurtenances, to build or cause to be built upon, house or place of worship for the use of the members of the Methodist Episcopal Church of the United States of America."

Trustees

"June 15, 1843. This indenture made between William Foster, Casper Yost, James L. Yost, Michael Umberger, Henry Whitman, William Newland, Abraham Umberger, David Sharitz, and David Umberger, successors to William Newland, Solomon Harkrader, Leonard Umberger and Mathias Darter, who were original trustees to whom was conveyed 1¼ acres of land for Salem Camp Ground by John Umberger and wife for the use and benefit of the Methodist Society of one part and Isaac J. Leftwich of the other part. For and in consideration of $60.00 current money of the United States, doth grant and sell to Isaac J. Leftwich, certain tract of land on Reed Creek, adjoining the lands of Isaac J. Leftwich and surrounded on all sides by his land, except cabins and fixtures owned by private individuals. Signed, Casper Yost, William Foster, James L. Yost, William Newland, Henry Whitman, David Umberger, Joseph Sharitz, Michael Umberger and Abram Umberger."

It appears from the court records that Salem Camp Grounds were also used for school purposes.

"School Article for the Camp Ground

"An article of agreement made and entered into between John J. Head of the one part and the undersigned subscribers of the other part.

"The said Head doth bind himself to teach an English School, consisting of reading, writing and arithmetic for the term of six months for $5.00 per scholar. He will teach the English Grammar and Geography for six dollars per scholar. Said Head doth bind himself to pay due attention to this school and use his best efforts to advance the scholars, agreeable to the several capacitys, and understandings, and we the undersigned do bind ourselves to furnish said Head a regular house to teach in and also to pay the said Head the several sums to our names when school expires. Said school will commence on the Monday in April, 1833. Subscribers names: John Utt, 2; John Umberger, 1; Leonard Wyrick, 1; Martin Wyrick, 2; Frances Tompson, 1; Jacob Hounshel; Solomon Harider, 1."

That the said Head did not comply with the contract to teach school, is proven by the fact that William Newland and others instituted court proceedings against Head to collect various debts. The action was taken in the summer after the above contract was made in April.

We have been unable to find the exact location of the Salem Camp Ground but judging from the names of the citizens who figured in it and the school contract, it must have been a few miles west of Wytheville, possibly in the neighborhood of Mount Pleasant or further west.

The John Newland, who figured in the Asbury Camp Ground, had three sons, Joseph, James and William. A William Newland, who resided on lower Black Lick, was one of the trustees of the Salem Camp Ground and it is reasonable to suppose that he was a son of John Newland of Asbury.

ASBURY

The first Asbury Church stood on a knoll, near the home of William H. Fisher, the present site of W. H. Fisher's barn. The land was deeded by John and James Newland, for a Methodist Episcopal Church, on the 24th day of December, 1825, to the following trustees: Zachariah

Mitchell, Casper Yost, David Horn, John Gannaway, Lewis S. Marshall, Peter Keesling, John Phillippi, William Scott and George Phillippi.

This building was used as a place of worship until about 1864, when arrangements had been made for the erection of a new building for worship. The lumber was on the ground, when a rumor was circulated that all of the Methodist Churches would be confiscated by the Federal forces. The citizens of the neighborhood gathered at night and removed the lumber to another site where the present church stands.

Shortly thereafter the present church was erected. It has since been remodeled and Sunday School rooms added.

Asbury is the oldest Methodist organization in Wythe County holding continuous service.

Asbury Church and Camp Ground were named for Bishop Asbury, an outstanding exponent of Methodism. He died in Spottsylvania County, Virginia, March the 13th, 1816 and is buried in a vault beneath the pulpit in Eutaw Street Church, Baltimore, Maryland.

WYTHEVILLE METHODIST CHURCH

The first Methodist Church in Wytheville was probably built in 1827, as we find that on the first day of January, 1827, William Rider and wife, Christina, deeded lot No. 14, in the Town of Evansham, to Trustees Henry Whitman, Adam Saufley, William Pattison, Casper Yost and Lewis S. Marshall, for a Methodist Episcopal Church. There is a tradition that Andrew Jackson spent the night at Saufley's Tavern and attended service at this church on a Sunday, when enroute to Washington to be inaugurated.

Later, a second church was built, for the records show that on the 8th day of March, 1838, John Haller and wife, Cathrine, deeded a half lot in the Town of Evansham, located on the road leading from Wythe County Court House to Tazewell, for the purpose of erecting a Methodist Episcopal Church thereon, to the following Trustees: Casper Yost, William H. Foster, Henry Whitman, William Pattison, Michael Moyers, James St. Clair, Thomas Gibboney, Larkin Smith and James L. Yost.

On the 19th day of October, 1839, the Trustees of the New Methodist Church in the Town of Wytheville sold a lot located on the north side of West Monroe Street to Martin Kegley. The trustees were: Henry Whitman, William Pattison, Casper Yost, late trustees in the Town of Evansham (now Wytheville). The present surviving trustees: Casper Yost, William H. Foster, Henry Whitman, William Pattison, Michael Moyers, James St. Clair, Larkin Smith and James L. Yost. The lot sold to Martin Kegley was the site of the first church, which was a log building.

There was a marble plaque in the Tazewell Street Methodist Church to William H. Foster and is preserved to-day. It reads as follows:

DEDICATED
BY THE CHILDREN
TO THE MEMORY OF
WM. H. FOSTER
DIED DEC'R 22, 1869
AGED 64 YEARS
FOR 30 YEARS SUPERINTENDENT
OF THIS SABBATH SCHOOL

Mr. Foster was a native of Loudoun County, Virginia.

The third Methodist Church was erected at the corner of Church and Franklin streets. The deed follows:

For and in consideration of the sum of $900.00 of which $300.00 cash in hand is paid, and the residue with interest from date is payable on or before the 15th day of October next, as is evidenced by the bond of G. S. Bruce, C. J. Noel and W. W. Rich, bearing even date with this writing; we, the undersigned, bargained and sold and as soon as the balance of the purchase money is paid do promise to convey with good title that certain lot or parcel of land lying in Wytheville, Va., and the privilege connected therewith set out, described in a deed from Charles H. Fontaine and wife to Randall McGavock, trustee for A. J. McGavock, dated 15th of September, 1868, and recorded in the Clerk's office of Wythe County, Virginia, book No. 23, p. 328 unto such persons or trustees as be designated to us by the proper authorities of the Methodist Episcopal Church, South, to hold said lot for said church.

Given this the fifth day of June, 1883, under our hand and seal. J. H. Fulton, Sarah J. McGavock, Cynthia McG. Fulton, and Maggie M. McGavock.

This deed made this the 16th day of November, 1883, between Sarah J. McGavock, Margaret M. McGavock, J. H. Fulton and his wife, C. McG. Fulton, in their own right and J. Cloyd McGavock, J. H. McGavock and E. H. Ingle, trustees appointed by the will of Mrs. Abbie J. McGavock, deceased, duly probated in County Court of Wythe County, Virginia, the 14th day of August, 1877, and Randal McGavock, trustee under a deed executed by C. H. Fontaine to said Randal McGavock as trustee for the aforesaid Abbie J. McGavock of the first part and G. S. Bruce, W. W. Rich, William H. Sult, E. Dyer, J. M. Mc-Teer, P. Gallagher and C. J. Noel, trustees nominated by the proper authorities of the Methodist Episcopal Church, South and appointed as such by the Circuit Court of Wythe County, Virginia, at its September term, 1883, of the second part.

The third church, a brick structure, was erected in 1885, under the pastorate of the Rev. J. W. Smith, an untiring worker. Sunday School rooms and ladies' parlors have been added since.

One of the trustees of the first church was a man by the name of

Casper Yost, who figured in more church organizations in Wythe County than any single individual of his day. Beside donating the land on which Mount Ephraim was erected, he was trustee for several other churches and the two Camp Grounds.

MOUNT EPHRAIM

On October 10th, 1828, Casper Yost and wife deeded to the Methodist Episcopal Church, an acre and a half of land about a mile and a half south of Crockett. On this site was built Mount Ephraim Church which has been a place of worship for more than one hundred years. The trustees were Paulser Johnson, John Coleman, Leonard Umbarger, George Porter and Cornelius Brown.

The membership in 1846 was thirty-eight and among those whose names were on the church register were: Joel and Elizabeth Johnson, Simon and Malinda Umbarger, Charles and Mary Poff, Elizabeth and Alexander Cooper, David and Susan Gose, George and Margaret Porter, John and Annie Irvin, Lucinda and Margaret Thomas, Joseph and Mary Kegley, Joseph and Turley Hilton, Joseph and Mary Grubb, William and Eveline Hedrick, Charles and Jane Williams. Colored slave members were Edmond Gannaway Alsey and Jonathan Gose.

There have been four church buildings at this place. The first, built of logs, was erected near a small stream. The second, also a log structure, was burned in 1875 by the carelessness of campers, who were not apprehended.

When the second church was built higher on the hill, the first was used as a school house; and when the second was burned, the school house was repaired and used as a place of worship.

Work on the new, or third church, was started in 1875 and completed the following year. It was dedicated September the 24th, 1876, by the Rev. John M. McTeer.

The next, or fourth church, was erected in 1914 and dedicated on October the 26th by Bishop Waterhouse. Mount Ephraim is the third oldest permanent Methodist organization in Wythe County, Asbury (1825), Wytheville (1827) having precedence.

A number of Confederate Soldiers are buried in the cemetery at this place.

OLIVE BRANCH CHURCH

Olive Branch Church, the fourth oldest Methodist Episcopal Church in Wythe County and later called the Methodist Episcopal Church, South, is located in the southeast section of Wythe County, a short distance from Porter's Cross Roads. The church was organized March the 9th, 1833. The first trustees were: Joshua Percival, Wendell Swecker, Burgess Williams, Burrell Wall, John Nuckolls and Jacob

Fisher. There have been two or three church buildings at this place.

The Rev. James Fisher, who once resided in the neighborhood, was a leader in the community for many years. A memorial to him has been placed in the church, bearing this inscription:

> " 'The righteous shall be in everlasting remembrance.'
> The Rev. James Fisher was born Dec. 17, 1810.
> Died Dec. 27, 1888. Aged 78 years, 10 days.
> He was 60 years a faithful Christian, 2 years an exhorter and 47 years a faithful preacher.
> Full of faith and of the Holy Ghost, he served his generation with zeal and fidelity, and was not, for God took him. Many were the sheaves which he gathered for the Master."

FOREST CHURCH, IVANHOE

On the 31st day of August, 1870, S. J. Williams and wife and William B. Porter deeded to William M. Painter, George Jackson, John Walters, James T. Early and Benjamin Rowe, trustees, to them and their successors, a tract of land for the property of the Methodist Episcopal Church, South. This church property was to be used by other denominations of Christians, South, one-fourth of the time, should they so desire.

The Methodist church has since acquired entire control of the property and at present it is used exclusively by that denomination.

BETHEL CHURCH ON PEPPER'S FERRY ROAD

On the 10th day of Janary, 1856, John Cassell conveyed 80 perches of land to Harrison Baylor, Christopher S. Holston, Michael Myers, Elijah Dyer and William H. Foster, trustees for the Methodist Episcopal Church, South. On this land there has been erected a church.

The first building was a log structure, which was used for school purposes and a place of worship. A nice frame church has taken the place of the old log building, and an active congregation worships there at this time.

WHITE TOP CHURCH

Before the erection of the White Top Church in 1850 or thereabout the people of Austinville and community worshipped in a store building, which stood near Mr. John B. Jackson's store, the locality being known as Dotson's Hollow. In the early sixties the place of worship was in a school building near what is now known as the Gregory homestead. In the fall of 1874 the old Lead Mine Company erected the

White Top Church, near the site of the school building, for the benefit of the employees and the citizens of the community. This was the first church to be erected at Austinville for a hundred years. The land was donated by the Lead Mine Company for a cemetery and a church. Mr. John Shupe and son, who built the church, and Mr. Henry Stoots, were the first persons buried in the cemetery which at present contains over five hundred graves.

Mr. William J. Jackson was superintendent of the Sunday School, almost the entire time from the erection of the church until it was abandoned in 1907. The Rev. Richard N. Price was the first pastor of the White Top congregation. Other ministers serving this congregation were: Revs. Henry C. Neel, S. T. M. McPherson, William Mitchell, R. A. Owens, D. P. Hurley, John H. Kennedy, James Fisher and Rush Jackson. The last pastor was the Rev. J. T. Guy and during his ministry the church was moved a distance of two miles near Austinville. The new church was dedicated as Trinity during the summer of 1907 by the Rev. W. M. Morrell, Presiding Elder of the Wytheville District.

In May, 1938, the Trinity building was abandoned on account of being unsafe and a new one has been erected.

The Lead Mine Company did not deed the property to the church but gave the congregation the right to hold services. When it ceased to be a place of worship the land reverted to the company. Some of this information was furnished us by Mr. James Freeman, oldest member of the church, through the courtesy of Mrs. T. W. Jackson.

GLENWOOD CHURCH

"A deed made this, the 20th day of January, 1875, between J. W. McGavock and wife Emily M. McGavock of the first part, and William Sayers, Nathan Dyer, and William R. Wheeler, trustees, of the Methodist Episcopal Church South, of the second, doth give to said trustees a lot near Barren Springs Furnace, the property being situated in Wythe County, near Barren Springs, at the intersection of the Indian Grave Road and the Greenbrier Road and bounded as follows: * * * * * The mineral right is reserved." On this property was built the Glenwood Church, where regular services continue to be held.

HIGH ROCK CHURCH

On June the 30th, 1869, David Graham deeded two acres of land at High Rock, on Reed Island to Samuel V. Wheeler, Charles W. Lyons, James S. Stephens, Jacob Swecker and William Sayers, trustees for the Methodist Episcopal Church, South. The church building which was erected was a log structure and was used for both a place of worship and a school. It was doubtless abandoned as a place of worship after the organization and erection of Glenwood, as some of the trustees served at both places.

GREEN CASTLE CHURCH

On the first day of May, 1876, an agreement was made and entered into between Ephraim Copenhaver, trustee for the Lutheran Church, of the one part, and John M. Porter, Rufus M. Wampler, David H. Porter, Eli Hillenberg, James A. Johnston, L. P. Wampler and Charles Poff, trustees of the Methodist Episcopal Church, South, of the other part, for a plot of land on which Green Castle Church stands. A deed to this land was executed by John King to Charles Poff, Rufus Wampler, Ephraim Copenhaver and Jacob Stanger, trustees, about the year 1852 or 1853, reading as follows: "Bargained and sold to John M. Porter and others, trustees, for the Methodist Church all the rights, title and privileges hitherto vested in the said Lutheran Church to the aforesaid lot of land, about two acres and a half. The Lutheran Church doth hereby surrender all its rights and privileges to the aforesaid trustees. Ephraim Copenhaver, Trustee."

After the church was purchased by the Methodist congregation, the name was changed to King's Grove.

MACEDONIA CHURCH

Macedonia Methodist Episcopal Church, South, was located on Black Lick not far from Marvin Church. It was erected in 1843. On June the 26th, 1845, Mary Newland, Eliza and Margaret Davis deeded land for a Methodist Church to the following Trustees: Solomon Harkrader, Robert N. Ward, Samuel Y. Lloyd, James Doak, Edley Doak, Nicholas W. Winn and Austin Miller.

Macedonia Church was destroyed by fire in 1879. The disposition of the land is shown in the following deed:

"This deed, made this the 14th day of February, 1885, between Edley Doak, John C. Brown, William F. Lloyd and Canara D. Doak, all of the County of Wythe, State of Virginia, of one part, and Stephen A. Umberger, of the County and State aforesaid, of the other part: Witnesseth, that in consideration of the sum of $25.00, the parties of the first part grant, bargain and sell all rights, title and interest in and to a certain lot or parcel of land lying on the waters of Reed Creek, in the Black Lick neighborhood, known as the Macedonia Church. This property was sold by an act of the Legislature of Virginia and the proceeds are to be used for the erection of a new church. Signed by Edley Doak, J. C. Brown, W. F. Lloyd and C. D. Doak."

After Macedonia was burned, a new church was erected on Reed Creek, in the same neighborhood, which was called Marvin. There is a flourishing congregation at this place and there is a large cemetery adjoining the church grounds. The late Secretary of Labor, William Doak, is buried here.

NEW HOPE

New Hope Methodist Episcopal Church was located north of Crockett, in what is now the Groseclose Mill neighborhood. The land was purchased from Joseph Hilton and wife Mahala, as of deed dated December 17, 1850. The trustees were: Mathias Tarter, Andrew Catron, Robert N. Ward, Nathan Henley, Joseph Wyrick, William Catron and James Lanter. This church was burned and later a new one was erected on the Lee Highway and called New Bethel. The New Hope membership was transferred to New Bethel, where at present there is a flourishing congregation.

GRAHAM'S FORGE CHURCH

Although unable to ascertain the date of the organization of a Church at Graham's Forge, it is safe to state that it was prior to 1875, as Mr. W. D. Sanders informs us he attended Sunday School there at that time. Before the erection of the church in 1901 services were held over the store of Graham, Robinson & Company.

The following is a deed found in the records:

"On May the 11th, 1901, John W. Robinson, B. G. Robinson, Nannie W. Graham, David Graham, William T. Graham, Charles T. Graham, Robert C. Graham, James M. Graham and others deeded one lot at Graham's Forge to John W. Robinson, H. J. Mathews, George W. Baker, David V. Fink, Jason L. Runion, William T. Graham, Robert T. Keesling, G. Burton Sanders, trustees, for the Graham's Forge Methodist Episcopal Church, South, of Wythe County and their successors."

FOSTERS FALLS CHURCH

In the establishment of this church the records carry the following:

"This deed made this, the 13th day of February, 1902, by and between Archer A. Phlegar, one of the Receivers of the Virginia Iron, Coal and Coke Company, party of the first part, and J. D. Painter, Geo. P. Chaffin, M. H. Jackson, J. J. Baker, J. D. Dyer, Jas. A. Dyer and John Jackson, Trustees of the Methodist Episcopal Church, South, parties of the second part, doth hereby grant, bargain and convey a tract or parcel of land near Fosters Falls, Virginia."

At the time of the conveyance there was an active operation of Iron mines at Fosters Falls and a large number of people resided in that community. A nice frame house of worship was erected. However, since the closing of the furnace and mines, the congregation has been depleted in membership. There was an organization at this place before the church was erected. A school house was used for a place of worship.

MOUNT ZION

Mount Zion, Methodist Church, is located on the Ceres road in the upper Black Lick section. There is still a semblance of an organization and services are held occasionally. The land for the church building was given by Jacob Miller.

EVERGREEN CHURCH

Land was donated by W. H. Fry for this Church and the building was dedicated in the summer of 1887. The trustees were: Daniel Sharitz, Thomas W. Fisher, Samuel Houseman, W. H. Fry and John Burgiss.

FAIRVIEW CHURCH

About 1875 a Sunday School was organized at Gravel Hill School House. Sunday School and preaching were held at this place for a number of years. About the year 1890 a number of citizens of the neighborhood decided to erect a church which was called Fairview and dedicated in September, 1891. The land was given by W. C. Marshall. Among those who served on the building committee and, later, elected the first Trustees were: H. J. Crowgey, D. M. Sharitz, S. A. Kegley, B. F. Brown, F. T. Umberger and W. H. Simmerman.

B. F. Brown is the only member of the building committee or Board of Trustees now living. He still resides in the neighborhood and is an active member.

MOUNT PLEASANT CHURCH

"On the 21st day of May, 1867, Abraham Umberger and wife, Elizabeth J. Umberger, deeded land to Joseph Sharitz, Guy Sharitz, A. Umberger, Levi Umberger, L. M. Yost, T. K. Harkrader, Johiel F. Umberger, Trustees of the Methodist Episcopal Church, South, known as Mount Pleasant."

The above is the only deed we have been able to find but we think it is safe to state that services were held at this point prior to that date. It was the logical place for the community center. The first church was a log building and at one time served as a school house, as well as a church. The present church is a commodious structure, located on a hill, giving an excellent view of the surrounding country. It is immediately on Federal Route No. 21.

SILOAM CHURCH

We find the following record:—"On the 4th day of April, 1874. George W. Hudson and his wife, Jane, of the first part, and Madison

H. Dean, William Hudson, Samuel P. Hall, Joseph Shaffer, John M. Bunts, John Hudson, George W. Armbrister, Joseph W. Hollandsworth, William J. Johnston, and George W. Hudson, Trustees, bargained and sold 1 acre of land to the parties of the second part of the church known as Siloam, to be used as a school house and a house of worship by the Methodist Episcopal Church, South, and when not occupied by the Methodist to be used by other Protestant denominations, as a house of worship. When not used as a house of worship the land is to return to the heirs of George W. Hudson."

ANOTHER CHURCH

The following record refers to a church which has passed out of existence:

"On the 20th day of April, 1876, Michael Wisely, Sr., and Barbara Anne his wife, sold to Isaac Wiseley, John W. Grubb, Michael Wisely, Jr., Hiram Miller, of the County of Wythe, and the State of Virginia, Trustees of Methodist Episcopal Church of the United States of America, a plot of land adjoining the land of J. A. Bourne." This was to be used to erect a place of worship and the church was located a short distance west of Zion Lutheran Church. The membership was small and services were discontinued in a few years.

ST. MARKS OR HUDDLE MEMORIAL

The following deed, copied from the records, explains itself:

"On June the 2nd, 1904, William D. S. Huddle, in consideration of the sum of $1.00 and the love for the Methodist Episcopal Church, South, doth release, bargain, grant, sell and convey to Robert P. Williams, G. W. Dunford, Robert E. L. Huddle, B. F. Porter, W. C. Davis and others, trustees of St. Mark's Methodist Episcopal Church, South, of the Wytheville Circuit, Holston Conference, and their successors in office, one acre of land and the interest in the school house lot."

CALVARY CHURCH

In establishing the history of Calvary Church we quote this deed:

"On the 2nd day of June, 1904, George W. Gleaves and Isabella C., his wife, in consideration of the sum of $1.00 and love for the Methodist Episcopal Church, South, do grant, bargain, sell and convey, unto John S. Johnson, J. E. Groseclose and others, trustees of Calvary Methodist Episcopal Church, South, Wytheville circuit, Wythe County, on the waters of Cripple Creek, two acres of land, more or less, being a portion of the land on which George W. Gleaves now resides and the use of the spring west of said tract of land and south of the road."

PINE GROVE OR GROSECLOSE CHAPEL

"This deed made the 10th day of August, 1894, by and between R. L. James of the first part and J. H. Groseclose, D. J. Horn, _____DeBord, J. G. Keesling, and R. L. James, Trustees of Pine Grove Methodist Episcopal Church, South, of the second part, all of the County of Wythe, State of Virginia. Witnesseth: that for and on consideration of the sum of $11.25 cash in hand, receipt of the same hereby acknowledged, the party of the first part doth bargain, sell and transmit with full covenant of general warranty, unto the aforesaid Trustees and their Successors, a certain parcel of land lying and being in the aforesaid County and State, on the waters of Cripple Creek, in trust that said premises shall be used, kept and maintained and disposed of as a place of Divine Worship for the use of the ministry and membership of the Methodist Episcopal Church, South; subject to the discipline, usage and ministerial appointments of said Church. The said tract contains 1⅝ acres more or less. Signed, J. R. James."

QUAKER CHURCH

On July 2, 1882, James Kyle and wife Julia Kyle gave the land in the Town of Speedwell for a Quaker church, which they erected. Mrs. Kyle was the prime mover in the enterprise. There were very few persons of that faith in the neighborhood and after the death of Mrs. Kyle only occasional services were held. About 1898-1900 through the instrumentality of Dr. Alexander Phillippi the property was acquired by the Lutherans and the church called St. Andrews. Regular services were held at this place for several years, when the members were transferred to other points. Only occasional services are held there at this time.

This is the only Quaker church ever erected in Wythe County. Mrs. James Kyle was a devout Christian woman and wielded a tremendous influence for good in the neighborhood. The writer remembers when she was Superintendent of the Sunday School at Fleming Methodist Church. The Kyle family frequently attended service at Fleming and Speedwell churches.

MT. CARMEL OR FLEMING CHURCH

Mt. Carmel Church was located on Cripple Creek, about two or three miles northeast of Speedwell. On June the 6th, 1846, John A. Sanders and wife Elizabeth Sanders, deeded land to Stephen Porter and George A. Sanders, Trustees, for a Methodist Episcopal Church. The acknowledgement to the deed was taken by William N. Chatwell, a Justice for Wythe County.

The first church was named Fleming, later changed to Mount

Carmel. A short time after the close of the War Between the States the name was changed again to Fleming and so remains to the present time.

The church was named for David Fleming who grew to manhood in this county and became a noted preacher. He married a Miss Miller, of Hawkins, Tenn., and died shortly after the close of the War Between the States.

The first building was a large frame structure with a gallery. For a number of years there was a large and flourishing congregation. This building was torn down and about 1885-86 a new one erected, which was later burned. A new and smaller building has since been erected on the site, thus making three churches in all to have been at this place.

The second church was burned February the 25th, 1930. Services were held at a neighborhood school house until the erection of the third church, which was dedicated August the 21st, 1932.

Before the War Between the States, a large number of slaves in the neighborhood attended service here, occupying the seats in the gallery, which accommodated a hundred or more people. The writer can remember in the 70's or early 80's when a number of the colored people still attended service at Fleming on special occasions.

GLADE CHURCH—MOUNT ZION

Searching for a record of this church, we find the following deed:—

"October 16, 1875.

"This deed made between John Aker and Margaret J. Aker, his wife, in the County of Wythe, State of Virginia, of the first part and T. R. Dunford, George Arnold, A. Arnold, W. F. Fry, John Aker, Trustees of the Glade Methodist Episcopal Church, in County of Wythe, State of Virginia, of the second part. Witnesseth: That the said party of the first part for and in consideration of the sum of $2.00, the receipt of which is hereby acknowledged, do grant, bargain, sell and convey unto the said named trustees and successors in office forever, a certain tract or parcel of land lying and being in the County of Wythe, State of Virginia, to have and to hold the said tract or parcel of land with all the appurtenances, unto the said-named trustees and their successors in office, duly appointed in trust that the said premises shall be kept, used and maintained and disposed of as a place of Divine Worship, the use of the ministry and members of the Methodist Episcopal Church, in the United States of America." The name of this church has since been changed to Mount Zion, and is located in what is known as West Piney and has a substantial membership. It serves a section of the county in which there is no other church organization.

FAIRVIEW CHURCH
(South of Rural Retreat)

The establishing of a church at Fairview is shown by the following record:—

"March 5, 1889. This deed made by and between, James P. Littz, and America F. Littz, his wife and Polly Littz, parties of the first part, of the County of Wythe and the State of Virginia, and J. S. Clark, D. B. Vaught, A. M. Steffey, Elbert S. Keesling, James P. Littz, M. F. Littz, Henry Neff, Isaac P. Buck, J. W. Arney, Trustees, of the Methodist Episcopal Church, South, parties of the second part of the same county and state: Witnesseth: that for and in consideration of the love of God and further consideration of $1.00 in hand paid, the receipt of which is hereby acknowledged, they, the said parties of the first part, do convey, with covenant of general warranty, to the said parties of the second part, Trustees and their successors in office forever, for the purpose of building a house of worship and for cemetery purposes, one acre of land, more or less, lying on the headwaters of Reed Creek.

It being understood that the Lutheran ministers and the congregation of the Evangelical Lutheran Church, are to have the privilege of occupying said house of worship, one-fourth of the time and to pay one-fourth of the expense when the building is completed. Signed, J. P. Litz, America Litz, Polly Litz."

Later the Lutheran congregation disposed of its interest in the property and the members were transferred to Grace Lutheran Church, Rural Retreat. The Methodists have a very active organization there at this time.

CROCKETTS CHAPEL M. E. CHURCH, SOUTH
CRIPPLE CREEK, VA.

We are indebted to the Rev. J. W. Morris for the following account of Crockett's Chapel:

"The Methodist Church here was started by the Revs. T. C. Vaughan and John Bird, local preachers and 'Doc' Williams and Robert Akers, Exhorters, all of Grayson County. They started preaching here in the old Pack School House, near where the bridge now crosses the mill pond, which was located on the south side of Cripple Creek. This resulted in a Methodist class being organized in the schoolhouse with Abner Hines as Class-leader, and William Pack and J. W. Brown with others as pillars in the Church. The Post Office then was called Beverly. Nearby was Beverly Furnace and later Beverly Mill was built.

"Later there was established a circuit called 'Iron Mountain Mission' and this was one of the preaching places. And the Rev. J. H. Kennedy was sent here as pastor. The Rev. Kennedy and James S. Crockett conceived the idea of building a church. The work was begun in 1888. Soon after this in the same year Mr. Crockett died, but the work was carried on to completion, and the church was named in his honor, 'Crocketts Chapel.' The window behind the pulpit also bears his name. The land was given by Crockett and Company and the deed was later made by William R. Crockett, administrator. Abner Hines, J. W. Brown, William Peck, Mrs. Bralley and perhaps another one were the original Trustees.

"The first church was dedicated by the Presiding Elder of Wytheville District, the Rev. W. W. Pyott preaching from the text, Proverbs 29:1: 'He, that being often reproved hardeneth his neck, shall suddenly be destroyed, and that without remedy.'

"Then as the congregation grew, a need was felt for a more commodious building, and so the church was re-modeled. This was done during the pastorate of the Rev. L. M. Burris, who was here from 1922 to 1926. When completed, our Wytheville District Conference was held in the new church, also while the Rev. Burris was here. This time the church was dedicated by the Rev. John Moore Crowe, then stationed at Wytheville. Mr. William A. Painter was the leading man in this new movement. Mr. Painter died December 19, 1937."

SPEEDWELL CHURCH

Speedwell Church is located about one mile west of the Town of Speedwell, in the Cripple Creek valley and only a short distance from the site of the first Speedwell Furnace, which was erected in 1792 and around which clusters names of persons, who were not only the makers of history in Wythe County and Virginia, but of other states.

On the 15th day of June, 1841, William Ward and wife, Mary, sold a tract of land for the erection of a Methodist Episcopal Church of the United States of America to the following Trustees: John Gannaway, Sr., James H. Piper, Seymore W. Gannaway, Thomas Gannaway, David Whitman, Peter Keesling and Stephen Porter.

The first building erected was a brick structure, the bricks having been made in that locality. After a number of years this building became unsafe, on account of the cracking of the walls. It was torn down and a frame church erected on the site.

There is a cemetery adjoining the church, in which is the resting place of the remains of Col. James H. Piper, one of the first trustees.

The initial movement for the organization of a church at Speedwell was held at the home of Col. Piper at which time William Ward was elected Class Leader. After the death of Col. Piper, September the 8th, 1854, at Grayson Sulphur Springs, his widow, formerly Miss Frances Smyth, was married to the Rev. John M. McTeer.

BETHANY METHODIST CHURCH

Bethany is located on the Highway leading from Austinville to Poplar Camp. There have been two churches at this place. On October the 6th, 1846, Elizabeth Chaffin conveyed two acres of land to trustees for the purpose of erecting a Methodist Episcopal Church thereon. The trustees were: James N. Peirce, James Stephens, Joseph McC. Baker, William Crawford, Sr., James Fisher.

The first church was a large frame structure with a gallery. So far as we have been able to ascertain, there were three churches of this type in Wythe County, viz: Bethany and Fleming, Methodist, and St. Peters, Lutheran.

The second church was erected on a lot adjoining the one on which the first church stood. The deed follows:

"This deed made June the 14th, 1902, between M. J. Jackson and Maggie Jackson, his wife, parties of the first part, and W. J. Jackson, M. H. Jackson, M. J. Jackson, W. H. Dean and N. P. Oglesby, trustees and their successors in office of the Bethany Methodist Episcopal Church, South, parties of the second part. Witnesseth: for and in consideration of the love we bear for the cause of Christ and for our earnest desire to promote His heritage on earth, the said parties of the first part do give, grant and convey to the said trustees and their successors in office, a certain tract of land adjoining the lot on which Bethany church now stands. The mineral right not conveyed."

The second church is a large commodious building and together with the nearby school building serves as a community centre. There is an active congregation and Sunday School.

CEDAR HILL CHURCH

Cedar Hill Church, located three or four miles east of Wytheville on the Lee Highway, is among the oldest Methodist churches in the county.

In the records we find the following:

"On the third day of October, 1843, Jacob Davis deeded one-fourth of an acre of land, for a Methodist Episcopal Church, to the following trustees: Thomas Bohanon, William H. Foster, Harrison Baylor, William Simmerman, George Riggle, James Graham, William Huffard, Larkin Johnson and Abraham Davis."

The first building was constructed from logs and stood about one hundred yards north of the present church. It was used for school purposes as well as a church, in the beginning.

SECOND CEDAR HILL CHURCH

The second church at Cedar Hill was erected in 1890 as will be seen from the following deed:

"On the 24th day of April, 1890, between J. A. Walker, trustee for R. R. Moore, parties of the first part, and H. G. Bourne, W. H. Taylor, F. H. Davis, D. S. Brown and A. J. Armbrister, trustees for the Methodist Episcopal Church, South, parties of the second part. Witnesseth: for and in consideration of the sum of $50.00 paid cash on January the 31st, 1890, the said parties of the first part do hereby grant and convey unto the said parties of the second part, a certain tract or parcel of land situated in the County of Wythe, on the McAdam road four miles east of Wytheville, containing one acre, more or less, with special warranty. It is further agreed between the parties of the first and second part, that in the event this lot of ground ever ceases to be used and occupied as a church property, then the same to revert to R. R. Moore or his heirs and the title shall be reinvested in him or them. But the trustees shall have the liberty to remove any and all buildings erected by them on said lot. Signed, R. R. Moore and James A. Walker."

Mr. A. J. Armbrister is the only surviving member of the trustees.

There is still an active congregation at this place and Sunday School and preaching service are held regularly.

SLATE SPRINGS CHURCH

On March 13, 1855, David Fisher executed a deed to Absalom Fisher, Reuben Fisher, Jacob Davis, H. J. Fisher and George Sanders, trustees of the Methodist Episcopal Church, for one acre of land, including the Slate Spring Church on Walker's Branch. The stream on which this church stood was also called Beaver's Branch. Judging from the wording of the deed mentioned above, the building must have been erected some time before the deed was executed.

After the organization of Huddle Memorial and Calvary congregations, the Slate Spring building was sold to the Baptist organization, June the 3rd, 1905. The Rev. W. A. Gaines, of Wytheville, was the pastor. After a few years the work was discontinued and the building sold.

MOUNT MITCHELL CHURCH

This church is located on the Lakes-to-Florida Highway, about six miles north of Wytheville. There is an active congregation and Sunday School. It is the community centre at that place.

The deed follows: "This indenture made this the 24th day of May, 1876, between J. W. Tarter and Susan M. Tarter in the County of Wythe, and State of Virginia, parties of the first part, and J. W. Tarter, Joseph Lindamood, A. Repass, Elijah Tarter, and G. J. Neese, of the County of Wythe, and the State of Virginia, trustees of the Methodist Episcopal Church of the second part: Witnesseth, that the said party of the first part, for and in consideration of the sum of $1.00, the receipt of which is hereby acknowledged, do grant, bargain, sell, confirm and convey unto the said above-named trustees and their successors in office forever, a certain tract of land, lying and being in the County of Wythe, State of Virginia, bounded as follows: * * * * * * on the east side of Tazewell and Fancy Gap Turnpike."

POPLAR GROVE

"On the 16th day of May, 1876, land was given by Joseph Umberger for Stony Fork Methodist Episcopal Church in United States of America and the Lutheran Church of Wythe County. Trustees were: Joseph Lindamood for the Methodist Episcopal Church, and for the Lutheran Church, Joseph Hedrick, Andrew Thompson and Jacob Felty."

This church was about nine miles north of Wytheville on the Tazewell and Fancy Gap Turnpike. It has long since become extinct and the building has been torn down.

MAX MEADOWS CHURCH

From the records we quote the following, which gives the origin of the M. E. Church, South, of Max Meadows.

"This deed made July 2, 1891, between the Max Meadows Land Company, party of the first part and S. D. Sanders, Robert Blair, W. J. H. Robinson, A. G. Crockett, Adam Collins, Wythe Graham, J. B. Bridges, Trustees of the Methodist Episcopal Church, South, parties of the second part, for and in consideration of the erection of a building (not to cost less than $1,200.00) and the sum of $5.00, the party of the first part bargained and sold to the parties of the second part a lot or parcel of land in the Town of Max Meadows, Wythe County, Virginia." This church was burned in February, 1917.

The date of the erection of the new church, which is a beautiful brick structure, was 1919, when it was begun under the pastorate of the Rev. J. H. Umberger. It was dedicated in May, 1920, under the pastorate of the Rev. L. D. Mayberry, who served the charge for five years.

RURAL RETREAT METHODIST CHURCH

The Rural Retreat Methodist Episcopal Church, South, is located in the northern section of the town. The lot for the erection of the church was purchased from Rufus Hawkins and wife, Betty, as of deed dated December the 19th, 1885. The first Trustees were: John W. Spence, Henry A. Effort, William F. Lloyd, John C. Brown, George

W. Freeman, Philip T. C. Snavely, Peter P. Keesling, Andrew J. Davis, J. M. Phillippi, Jasper Nelson, Emory W. Steffey.

The first church building was frame and was used for a number of years until the membership outgrew the seating capacity. A beautiful brick structure with Sunday School rooms and every modern convenience has since been erected on the west side of the street, to accommodate the large and growing congregation.

CHRISTIAN CHURCHES

BETHPAGE CHURCH

Bethpage church was located one mile west of Wytheville on land deeded to the Trustees by Martin Kegley and wife, Susan Kegley. Trustees, Archie Hoilman and William Pattison. Date of deed Dec. 11, 1867. First pastor was the Rev. D. A. Snow and there was a large and flourishing congregation. The church was burned December the 14th, 1878.

The congregation erected a new church on West Main street on a lot donated by David Sexton. The new church was dedicated October the 9th, 1879. Thus it will be seen that the new church was erected in less than a year after the loss of Bethpage. During the erection of the building, services were held in the various churches of the town, principally the Presbyterian. The Church is now known as the Main Street Christian Church of Wytheville, the Rev. C. B. Livesay, pastor.

BEREA

The first church that was erected May 26, 1850, on this site was Methodist, as shown by the deed of October 12, 1867. The trustees were Abram Frye, John Irvine, Michael Umberger, Absalom Fisher and Thomas Fisher, trustees for the M. E. Church, South. The church building was later sold to the Christian Church with D. A. Snow, John G. Kegley, Doctor C. Kegley, Jacob Grubb, as Trustees. There is an organization there at the present time with the Rev. C. B. Livesay, as pastor.

GALILEE CHRISTIAN CHURCH

Galilee church is located about five miles south of Wytheville on U. S. Route 21. George W. Kegley, one of the outstanding members of the Christian church in that neighborhood, was largely instrumental in the organization and erection of a church at that point. On Sept. 10, 1886, a lot was purchased from John J. Bateman and wife. The Trustees were: John G. Kegley, A. J. Grubb and Ranson Murray. An active congregation has continued since the erection of the

An active congregation has continued to worship here since the erection of the church.

The church was dedicated August the 14th, 1887.

PETUNIA CHURCH

In 1890 R. K. Shores, who had resided in Wytheville for many years, removed to the country. Shortly after locating there he organized a Sunday School in the neighborhood school house. Mr. Shores continued his work in that section and in 1894, the Rev. D. A. Bridle organized the "Church of Christ" at Petunia. R. K. Shores and James H. Daugherty were appointed Elders and A. H. Shores was elected clerk and treasurer.

Mrs. L. F. Shores, the widow of R. K. Shores, and A. H. Shores gave the land for the erection of the church.

CATHOLIC CHURCHES

ST. MARY'S CATHOLIC CHURCH

St. Mary's Catholic Church is located in the eastern section of Wytheville, on land given by Capt. John P. Mathews for a church site and cemetery. Mr. Mathews lived at what is known as "Hedgefield" and the land donated was a portion of that farm.

The church was dedicated on August the 10th, 1845, by Rt. Rev. Bishop R. V. Whelan, of Richmond, Virginia. The station at that time was in charge of the Rev. Father Edward Fox, who was resident priest at Lynchburg, Virginia, and made the trip by stage coach. A number of people of note are buried in the cemetery.

Deed—"John P. Mathews and wife, Malvina, for and in consideration of the sum of one dollar, current money of U. S., do grant, bargain and sell unto the said Richard V. Whalen and his successors, a certain parcel of land in the county of Wythe, a certain parcel of land in trust to the sole use of the Catholic congregation in religious worship and in no other manner. April 11, 1846."

NEW ST. MARY'S CHURCH

The new St. Mary's Church with Priest house attached, located on East Main Street, Wytheville, Va., was dedicated Sunday, July the 25th, 1937, by The Most Rev. John J. Swint, D. D., Bishop of Wheeling, West Virginia. He was assisted by the Rev. Michael McInery, Belmont Abby, North Carolina, the Rev. Raymond J. Judge, Pastor and the Rev. George I. Walter, Assistant Pastor of the Wytheville Church. The new church and home cost approximately $13,000.00 and is complete in every respect. The old church is being kept as a shrine, where services are held annually on Memorial Day.

The first St. Mary's Catholic Church in east Wytheville, which is the oldest original church building in the county. It lacks but a few years of being a century old, having been built in 1844-45.

ST. PATRICK'S CHURCH

St. Patrick's Catholic Church is located south of Speedwell on U. S. Route 21. The date of the erection of the first church, we have been unable to ascertain. On June the 26th, 1875, Daniel Long and Ellen Murphy, his wife, deeded to Bishop John J. Kane, Bishop of Wheeling, a lot on Dry Run on which a church has been erected. A cemetery adjoins the church. A second church was erected there later. The church at that place is served by the priest in charge of the Wytheville parish. It is possible that the first church was erected a number of years before the deed was recorded as there was a great influx of Catholic people in that locality in the forties.

Prior to the erection of the first church, services were held in a number of homes in the community, namely, Daniel Long, James O'Connor, Michael O'Donnell and Michael Harrigan.

Father Edward Jenkins was in charge of the work when the second church was erected.

The church records show the following:

"July 26th, 1877: This is to certify that St. Patrick's Church on Dry Run, Wythe County was, after being repaired, reblessed and the graveyard adjoining consecrated by the Most Rev. John J. Kain, Bishop of Wheeling, W. Va. The eastern corner of said graveyard was reserved and set apart for the burial of unbaptized infants. Signed, Joseph Mullen, Pastor."

While the court record shows that the deed was executed in 1875, there must have been a church there for a number of years, as it was repaired in 1877. While we have been unable to get the exact date of erection, we have been informed that it was erected either a short time before, or just after, the War Between the States. From the facts obtainable, we are of the opinion the date was before the War Between the States.

BAPTIST CHURCHES

WYTHEVILLE BAPTIST CHURCH

This Church was organized in Wytheville in 1883 with an enrollment of thirteen members. The first pastor was the Rev. C. J. Woodson, who served for two years. The church on Tazewell street in which they first worshiped was purchased from the Methodist congregation. On May the 6th, 1891, the Rev. John W. Mitchell was called and served until August the 6th, 1894. It was during his ministry that the church street building was erected. On October 9, 1898, a reorganization of the church was held and a covenant and new articles of Faith adopted.

The present brick church was erected in 1916. The corner stone was laid by Wytheville Fraternal Lodge No. 82 A. F. and A. M. during the pastorate of the Rev. W. E. Abrams. M. L. Harrison, J. M. Sudduth and W. E. Fulton were appointed trustees, to negotiate for funds from the Home Mission Board of the Southern Baptist Convention to assist in financing the project. The present pastor is the Rev. R. J. Kirby, under whose leadership the church has grown and prospered.

LIBERTY GROVE BAPTIST CHURCH

Liberty Grove Church is located about midway between Jackson's Ferry and Poplar Camp on a plot of ground belonging to the farm of the late J. W. Jackson.

The church was organized on the first Sunday in November, 1919, and it was dedicated by the Rev. Oliver Shank in August, 1920. The trustees appointed were: J. W. Jackson, J. E. Bryant, and J. C. Mabry.

The Rev. James E. LaRue built the church and served as its first pastor.

The church now has an active Woman's Missionary Society, a growing Sunday School, and a recent organization of its young people.

The congregation, under the leadership of its present pastor, the Rev. D. K. Kesler, is planning the erection of a new and larger building.

STONY FORK BAPTIST CHURCH

Stony Fork Baptist Church is located on West Stony Fork Creek, near the foot of Walker's Mountain, north of Wytheville.

The church was erected in 1914-15 on land obtained from Mrs. Josephus Brady. The building is a small frame structure. There is an active organization under the leadership of the Rev. J. I. Brinkley, of Wytheville.

SUMMIT CHURCH

The Summit Baptist Church, located in the eastern portion of Wythe County was organized in 1898 by the Rev. T. M. Bane. The Church was erected on land purchased from J. R. Short.

At present the church is served by the Rev. J. I. Brinkley, of Wytheville and a minister from Pulaski. Sunday School is held every Sunday.

PENTECOSTAL HOLINESS CHURCHES

The following has been contributed by the Rev. C. J. Peyton, Pastor:

The Pentecostal Holiness Church of Wytheville, Va., was organized October 22, 1916, with the Reverend David Nicewander acting as chairman. Mr. H. J. Hearn was elected as deacon. Mr. Alex. Hearn was elected as clerk. Mrs. H. J. Hearn was elected as treasurer. Church trustees: W. M. Waller, Emmett Williams, Alex Hearn. Committee on Foreign Missions: Mrs. A. V. Kesling, Mrs. E. O. Patterson, Rev. David Nicewander. Charter members: H. J. Hearn, Mrs. E. O. Patterson, Mrs. John Shelton, Mrs. H. J. Hearn, Mrs. Andy Robinson, Alex. Hearn, Miss Virginia Hearn (now Mrs. Owens Waller), Mrs. Alex. Hearn, Mrs. Frank Hoback, Mrs. Fannie Dickens, Joseph Hearn, Mary Hearn, William Hearn, and William Fuller.

Charter members who are yet members of the church are: Mrs. E. O. Patterson, Mrs. John Shelton, Mrs. Owens Waller, Mr. and Mrs. Alex Hearn.

The building which is used for worship now was purchased by the church November 27, 1916.

The organization continued as an independent Pentecostal Holiness

Church from 1916 until 1921 when it became part of the Virginia Conference.

Austinville Pentecostal Holiness Church was organized in the year 1933 by the Reverend Charles McDaniel.

Bakers Chapel Pentecostal Holiness Church was organized in the year 1918 by the Reverend J. T. Baker.

Ivanhoe Pentecostal Holiness Church was organized in the year 1919.

Seven Springs Pentecostal Holiness Church, Speedwell, Va., was organized in the year 1918.

Liberty Hill Pentecostal Holiness Church was organized in the year 1916.

St. Paul Pentecostal Holiness Church was organized in the year 1917.

MOUNTAIN VIEW CHURCH

Mountain View Methodist Episcopal Church, South, is located on the Grayson and Raleigh Turnpike about ten miles north of Wytheville. The land on which the church was erected and the lumber for the building were given by Elijah Smith and wife Margaret. They also gave land for a cemetery with the understanding that all burial plots were to be free.
The church was erected in 1894 and was dedicated in May, 1895 by the Rev. Charles Kelley.
The first trustees were: Elijah Smith, Alexander Smith, B. F. Spraker and D. A. Smith, all of whom are dead.
Mr. and Mrs. Elijah Smith were members of St. John's Lutheran Church for a number of years but after the erection of Mountain View Church had their membership transferred to the latter place because of its accessability. This information was furnished us by Mr. George G. Smith, a son of Mr. and Mrs. Elijah Smith.

COVETON CHURCH

Coveton Methodist Episcopal Church, South, is located in Crockett's Cove and was erected on land donated by S. C. Davis and wife. A small neat frame building was erected about 1895 to accommodate the congregation which is not large.

THE BRICK CHURCH IN THE COVE

What is known as the battle of the Gap of the Cove was fought on Tuesday, May 10th, 1864. The Federal forces, commanded by Col. William Woods Averell, a New Yorker and a graduate of West Point, came through Bland County over the Grayson and Raleigh Turnpike.

The Gap of the Cove had been fortified by the Confederates under General John H. Morgan. The Federals were trapped and after a hard fight, retreated. Some of the wounded Federal soldiers were left in the Brick Church and were found the next day by people living in the neighborhood. They were given food and their wounds dressed.

The bricks for the erection of the church were made on the ground by a Mr. Wesley Johnson, of Wytheville, who was the contractor.

The Brick Church in the Cove is the second oldest original church in Wythe County.

SEVENTH-DAY ADVENTIST CHURCH

The only Seventh-day Adventist Church in Wythe County is located on Eleventh Street in the Town of Wytheville.

The Church was organized in 1932. The trustees were: B. F. Conerly and W. O. Berry. The church is served at present by the Galax pastor.

NOTE TO KIMBERLING CHURCH

An interesting story concerning the original church has been disclosed by Mr. S. S. Cassell and is as follows: The first pulpit at Kimberling Church was made of walnut and placed across a corner of the church, an unique position for a pulpit. When the church was rebuilt in 1856 the discarded pulpit was purchased by Mr. Michael Cassell for fifty cents and used in his barn as a grain bin. Later, it was converted into a bookcase and presented to Corinth Sunday School where it remained until 1930 when it was again discarded. It, then, became the property of Mr. S. S. Cassell, the son of Mr. Michael Cassell, and is used in his home as a bookcase at the present time.

---o---

JOHN ALFRED MOREHEAD

A history of the churches of Wythe County would not be complete without mention of a minister who attained world wide fame as a churchman and on whom were conferred definitely high honors as a benefactor.

It would be a pleasure to give the history of every minister in each denomination who went out from our midst but it is impossible to do so. However we feel that our readers will agree that the Rev. Dr. John A. Morehead deserves special mention. Dr. Samuel Trexler has written a book entitled "John A. Morehead Who Created World Lutheranism" which gives a most delightful account of the life of this man whom Wythe County is proud to claim as a son. Although born in Pulaski County, where the first twelve years of his life were spent, he grew to manhood in Wythe County, studying in its schools, went from thence to Roanoke College, married in Wythe County and was bound to it by ties of relationship to many families, and linked especially with the history of St. John's Lutheran Church.

Born February the 4th, 1867, the second son of James Morehead and Barbara Catherine Yonce Morehead, he bore the mixed heritage of Scotch-Irish and German-Dutch blood.

His paternal family name was Muirhead, a family of Scotch-Irish Presbyterians when they came to America. The name was soon changed to Morehead. It was from the maternal German-Dutch line that Lutheran influence came which gave to the world "The Best Known Lutheran in the World", as he was spoken of by his biographers.

His education began in the country schools near his home, after which he attended Roanoke College from which he graduated with the degree of Bachelor of Arts in 1889. Following this he studied at the Lutheran Theological Seminary in Philadelphia, graduating in 1892. He also studied at the Universities of Berlin and Leipzig in 1901-1902. In 1902 Roanoke College conferred the degree of Doctor of Divinity upon him.

He was married to Nellie Virginia Fisher, October, 1892, in

Wytheville and the same year was ordained to the ministry, his first chage being in Burkes Garden, where he remained two years. Next he became pastor of the First English Lutheran Church in Richmond, Virginia. In 1898 he was made President and Professor of Systematic Theology at the Southern Lutheran Theological Seminary in Charleston, South Carolina. After five years he became President of Roanoke College, remaining sixteen years.

He was President of the United Synod of the South 1910-1914.

He left the Presidency of the college to become Chairman of the European Commission of the National Lutheran Council, traveling throughout Europe for the next four years. Elected President of the first Lutheran World Convention at Eisenach 1923 he served in that capacity through the gatherings at Copenhagen 1929 and in Paris the year 1935 when he was retired and made honorary president for life.

Trexler says: "Dr. Morehead's work is unparalleled in the history of the Christian Church. He organized agencies that saved the lives of millions. From the Urals to the Pyrenees his name is still a household word." He preached the opening sermon at the second Convention in Copenhagen when 885 delegates, including the King and Queen of Denmark, gathered from all parts of the world.

He made thirty-eight round trips across the Atlantic in the course of his travels for the Lutheran Council and World Convention.

He directed the spending of $10,000,000.00 raised for relief in Europe by the Lutheran Churches of America. During his assignment in Russia ten thousands of every race, color and creed were fed.

Dr. Morehead was deluged with decorations and degrees received on both sides of the Atlantic. These honors came to him in recognition of his post war relief work for furthering unity among Lutherans.

In Paris he was honored by a degree of Doctor of Theology by the University of Sorbonne.

He was awarded the Knighthood and Cross of the Order of Dannebrog by the King of Denmark in 1930.

He was made a Knight of the Order of the White Rose, First Class, by Finland in 1932.

President Hindenburg awarded him the German Red Cross.

Pennsylvania College made him a Doctor of Laws in 1921.

The University of Leipzig made him a Doctor of Theology in 1922.

Elizabeth University, Hungary, created him a Doctor of Sacred Theology in 1929.

Four countries, Germany, Finland, Sweden and Denmark proposed him for the Nobel Peace Prize and efforts were made in America to have the request made, through the proper channels, to President Roosevelt but before the matter could be consummated Dr. Morehead had passed away.

From the Lutheran of June the 11th, 1936: "There is a tradition that Dr. Morehead was the first civilian who crossed the line from France to Germany after the World War. He went to Berlin, enroute to Sweden, as a helper of an American "Doughboy" who was deputed to carry mail from military authorities in France to Military authorities in the capital in Germany."

Dr. Morehead died in Salem, June the 4th, 1936, a few hours after the burial of his wife. He was buried by her side in the cemetery at that place.

FOUR OUTSTANDING MEN

Possibly, Wythe County has never had within its borders four men of more outstanding character who exerted a greater influence over the early civic and religious life than the Rev. "Father" George D. Flohr, the Rev. Mr. John Stanger, the Rev. Mr. Jacob Repass and the Rev. Mr. Casper Yost. The first three were identified with the Lutheran, Presbyterian, and Reformed Churches and the latter with the Methodist Episcopal Church.

A brief sketch of the Rev. "Father" Flohr was given in the history of St. John's Church.

The Rev. Mr. John Stanger was born in Germany June 10th, 1765. Died October the 14th, 1848. Buried in Zion cemetery. He was educated at Tubiugen University, Kirkheim, Germany and is supposed to have come to Wythe County, Virginia, some time before 1790, as he was licensed to perform marriage ceremonies in that year. He had both the degrees of M. D. and D. D. conferred upon him. He represented Wythe County in the House of Delegates and was also one of the Justices of the court.

He resided about three miles east of Rural Retreat on the property now owned by Mr. Victor King. He married Magdelene Wampler. The following inscription is on his tomb stone: "Let no rude hand deface this stone, nor hasten wasting time in removing this memorial, that he lived and loved and that here rests the remains of one whose memory the survivors of his home would cherish and praise." The grave stone is rapidly deteriorating and in a few years will be unreadable.

Jacob Repass (Rayboss, Rebass) is buried at St. John's cemetery north of Wytheville, near the grave of "Father" Flohr. The inscription reads: "Born August 19, 1737. Died June 21, 1814," and is in Latin. It is evident that he came to Wythe County about 1780, or before, as a deed at Christiansburg shows that he took up land here in 1781 and 1782. He lived at what is now known as the Morehead place, where Mr. G. B. Morehead resides.

Both the Rev. Mr. John Stanger and the Rev. Mr. Jacob Repass resided in Wythe County several years prior to 1790, when Wythe County was formed. We find the following:

ORDER BOOK WYTHE COUNTY COURT

"On June the 22nd, 1790, at Stophel Simmermans, Present: James

McGavock, William Davis, Robert Sayers, William Ward, William Thompson, Andrew Boyd, James Newell, John Adams, Jehu Stephens, John T. Sayers. Gentlemen. On motion of John Stanger, who produced proper credentials, a license is granted him to solemnize the rites of matrimony according to the ceremonies of the Lutheran Church, he having, with John Harkrader his surety, entered into and acknowledged their bond in the penalty of 500 Pounds, conditioned according to law."

"Jacob Raypass the same according to the ceremonies of the Presbyterian Church."

CASPER YOST

The Rev. Mr. Casper Yost came to Wythe County in the early part of 1800 and was a staunch Methodist and wielded a strong influence for his church. He was a trustee in a number of the churches and Camp Grounds. He was born at Harper's Ferry May 7, 1785, married Euphrima Bickle Feb. 17, 1806, died January 4, 1850 and is buried in Wytheville in the West End cemetery. He was a member of the Methodist Church for 48 years.

He resided on a farm about three miles west of Wytheville and south of Mount Pleasant church.

His father owned a gun factory at Harper's Ferry and is supposed to have manufactured arms for the Revolutionary soldiers.

REFERENCES

Court records of Wythe County (formerly Fincastle, Montgomery) at Wytheville and Christiansburg.

Church records of the following church organizations: St. Paul's Lutheran, St. John's Episcopal, Wytheville Mount Tabor Presbyterian, Wytheville Presbyterian, Anchor of Hope Presbyterian.

Sermons and Essays, in two parts, the first containing Popular and Evangelic Sermons by the late Rev. G. D. Flohr, of Wythe County, Virginia. Translated from the original, by several ministers of the Evangelical Lutheran Church. The second containing sermons and Essays, for the most part by living ministers. Published by J. T. Tabler 1840.

The History of the Lutheran Church in Virginia and East Tennessee, edited by C. W. Cassell, W. J. Finck and Elon O. Henkel. Published by the Lutheran Synod of Virginia, 1922.

Origin and Defense of Camp-Meetings, by the Rev. S. D. Gaines 1871. Printed at the Southwest Virginia Enterprise Office, Wytheville.

Diamond Jubilee Address on the History of Abingdon Presbytery, by the Rev. Goodridge A. Wilson, Jr., D. D. April 21, 1936.

Tombstones in St. John, Zion and West End Cemeteries.

Minutes of Hanover Presbytery.

Memorials of Methodism in Virginia, by the Rev. William W. Bennett, D. D. Published 1871.

John A. Morehead Who Created World Lutheranism, by Dr. Samuel Trexler.

We wish to thank Mr. Frank R. Brown for his interest and assistance in the compilation of data.

CHATAIGNE'S
VIRGINIA GAZETTEER

— AND —

CLASSIFIED BUSINESS DIRECTORY,

1893-94.

J. H. CHATAIGNE,

COMPILER AND PUBLISHER,

RICHMOND, VA.

Pps. 1266 - 1283 are reproduced herewith.

PRICE, - - $6.00.

Entered according to Act of Congress, in the year 1893, by J. H. CHATAIGNE, in the office of the Librarian of Congress, at Washington, D. C.

WYTHE COUNTY.

Value of real estate 1892, ... $3,365,955.00
State tax on real estate, ... 13,470.76
Value of personal property, ... 1,054,370.00
State tax on personal property, ... 4,217.48
Capitation tax, . . White, $2,843; colored, 479.00
Population 1890, . White, 14,826; colored, 3,192

Wythe county was formed from Montgomery in 1790. Its county boundaries are Bland on the north, Carroll and Grayson on the south, Pulaski on the east, and Smyth on the west. The greater part of the county is a mountain valley, included between Brush mountain on the northwest and Iron mountain on the southeast. There are several other mountains within the county, the two largest of which are known as Walker's and Dick mountains, dividing the county into three fertile valleys—Walker's Creek, Wythe Valley and Cripple Creek. Wythe Valley is an elevated table land, about 2,000 feet above the level of the sea.

The Norfolk and Western railroad extends through the middle of the county from northwest to southeast, furnishing most excellent transportation facilities. The county is watered by New River, Reed Creek, Cripple Creek, Walker's Creek and Peak Creek. The soil is well adapted to raising grain and the grasses.

Wytheville, the county seat, is on the line of the Norfolk and Western railroad, 248 miles southwest from Richmond, and 55 miles from Abingdon, and contains a population of 3,000. The vicinity is rich in minerals, iron, lead, zinc and coal being abundant.

The town is well supplied with schools and churches, and the society is excellent, being largely augmented during the summer months by visitors from all parts of the south and southwest. A fine mineral spring has recently been discovered near by, and its waters are conveyed in pipes to the centre of the town, forming a no inconsiderable attraction to visitors.

Within a short distance of Wytheville is located the State fish hatchery, which under skillful management, is rapidly supplying the waters of Virginia with an abundance of the best varieties of fish. As a business centre Wytheville presents a more attractive appearance than any other town in Southwest Virginia. Wythe has an area of about 567 3-4 square miles.

Courts.

The CIRCUIT COURT of the 15th circuit meets at Wytheville on the 2d Monday in February and September.
Judge, Samuel W WIlliams.
Clerk, Wm B Foster.
The COUNTY COURT meets at Wytheville on the 2d Monday in each month.
Judge, Wm E Fulton.
Clerk, Wm B Foster.

County Officers.

Sheriff, J R Harkrader.
Surveyor, Jas M Gibbony.
Treasurer, J W Repass.
Commonwealth's Attorney, J L Gleaner.
Commissioner of Accounts, A A Campbell.
Superintendent of Poor, Daniel Cassell.
Superintendent of Schools, Geo R Huffard.
Comm'r of Revenue, Joseph Shaffer and J R Hilton.

MAGISTRATES.

T J Obenchain, J P M Huddle, G M P Keesling, N W Buford, R P Cooper, R P Williams, H M Henser, John M Bunts, W B Ryan, J E Brown, J Gratt Crockett, Joseph Hedrick.

SUPERVISORS.

Jas H McGavock, J L Lindamood, John A Bourne, William M Painter, Wm A Harkrader.

CONSTABLES.

Joseph M Cassell, Jno T Moyers, Wm H Wyrick, Thos S Davidson, J Marion Davis.

Post-offices.

Austinville, JOHN C RAPIR.
Barrow Springs.
Bertha, T K Calfee.
Catron.
Cedar Springs, MARY J HONAKER.
Clarks.
Cripple Creek.
Crockett Depot, J H Wilson.
Etter.
Favonia, Ellen C Walton.
Foster's Falls, J A DYER.
Graham's Forge.
Ivanhoe, F A GROVE.
Max Meadows, C S Bridges.
Newberry Mills.
Noble, W H NYE.
Patterson, Chas S Lucas.
Petunia, A H Shores.
Red Bluff, S C BRALLEY.
Rural Retreat, J W Davis.
Speedwell, J M James.
Walton Furnace, H E Blair.
Wytheville (c h), W R Repass.

Agricultural Implements.

FOOTE & JOHNSON, Wytheville
Huffard & Brown, Wytheville
Sexton G S & Co, Wytheville
Sult M M, Wytheville

Attorneys at Law.

BLAIR & BLAIR, Wytheville
Bolling & Stanley, Wytheville
Buford H D C, Wytheville
Caldwell J W, Wytheville
Campbell A A, Wytheville
CROCKETT ROBERT, Wytheville
Fulton J H, Wytheville
Fulton W E, Wytheville
Gleaves J L, Wytheville
Heuser H M, Ivanhoe
Holbrook & Thomas, Wytheville
Kegley W B, Wytheville
Pierce D S, Wytheville
Poage W R, Petunia
Poage W S, Wytheville
Powell J J A, Wytheville
Rector Wm, Ivanhoe
Sayer Robert, Wytheville
Walker & Caldwell, Wytheville
YOST W L, Wytheville

Auctioneers.

Harrison L D, Wytheville

Bakers.

Beuchler G T, Wytheville

Banks.

Bank of Wytheville, J G Brown cashier, Wytheville
Farmers Bank of Southwest Virginia, V C Huff cashier Wytheville
WYTHEVILLE INS & BANKING CO, H J Heiser cashier, (see adv) Wytheville

Barbers.

Gibson P R, Wytheville
Harper J A, Wytheville

Billiards & Pool.

Clayton J P, Wytheville

Boarding.

Crockett S S Mrs, Wytheville
Gibbony Jane Mrs, Wytheville
Hurt Mary Mrs, Wytheville
Lackey Julia Mrs, Wytheville
Lewis Jane Mrs, Foster's Falls
Noel M E Mrs, Wytheville
Percival Sarah Mrs, Speedwell
Richardson Charlotte Mrs, Wytheville

Booksellers & Stationers.

Heuser Bros, Wytheville

Boot and Manufacturers and Dealers.

Blackwell R P, Wytheville
Brady J, Wytheville
Hagan J H, Wytheville
Rosenheim & Trinkle, Wytheville

Brick Manufacturers.

Huffard S R, Wytheville

Butchers.

Hawke & Rider, Wytheville

Carpenters and Builders.

Blair & Sampson, Red Bluff
Cox James A, Fosters Falls
Grubb Elbert, Petunia
Hines James, Red Bluff
Lindamood L A, Petunia
Musser F H, Rural Retreat
Odell D H, Austinville
Pierce Bros, Ivanhoe
Scott J A B, Rural Retreat
Vaught Jas, Cedar Springs
Wright Sam'l F, Cedar Springs

Cigar Manufacturers.

CRABILL A B, Wytheville

Clothing.

Bergman S, Wytheville
Frank & Co, Wytheville
Stern Nathan, Wytheville

Carriage, Coach & Wagon Manufacturers.

Brally W H & Co, Red Bluff
Creger Sons, Wytheville
FOOTE & JOHNSON, Wytheville
Jones William, Red Bluff
Myers W A, Rural Retreat
Sells & Gormany, Rural Retreat

Sult & CO, Wytheville
Walls E W, Cedar Springs

Carriage Material.

FOOTE & JOHNSON Wytheville

Coal and Wood Dealers.

Calfee L D, Wytheville
Callaghan & Yates, Newberry Mills
Ward J E, Crockett Depot

Commissioners in Chancery.

Campbell A A, Wytheville
Powell J J A, Wytheville

Commission Merchants.

Carrico & Bourne, Wytheville

Confectioners.

Bailey D C, Wytheville
Bailey E H, Wytheville
Beuchler G T, Wytheville
Wolfenden W C, Wytheville

Dentists.

Eversole E C, Rural Retreat
Farmer, Haller & Ewald, Wytheville
Porter Wm, Red Bluff
Umbarger E W, Wytheville

Distillers.

Candler R D, Rural Retreat
Hoback Joseph, Speedwell
Marshall C M, Foster's Falls

Druggists.

Aumann & Co,	Wytheville
Buck W W,	Rural Retreat
Candler R D,	Rural Retreat
Pepper C T,	Rural Retreat
Poage R L,	Wytheville
Puckett John H,	Ivanhoe
Pucket & Hudle,	Red Bluff
Shore R K,	Petunia
Walker Allen P,	Wytheville

Dry Goods.

Gibboney D K & Co, Wytheville
Richardson C Mrs, Wytheville

Dyers.

Brown W E, Wytheville

Fertilizer Manufacturers and Agents.

Coley W M,	Crockett Depot
Foote & Johnson,	Wytheville
Neff N W,	Rural Retreat
Sexton G S & Co,	Wytheville
Snavely J M,	Rural Retreat
Spiller W H,	Wytheville
Ward J E,	Crockett Depot

Florists.

Vaught Ordelia Miss, Cedar Springs

Furniture Dealers.

Rich W W, Wytheville

Seagle J F & Son, Wytheville

General Merchants.

BLAIR C D & CO, Walton Furnace
Boyer C Q, Wytheville
Bruce G S & Co, Wytheville
Calfee, Robinson & Co, Barren Springs
Candler R D & Co, Rural Retreat
Consolidated Mining Co, Foster's Falls
Dake N S, Rural Retreat
Earley J J, Ivanhoe
Fisher S O & Bro, Cedar Springs
Foster's Falls Manfg Co, Foster's Falls
Gammon A A & Son, Rural Retreat
Graham & Robinson, Graham Forge
Harrison Luther D, Wytheville
Hemetite Iron Co, Foster'sFalls
Hicks J M, Rural Retreat
HONAKER J R, Cedar Springs
Indian Camp Mining Co, Austinville
Jackson M, Rural Retreat
James J M & Co, Speedwell
L C W Co, Cedar Springs
Leslie J W, Crockett Depot

Lobdell Car Wheel Co, Max Meadows
Miller W H, Noble
Moore J W, Speedwell
New River Mineral Co, F W Masters agt, Ivanhoe
Painter J D & Bro, Ivanhoe
Painter Wm M & Son, Ivanhoe
Perry H G, Rural Retreat
Phelps E McG, Wytheville
Prichett & Bro, Rural Retreat
Robinson & Blair, Max Meadows
Rowe & Walters, Rural Retreat
Shenandoah Furnace Co, Foster's Falls
Shores R K, Petunia
Spence J W, Rural Retreat
Spiller W H, Wytheville
Sudduth & Hershberger, Wytheville
Swecker M P, Ivanhoe
Ward J E, Crockett Depot
Wilson & Kincer, Crockett Depot
Wolfender W C, Wytheville
Wythe Lead & Zinc Co, Austinville

Grocers.

Baldwin & Co, Wytheville
Bralley A J & Son, Wytheville
Gibbony D K & Co, Wytheville
Lindamood W M & Bro, Wytheville
Saxton G S & Co, Wytheville
Topham Bros, Wytheville
Wappett T P, Wytheville

Hardware.

Huffard & Brown, Wytheville
Sult M M, Wytheville

Hotels.

Brown J H, Rural Retreat
Candler Emma Mrs, Rural Retreat
Commercial House, C L Price Ivanhoe
FARMERS, J S Mahady prop. (see adv) Wytheville
Foster's Falls Hotel, Foster Falls Mangf Co props, Foster's Falls
Fourth Avenue, G J Holbrook, Wytheville
Hancock House, J A Barnitz, Wytheville
Hotel Boyd, W B Preston prop, Wytheville
Ivanhoe Inn S R Smith, Ivanhoe
Percival S E, Speedwell
Petunia, James Cline, Petunia
Price C L, Red Bluff
Smyth E M, Red Bluff
Snavely J M, Rural Retreat
VIRGINIA HOUSE, W A

Street, (see adv) Wytheville
Ward J E, Crockett Depot

Ice Companies.
Wytheville Ice and Dairy Co, Wytheville

Insurance Agents.
Brown J G, Wytheville
Davis E M, Rural Retreat
Ewald S F, Wytheville
Withers R E & Co, Wytheville

Insurance Companies-Fire.
Petersburg Savings and Insurance Co, Wytheville
Virginia Fire and Marine, Wytheville
Virginia State, Wytheville
WYTHEVILLE INSURANCE AND BANKING CO, (The) (see adv) Wytheville

Iron Fencing.
GREENAWALT F B & CO, (see adv) Wytheville

Iron Founders & Machinists.
Coldicott C R, Cedar Springs
Foster's Falls M and M Co, Foster's Falls
Hushour W H, Cedar Springs
Killinger J B, Cedar Springs
Lobdell Car Wheel Co, White Rock

McDonald E H, Wytheville
New River Mineral Co, Red Bluff
WYTHEVILLE FOUNDRY & MACHINE CO, (see adv) Wytheville

Land Agents.
Carnahan John W, Petunia

Laundries.
Wytheville Woolen and Knitting Mills Co, Wytheville

Leather and Findings.
Ewald J H & Bro, Wytheville

Lithia Waters.
Cove Lithia Springs, Crockett
Thomas & Co, Wytheville
Wytheville Lithia Springs, G W Nye, Wytheville

Livery Stables.
Candler R D, Rural Retreat
Harkrader & White, Wytheville
Hatcher A D, Wytheville
Gammons A A & Son, Rural Retreat
Gibboney D K, Wytheville

Marble Works.
GREENAWALT F B & CO, (see adv) Wytheville

Merchant Tailors.
Crowder & Rider, Wytheville

Millinery.

Richardson C Mrs, Wytheville
Short T B Mrs, Wytheville
Sullivan Jennie Miss, Wytheville

Mills—Corn & Flour.

BISHOP N W & SON, (see adv) Wytheville
Callaghan's, Newberry Mills
Fishers Mill, S O Fisher & Bro, Cedar Springs
Foster Falls Mills, Foster's Falls
Galena Mills, Austinville
Graham & Robinson, Red Bluff
Keesling & Son, Cedar Springs
Kyle James, Speedwell
Neff B H, Rural Retreat
New River Mineral Co, Red Bluff
Perkins J R, Crockett Depot
Raper Wm & Co, Red Bluff
Robinson E H, Red Bluff
Rusling E S, Rural Retreat
Shores R K, Petunia
Simmerman R L, Walton Furnace
Slater Frank, Crockett Depot
Staley E H, Rural Retreat

Mills—Knitting.

WYTHEVILLE WOOLEN & KNITTING MILLS CO, (see adv) Wytheville

Mills—Saw & Planing.

Alford R J, Austinville
Baughman C D, Rural Retreat
Buchanan W M, Rural Retreat
Edwards W J, Ivanhoe
Foster's Falls, Foster's Falls Mfg Co, Foster's Falls
Graham & Robinson, Foster's Falls
Harvey E P, Noble
Horne D J, Cedar Springs
Keesling & Son, Cedar Springs
Litteral Geo, Ivanhoe
Petunia, R K Shores, Petunia
Rich W W & Son, Wytheville
Sexton G S, Wytheville

Mills—Woolen.

Callaghans & Yates, Newberry Mills
WYTHEVILLE WOOLEN & KNITTING MILLS CO, (see adv) Wytheville

Millwrights.

Bralley G F, Red Bluff
Cline James, Petunia
Collins A M, Foster's Falls

Danner J A, Austinville
Grubb E L, Petunia
Kitts N G, Cedar Springs
Lambert Robert, Red Bluff
Warden Thos, Red Bluff

Mines—Coal.
Brown Robert, Petunia
Tiffert H A, Rural Grove
Waddle K, Petunia

Mines—Iron.
Blair Jerome, Walton Furnace
Bralley S S, Red Bluff
Consolidated Mining Co, Foster's Falls
Deep Well Ore Bank, Foster's Falls
Foster's Falls Manufacturing Co, Foster's Falls
Hammer Ore Bank, Foster's Falls
Hamatite Ore Bank, Foster's Falls
Hudson G W, Red Bluff
Lobdell Car Wheel Co, Ivanhoe
New River Mineral Co, Ivanhoe
Penna Zinc and Iron Co, Ivanhoe
Sanders C F & Bro, Walton Furnace
Sayers R, Speedwell

Shenandoah Furnace, Foster's Falls
Walters John P, Petunia

Mines—Zinc.
Bertha Zinc Mine, Bertha
Wythe Lead and Zinc Co, Austinville
Wythe Mining Co, Wytheville

Newspapers.
Ivanhoe News (indep, Friday), Ivanhoe
Patriot and Herald (weekly, Rep), Repass & Repass managers, Wytheville
Rural Retreat Times (Dem), Rural Retreat
Southwest Virginia Enterprise (semi-weekly, Indep), Enterprise Publishing Co, Wytheville

Photographers.
Carnahan J E, Wytheville
Noel Walter, Wytheville

Physicians.
Buck W W, Rural Retreat
Crockett A G, Max Meadows
Gleaves C W, Wytheville
Graham J T, Wytheville
Gunners A P, Foster's Falls
Haller J P, Crockett Depot

Moore John H,	Ivanhoe
Pepper C T,	Rural Retreat
Phipps J M,	Rural Retreat
Pierce J B,	Ivanhoe
Pierce William,	Red Bluff
Ribble W H,	Wytheville
Robinson C R,	Ivanhoe
Robinson E H,	Red Bluff
Saunders R W,	Walton Furnace
Stran W R,	Rural Retreat
Thomas E A,	Wytheville

Plumbers & Gas Fitters.

Mill J H, Wytheville

Printers—Book & Job.

Enterprise Publishing Co, Wytheville
St Clair D A, Wytheville

Provision Dealers.

Painter & Carson, Ivanhoe

Real Estate Agents.

Withers R E & Co, Wytheville

Restaurant.

Otey C U,	Wytheville
Perry Charles,	Wytheville
*Trigg E & Son,	Wytheville

Saddlers & Harness Makers.

Ewald J H & Bro, Wytheville

FOOTE & JOHNSON, Wytheville
Sexton J C, Wytheville
Wampler L P, Crockett Depot

Saloons.

Beville J M, Wytheville
Brady J C, Wytheville
Otey C U, Wytheville

Sash, Doors and Blinds.

Wytheville Manufacturing Co, Wytheville

Sewing Machines.

Singer Manufacturing Co, M D Beckett agt, Wytheville

Schools and Academies.

Ashburg Academy, Cedar Springs
McDonald Institute, E M McDonald, Wytheville
Pettit M A Mrs, Wytheville
Petunia, Petunia
PLUMER MEMORIAL FEMALE COLLEGE, Rev J H Alexandria principal, (see adv) Wytheville
Trinity Hall (Female) School, Rev A Phillippi prin, Wytheville
Wytheville Female Seminary,

Mrs T R Dew prin, Wytheville
Wytheville Male College,
Brown prin. Wytheville

Stoves and Tinware.

Palison G H, Rural Retreat
Patterson C E, Wytheville

Tailors.

Rider & Crowder, Wytheville

Tanners and Curriers.

Ewald J H & Bro, Wytheville
Wampler L P, Crockett Depot

Telegraph Companies.

Western Union, Wytheville

Undertakers.

Lambert William,
      Rural Retreat
Lindsey C S & Son,
      Rural Retreat
Pierce Bros & Van Doren,
      Ivanhoe
Rich W W, Wytheville
Seagle J F & Co, Wytheville
Stately E P, Rural Retreat

Watchmakers and Jewelers.

Funk E M, Wytheville
Heilig A M, Wytheville
Neighbors W H, Wytheville
Scott J A B, Rural Retreat

Principal Farmers.

Austinville.-Chas A Jackson, W J and J C RAPER, W S Thorn, Mrs Chaffin, T J Gregory, Wm Jackson, Frank Chaffin.

Cedar Springs.-E S Keesling, J C Killinger, A P Scott, M F Newland, J H Wissler, G M P Keesling, P P Keesling, S O Fisher, G B Stone, E Vaught, H T Vaught, Jno Horne, Jas Denting, M Bermington, W L Mitchell, W R Pierce.

Crockett Depot.-D H Porter, Ephraim Copenhaver, J L Copenhaver, J P Copenhaver, Issac King, John King, H W King, J J King, D C Kincer, T F Dix, A J Hilton, A J Rosenbaum, R P Cooper, E A Andrews, C A Williams, J A Johnson, S S Etter, M M Waumpler, A A Waumpler, I T Waumpler, S K Ling, G M Wholford, W P Copenhaver, J T Leedy, J C Groseclose, E R Wyrick, W W Headrick, J T Kinser, J M Porter.

Foster's Falls.-N P Oglesby, Thos M Jackson, W W Chaffin; W J Raper, L E Painter, J E Brown, Falls Mining & Manfg Co, J J Baker, S D Saunders, J P M Saunders, Frank Carter, A M Chaffin, R M Tipton.

Ivanhoe.-Robt M Early, Jno P M Simmerman, L E Painter,

M F Porter, Marion F Jackson, James Sisk, Thomas Pearman, James Fisher, J T Early, W O Moore, Andrew Umbarger, R E L Simmerman, Thomas Blair, Richard Jackson, John Jackson, W M Painter, R E L Huddle, B F Kitchen, G W Dunford.

Max Meadows.-J H McGavock, J R & JC McGavock W B Graham, J G Kent, J P Sheffey, Mrs E V Simmerman, C C Allison.

Noble.-Byron Crockett, Jno A Bourne, E R Ward, Geo A Lambert, J A Ward, A B Nye, R E L Clark, Daniel Umbarger, Joseph Coley, Jno Chatman, Geo Clark, J W Ross.

Petunia.-John T Shuretze, R K Shores, Rufus King, Posy Walters, Michael Walters, Charles Covin, Pucket Umbarger, Austin Umbarger, Kent Creger, Simon Umbarger, Alex Umbarger, Samuel Six, John Sult.

Red Bluff.-Jas Blair, G W Hudsor, S S Bralley, S C Bralley, J H Huddle, G S Bralley, G O Hollandsworth, E H Robertson, J P M Simmerman, Rufus Jackson, Jno Wright.

Rural Retreat.-W G Howe, S W Repass, M Cassell, J C Brown, Stephen Umbarger, Josiah Brown, J E Goodman, P W Hounshell, W F Lloyd, C D Doak, Josiah Leedy, Jos L Lindamood, Rufus Brown, W S Neff, C K Coley, S S Etter, W A Buchanan, Joel Cormany, D F Copenhaver, A J Rosenbaum, J H Buck, T S Lambert, Sal Buck, J Y Walters, Z M Neff, Mrs N M Stran.

Speedwell.-J A Sanders, N W Buford, S L Porter, A L Porter, S S Simmerman, L R Ward, H M Ager, E P Harvey, John Rodgers, Thos Cassell, John O'Conner, G W Hufford, J N Coley, J C James, D M Lanter, J M Davis, Ephraim Crigger, Joseph Clyne, John Ward, D E James, John Benington, Sam Arnold.

Walton Furnace.-Jerome Blair, S F Watts Jr, R L Simmerman, Robt Ward, Geo W Armbrister, T J Porter, W F Blair, C F Sanders & Bro, Dr R W Sanders, E H Robinson, Geo W Hudson, W R Hudson.

Wytheville.-Jas Shaffer, R C Kent, G B Repass, Mrs E S Trinkle, J G Kegley, Henry Bourne, R R Moore, T A Marshall, W C Marshall, S P Browning, J M Wilson, Mrs A B Lawson, J H Pattison, R A Calfee, Samuel Cassell, M B Cassell, E C Burton, H J Crowgey, R H Crowgey, John Williams, Simon Umberger, M L Umberger, Jos Fisher, Jacob Fisher, R N Pendleton, Mann Pendleton, C R Fountain, Wm Crockett, J G Crockett, S R Crockett, N H Repass.

A Short Historical and Physical Description of Wythe County, Virginia.

Showing all its Mineral, Agricultural and Commercial Resources and Prospects. : : : :

Published by Order of Its Board of Supervisors for distribution at the Jamestown Ter-Centennial Exposition. 1907. : : : :

Compiled by H. M. Heuser, Wytheville, Virginia.

ENTERPRISE JOB PRINT,
Wytheville, Va.

Reproduced with permission
of Mr. Paul Heuser, son of Mr.
H. M. Heuser.

Wythe County.

Is one of the garden spots of the Old Dominion, and is one of the oldest of the Southwestern tier of Counties. It was formed from Montgomery County in 1790 and named for Geo. Wythe, one of the signers of the Declaration of Independence.

It contains an area of almost 500 square miles, one twelfth of which is yet in virgin forest, with acres of fertile soil indifferently farmed; with mountains of ore and coal undeveloped, and with many unharnessed streams hurrying away to the sea. This region of Bluegrass hills and fertile valleys is one of marvelous beauty and of great possibilities.

It is traversed through the central part by the main line of the Norfolk & Western Railway Company, and on the south side of the County by its North Carolina and Speedwell extensions, making 75 miles of main line and 16 miles of side track in the County.

Wytheville, the County seat, is 270 miles from Richmond, 240 miles from Washington City, 335 miles from Norfolk, 71 miles from Bristol and 80 miles from Roanoke.

Wythe County has over 600 miles of turnpike roads and 60 miles of macadamized roads, two local telephone lines and one long distance line, thus bringing every section into close touch.

Her population is 20,000 whites and 2,-000 colored. The total valuation of property for 1906 was, land and improvements, $3,267,017, personal property, $1,125,-792, making a total of $4,392,709.

This is the valuation for purposes of taxation and is about one third of its market value. But with this low valuation the rate of taxation thereon for State, County and District purposes will average about $1.25 upon each $100. The work animals and stock cattle and sheep were assessed in 1906 at nearly $300,000.

Topography.

Wythe County lies in the Appalachian Division of the State, at an average elevation of 2200 feet above sea level.

Whilst more properly speaking it is a plateau region, it is also a prolongation of the Valley of Virginia, traversed by three mountain ranges generally running from northeast to southwest. The uplands as well as smooth bottoms are very productive. Some of the latter have a loamy soil five feet deep.

The mountains are rugged and broken, with several peaks nearly 4000 feet high. They are filled with abundant stores of mineral wealth and clothed with fine virgin forest.

Soil.

Generally the soil is rather dark limestone, though some is gray; and in the mineral belt it is red. The mountain ridges are either sand or slate, all having a clay subsoil.

Geology.

Wythe County, from Southern to Northern border, holds the rocks of nearly all the epochs and their sub-divisions: Huronian, Cambrian, Potsdam, Oriskany and Proto-Carboniferous. In nearly every era so represented, Nature, with a lavish hand has deposited some of her best and most useful ores. Alternating with each other on the south side are wonderful and extensive veins and deposits of iron, lead, zinc, and manganese ores of extraordinary purity. Through the centre, red slates, shale, brown sand stones, lime stone and marble. While in the north will be found brown and semi-magnetic iron ores, lying close to workable veins of semi-bituminous and semi-anthracite coal. Lying between these belts and interlaced with them are fine belts of well watered grazing and farming lands of a high order.

Within the limits of this County are an extent and variety of mineral and agricultural lands which taken together, are unsurpassed by the same area anywhere else in the United States.

Minerals.

The minerals of this County are immense in quantity and value. They were known and worked in a primitive fashion 150 years ago, and include lead, zinc, iron, manganese ores, coal, marble, limestone, soapstone, kaolin and sand. The southern part of the County, or the developed mineral belt,—is dotted with the ruins of old charcoal furnaces, forges and smelting works. These have been supplanted by the immense hot blast furnaces of modern date now visible at Austinville, Ivanhoe and Max Meadows.

Lead and Zinc.

These ores are found side by side through a considerable belt of this County and are of great value and purity.

Lead was first discovered at Austinville on New River, about 1750 by Col. Chiswell. He was a British officer who established Fort Chiswell a few miles distant in 1756. These mines have yielded lead and zinc almost continuously since their discover first utilized them in a very primitive manner. Some years later when Col. Chiswell was attending the "King's Council" at Richmond, he gave such glowing accounts of the richness of his find that some arrogant wiseacre questioned his truthfulness. This precipitated a fight, in which, tradition says, Col. Chiswell slew his challenger with his sword.

At these same mines many bullets were moulded for the "Patriots of 1776."

Here our hardy mountaineers got the lead they used so successfully on Ferguson and his Redcoats at Kings Mountain. And they supplied the Southern Confederacy with nearly 5,000,000 pounds of its lead during the Civil War.

The zinc is unsurpassed in quality, being the standard spelter of the United States Government. Many specimens have shown by analysis 96 per cent. and 99 per cent. metallic zinc. Much zinc has been mined at Austinville and Bertha, but was carried to Pulaski City and other places to be smelted.

Many shafts have been worked also at Forneys, Ivanhoe and at Cedar Springs in this County, and surface indications appear at various places between these points.

Iron.

Iron ore being found in such profusion in Wythe County, it is not surprising to learn that David Peirce, an emigrant from Pennsylvania, made pig iron at his "Poplar Camp" furnace as early as 1779.

The "Raven Cliff" furnace was built in 1810, the "Little Wythe" in 1819, the "Cedar Run" in 1832, and from then until 1882 at least twelve more charcoal, cold-blast furnaces were erected and operated, when the large hot-blast ones came into vogue. Forges were also erected at an early day in Wythe County. Among the first was that of David Peirce on Cripple Creek, near Ivanhoe, in about 1800. Prominent among the others were Porter's, Bell's, Huddle's and Chatwell's. The largest and most successfull, however, was that of David Graham, on Reed Creek, first built by him in 1828, at what is still known as Graham's Forge.

¶On the south side of the County, following the trend of Iron Mountain from east to west, are a series of veins of what is locally called Limonite, Hematite and Mountain ores, of immense value and extent. They show from 47 to 58 per cent. metallic iron. Some of the ore at Rich Hill, Ivanhoe and other points may be classed within the Bessemer standard This section contains the old furnaces and forges and most of the modern ones, and covers miles of territory. The finest of charcoal iron has been made in this County as low as $9.00 per ton. The iron in Lick Mountain, Walker's Mountain and Draper's Mountain has not been so extensively developed, but shows from 45 to 54 per cent. metallic iron. It reveals frequent and extensive deposits of semi-Magnetic, Manganiferous and Oriskany iron ores, accompanied by that system of rocks to which they geologically belong.

Coal.

Along the base of Little Walker's Mountain, traversing the northern part of the County and spreading considerably near Max Meadows, are out-crops of hard and soft coal in veins from 8 inches to 8 feet in thickness. This has been but little developed, although various openings have been made from time to time—to the north of Rural Retreat and Max Meadows and on Stony Fork near Wytheville. The black smiths prefer this coal for their fires. It burns nicely in grates and some mined by Col. Boyd on Stony Fork some years before his death made a good quality of coke. At no point is this coal more than six miles from the railroad. It will eventually occupy a more important position commercially than at present.

Manganese.

This ore is found in considerable quantities through the entire iron belt. Often combined with and again entirely distinct from the iron ore.

Copper.

Small veins and very fine specimens have been found in the County near Ivanhoe, Max Meadows and Mt. Airy, but it is not positively known to exist in any considerable quantity.

Marble.

Variegated marble is found generally through the County. Brown, red and almost white are also found. Upon Cripple Creek, to the north of Wytheville and north of Rural Retreat. It has not been extensively quarried because of the small local demand.

Kaolin and Alumina.

A considerable deposit of kaolin is found on Lick Mountain, south of Wytheville, as well as clay containing a high per cent. of alumina.

Limestone.

Exists in abundance in almost every section of the County. It is successfully used for lime, furnace fluxing, building purposes and for road metal.

For this reason cement works should succeed here.

Sandstone and Sand.

Grindstone and whetstone rocks of good quality are abundant on Stony Fork of Reed Creek.

The granite-like sandstone of Sand Mountain always furnished the Hearth Rock for the charcoal furnaces, and there is an inexhaustible supply left.

Other sections of this mountain will furnish abundant material for glass-making.

Timber.

The large boundaries on the south side of the County have generally been converted into charcoal by the furnaces. But they are still to be found in the northern section of the County, containing white, red, black and chestnut oak, hickory, locust, maple, cedar, poplar, walnut, pine, ash and chestnut.

General Products.

Those articles generally raised in the Temperate Zone—whether belonging to the animal or vegetable kingdom—succeed in an admirable degree in this County, and bring good returns throughout the year

Some of our citizens give special attention to stock-raising; others to vegetables; others to fruit; others to poultry; others to bees, and so forth. The maximum yield of potatoes has been about 300 bushels per acre; of cabbage about 40,000 lbs.; from 35 to 55 bushels of wheat and from 60 to 100 bushels of corn to the acre. Of course the average is lower.

Tobacco, peanuts and sweet potatoes mature with us, but not to the same degree of perfection as in the Tidewater and Southside sections of the State.

Asparagus and celery grow here to perfection. Much of our bottom lands will yield crops of celery as abundant, as crisp, as fine flavored and with as good keeping qualities as can be produced anywhere.

In many respects the crops of 1906 were not up to the general average, but a few figures will serve to show the variety and value of some staple products of Wythe County. The following shipments were made from our depots last year:

12,000,000 lbs. Cabbage or 600 car loads,
200,000 bu. Potatoes " 400 " "
300,000 bu. Apples " 300. " "
6,000 crates Eggs " 215,000 doz,
5,000 coops Poultry or 100,000 chickens
280,000 lbs. Dressed Fowls,
7 car loads Butter,
5 " " Onions,
25 " " Live Hogs,
250 " " Cattle,
120 " " Sheep and Lambs.

This does not include hundreds of car loads of export logs, scores of car loads of tan bark, flour, feed stuff, wool and our various mineral waters.

The variety, the value and the quality of these products are elements of wealth, industry and prosperity that are not only present but perennial. Every summer shower reveals upon our hilltops that "everlasting covenant," which tells to each generation that seed time and harvest will return as long as the earth stands. The appetite of the Industrial World may in a few cycles consume our timber, and our ores; and so completely harness every unit of our water power that development along these lines will have passed the meridian of its prospects.

This can not be said of our farming, grazing and fruit crops. For as our soil is more scientifically and intensively handled, so will the quality and the quantity of its products increase with geometrical proportion.

There is stimulation and hope of bountiful harvests, large fruitage, and fat cattle being made more abundant each succeeding year. The zenith of Wytle County's agricultural possibilities will come with the millenium.

Fruit.

Fruit deserves especial mention because in recent years some of our citizens have given marked attention to fruit culture—in field and garden—and both with success. Fruits and berries raised here, in size, flavor, keeping and bearing qualities are second to none. Some new orchards have already yielded crops bringing from $1500 to $3500 in the field.

Apples, pears, quinces, cherries, plums and grapes grow to perfection here. Peaches are also fine but not as sure. Strawberries, raspberries, currants and other similar small fruits are indigenious to our soil and yield luscious crops.

As our people become more familiar with their culture the yield will of course be better. Thousands of trees are annually planted in this County.

Particular Industries.

The mining and manufacture of iron, lead and zinc is at present very large. The iron furnace at Max Meadows has a daily output of nearly 200 tons and is one of the best equipped plants in the South. The iron furnace at Ivanhoe has a daily output of about 80 tons.

At Austinville, during the past three years, new and improved machinery to the value of $200,000 has been added to the lead and zinc furnaces there. Iron ore is mined and washed at Patterson, Rich Hill, Barren Springs, Red Hill, Sanders, Tipton, Crawford, Foster Falls, Hematite, Locust Hill, Ivanhoe, Cripple Creek, Speedwell and perhaps other smaller places.

Large roller flour mills and large saw mills are found in every district.

Wagon factories, woolen mills, ice factories, foundry and machine shops, sash and blind factories and grain cradle factories supply a large part of our local demand for these things.

Produce dealers, stock raising, fruit, poultry and dairy products are each a large source of revenue.

Enterprising parties would do well here in the following lines of business:

Viz: Canning factories, wood working factories, cement works, fertilizer, brick and glass making. Any power plants needing motor power:—Because, we have the needed raw material, and fuel supply so near. Because the local demand for these things is good, and being on the main line of a great Railway System the facility for distribution is good. Because the weather is favorable and the water is pure. And because our laborers are generally intelligent and all speak the English language.

Water.

Pure, cool limestone and freestone springs exist in abundance. Some bold enough to run a corn-mill within 100 yards of their source.

Mineral springs are frequent and much used, viz: Bromide-Arsenic, Lithia, Chalybeate, Alum and Sulphur.

Climate.

The climate is delightful and invigorating: for Wythe County's altitude makes her people doubly blessed in that they are free from epidemics and mosquitoes. In temperature we are a happy mean between the rigors of the North and the humidity of the more Southern heat. Our summer nights are always cool enough for light covering. They are ideal for tourists or camping fishing parties.

The average temperature of Wytheville, the County seat of Wythe County, for 33 years is as follows:

Summer 71 degrees
Winter 34 degrees.

As compared with Asheville, N. C., a noted resort 200 miles further south, and with same elevation, about 2300 feet, our annual average is only 1 degree colder, but we have one-fourth less fog than Asheville.

As compared with some famous European resorts, examine the following table:

	Summer	Winter	Year
Geneva	70.3	34.	52.7
Vienna	71.8	38.7	55.3
Wytheville	71.	34.	52.5

The following table shows for 33 years the monthly average of normal temperature and precipitation:

	Temperature	Rainfall
January,	33. degrees.	3.03 inches.
February,	35.1 "	3.38 "
March	42.3 "	3.80 "
April	52. "	3.05 "
May	61.4 "	3.80 "
June	68.7 "	4.20 "
July	72.6 "	3.73 "
August	70.5 degrees.	4.51 inches.
September	63.6 "	3.39 "
October	53.6 "	2.74 "
November	43. "	2.21 "
December	35.3 "	2.77 "

General average temperature per year, 52.6 degrees. Total of general average rainfall per year, 40.61 inches.

Education and Religion.

Our County has about 90 public schools enrolling something like 3600 pupils. Several have high-school departments for the more advanced students. Our school facilities and buildings are being improv-

the modern machinery in contrast with the crumbling ruins of the primitive furnaces.

The old stone Shot Tower, at Jackson's Ferry. on a bluff overlooking New River—230 feet high, from the water level.

The Boiling Springs—where an entire creek gushes at once from the ground. All of these places will charm you.

If you are a disciple of Isaak Walton—Cripple Creek, Reed Creek or New River will afford you abundant employment, for in these streams are the finest of game fish. Along their banks is scenery that rivals both Scotland and Switzerland.

Notable Incidents.

No great battle has been fought in Wythe County, nor has the accident of birth made it the home of a President. Both Jefferson and Jackson have visited our people in the days of the stagecoach. Whilst in the days of the pullman palace cars the sturdy Cleveland and strenuous Roosevelt have both been delighted to see us *viam*.

A drive to the farming country in any direction will rest you with an ever changing panorama of verdant slopes, fertile valleys, sparkling streams, browsing cattle, blue mountains, growing crops and busy men and women.

If you have a turn for mountain climbing, fishing, exploring or sight-seeing, you can easily put in the season. A trip to Chimney Rocks, on Lick Mountain, 4000 feet high and only 5 1-2 miles from Wytheville, will give you a glorious view of the northern and eastern part of the County.

Two miles east on the same mountain will be found a natural curiosity of considerable rarity. The Ant Hills, being several acres taken up by their immense heaps, in and out of which constantly pour millions of these voracious insects.

A trip to the U. S. Fish Hatchery will pay you.

There are several caves in the County. Several old Indian burial grounds.

Then trips to the mineral section—to see the various mines, the furnaces,

ed each year. Besides these, there are a number of private schools of a high order.

Her citizens are law-abiding, and grateful to Providence for the many spiritual and temporal blessings they enjoy. But few communities could be found in the State where there are more schools and churches than in Wythe County. There is not a single bar-room, distillery, or brewery in the County.

The following denominations are represented: Lutheran, Southern Methodist, Presbyterian, Baptist, Catholic, Episcopal, Christian and Northern Methodist among the whites; and the colored people are pretty evenly divided among Northern and Southern Methodist and Baptist.

Places of Interest.

During the summer months a large number of visitors make their home in Wytheville. There are numerous places of interest in the County to make their stay pleasant as well as healthful. There are innumerable places along the water courses or upon the mountains for picnic parties.

193

Tourists, Investors, and Home-Seekers

Don't buy level wastes of sand in the mosquito belt but come to the blue-grass section and purchase first-class lands where the climate is fine and the water is pure.

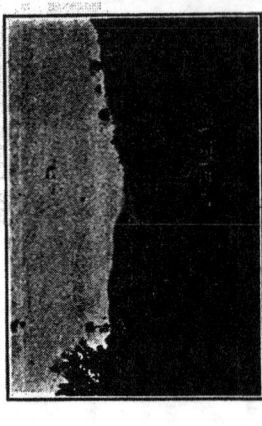

NEW RIVER SCENERY AT JACKSON'S FERRY.

The citizens of Wythe County are active, law-abiding and brave. The first settlers were English, Scotch-Irish, German, Irish and a few French.

For years it was a military out-post with a boundless hunter's paradise to the west. From 1770 and for a quarter of a century afterwards, thousands of pioneers passed through here to Kentucky and Tennessee.

The old "Wilderness Road" from Draper's Meadows to Cumberland Gap, often trodden by Boone and others, goes by Fort Chiswell and what is now Wytheville. Whilst the pioneer was contending with the red man, the tide of emigration began to pour in and push to the west and southwest. In those stirring times our civilization began. From that day to the present Wythe County men have taken prominent part in developing the history of Virginia.

She was at Pt. Pleasant against Cornwallis, at King's Mountain with Campbell and with Clark at Vincennes. During the war of 1812, her citizen, Gen. Alex. Smith defeated the British at Lake Erie. Among the captured stores at this encounter was a Dutch bell, cast in Hamburg, which Gen. Smith brought home. A few years later he made Wythe County a present of it and for more than 80 years it has hung in the Court-house and been used to announce the opening of court.

Wythe County sent many volunteers to the Mexican war also.

When the Civil war began in 1861, her gallant boys were among the first to the front. Every battle field from Manassas to Appomattox contains the remains of Wythe County soldiers. Our own cemetery holds the mortal remains of two generals who at different times commanded the immortal "Stonewall Brigade." When this celebrated Brigade was first so named, in one of the regiments composing it, was more than one company of Wythe County men.

Wythe County, in all, furnished about 1500 men to the Confederacy, and none to the Federal army.

In the Spanish war, she sent one full company to the field. Many of these boys re-enlisted and have since served with distinction in the Phillipines.

PART OF OLD FORT CHISWELL USED AS A NEGRO CABIN UNTIL RECENTLY DESTROYED BY FIRE. ERECTED IN 1755.

AN OLD LUMBER CAMP, NEAR MAX MEADOWS. VA.

NEW COURT HOUSE. WYTHEVILLE VA.

ONE OF OUR JACKS.

A THOROUGHBRED PERCHERON.

A THOROUGHBRED SHORT HORN.

WYTHE COUNTY BLOOD HOUNDS.

A FEW WYTHE COUNTY SHEEP IN MID-WINTER.

JACKSON'S SHOT TOWER NEAR JACKSON'S FERRY. ERECTED IN 1808.

CONVENT AND SCHOOL, WYTHEVILLE, VA.

SOME SUCKLING COLTS IN WYTHE COUNTY.

A DAILY SCENE AT RURAL RETREAT WHEN CABBAGE SEASON IS OPEN.

WYTHEVILLE.
View from Pine Ridge, one-half mile west of the town.
From Photo. by W. A. Johnston.

WYTHEVILLE:

Illustrated Prospectus

—— OF THE ——

CONTAINING DESCRIPTIONS OF ITS SCENERY, CLIMATE,
LOCATION, NATURAL RESOURCES AND OTHER
INDUCEMENTS TO TOURISTS AND THOSE
SEEKING A MOST DELIGHTFUL
SUMMER RESORT.

Published by the Board of Councilmen of the
Town of Wytheville.

Reproduced through the courtesy of a Friend.

WYTHEVILLE:
P. A. ST. CLAIR. PRINTER.
1887.

Some of the Natural Advantages of Wytheville
AS A
SUMMER RESORT.

IT is 2300 feet above the sea level—its air is pure and bracing.

It is entirely free from Malaria and is subject to no epidemic diseases.

The town is beautifully laid off in squares, with wide streets, and spacious yards.

It is situated on the Norfolk and Western Railroad, and has a Telegraph office in the center of the town.

It is the center of a network of country roads, many of which afford delightful drives.

It is situated in the famous blue-grass region, where the grass is of spontaneous growth and covers all uncultivated lands with an emerald green.

It contains an ever flowing fountain of excellent Alum-chalybeate water on Main Street, *free to all.*

Its church facilities are superior to those of any summer resort in the State.

Wytheville as a Summer Resort.

 THERE is no spot in the Appalachian Chain of Mountains, from the Canada line to the Gulf of Mexico, that offers a more desirable and delightful summer resting place than the town of Wytheville. It is situated in a cradle like depression on the summit of the Alleghanies, near that happy parallel of latitude, "where the frosts of winter bite not and the pestilences of summer stalk not forth," and is in the center of the largest white belt on the health map of the United States. By reference to this map the health seeker will discover that the few white belts upon it mark the areas where, alone, total exemption from malarias and epidemics may be found.

During the summer months a pleasant mountain breeze cools the heat of the midday, and a blanket is requisite for comfort during the night. The air is pure, sweet, and light enough to be exhilarating, and there are no morning fogs to dampen the spirits or chill the frame. A chalybeate spring of fine tonic properties flows from a fountain near the center of Main Street, and its restorative waters are free to all. Delicate ladies and feeble children are especially benefited by the use of this water. It acts quickly upon the system, and is regarded by many, who have tested its virtues, as fully equal to the famous Alleghany Springs in relieving dyspepsia, and similar complaints.

For a number of years Wytheville has been known as the metropolis of the wealthy and picturesque section of South-west Virginia. Its churches are numerous; its colleges and schools excellent; its streets are broad and clean; and its people warm hearted, cultivated, and hospitable. No town of its size in the South can boast of a more refined and elevated society: it delights in all enjoyments, sports, and recreations that are pure and healthful, but quietly, though firmly, refuses to be drawn into the vortex of useless extravagance and fashionable follies. In this respect it presents a striking contrast to many other places of resort where a shoddy display of style is too often the first and only consideration, and comfort and content are the last, if indeed, they be not entirely ignored.

To the weary invalid wishing to recruit his health and strength; to the women and children of the South who desire to escape from the heat of midsummer's sun; to the exhausted business man and tired professional, craving relaxation and rest, she extends her invitations; assuring them that many have accepted in the past and but few, if any, ever regretted it ; for, within her limits, the Goddess of Health has often cooled the fevered brow; changed the pale lilies to bright roses; cleansed the blood from its foul poisons of malaria; restored tone to the depressed nerves; infused strength to the emaciated frame; supplanted despair with hope; created new sources of happiness, by making grief forget her woes; taught folly to be wise, and prolonged human life.

Location of the Town.

WYTHEVILLE is situated on the Norfolk and Western Railroad, 133 miles west of Lynchburg, Virginia, and 71 miles east of Bristol, Tennessee, the western terminus of the Road. It is located near the center of South-west Virginia, owing to which fact as well as to its excellent system of turnpikes, it is the largest town in that section of the State, (containing a population of 3,000,) and has an immense trade with the neighboring counties off of the railroad—the large canvas covered country wagons from Grayson, Carroll, Bland and other counties being daily visitants to its streets.

Wythe County is included within the far famed blue grass region of Kentucky and Virginia, which, to be appreciated, must be seen. Here the grass grows spontaneously in woodland or on open plain, without care and without cultivation, carpeting the whole landscape with dark green from early spring until late in the fall, affording a luxuriant pasturage to numberless herds of cattle. Many of these cattle are shipped as beeves to Baltimore and other eastern cities where a Southwest Virginia steak is considered a delicacy equal in flavor to the Linhaven Oyster of the Eastern Shore, or the Canvasbacked duck of the Delaware.

Climate.

THE first question that suggests itself to any person seeking a summer home, is the character of its climate. Wytheville, appropriately called the "Mountain City" is located near the crest of the Alleghanies, 2,300 feet above the level of the sea Hence, not a day passes without a refreshing breeze, while the nights, owing to the dry and rarified atmosphere, rapidly cool, so that not a single one passes but that a blanket becomes a necessity before morning. Below will be found statistics, carefully compiled, showing the comparative temperature of Wytheville with a number of the famous health resorts of Europe.

	Spring.	Summer.	Autumn.	Winter.	Year.
Geneva, . . .	52.2	70.3	54.2	34.0	52.07
Turin, ...	53.7	71.5	53.8	33.5	53.1
Vienna, . . .	56.2	71.8	54.6	38.7	55.3
Milan, ...	54.9	72.8	55.9	36.1	54.9
Wytheville, .	52.	70.6	53.	32.3	53.

An observation for 19 consecutive years shows the following average monthly temperatures for Wytheville.

January 25	July 73
February 37	August 71
March 43	September 63
April 52	October 54
May 61	November 42
June 68	December 35

The rainfall in summer though frequent enough to refresh the atmosphere and keep the ground moist, consists principally of mountain showers which, owing to the natural drainage of the country, occasion little inconvenience, as the surplus water quickly runs off and leaves the grass and herbage green and luxuriant.

The following statistics will show the average rainfall :

Spring.	Summer	Autumn.	Winter.	Year.
10.6	11.9	9.5	9.8	41.9

Hotels and Boarding Houses.

THE Hotels of Wytheville are commodious, airy, cleanly and well kept, and for politeness and attentiveness of servants are proverbial. For a further description of them, reference is made to the advertisements in the back of this book.

The boarding houses are a peculiar feature of the town.

From Photo. by W. A. Johnston.

VIEW FROM BOYD'S HILL.

Many of the best families in the place, who can place spare rooms at the disposal of visitors for the summer months, do so, thereby supplying them with all the comforts and surroundings of a home without the worry incident to keeping house. Frequently several families, or friends, from the southern, or eastern cities, club together and secure one boarding house with ample room for their accommodation. Thus they can select their company and provide their own amusements entirely free and independent of the restraints incident to a life at the springs. The yards to most of the boarding houses are large and beautifully turfed, affording excellent play-grounds for children.

For a list of those desirous of taking boarders the present summer, address, D. Kyle Gibboney. See also advertisements.

Walks and Drives.

THE Main street of the town which is 90 feet wide and a mile long, has paved sidewalks, from one end to the other, affording to pedestrians a comfortable walk, in any weather. All of the more prominent cross-streets are also supplied with either excellent rock or plank walks. But during the summer months there is little need to confine ones-self to these, since the thick and springy turf on the commons, in the suburbs of the town, affords a more pleasant and comfortable walk than can be devised by the ingenuity of man. Those desiring to extend their rambles further will find in the woodland streams, the wild mountain flowers, the commanding hill tops which overlook the town, or the secluded dell, whose soft velvety carpet is rarely pressed by the foot of man; or, later in the season, the mountain side decked as a bride with its robe of waxy white ivy blossoms, shaded by dark green leaves, or with the bright blooming rhododendron the queen of flowers, something to charm the eye and captivate the thoughts with each recurring visit.

To those preferring a drive, the town affords excellent liveries, The Macadamized road, originally constructed as the great Valley thouroughfare for stages and other vehicles, before the railroad had penetrated this region, runs through the town. This road which extends from the Seven Mile Ford in Smyth County as far east as Staunton, Virginia, affords a delightful

From Photo. by W. A. Johnston.

MAIN STREET, WYTHEVILLE.

drive. Bordering it on either side may be frequenlty seen those. large boundaries of pasture lands, for which Wythe County is so noted, dotted over with hundreds of fat cattle. Other roads, though not metaled, afford equally pleasant drives in summer, as you follow them to the Fish Hatchery, or the Chimney Rocks, or the Grayson Springs, or the Lead Mines, or Ivanhoe Furnace or other places of equal interest within easy access of the town.

Mineral Waters.

MANY persons are induced to undergo the noise and confusion and fashionable display of a life at the springs for the sake of drinking its waters, for the recuperation of their health. Wytheville affords the latter to its fullest extent, as many who have tried its life giving waters will testify, while in the secluded retreat of a private home, the annoyances are avoided. From a fountain on Main street continually flows a stream of Alum-Chalybeate water, which for medicinal purposes is unexcelled, having proved itself to be both a tonic and a specific for the most confirmed cases of dyspepsia. The Cove Lithia Springs are only a few miles from the town and its waters are brought in daily and are for sale at the drug stores and hotels. The Sharon Alum and the Grayson Sulphur Springs, both celebrated, are also within easy access.

Amusements.

THE Wytheville German Club, composed of the young gentlemen of the town, an organization which has been in existence for several years, gives a select German at one of the hotel ballrooms once a week. To these are added other hops or Germans given by individuals, from time to time, for the pleasure of their friends or guests, so that rarely a week passes during the gay season without two or three large entertainments. For other less general amusements, many of the summer visitors club together for the purpose of excursions, or picnics, or private charades, as the case may be.

From Photo. by *W. A. Johnston.* WALTER'S BRIDGE, N. & W. R. R. (90 feet high).
Located 3 Miles west of Wytheville, next to the highest bridge on the line of the Norfolk and Western Railroad.

Interesting Mineral Features around Wytheville.

BY CAPT. CHAS. R. BOYD, AUTHOR OF MINERAL RESOURCES OF SOUTH-WEST VIRGINIA.

ADDED to the other numerous attractive features, to which the region surrounding Wytheville may justly lay claim, are those of an unusually beautiful and valuable character, which owe their richness, beauty, variety and attractiveness to the peculiar disposition of the massive rock and ore formations, and Mineral Deposits. In positions accessible to the miner and the tourist they lie, alternating, in the different series of stratification, with excellent grass and grain lands—broad slopes of green pastures and waving grain, running back into the blue mountains, whose shaded sides and bowered retreats are the storehouses from which issue the crystal springs that join below in silvery streams whose flow is perennial.

Any attempted description with the pen only mars the beauty and splendour of the matchless arrangement; and to see it, as it is written in faultless lines and with incomparable art by the hand of nature, only, can either its beauty or the charming design of its composition be appreciated.

Fifteen miles away, in Wythe County, are the ancient mines with the bright blue ores of lead and the fretted white and yellow incrusted ores of zinc, which, in the infancy of the great republic, supplied the greater part of the lead used by the patriots of '76, and a very great part of that consumed by Lee's soldiers, in the late war. These massive bands of ores, of more than two hundred feet vertical thickness, lining that margin of the great Valley of Virginia for nearly forty miles in this County, are now supplying the Zinc and Lead ores from which the purest metals of either are manufactured, in the whole

From Photo. by Walter Noel.

CHIMNEY ROCKS.
A view of the rocks from the rear, showing Wytheville in the distance.

country; and their reduction at works within a short and pleasant drive from Wytheville, is an accomplished fact.

But a stone's throw of these, south, is the great floor or bed rock series, underlying all this formation, much of which carries free gold; and around it and running with it, throughout the Cripple Creek-New River basin, are those unusual and profuse deposits of Bessemer brown Iron ores which are so attracting the earnest attention of all capitalists and investors, as to cause the erection of costly furnaces and reduction works, which are now, and will soon be on a much more extended scale, engaged in the production of metal which is eagerly purchased by all manufacturers of Iron and Steel.

In the great diversified bands of Limestones, Sandstones and Slates, nearer the middle of the County, and enveloping Wytheville, are many deposits of pure and excellent Iron Ores, Manganese Ores, Ores of Copper, and the whole so placed as to be unusually convenient to the main stem and branches of one of the most efficient and best equipped lines of railway in the world—The Norfolk and Western Railroad.

The unequal solubility of these great bands of limestones has caused to be formed, in the course of time, by the action of nature's powerful erosive forces, caves and cliffs of marvelous beauty.

Some of these ledges are beautiful variegated marble; others are pure limestone, with delicate fossils traced between the close bands, and still others are the valuable magnesian deposits from which the Cement of commerce is made.

Toward the northern margin of this great valley of wooded hills and emerald vales, some powerful convulsion of nature has thrust these great limestones up against those equally great and important formations which hold, in the bosom of that long line of hills, the valuable deposits of Coal and Carbonate of Iron, which will soon cause that side of the County to take high rank among the ore and coal producing regions of the country. Down, under these massive bands, are great basins of Salt, and floating under the convexed arches of the stratifications, just north of them, are inexhaustible lakes of Petroleum.

TOWN OF WYTHEVILLE.

Along the flanks of the great North Mountains the Iron ores with their blood red streaks and those of ochreous tint add value to these elevated areas, wooded to their summits with all the forest growth of this healthful latitude.

Wytheville, is thus surrounded with everything in Nature that can make it beautiful and attractive; and still within the radius of an easy days drive, over mountains whose elevations afford so many points from which to view these changing scenes of more than romantic beauty, the tourist can look at the broad outcropping surfaces of inexhaustible stores of Gypsum, so valuable to restore the fertility of impoverished lands and so much in use, as plaster of Paris, for architectural purposes.

Then, should Wytheville still require other aid than the matchless resources, already described, with the Thermal and Mineral waters that flow from this great variety of mineral bearing rocks, she could convert herself into a sanitarium and by their sure and well tried merits cure all the ills that flesh is heir to

Should, then, the early construction of contemplated railways be accomplished that would bring the Coal and Coke of the counties in the Cumberland plateau, and those of Wythe and Rich Valley, into close contact, at Wytheville, with the ores derived from the vast deposits named above, the beautiful streets of the town, would soon, in addition to those already erected, be lined with costly and elegant residences! and all the favorable locations be occupied with establishments especially adapted to the making of all grades of Iron and Steel and to the production of the fruit of the loom, and the heart of the tourist and pleasure seeker would be gladdened by all these additional facilities for enjoyment.

CONCLUSION.

To attempt to enumerate the attractions of Wytheville and the surrounding country in the limited space allotted us would be the height of folly. A mere sketch or outline is all that could be expected. This we have drawn with the hope of exciting the interest of those seeking a change of climate and location, either permanently or transiently for the sultry months of summer, feeling assured that a closer inquiry will induce them to give our section a trial.

To one and all we extend a hearty invitation. To the seeker after health we would say that many who have preceded you have pronounced high encomiums on the place; to the tourist, our natural scenery is unsurpassed; to the capitalist, our inexhaustible beds of minerals, notably iron and lead are already creating great excitement among investors. Recent analyses by eminent chemists and explorations by distinguished geologists show the iron ores of Cripple Creek Valley in this county to be superior both in quantity and quality to those of any other district in the South for the purpose of making the highest grades of iron. Railroads are already projected which when completed will open up to the world a country the superior of which the sun in its daily course never shone upon.

In conclusion it has been our endeavor to state the facts as they are, realizing not only the folly but the wrong of attempting to inflate the reputation of any section, in these days of intelligence, by any exaggerated statements or highly colored pictures. It is not our desire however that any should take our statements as true without verification. We invite inquiry. Look on the atlas, look at the United States health reports, look at statistics in mining and manufacturing papers with regard to the quality of the minerals, look at the immense sales that have recently been made in the county and finally, if possible, come and look at the country yourself, and be assured in advance of a hearty welcome.

TOWN OFFICERS—ADVERTISEMENTS.

TOWN OFFICERS,

B. W. TERRY, Mayor.

COUNCIL.

J. W. CALDWELL, Pres.   CHAS. A. EWALD,
S. C. LaHUE,   T. J. BOYD,
H. B. MAUPIN,   JAS. F. SEAGLE,
E. C. DEUEL,   I. FRANK,
G. T. BEUCHLER,   H. G. WADLEY.
GEO. R. DUNN,   GEO. H. WILLIAMS.

WM. B. FOSTER, Clerk.
S. J. WILKINSON, Chief of Police.

ADVERTISEMENTS.

PRIVATE BOARDING HOUSE,

ADJOINING FOURTH AVENUE HOTEL.
CENTRAL PART OF TOWN—ELEGANT ROOMS.

Board per day, ... $ 1.50
"   "   week, ...   8.00
"   "   month, ... 30.00

Address:
MRS. JULIA C. LACKEY.

BOARDING HOUSE.

The most central Boarding House in Wytheville is a large three story brick building, situated on Main Street, with elegant rooms, large halls, front and back porches. It also has a front and back yard.

For particulars apply to
MISS JANIE K. GIBBONEY.
Wytheville, Va.

ADVERTISEMENTS.

BOYD'S HOTEL,
WYTHEVILLE, WYTHE COUNTY, VA:
AT THE DEPOT OF THE
NORFOLK AND WESTERN RAILROAD.

132 miles South from Lynchburg, and 72 miles East from Bristol, Tennessee; and at an elevation of 2300 feet above the level of the ocean.

A large brick-house, four stories high above the basement.

Two never-failing Springs, of mild limestone water, near the Hotel; a large Cistern, of pure rain-water, in the yard; Mineral Water (shown by analysis of Professor Mallett, of the University of Virginia, to contain valuable medicinal qualities) flowing from pipes in the heart of the town.

Board, at moderate rates, by the day, week, or month. Board, at very reasonable rates, can be had at several other hotels in the town, and with private families, in the town and neighborhood, and at several pleasant and well kept Watering Places, conveniently reached from this Depot.

Persons stopping at this Hotel, and desiring to change to some other boarding-house, will cheerfully be afforded all information and facilities for doing so.

Good horses and carriages may be had at Livery Stables in the town.

The town of Wytheville is located near the center and most elevated part of the beautiful Mountain Region of South-west Virginia, (a region filled with iron, coal, zinc, copper, gypsum, salt, manganese, and many other minerals), at an elevation of 2300 feet above the level of the sea; and with an atmosphere, for its purity and pleasantness, especially in the summer and fall seasons, unsurpassed and rarely equaled by that of any other locality. It has a population, numbering nearly or quite 3,000, and is well supplied with Churches for the various denominations, and with good Schools, and Mercantile Houses, and sundry Manufacturing Establishments.

THOS. J. BOYD,
Proprietor.

April, 1887.

ADVERTISEMENTS.

FOURTH AVENUE HOTEL,
Wytheville, Virginia.

The handsomest and most attractive building in the City, situated at the junction of Main and 4th Avenue, the most central and fashionable point, offers, the most inviting accommodations for guests at reasonable rates.

The Hotel is new and complete in all its apartments and appurtenances. The rooms are large, airy and elegantly furnished, spacious halls and verandas; baths, hot and cold. The hotel is provided with the best fare the market affords. Telephone Exchange with all the principal points in the City, and Western Union Telegraph Office on opposite square.

Rates per day, ... $ 2.00
Rates per week, ...   12.50
Rates per month—special, according to room or number of rooms desired.

Free Omnibus to all trains.

ADVERTISEMENTS.

SUMMER BOARDERS WANTED.

Large Airy Rooms—Grassy yard.

Location, one square from Main Street.

Address:

MRS. JANE FOX,

Wytheville, Va.

MRS. M. E. NOEL'S
BOARDING HOUSE,

MAIN STREET,

WYTHEVILLE, VIRGINIA.

Pleasant Location—Terms Reasonable.

MRS. RICH'S BOARDING HOUSE,

MAIN STREET,

Convenient Location—Comfortable Rooms. Has been a popular boarding house with Summer Visitors the past 15 years. Address:

MRS. MARY T. RICH,

Wytheville, Virginia.

GLENBROOK.

Large and commodious dwelling, beautifully situated in grove. Ample playgrounds, beautiful walks all around, spring and cistern. Within ten or fifteen minutes walk of Post Office, Fountain, and Main Street. Everything will be done to make it an attractive and pleasant summer retreat.

TERMS:—$25.00 per month; $7.00 per week; children and nurses half price. Special rates to families, made known on application. Address

P. O. Box 54. THOS. C. MILLER.

ADVERTISEMENTS.

SUMMER BOARDERS WANTED.

Large grounds, good shade and walks, fine air, pleasant rooms, commanding view, retired situation.   Address

MRS. ELLEN C. CALDWELL.

MRS. E. A. OBENCHAIN'S
BOARDING HOUSE,
MONROE STREET,
WYTHEVILLE, VIRGINIA.

Can accommodate Sixteen Boarders. Large front yard, well shaded. Convenient to all Churches.

WYTHEVILLE MALE ACADEMY,
(MILITARY.)

Session 1887–8 Commences September 7, 1887.

Full Corps of Instructors. Boarding department under the supervision of the principal.

TUITION:—

English course, per session of 40 weeks $40.00
Classical   "   "   "   "   "   " 50.00
French and German, ... 10.00

For further particulars apply to

A. A. CAMPBELL, A. M.,
WYTHEVILLE, VIRGINIA.

ADVERTISEMENTS.

HANCOCK HOUSE,

CORNER OF MAIN AND FOURTH STREETS,

WYTHEVILLE, VIRGINIA.

L. D. HANCOCK, Proprietor.

———•———

This House is open for reception of Guests, the Proprietor will be pleased to meet and accommodate all who choose to call on him. He promises polite attention, and as good fare as the market affords.

Two large sample rooms for commercial travellers. Good Livery Stable on lot.

TELEGRAPH OFFICE IN HOTEL.

April, 1887.

WESTERN HOTEL.

R. K. SHORES, Proprietor.

On Main Street and within 100 yards of Chalybeate Fountain.

Terms:—Board per day . . . . $ 1.00 to $ 1.50
      "   " week 5.00
      "   " month . . . . . . 15.00 to 25.00

Governed according to rooms occupied. Every necessary attention to make quests comfortable.

BOARDING HOUSE,

EAST END OF MAIN ST.

NEW HOUSE AND NEW ROOMS.

Terms:—$1.00 per day; $25.00 per month. Half price for Children and Servants. Address:

MRS. S. S. CROCKETT,

Wytheville, Virginia.

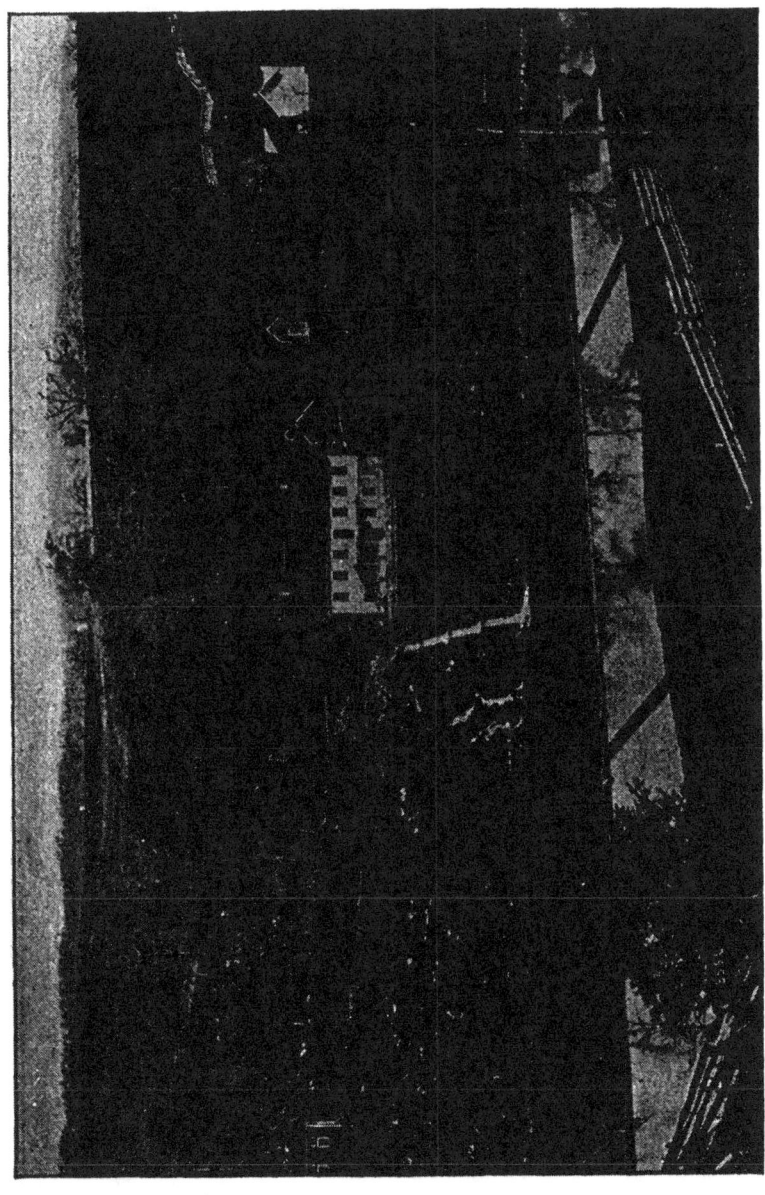

Railroad view of the U. S. FISH HATCHERY. Located 3 miles from Wytheville.

ADVERTISEMENTS.

PLUMER MEMORIAL FEMALE COLLEGE,
WYTHEVILLE, VIRGINIA.

W. S. PLUMER, D. D., LL. D.

Next Session Begins September 15, 1887.

REV. S. R. PRESTON, M. A., PRESIDENT.

Assisted by an Excellent Corps of Teachers.

Board, fuel, light, &c., with Collegiate course, including Latin, Calisthenics, Book-keeping and Vocal Music in class, $168. FOR ENTIRE SCHOOL YEAR.

Art, Music, German, French and Elocution THOROUGHLY taught.

Unusual advantages in French and German—the teacher is a native of Holland.

Location, Climate, Surroundings, all combine to make a delightful SCHOOL-HOME for girls.

Send for Catalogue to the President,

REV. S. R. PRESTON,
Wytheville, Virginia.

ADVERTISEMENTS.

WYTHEVILLE SEMINARY.

This institution for young ladies and little girls will begin its Second Session on the 15th of September, 1887, with a full Corps of competent teachers.

Modern Languages by a native. Special attention given to Music.

For further particulars, address

MRS. THOS. R. DEW,
Wytheville, Virginia.

MRS. B. B. SHORTT,

Wytheville, Virginia.

MILLINARY AND LADIES' NOTIONS,

JEWELRY AND FANCY GOODS,

EMBROIDERY STAMPING A SPECIALTY,

BUTTERICK'S FASHION PATTERNS,

HAIR AND HAIR GOODS,

Rubber Printing Business and Name Stamps, Stencils, Key Checks, &c.

THE BEST SEWING MACHINES.

WM. H. NEIGHBORS,
THE LEADING JEWELER,
WYTHEVILLE, VIRGINIA.

DEALER IN

Fine Watches, Jewelry, Silver and Plated Ware, Clocks, Spectacles, Eye Glasses and Optical Goods.

WATCH REPARING A SPECIALTY.

Opposite Farmers' Bank.

ADVERTISEMENTS.

COVE LITHIA WATER.

NATURE'S SPECIFIC REMEDY FOR

GRAVEL, AFFECTIONS OF THE KIDNEYS AND BLADDER, RHEUMATISM, DISORDERED STOMACH, IMPAIRED DIGESTION AND DISEASES PECULIAR TO FEMALES.

The spring from which this water is obtained is situated seven miles from Wytheville in Crockett's Cove.

Board can be had at the beautiful country home of Mr. Wm. G. Crockett, who lives near the spring, at Twenty Dollars per month, by those who prefer to use the water from the Spring.

It is kept for sale at the drug stores in Wytheville, and is shipped in cases of 1 doz. half-gallon bottles to all parts of the country for $4.00 per case, delivered on cars at Wytheville.

Send for pamphlet, giving testimonials of the wonderful curative power of the water.

CROCKETT & THOMAS,
Proprietors.

P. O. Box 47.
WYTHEVILLE, VIRGINIA.

From Photo. by Walter Noel.

CROCKETT'S FALLS.
One mile South from Wytheville.

ADVERTISEMENTS.

R. L. POAGE & CO.,
DEALERS IN
Drugs, Medicines and Chemicals,

Perfumery, Soaps, Combs and Brushes, Trusses, Supporters, Shoulder Braces, Fancy and Toilet Articles, Kerosene Oil, Lamps and Chimneys.

Glass, Putty, Paints, Oils, Varnishes and Dye Stuffs,

☞ Prescriptions Carefully Compounded at ALL hours. ☜

WYTHEVILLE, VIRGINIA.

H. J. HEUSER & CO.,

REGISTERED PHARMACISTS,

AND DEALERS IN

STATIONERY, PAINTS, OILS, ETC.

WYTHEVILLE, VIRGINIA.

ADVERTISEMENTS.

AUMANN'S DRUG STORE,

MAIN STREET,
WYTHEVILLE, VIRGINIA.

Full Line of Pure Drugs and Medicines,

Toilet Articles, Perfumery, Cigars and Tobacco, Paints and Oils, etc., Constantly on hand.

SODA AND MINERAL WATERS.

Especial attention is called to the COVE LITHIA WATER, and that remarkable healing and alterative water—the BROMINE-ARSENIC, descriptive pamphlets of which will be furnished on application. Respectfully,

JAMES AUMANN, M. D.

W. A. JOHNSTON'S

The Leading Photograph Gallery

Of the South-west, and for the production of Fine Photographic work, Equal to any in the State.

SOUTHERN VISITORS

And all others visiting Wytheville, wishing any work in the Photographic line, will find they will be given entire satisfaction at W. A. JOHNSTON'S PHOTOGRAPH GALLERY.

MAIN STREET,
WYTHEVILLE, VIRGINIA.

ADVERTISEMENTS.

STERN BROTHERS,
ONE PRICE CLOTHIERS,
HATTERS, AND GENTS' FURNISHERS
(SPECIALTIES.)

FINE CLOTHING, CUFFS, GOLD AND
SILVER SHIRTS, COLLARS AND NOBBY
NECKWEAR, TRUNKS, VALISES AND UMBRELLAS

MAIN ST. OPPOSITE POST OFFICE.

WYTHEVILLE, VIRGINIA.

☞ Clothing made to order—A FIT GUARANTEED. ☜

HEUSER BROTHERS,
BOOKS, JEWELRY, WATCHES,
Clocks, Stationery, Artists' Materials,
Wall-paper, Frames, Fancy Goods, &c., &c.,
PIANOS, ORGANS.
☞ Fine Watch work a specialty. ☜

R. P. BLACKWELL.   W. E. THOMAS.

R. P. BLACKWELL & CO.
Dealers in and Manufacturers of
FINE BOOTS AND SHOES,
LEATHER AND FINDINGS.
WYTHEVILLE, VIRGINIA.

TERMS: Strictly Cash.

ADVERTISEMENTS.

MRS. C. RICHARDSON'S
MILLINERY AND NOTION STORE,
MAIN STREET,
WYTHEVILLE, VIRGINIA.

A large stock of the latest styles of Millinery and Ladies' Notions kept for sale, at the lowest prices. Call and examine.

MRS. R. D. ROSENHEIM,
MILLINERY AND LADIES' NOTIONS,
COR. MAIN AND FIRST STREET,
Wytheville, Virginia.

Dealer in the latest styles of Ladies Hats, Bonnets, Fancy Articles and Underwear.

S. F. EWALD,

DEALER IN

Boots, Shoes, Hats, Trunks and Valises,

LADIES', MISSES' AND CHILDREN'S
FINE SHOES A SPECIALTY.

ADVERTISEMENTS.

GREEN & GIBBONEY,

DEALERS IN

DRY GOODS, NOTIONS, CLOTHING,

HATS, BOOTS AND SHOES,

Heavy and Fancy Groceries of all kinds.

G. S. BRUCE,

WHOLESALE AND RETAIL DEALER IN

GENERAL MERCHANDISE,

Salt, Plaster, Iron, Lime, Bacon, Lard, Butter, Chickens, Eggs, etc., etc.

WYTHEVILLE, VIRGINIA.

From Photo. by W. A. Johnston, View of MAIN STREET, December 8th, 1885. Snow fell to the depth of 24 inches on a level. An unprecedented occurrence in the history of the town.

ADVERTISEMENTS.

W. H. SPILLER,

DEALER IN

DRY GOODS, NOTIONS,

Gents' Furnishing Goods,

Boots, Shoes, Hats,

Wooden and Willow-ware,

Queensware, Groceries, &c.

Carpets, Oil Cloths, &c., &c.

Telephone No. 21.

WYTHEVILLE, VIRGINIA.

FRANK & COMPANY,
LEADING CLOTHIERS
AND GENTS' FURNISHERS,

UNDER SEXTON'S HALL,

WYTHEVILLE, VIRGINIA.

☞ Merchant Tailoring a specialty.

J. B. BARRETT & CO.,
DEALERS IN REAL ESTATE,

Have on hands several very valuable properties for sale, Iron, Coal, Lead and Zinc ore. Also Timbered land and farm.

☞ Mineral land a specialty. ☜

Address: Wytheville, Wythe County, Virginia.

ADVERTISEMENTS.

E. McG. PHELPS,

DEALER IN

Dry Goods, Notions, Boots, Shoes and FAMILY GROCERIES,

☞Rogers Bros.' Silverware, Watches and Jewelry a specialty.

WYTHEVILLE, VIRGINIA.

LUTHER D. HARRISON,

General Auctioneer & Commission Merchant,

COR. MAIN AND FIRST STREETS.

WYTHEVILLE, VIRGINIA,

Opposite Farmers' Bank of South-west Virginia,

Attends to all Sales of Real and Personal Property—Solicits Consignments—Quick Sales and Prompt returns—Full Lines of Goods always on hand—Auction Sales every Saturday and on Court days opposite Court-House.

From Photo. by W. A. Johnston.

ST. MARY'S ROMAN CATHOLIC CHURCH, Wytheville.

ADVERTISEMENTS.

MAUPIN & BRUCE,
DEALERS IN
Hardware, Stoves, Agricultural Implements,
PAINTS, OILS AND VARNISHES.

AGENTS FOR

Champion Mowers, Reapers, Binders and Grain Drills, Superior Pumps,

Geiser Manufacturing Co.'s Engines, Saw Mills, and Threshers.

WYTHEVILLE, VIRGINIA.

JOSEPH EWALD,
MAIN STREET,
WYTHEVILLE, VIRGINIA,
DEALER IN
GENERAL HARDWARE,
Agricultural Implements, House Furnishing Goods, Stoves, &c., &c.

C P. McWane,   N. L. Look,
H. E. McWane,   C. F. Lincoln.

C. P. McWANE & CO.,
FOUNDERS, MACHINISTS,
AND MANUFACTURERS OF

Chilled Plows, Hill-side Plows, Saw Mills, Water Wheels, Cider Mills, Steam Cutters, Corn Shellers, &c.

WYTHEVILLE, VIRGINIA.

ADVERTISEMENTS.

CLARK, BLESSING & CO.,
SAW AND PLAINING MILL,

Manufacture Tobacco Box Shooks, Staves, Bands, Barrel Hoops, Dimension Stuff for furniture, Agricultural Machinery, Wagons, Plow Beams, &c., &.

AND OWNERS AND PROPRIETORS OF

Clark's Alum Springs ot Clark's Summit

On the Norfolk and Western Railroad, which is highly recommended for diseases of the skin and Scrofula, Chronic Diarrhœa, Dysentery, Catarrh of the stomach and intestines, Diabetes Insipidus, Lead Colic and Hemorrhages.

Kept for sale at drug stores in Wytheville and shipped to all parts of the Country in cases of 1 doz. half gallon bottles at $3.50 per case, delivered on cars.

P. O. Box 47.   Address:
WYTHEVILLE, VIRGINIA.

WALTER NOEL'S
NEW PHOTOGRAPH GALLERY,

EAST END MAIN ST.
WYTHEVILLE, VIRGINIA.

☞ Reception room on first floor — High-Class work only. ☚

G. T. BEUCHLER,
BAKER AND CONFECTIONER,

Dealer in

Fancy Groceries, Cigars and Tobacco.

MAIN STREET,
WYTHEVILLE, VIRGINIA.

ADVERTISEMENTS.

J. F. SCOTT,

OPP. FARMERS' BANK.
WYTHEVILLE, VIRGINIA.

GENERAL CONFECTIONERY,

Finest Candies always on hand, Cigars, Tobacco, and Tropical Fruits of all kinds.

E. H. BAILY,

Fine Cigars, AGENCY FOR & Smokers
Tobaccos TANSILL'S PUNCH 5¢ Articles,

Tropical Fruits and Choice Confectioneries.

Two doors East of Post Office,
WYTHEVILLE, VIRGINIA.

L. S. IRVINE & CO.,

DEALERS IN

Live Stock and Fresh Meats.

CREGER & CLIFT,

DEALERS IN

First-Class Fresh Meats.

ADVERTISEMENTS.

Jno. H. Ewald.   A. R Ewald.

J. H. EWALD & BRO.

Manufacturers and Dealers in

Leather, Saddles, Harness,

BOOTS, SHOES, SADDLERY-HARDWARE AND SHOE-FINDINGS.

EWALD BLOCK, MAIN STREET,

WYTHEVILLE, VIRGINIA.

Paid up Capital $100,000.

ISAAC J. LEFTWICK, President.   V. C. HUFF, Cashier.

Farmers' Bank of South-west Virginia,

WYTHEVILLE, VIRGINIA.

Organized in 1873.

Particular attention given to collections and correspondence.

CORRESPONDENTS AND REFERENCE.

Hanover National Bank, New York.
National Exchange Bank, Baltimore.
Planters' National Bank, Richmond, Virginia.
People's National Bank, Lynchburg, Virginia.

ADVERTISEMENTS.

Paid up Capital $50,000.

GEO. R. DUNN,
President.

G. S. BRUCE,
Vice-President.

JNO. G. BROWN,
Cashier.

BANK OF WYTHEVILLE,

WYTHEVILLE, VIRGINIA.

Organized in 1882.

CORRESPONDENTS AND REFERENCE.

Kountze Bros., New York.
J. J. Nicholson & Sons, Baltimore.
State Bank of Virginia, Richmond.
National Exchange Bank, Lynchburg.

Established in 1862.

WYTHEVILLE DISPATCH,

F. H. TERRY, Editor and Owner.

With over Two Thousand Readers.

Wytheville, Virginia, is the central and largest town in a radious of seventy miles of the wealthiest section of the State, and opens to the City Merchant and Manufacturer a valuable market for both sale and purchase; it being the trading point of the four Counties of Wythe, Bland, Grayson and Carroll, and the principal summer resort of the South-west.

ADVERTISEMENTS.

GEO. S. SEXTON & CO.,
DEALERS IN

Family Groceries, Agricultural Implements,

Frick & Co.'s Steam Engines and Saw Mills, Superior Grain Drills, Buckeye Mowers and Reapers, Fertilizers, William Penn Harrows, New Home Sewing Machines, &c.

☞Country Produce Bought and Sold.☜

Store rooms in "Sexton's Block."

WYTHEVILLE, VIRGINIA.

WOLFENDEN BROTHERS,
DEALERS IN

Confectionery, Fruits, Family Groceries,

China and Glassware, Toys, Fancy Articles, Fine Jewelry and Silverware.

☞One door East of the 4th Avenue Hotel.☜

WYTHEVILLE, VIRGINIA.

TOPHAM BROTHERS,
DEALERS IN

General Merchandise and Produce,

WYTHEVILLE, VIRGINIA.

From Photo. by W. A. Johnston. FOURTH (or "Boyd") AVENUE. A new Street.

ADVERTISEMENTS.

FOOT & JOHNSON,
BUILDERS OF
Fine Carriages and Wagons,
MAIN STREET,
WYTHEVILLE, VIRGINIA.

Write for Catalogue and prices before buying.

SULT SHRADER & CO.,
WYTHEVILLE, VIRGINIA.
Manufacturers of all kinds of
Carriages, Buggies, Spring & Farm Wagons,
THE MORRISON SPRING BUGGY A SPECIALTY.

Repairing done on short notice. Prompt attention given to all orders—Satisfaction guaranteed.
Shops on Corner of First and Monroe Streets.

W. W. RICH & SON,
Manufacturers and Dealers in
Furniture, Chairs, and Mattresses,
WYTHEVILLE, VIRGINIA.

A full stock kept on hand at their Ware-Rooms. Lumber of all kinds dressed, and for sale at their Factory.

UNDERTAKING:—Prompt personal attention paid to all orders, on the shortest notice.

MAPLE CASCADE.

From Photo. by W. J. Johnston.

ADVERTISEMENTS.

THOMAS P. WAPPETT,
GROCER,
MAIN STREET,
WYTHEVILLE, VIRGINIA,

Keeps on hand a choice stock of Groceries and Canned Goods, Sole Leather, Calf-skins, Nails, Liverpool and Virginia Salt, Landreth's Garden Seeds in bulk and in papers.

WYTHEVILLE MARBLE WORKS,
REPASS, CROSBY & DAVIS, Proprietors.
WYTHEVILLE, VIRGINIA,
Dealers in and Manufacturers of

Granite Monuments, Iron Fencing and all kinds of
CEMETERY WORK.
Done on short notice. A large assortment of work always on hand. Particular attention given to orders from a distance.

J. C. SEXTON,
Manufacturer of all kinds of

Saddles, Especially Fine Letort's Shafto
Somerset and Sexton's Improved Ladies' Saddles,
Carriage and Wagon Harness, Bridles and Collars,
MAIN STREET,
WYTHEVILLE, VIRGINIA.

VIEWS.
Persons desiring Views of Wytheville and vicinity, can obtain the same by applying at W. A. Johnston's Photograph Gallery, Wytheville, Va.

ADVERTISEMENTS.

J. HAL. GIBBONEY & CO.,
Insurance Agents, Undertakers & Dealers in Furniture,
House-Furnishing Goods, Bedding, Carpets, Sewing Machines, &c.

WYTHEVILLE, VIRGINIA.

Large stock of fine and cheap Wood Coffins, Cloth Caskets, Metallic Cases, Robes, &c., at the lowest prices, and prompt personal attention day or night.
Telephone: Store, No. 28, dwelling No. 27.

C. N. OTEY,
BILLIARD HALL,
McGavock's Corner,

WYTHEVILLE, VIRGINIA.

A. D. HATCHER,
LIVERY STABLE,
One square from Fourth Avenue Hotel and Hancock House.

Will furnish at all times Fine Carriage, Buggy and Hack Teams and Saddle Horses at reasonable prices. The patronage of visitors is specially solicited.
Telephone communication with Hotels and Boarding Houses.

TRIGG & JOHNSON,
OMNIBUS LINE,
To and from Depot. Meet all trains and accommodate all travel in and about the City.

Telephone call, No. 23.

ADVERTISEMENTS.

E. DYER,
MERCHANT TAILOR,
MAIN STREET,
WYTHEVILLE, VIRGINIA.

Will furnish suits; or make and trim, or make, where the goods are furnished by the customer. And in order to give work to sewing women, will cut common suits for 50 cents, fine suits $1.00 as heretofore.

☞A large line of samples always on hand.☜

Wm. Farmer, M. D., D. D. S.   Walter Stuart, D. D. S.

FARMER & STUART,
DENTISTS,
WYTHEVILLE, VIRGINIA.

(Nitrous Oxide Gas and other painless processes for extracting, &c.)   Telephone No. 22.

CHAS. W. GLEAVES, A. M., M. D.
Office at Residence,
FOURTH AVENUE.

M. M. CALDWELL,
Attorney at Law and Notary Public,
WYTHEVILLE, VIRGINIA.

All legal business attended to with promptness and fidelity.

ADVERTISEMENTS.

WM. TERRY,
ATTORNEY AT LAW,
WYTHEVILLE, VIRGINIA.

F. S. BLAIR,
(Late Attorney-General of Virginia)

Has Law Offices at Wytheville, Virginia.

Where he will attend to all business confided to his care in the several Courts, State and Federal, of Virginia, and in the Supreme Court of the United States.

H. D. C. BUFORD,
ATTORNEY AT LAW,

Will practise in the Courts of Wythe, Grayson and Bland.
McGavock Building,
WYTHEVILLE, VIRGINIA.

BEN. W. TERRY,
ATTORNEY AT LAW AND NOTARY PUBLIC,
Wytheville, Virginia.

ADVERTISEMENTS.

CALLAGHAN & YATES,
Manufacturers and Wholesale Dealers in

Best Full Roller Flour, Meal, Mill-Feed and Wool, Woolen Goods, Yarn, and General Merchandise,

Kent's Mills, Virginia.

CHURCH DIRECTORY.

METHODIST EPISCOPAL CHURCH (SOUTH),
CHURCH STREET,
REV. K. C. ATKINS, PASTOR.

PRESBYTERIAN CHURCH,
CHURCH STREET,
REV. J. I. VANCE, PASTOR.

ST. JOHN'S EPISCOPAL CHURCH,
EAST MAIN STREET,
REV. MERCER P. LOGAN, PASTOR.

LUTHERAN CHURCH,
WEST MAIN STREET,
REV. ALEX. PHILLIPPI, PASTOR.

CHRISTIAN CHURCH,
WEST MAIN STREET,
REV. F. F. BULLARD, PASTOR.

ST. MARY'S ROMAN CATHOLIC CHURCH,
EAST MONROE STREET,
REV. JOHN McBRIDE, PASTOR.

MISSIONARY BAPTIST CHURCH,
CHURCH STREET,
REV. A. J. BOLT, PASTOR.

NYE LITHIA SPRINGS,
WYTHEVILLE, VA.

On the Norfolk & Western railroad, with an elevation of 2,360 feet above the sea level, and a mean temperature of 52 degrees, giving one of the healthiest resorts from all the Malarial and Febrile diseases of the lowlands of the United States. Of easy access; one-half a mile from the city, one-fourth from the newly laid off city of Newberry, on the Meadam road, a pleasant walk or drive, surrounded by a beautiful orignaal oak grove, where a commodious hotel will soon be erected for the accommodation of those seeking pleasure as well as health.

Unsurpassed for health and scenery, recreation and pleasure

For the purity and strength of the water, the first in the United States.

FOR ALL

Sick Headache and Morning Sickness, Diseases of the Stomach, either in Gestation or from Indigestion, Kidneys, Bladder, Gout, Rheumatism, Insomnia, Uric Acid Deposit or Brickdust in the Urine, Hemorrhage or Blood in the Urine, Gravel, Nervousness of Brain Workers, Acute and Chronic Bright's Disease, Diabetes, Typhoid and other Fevers.

Reproduced through the courtesy of a Friend.

No person that ever used it but praise it, neither will any one after trying it ever use any other mineral water but the Nye Lithia Springs Water, at Wytheville, Va.

Write a postal card for any information desired, or come to the Springs and see for yourself, and drink fresh from the ever-flowing, health-giving fountain. If you can not come, get the water from your wholesale druggist or order direct from the Springs. Special freight rates to all, by the case or car load lot. Try it if you are suffering with disease.

Comparative statistics of various mineral springs will also be furnished, showing the lightness and pureness of the Nye Lithia Springs Water, with full analysis, duplicated, enough to satisfy the most sceptical, on request.

Any person suffering with serious chronic disease, and too poor to buy the water, upon satisfactory evidence of the fact, it will be furnished them at the cost of vessels.

The number of persons who have used the water for diseases of the stomach, kidneys, bladder and various other disorders, are too numerous to mention, much less than to burden the reader seeking information for restoration to health, with other testimonials. If desired, any additional information will be given on application.

Chlorosis in young ladies, so often seen at the beginning of womanhood, Constipation, Neuralgia, Anemia, Torpid Liver, Swelled Feet, Dropsy, the BEST Remedy.

THE NYE LITHIA SPRINGS.

These Springs were used by their ancestors more than half a century ago for rheumatism. The remains of Indian village relics within fifty yards indicate they, too, had knowledge of its medicinal virtues, and doubtless used it for like diseases as their white brethren have done in more recent years.

MINERAL SPRINGS.

As mineral springs contain restoratives given forth from nature's laboratory, held in solution in pure Water, as in the NYE LITHIA Springs, containing more Lithia, the great uric acid solvent, than any other spring in the United States or the world now known, in proportion to its solid contents, and less deleterious matter than any other water put upon the market. Many waters holding in solution so much inorganic matter, to irritate the stomach or congested kidneys, thereby increasing the tendency to Bright's disease and gravel, either in the kidney or the bladder, instead of being a solvent for the stone, as is the case with the NYE LITHIA SPRINGS WATER.

LITHIA

Has long been known as a solvent for gravel in the bladder, or that condition known as sand in the urine. Its name derived from a Greek word signifying a solvent for a stone, hence its indication and use as a remedial agent in all affections of the bladder, such as gravel, with acute and chronic irritation or inflammation of its mucus membrane, caused often by the uric acid filtering through the kidneys forming stone with all its accompanying ills, such as Ischuria and Dysuria, with death ultimately curling the sufferings of the person affected, unless this condition of the system be corrected. This uric acid in the system, going through the kidneys into the bladder, forming a sediment, often in the kidneys—nephritic calculi—or irritating them to such an extent that acute and chronic Bright's disease results, is frequently complicated with hemorrhage. Then every source will be sought for a cure when too late; the kidneys are disorganized, and death ends the scene and sufferings.

This troublesome affection in the majority, in fact in all instances, is owing to the undissolved uric acid and urate of sodium, in all of which diseases the free use of the NYE LITHIA SPRINGS WATER will fulfil the indication of the dilution and neutralization of this acid and its compounds.

The use of the NYE LITHIA SPRINGS WATER meets the required treatment of the system as long ago pointed out by that eminent French surgeon, Petit, and the greatest of English pathologists, Garrod, in all arthritic diseases. The carbonate, particularly shown by the experiment of Dr. Alexander Ure, of London, the most celebrated chemist of modern times, has power to dissolve the gouty deposit, as also that of gravel in the bladder. Why not prevent its formation?

In the rheumatic and gouty condition of the stomach, as well as that of the convivial a potu, with acidity and fermentation, and all the sufferings of indigestion resulting, headache, nervous prostration and insomnia, the free use of the NYE LITHIA SPRINGS WATER before, at and after meals will give more relief than any known mineral water or remedy. Try it.

Any one inclined to gravel indicated by a pink stain left in the urinal after the urine has been thrown out, will find it disappear and prevented by drinking a glass of the NYE LITHIA SPRINGS WATER before or soon after each meal and at bed time, thus avoiding gravel with all its horrors.

FOR NERVOUSNESS.

It is especially adapted to those cases of nervous excitement which follow nerve exhaustion, nervous irritation and insomnia from over work, or in all nervous irritation that follows starved nerve conditions in Brain workers. In all cases of over work of the nervous system followed by a long train of symptoms of nervous prostration, uric acid or brick dust sediment in the urine, the NYE LITHIA SPRINGS WATER, upon the whole, is one of the best remedies known.

Its field of remedial influence is a wide one, and it should be better known and more often used by those suffering with diseases relating to the organs of the system having to carry off the waste of the tissues, which if neglected, as is too often the case, result in those diseases of the kidneys—Bright's—and the blad-

having percolated through any marshy district or lowlands, but surrounded by majestic mountain scenery. *No malaria ever occurred in this pure mountain air.*

Those seeking health or recreation can find their heart's desire by visiting the

NYE LITHIA SPRINGS,

At Wytheville, Va.

HOW TO USE IT.

The manner of using the NYE LITHIA WATER is to be determined by the tolerance of the stomach. Those with troubles of this organ are to take a glass on arising, half an hour before eating, and at all regular meals. It may be taken at any time during the day.

For insomnia, a large glass taken warm or hot before retiring, or before night. With some it acts well to take it cold and at the principal meals, and a glass at bed time.

For uric acid, gout or rheumatism, to be used freely, several glasses during the day, avoiding all forms of alcoholic beverages and highly seasoned or spiced food.

For Bright's disease of the kidneys and of the bladder, the NYE LITHIA SPRINGS WATER to be used only, not changing for water having a large amount of matter in solution.

For brick dust sediment, gravel, and in all abnormal conditions of the urine, the Water to be taken often and till all deposit disappears and the normal condition of the organs are resumed.

For diabetes and other diseases, further in-

---

disease of the kidneys, producing dark patches over the body, but more often on the face and hands with tan, the Nye Lithia Springs Water, taken freely several times a day, and an occasional bath to the face and discolorations, will restore the skin to its original soft, healthy condition, better than any cosmetic known.

For bronzing of the skin, due to chronic malarial poisoning of the system, the water will prove an invaluable remedy, restoring the functions to their wonted vigor and the skin to healthy action, dissolving the deposited pigment, enabling the circulation to carry it off.

THE CHALYBEATE SPRING.

A Chalybeate Spring by the side of the high grade LITHIA SPRINGS, containing the most essential element in restoring the chlorotic female, living in the smoke-laden, contaminated atmosphere of a city life, where the blood globules are deficient in their most essential health giving constituent, haematosin, the use of this and the Lithia Water, containing as they do the peroxide of iron, as it comes forth from nature's labratory, will bring the bloom of health to the cheeks of the chlorotic female deprived of the pure water and atmosphere, as the city mortality reports bear record of the many thousand young ladies that have gone into premature decline simply for the want of such elements as this water supplies. With the pure atmosphere of this altitude they can here find the most desirable boon, pure air and water, for the restoration to health, the LITHIA WATERS never

---

der that make life a miserable burden every year to many thousand persons.

AS AN APPETIZER.

A glass of the Water on arising in the morning, as an appetizer and promoter of digestion when the stomach has long suffered from *atonic*, rheumatic or gouty acidity, will give more relief than any other remedy.

LADIES

Suffering with Morning Sickness, and many other nervous disorders peculiar to their system during gestation, often with impaired digestion, acidity of the stomach, flatulency, general debility and uterine troubles, reflecting irritation to the bladder, producing one of the most distressing of all their affections, Dysuria, will find the NYE LITHIA SPRINGS WATER used freely, gives relief to these their most grievous annoyances whilst in this state as well as that of maternity.

Sick headache and neuralgia, that annoy most all ladies, more particularly while *enceinte*, the NYE LITHIA SPRINGS WATER has proved a *sine qua non*, as well as for so many ills to which their sex is heir, because of their peculiar physiological construction of their system and its functions during this period of their most important career in life.

Verbum sat sapienti in this connection.

FOR THE COMPLEXION, ETC.

For beautifying the complexion and clearing it of pimples and the skin of bronzing or sallowness, often caused by derangement of the stomach and torpid liver, whilst Addison's

formation us to the use of the WATER and diet will be furnished by the Resident Physician free on application. The NYE LITHIA SPRINGS WATER should be used to the exclusion of all others.

Consult the reports of those who have used the Water and been cured of disease.

SHIPPING.

In cases or carboys, at a reasonable price, within the reach of all who may not be able to visit the Springs.

The NYE LITHIA SPRINGS WATER has been kept for months without any deterioration or deposit of sediment, which makes it the more desirable for persons too feeble to travel, or unable to go to the Springs for the pure air surrounding them. They can get and use it, however, at their own homes in the cities, the more necessary particularly in the heated season, instead of the water usually furnished them from rivers filled with sewage and the bacteria of towns and cities along their banks, or if from wells, with all the seep into the alluvial soil and into the water, producing Typhoid Fever and all kindred diseases and Tuberculosis. This has recently been pointed out and elucidated by the celebrated Dr. Koch, of Berlin, as well as our own Dr. Samuel G. Dixon, of Brooklyn, and other eminent scientists, who with one accord place the cause of these and all other zymotic diseases in foul drinking water, thus the bacteria readily entering the circulation, disorganizing the blood globules and lodging in the tissues, produce decay and death instead of repair of the grand mechanism of the human system.

BRIGHT'S AND OTHER DISEASE CAUSES!

Statistics of the death rate of Bright's disease of the Kidneys in the city of New York, tabulated from the report of the Health Officers for the third week in October, 1890:

Total deaths from all diseases......,601.
From Bright's Disease............. 45.
Fourth week, ending October 31, 1890:
Deaths from all causes........... 602.
From Bright's Disease............. 56.

This being a fair showing for the contaminated water and atmosphere of a city life in the great metropolis of this country. In the *World's* issue for August 27th, 1891, will be found an account of "drinking from sewers," or the condition of the water supply to that city. A detailed report of President Wilson and Dr. Louis Balch, the Secretary of the Board of Health, may be read with profit.

How much better is it for any other city, supplied, as most are, from rivers, not even an attempt at filtering the water to clear it of the mud usually in it, much less the bacteria in it? Omnus casua mortis!

CERTIFICATES FROM TRIAL.

THOSE OF PHYSICIANS.

Dr. W. P. Haller, for many years an eminent physician of Wytheville:

I have been using water out of the NYE LITHIA SPRINGS for more than forty years. I never pass without drinking it, nor did I even before it was known to contain Lithia. I regard it as the best and softest water in Wythe county. A person can drink large draughts without any discomfort to the stomach. Its action upon the kidneys is direct and free. I consider it one of the most efficient waters in all that class of diseases tending to nervous exhaustion and gravel, either in the kidneys or bladder. In troubles of the stomach, either from indigestion or Morning Sickness, it is the best remedy. I have had a bottle in my house for sixteen months to test its purity, without any deterioration or deposit of sediment, showing it to be one of the purest waters known. I can, therefore, without hesitation, recommend it to the ladies as one especially useful for their many nervous troubles and irregularities. My wife used it with great satisfaction.

I do not hesitate to say that any one who may use it will likewise testify to its purity and curative virtues.

W. P. HALLER, M. D.

October 12th, 1890.

Of Col. R. E. Withers, M. D., ex-U. S. Senator from Virginia and ex-U. S. Minister to China.

At the request of Dr. Nye, I take pleasure in stating that the water from his Lithia Springs has been used freely for the past year or more by different members of my family, and has proved very efficacious in the relief of rheumatic and gouty affections, kidney and bladder troubles, and other complaints growing out of an excess of uric acid.

The analysis of the water shows it to be the most valuable and the strongest Lithia Water known, and I have no doubt of its efficacy in

the treatment of all the diseases for which Lithia Waters are usually found so advantageous. R. E. WITHERS, M. D.
Wytheville, Va., June 24th, 1891.

WYTHEVILLE, VA., June 18th, 1891.
I certify that I have prescribed the NYE LITHIA SPRINGS WATER in cases of congestion of the kidneys, complicated with hemorrhage, and in indigestion of ladies, with prompt benefit and relief. I take pleasure in recommending it as being a very pure and a high grade mineral water for such diseases, as well as nervous prostration, gravel and rheumatism, etc.
R. E. MOORE, M. D.

BRIGHT'S DISEASE

Of Dr. R. D. Huffard, Member of Virginia Medical Examining Board.

CHATHAM HILL, VA., July 7th, 1891.
DR. GEO. L. NYE:

Dear Sir: Yours of recent date is at hand. In reply will say that my experience with the NYE LITHIA SPRINGS WATER has been limited to two cases of Chronic Interstitial Nephritis (Bright's Disease), in which the urine contained respectively from 20 to 50 per cent. of albumen, and under the constant use of this water, the albumen has so completely disappeared that there remains at present but a trace. Indeed, in one case the patient was bordering on coma, and I had little hopes of giving him even temporary relief. Of course I did not rely on the water to the exclusion of other appropriate remedies, but think without

---

this water I would not have succeeded in giving them temporary respite from the ultimate results. I am confident from the results achieved in these two cases that the NYE LITHIA SPRINGS WATER will prove to be one of the best remedial agents in diseases of the kidneys and bladder, and that class of diseases depending on the uric acid diathesis, etc. I am yours very truly,
R. D. HUFFARD, M. D.

WYTHEVILLE, VA., June 16th, 1891.
I have used and prescribed the NYE LITHIA SPRINGS WATER with benefit. Judging from the analysis and the curative effects upon the many persons using it, I think it a valuable water, for the many troubles of the Stomach, Kidneys and Bladder, especially in the many forms of Gravel, more particularly the uric acid deposit in the urine. In Gout, acute and chronic Rheumatism, Typhoid and other Fevers, it will prove to be one of the most desirable remedial agents.
W. H. RIBLE, M. D.

WYTHEVILLE, VA., June 18th, 1891.
From the analysis of the NYE LITHIA SPRINGS WATER, I believe it to be a most excellent water for that class of diseases producing nervous exhaustion, irritation of the Stomach, Kidneys and Bladder, and contains more solvent for uric acid deposit or gravel than any other water.
C. W. GLEAVES, A. M., M. D.

Of Dr. W. H. Ribble, Jr., M. D.

WYTHEVILLE, VA., June 18th, 1891.
I have prescribed Water from the NYE LITHIA SPRINGS for the past two years, and fine it an excellent water in acid conditions of the Stomach, Rheumatic Gout, Kidney trouble, and all conditions dependent upon an excess of urea and uric acid in the system.
W. H. RIBBLE, JR., M. D.

WYTHEVILLE, VA., June 24th, 1891.
I have had no experience with the NYE LITHIA SPRINGS WATER, but basing an opinion upon the analysis furnished by distinguished chemists, I have no hesitation in saying that I believe the use of the Water will prove decidedly beneficial to all persons suffering from such troubles as are usually relieved by other similar waters.
V. C. HUFF, M. D.

Of Dr. Green, Member of Virginia Medical Examining Board.

Although I have had no personal experience in the use of the NYE LITHIA SPRINGS WATER, I have examined the analysis made by Prof. Dudley. Judging from the large amount of Lithium Carbonate contained in it, I think it would prove to be an excellent remedy for the treatment of the various affections in which this agent is indicated.

It is in REALITY a *Lithia Water*, which can not be truthfully said of many of the reputed waters of this class.
P. B. GREEN, M. D.

From Dr. Moore, late Surgeon in Confederate Army, and for thirty years a practicing physician.

Congestion of the Liver and Kidneys, with Bronzed Skin, relieved.

WYTHEVILLE, VA., Sept. 14th, 1891.

A lady patient from a Western State had been suffering with Congestion of the Liver and Kidneys from malarial influences for about three years, with a bronzed skin and general debility, accompanied with drowsy spells, often bordering on coma, from the urea retained in the circulation, when I directed her to use the water from the NYE LITHIA SPRINGS. After using the water for about three months she had but one attack, and that slight, during the time. Her skin soon cleared up and her general health so improved that she is like a new person. The liver and kidneys are now performing their work well, and I can truly say the action of this water in her case was wonderful.

R. E. MOORE, M. D.

Certificate of Dr. John M. Bailey, Receiver of the South Atlantic and Ohio R. R.

BRISTOL, TENN., June 15th, 1891.

Last winter I was greatly troubled with irritation in my bladder, having to get up several times to pass my urine during the night, with very uneasy and painful sensations extending to the surrounding organs. When I began the use of the NYE LITHIA SPRINGS WATER at Wytheville, Va., in less than forty-eight hours I experienced great relief, and in ten days I was entirely relieved, and have had no further trouble.   JOHN M. BAILEY.

Of Dr. S. R. Sayers, Surgeon in C. S. A. and a Director of S. W. L. Asylum.

WYTHEVILLE, VA., June 25th, 1891.

I have frequently prescribed the NYE LITHIA SPRINGS WATER with good results.

S. R. SAYERS, M. D.

Of Capt. F. S. Blair, ex-Attorney General of Virginia.

I have had occasion to use the NYE LITHIA SPRINGS WATER myself, and also members of my family, and cheerfully bear witness to its purity and medicinal virtues.

One of my sons had been afflicted with irritation of his bladder, his urine being thick and high colored. After using other mineral water for it without any relief, Dr. Sayers advised the use of the NYE LITHIA SPRINGS WATER. Prompt relief followed its use.

F. S. BLAIR.

LA GRIPPE AND COMPLICATIONS.

Certificate of Judge B. W. Lacy, Supreme Court of Appeals.

WYTHEVILLE, VA., July 31st, 1891

DR. GEO. L. NYE,

Dear Sir: I came to this place on the 10th of June last, still suffering from the effects of a severe attack of the Grip of unusual severity. A severe headache almost incapacitated me for work, and I had announced to my brethren that I would be compelled to give up all attempts at work. Dr. S. R. Sayers advised me to try the water from the NYE LITHIA SPRINGS, close by the town; I did so and used it freely and no other medicine. In a few hours I was relieved, and in a day or two began to grow strong again, and in one week I felt younger and stronger than I have for ten years. A friend from Richmond, Va., spending a few days here, in effort to shake off the effects of an attack like mine of Grip, complicated, in his case, with erysipelas, was induced to try the NYE LITHIA SPRINGS WATER, and in two or three days seemed to be rejuvenated, and returned to his business entirely restored to health.

Very truly yours,
B. W. LACY

Uric Acid Deposit.

Of Gen. James A. Walker, ex-Lieutenant Governor of Virginia.

I hereby certify that I used the NYE LITHIA SPRINGS WATER for the removal of a deposit of brick dust sediment in my urine. After using it for about ten days or two weeks the deposit entirely disappeared.

JAMES A. WALKER.

For Gravel and Kidney Trouble, with Hemorrhage, or Blood in the Urine.

MAX MEADOWS, VA., Aug. 19th, 1891.

Some five months ago I was attacked with Nephritic Calculi and suffered intense pain; my urine was loaded with blood and coloring matter, being very dark. Although attended by my physician, I continued to suffer for some weeks without improvement. I went to Wytheville to consult Dr. S. R. Sayers, and he advised me to use the water from the Nye Lithia Springs freely; that it would do me more good than any other medicine I could use. I drank copiously from the spring on my way up and on my return. It acted freely and promptly. I took some of the water home with me, and in two days I experienced great relief; my urine cleared up, and in three weeks I was cured. Since I began the use of the water I have passed five gravel. My general health is very good, I am free from pain and suffering, my urine has remained clear since the first use of the water. I am happy to state the use of the water fulfilled all that Dr. Sayers recommended it for, and what its action would be in my case, after having used medicines before without any relief or benefit.

JOHN H. DANNER.

For Gravel and Irritation of the Bladder, with Blood in the Urine.

WYTHEVILLE, VA., Sept. 4th, 1891.

I had been suffering for some time with Gravel, with great irritation of my bladder. My urine being scant and high colored, caused me much pain to pass it, there being some blood in the discharges. When I went to Dr. S. R. Sayers for treatment he advised me to use the water from the Nye Lithia Springs. In a day or two I experienced great relief. After using two gallons of the water I was cured entirely.

C. L. SCOTT.

For the Kidneys and Bladder—Passing Gravel from its use.

WYTHEVILLE, VA., Sept. 14, 1891.

I have been troubled more or less for two or three years with my kidneys and bladder, my urine being high colored. Last spring they gave me much pain and discomfort, when I began the use of the water from the Nye Lithia Springs, and did so for three or four weeks. Soon after using it I got easy and my urine cleared up. Whilst using the water I passed several gravel.

W. W. GRAHAM.

Nephritic Calculi, Etc., Etc.

DR. NYE: Having been a sufferer with nephritic calculi, and irritation of the kidneys and bladder resulting therefrom, after using the Nye Lithia Springs Water a few weeks I have been entirely relieved from all symptoms of the trouble named, and feel like a new man.

Very truly yours,
FRANK MYERS,
NEWBERN, N. C.

August 8th, 1891.

For Kidneys and Dysuria.
From Mr. W. W. Rich, manufacturer of and dealer in furniture.

WYTHEVILLE, VA., Sept. 14th, 1891.

I have been a sufferer with my kidneys for many years, my urine being high colored and diminished in amount, causing me much distress and an inability to pass it. After using the Water from the Nye Lithia Springs for several weeks, I received great relief, more than from remedies used for it, and I could pass my water freely from its use.

WM. W. RICH.

Congestion, with Hemorrhage from the Kidneys.

HANCOCK HOUSE, WYTHEVILLE, VA.,
September 4th, 1890.

When I came to Wytheville, on Aug. 22, I was suffering from hemorrhage from the kidneys, resulting from congestion. The discharges at every operation were very bloody, and continued so until I began the use of the water at the Nye Lithia Springs. I was here several days before I began the use of this water. After using the water two days the bloody discharge disappeared and my urine became clear as pure water and has continued so. I noticed a change for the better very soon after the first use of the water, and as before stated was relieved the second day. I never had anything to act so freely, quickly and pleasantly on my kidneys as this water.

B. J. KIMBRAUGH,
MEMPHIS, TENN.

Bright's Disease, with Hemorrhage, or Blood in the Urine.

I had been suffering with congestive nephritis, complicated with hematuria, for about five months, and having tried various remedies, under the direction of my physician, without any relief. By his advice I went to the NYE LITHIA SPRINGS at Wytheville, Va. In three or four days I called in Dr. S. R. Sayers, who advised me to continue the use of the Lithia Water. In a day or two I began to improve, my appetite and digestion became very good, and in two weeks all my trouble had completely disappeared. My general health has so much improved that I feel like a new person and can rest comfortably at night, which I could not do since the beginning of my illness. Ladies may communicate directly for full particulars if desired. I used no other remedy than the NYE LITHIA SPRINGS WATER.

MRS. M. S. WILSON,
IVANHOE, VA.

August 10, 1891.

Of Rev. G. W. Summers, of M. E. Church, S., Wytheville, Va.

This certifies that I have used, for eight or ten days, the NYE LITHIA SPRINGS WATER, with effect upon my system, toning it up and acting particularly well upon my kidneys.

G. W. SUMMERS.

October 18, 1890.

For Gravel.

I have used the Water from the NYE LITHIA SPRINGS for my kidneys and have been greatly benefited. I have been much troubled with gravel, and since I commenced the use of this water I have not suffered a single pain. It acts freely and pleasantly.

R. D. ROSENHEIM,
210 N. Liberty St., BALTIMORE, MD.

Sept. 12th, 1890.

Its action upon Kidneys and Uric Acid Deposits.

WYTHEVILLE, VA., Oct. 14th, 1890.

I have used the NYE LITHIA SPRINGS WATER for a few weeks, and can testify to its valuable properties in its action upon the kidneys and bladder. My urine showed red deposit in it. After using this water it cleared up entirely. I regard it of such value that people should know of its effect in these diseases.

ALFRED CLIFT

Eczema and Gravel.

I have used the NYE LITHIA SPRINGS WATER for eczema and received great relief. Furthermore, I have been troubled with a disposition to gravel, and the use of this water has given me relief. I consider this water a fine one, and that it is especially good in skin diseases.

M. L. KEESLING,
NEWBERRY, VA.

October, 1890.

Kidneys, Cystitis and General Poor Health cured by it.

NEWBERRY, VA., Aug 10th, 1891.

I had been a great sufferer for three years with my kidneys and cystitis, having been treated by my physician for nearly the three years. Part of the time he visited me three and four times a week, with little or no relief to my distress and sufferings. My health had become so poor I could hardly get about nor attend to my household duties, when Dr. S. R. Sayers advised me to use the Water from the NYE LITHIA SPRINGS. I began it, like all

---

other remedies I had so often tried, with doubts; but in a week's use I began to improve, and in three or four weeks I had so much improved that I felt like a new person. There was no mistaking the effects of the Water: when I got out of it a few days, I could feel the effects of the disease; on resuming it, relief would come again. Continuing to use it for a few months, my general health so improved that I can walk where I please, do my own work, and have as good an appetite and digestion as I ever enjoyed. All from the use of the NYE LITHIA SPRINGS WATER, and no other medicine from the first use of the Water a year ago.

Ladies suffering from such disease as made my life a miserable one can surely get relief by using this water.

MRS. MOLLIE TAYLOR.

Certificate of J. C. Allison, ex-Treasurer of Wythe County, Va.

WYTHEVILLE, VA., June 15th, 1891.

I have been a great sufferer with my bladder, with a deposit of gravel or sand in my bladder and urine. Since using the NYE LITHIA SPRINGS WATER I have derived great benefit from it, pass less deposit since I began the use of the water, the constant desire to pass my urine has ceased, and I am comparatively comfortable. Under its use my appetite and digestion has become very good. I regard it a very fine water for my class of diseases, as well as for nervousness and rheumatism. I have

used other Lithia waters, but this acts more promptly than any other.
J. C. ALLISON.

For Typhoid Fever and Kidneys.

WYTHEVILLE, VA., Aug. 3d, 1891.

My wife had been ill for some time with Typhoid Fever, and the disease had affected her kidneys in carrying off the poison, which gave her much pain and trouble. Drs. S. R. Sayers and C. W. Gleaves advised the use of the NYE LITHIA SPRINGS WATER, of which she drank freely, with relief in a few days to this one of her most serious troubles in the disease. So much comfort and relief followed its use that she continues to drink it in preference to any and all other water.
S. F. EWALD.

Kidneys and Appetizer.

My wife had long been a great sufferer with her kidneys, and the use of the NYE LITHIA SPRINGS WATER acted beyond any expectation, and the relief was greater than from any mineral water or remedy she had ever used. The effect was speedy and prompt. My daughter has been in poor health for quite a while, and this water acted as an appetizer better than any medicine she ever used to promote it.
A. J. HUFFARD,
WYTHEVILLE, VA.

October 24th, 1890.

Bladder and Urine.

I was troubled with my bladder and urine being unable to discharge but little water at a time, and that red and loaded with a mucus of a thick, ropy character, when I began and used perhaps some ten gallons of the NYE LITHIA SPRINGS WATER, after which all trouble passed away and my water is perfectly clear, gives me no further inconvenience. The relief was entirely due to the use of the NYE LITHIA SPRINGS WATER.
J. T. BURCH,
WYTHEVILLE, VA.

October 18th, 1890.

Kidneys and Bladder.

WYTHEVILLE, VA., Oct. 18th, 1890.

I was troubled with great irritation of my kidneys and bladder. My urine was loaded with a thick sediment on cooling. I had to void my water several times every hour and with great pain. I used freely of the NYE LITHIA SPRINGS WATER for perhaps a week, when my urine began to clear up, pain ceased, and I got comfortable; was relieved of the constant desire to pass my water. It gives me great pleasure to make this statement of the relief I obtained by the use of this water.
A. R. EWALD

Jaundice.

HANCOCK HOUSE, WYTHEVILLE, VA.,
October, 16.

I had jaundice and was very yellow. The bilious matter was passing through my kidneys; my urine was loaded with it. I drank freely of the NYE LITHIA SPRINGS WATER. It acted freely and promptly and my urine cleared up immediately.
B. T. CLARK,
Manager of the Hancock House.

Congestion of the Kidneys.

This is to certify that I suffered for some time with congestion of the kidneys. After using the NYE LITHIA SPRINGS WATER for it for about ten days I was entirely relieved.
JACOB FRANK.

Painful Urination.

WYTHEVILLE, VA., June 12th, 1891.

DR. NYE:

Dear Sir: My little girl, three years of age, was troubled with dysuria, having to pass her urine very frequently and with much suffering. The use of the NYE LITHIA SPRINGS WATER relieved her in two days.
Yours truly,
J. E. PERKINS.

Kidneys and Bladder.

MARSHALLTOWN, IA., March 20th, 1891.

I was badly afflicted with kidney complaint for several months, my urine being thick and dark brown, like coffee. I could not ride or scarcely walk. I was induced to try the water from the NYE LITHIA SPRINGS at Wytheville, Va. After using the water for three weeks I was entirely cured by it, using no other medicine. It is pleasant to drink and its curative powers are truly wonderful.
R. E. VANCOURT.

Nye's Lithia Springs Water for the past two months, and have realized great benefit from it, and recommend it to any one suffering from debility or nervousness.

MRS. JOHN T. SAYERS,
SALEM, VA.
September 8th, 1890.

For Nervousness.

Dr. Nye: *Dear Sir*: The Nye Lithia Springs Water is the best medicine for nervousness I ever used. Yours very truly,

D. C. HUFFARD.
July 4th, 1891.

Indigestion and Kidney Complaint.

VIRGINIA HOUSE, WYTHEVILLE, VA.,
July 4th, 1891.

Dr. Nye:

Dear Sir: I beg to inform you that I have been using your famous Lithia Water for some time, and I am happy to state that by so doing I have been cured of the complaint I had been troubled with, viz: indigestion and kidney trouble. I used the water freely and I found that it was conducive to sleep. I take great pleasure in recommending it to the use of any person who may be suffering from similar complaints. Very respectfully,

P. BROPHY, Sergeant,
Battery H, 3d U. S. Artillery.

Indigestion.

WYTHEVILLE, VA., June 10th, 1891.

I have been relieved entirely from indigestion by using the water from the Nye Lithia

---

Indigestion.

WYTHEVILLE, VA., Oct. 30th, 1890.

I have been using the Nye Lithia Springs Water with improvement in my digestion. Could I have procured the water more readily I would have gotten much more benefit. My appetite became very good from its use.

MRS. E. J. McCAW,
TUSCALOOSA, ALA.

Indigestion and Constipation.

My wife has been using the Water from the Lithia Springs for some time, being troubled with derangement of her stomach and protracted constipation. By using a glass in the early morning she has derived great relief, more than from the effects of medicines heretofore used. The trouble with her digestion has disappeared. For the particulars in her case, ladies may communicate directly with her. R. L. POAGE (Druggist),

WYTHEVILLE, VA.,
October 29th, 1890.

Sick Headache, Etc.

I can certify that my wife has been a sufferer for several years with sick or nervous headache, and after the use of the Nye Lithia Springs Water was greatly benefitted in general health and relieved entirely as to headache.

JNO. A. COOK.
WYTHEVILLE, VA.
October 30th, 1890.

Debility and Nervousness.

This is to certify that I have used Dr.

Indigestion and Irregularities, Etc.

WYTHEVILLE, VA., June 6th, 1891.

For sixteen years my wife could eat no supper nor could she eat fat meats or butter, and very little of any kind of food without fermentation, and great pain and suffering with her stomach. I had expended a great deal in effort to have her cured, but with little benefit. Life had become a real burden to her by her continued ill health, when she began the use of the Nye Lithia Springs Water. After the use of a gallon she had more relief than from all she had taken for it, and more use of the water has enabled her to eat meats, butter, and in fact anything she desires in comfort, and rest well at night, which she could not do before using the water. Her system has become normal under its use, which had not been the case for years before. Ladies may call upon her for full particulars, if desired, or communicate with her for the relief she obtained by the use of this water, after having tried many remedies, with no relief, for her stomach and digestion.

R. P. BLACKWELL.

Sick or Nervous Headache.

My wife having been a great sufferer for many years with periodical nervous or sick headache, with so much prostration resulting that many remedies have been tried, but the use of the Nye Lithia Springs Water has given more relief than any other article used. Her general health has become very good.

FRANK MEYERS,
October 12th, 1890. Newbern, N. C.

Springs. I recommend it to all who are afflicted the same way.
J. P. PRESTON.

Dyspepsia, Insomnia and Kidneys.

I have used the NYE LITHIA SPRINGS WATER, about one mile from Wytheville, Va., for about six weeks. I had been suffering for several years with dyspepsia, insomnia and trouble of the kidneys. I could not use fat meat or bacon at all. After using the water as above stated I could sleep well and eat bacon three times a day, which I had not done for years before.
J. W. MOREHEAD,
WYTHEVILLE, VA.

June 15th, 1891.

VIRGINIA HOUSE, WYTHEVILLE, VA., }
October, 1890. }

Several of my guests, during the summer, used the NYE LITHIA SPRINGS WATER, and with one accord gave it praise, and that their health had been greatly improved.
JOHN A. BARNITZ,
Proprietor Virginia House.

Nervousness and Rheumatism.

Of Col. R. Sayers, ex-Member of the Legislature of Virginia and ex-Sheriff of Wythe County, Virginia.

WYTHEVILLE, VA., June 15th, 1891.

DR. GEO. L. NYE:

Dear Sir: I hereby certify that one year ago I suffered a great deal from nervousness, especially at night. I commenced using the water from the NYE LITHIA SPRINGS and was soon relieved, so I can now eat a hearty supper and sleep soundly. I have for many years been afflicted with chronic rheumatism, each succeeding year a little worse, until I commenced the use of your LITHIA WATER. Since then, though not cured, I have suffered far less than usual, and been so much relieved that I can now go out at any time, which I could not do before. Very truly yours,
R. SAYERS.

Torpid Liver, Indigestion and Constipation.

WYTHEVILLE, VA., Aug. 25th, 1891.

For many years I have been troubled with torpid liver, indigestion and constipation, and after using the water from the NYE LITHIA SPRINGS for a couple of months, it regulated the action of my liver, my indigestion disappeared and my constipation was relieved. I can truly say that I never enjoyed better health in my life since I used this water.
A. J. BRALLY.

Mr. Massey, Manager of Wytheville Manufacturing Company.

WYTHEVILLE, VA., Aug. 27th, 1891.

My mother used the Water from the NYE LITHIA SPRINGS with marked and immediate benefit. Have used Lithia Water from other springs, and the celebrated Buffalo Water, and the NYE Water acted as promptly and more efficiently than any other has ever done.
THOS. MASSIE.

Congestion of the Liver and Kidneys.

NEWBERRY, VA., Sept. 1st, 1891.

Last winter my son was going to school in Wytheville, and became ill with congestion of the liver and kidneys. His eyes were yellow and his urine being thick and high colored. He lost his appetite and had to quit school for a week or more, when Dr. S. R. Sayers was called in to see him. He advised for his condition the use of the NYE LITHIA SPRINGS WATER. It acted like a charm. In one day's use he began to improve, and in ten days was relieved entirely. His urine cleared up and his appetite became good, when he resumed his place in school. The water has been used by other members of my family with great benefit.
DAVID A. RICH.

Dyspepsia and Headache.

Of Mrs. Gen. Alfred Moore.

DR. NYE:

Dear Sir: I take great pleasure in recommending the NYE LITHIA SPRINGS WATER, having used it for a year. I find especial benefit for dyspepsia and headache, also with great improvement in my general health.
Yours truly,
MRS. S. E. MOORE.

I take pleasure in adding my tribute to the virtues of the NYE LITHIA SPRINGS WATER. Its use for several months has afforded very decided benefit. MRS. J. B. BARRETT,
WYTHEVILLE, VA.

August 3, 1891.

Wytheville as a Summer Resort.

THERE is no spot in the Appalachian Chain of Mountains, from the Canada line to the Gulf of Mexico, that offers a more desirable and delightful summer resting place than the town of Wytheville. It is situated in a cradle-like depression on the summit of the Alleghanies, near that happy parallel of latitude, "where the frosts of winter bite not and the pestilences of summer stalk not forth," and is in the center of the largest white belt on the health map of the United States. By reference to this map the health seeker will discover that the few white belts upon it mark the areas where, alone, total exemption from malarias and epidemics may be found.

During the summer months a pleasant mountain breeze cools the heat of the midday, and a blanket is requisite for comfort during the night. The air is pure, sweet, and light enough to be exhilarating, and there are no morning fogs to dampen the spirits or chill the frame. A chalybeate spring of fine tonic properties flows from a fountain near the center of Main Street, and its restorative waters are free to all. It hots quickly upon the system, and is regarded by many, who have tested its virtues, as fully equal to the famous Alleghany Springs.

For a number of years Wytheville has been known as the metropolis of the wealthy and picturesque section of South-west Virginia. Its churches are numerous; its colleges and schools excellent; its streets are broad and clean; and its people warm hearted, cultivated, and hospitable. No town of its size in the South can boast of a more refined and elevated society; it delights in all enjoyments, sports, and recreations that are pure and healthful, but quietly, though firmly, refuses to be drawn into the vortex of useless extravagance and fashionable follies. In this respect it presents a striking contrast to many other places of resort where a shoddy display of style is too often the first and only consideration, and comfort and content are the last, if indeed, they be not entirely ignored.

To the weary invalid wishing to recruit his health and strength; to the women and children of the South who desire to escape from the heat of midsummer's sun; to the exhausted business man and tired professional, craving relaxation and rest, she extends her invitations; assuring them that, many have accepted it in the past, and but few, if any, ever regretted it; for, within her limits, the Goddess of Health has often cooled the fevered brow; changed the pale lilies to bright roses; cleansed the blood from its foul poisons of malaria; restored tone to the depressed nerves; infused strength to the emaciated frame; supplanted despair with hope; created new sources of happiness by making grief forget her woes; taught folly to be wise, and prolonged human life.

This photograph identified as Matt Gray's Barbershop, located in Bolling House where Durham's Restaurant is now operated. Notice the lattice behind which were public baths—also the built up shoe that Mr. Gray wears.

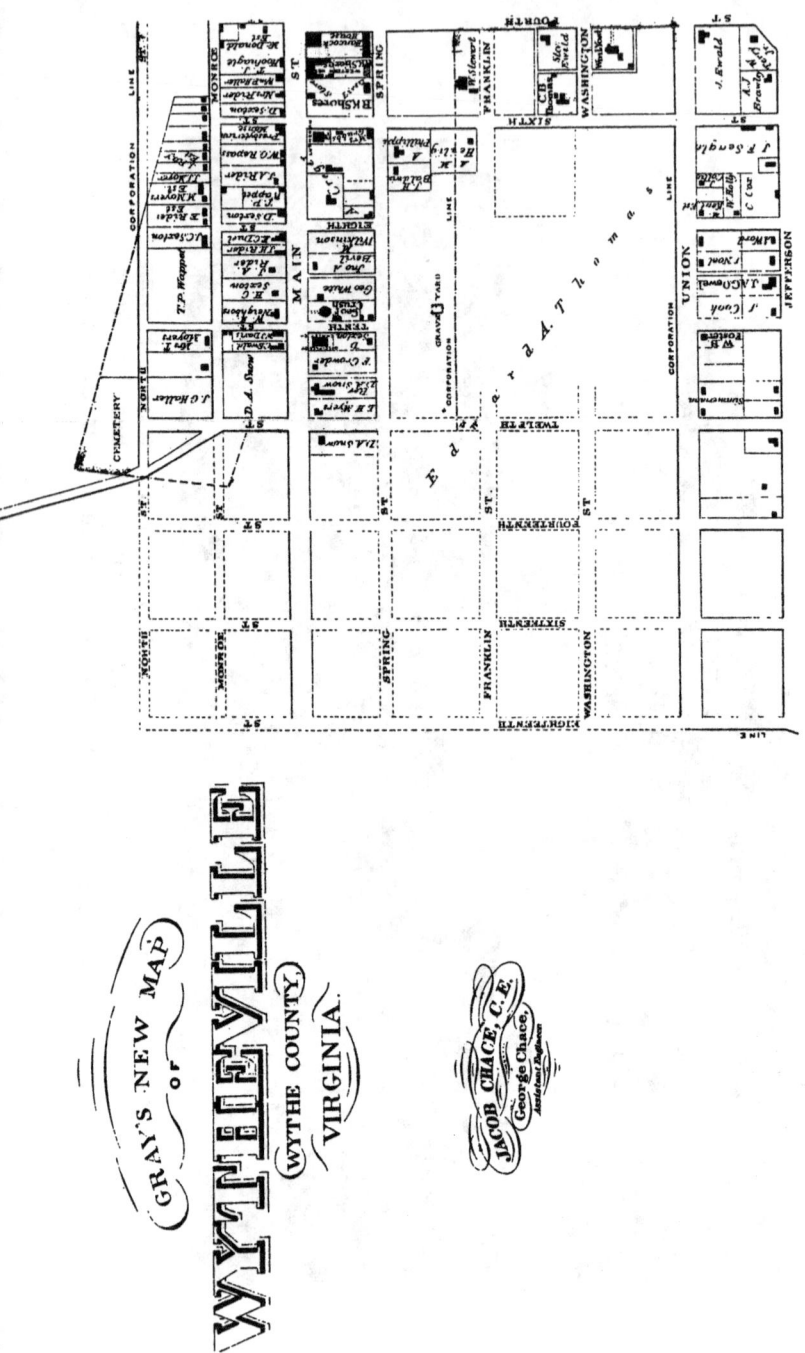

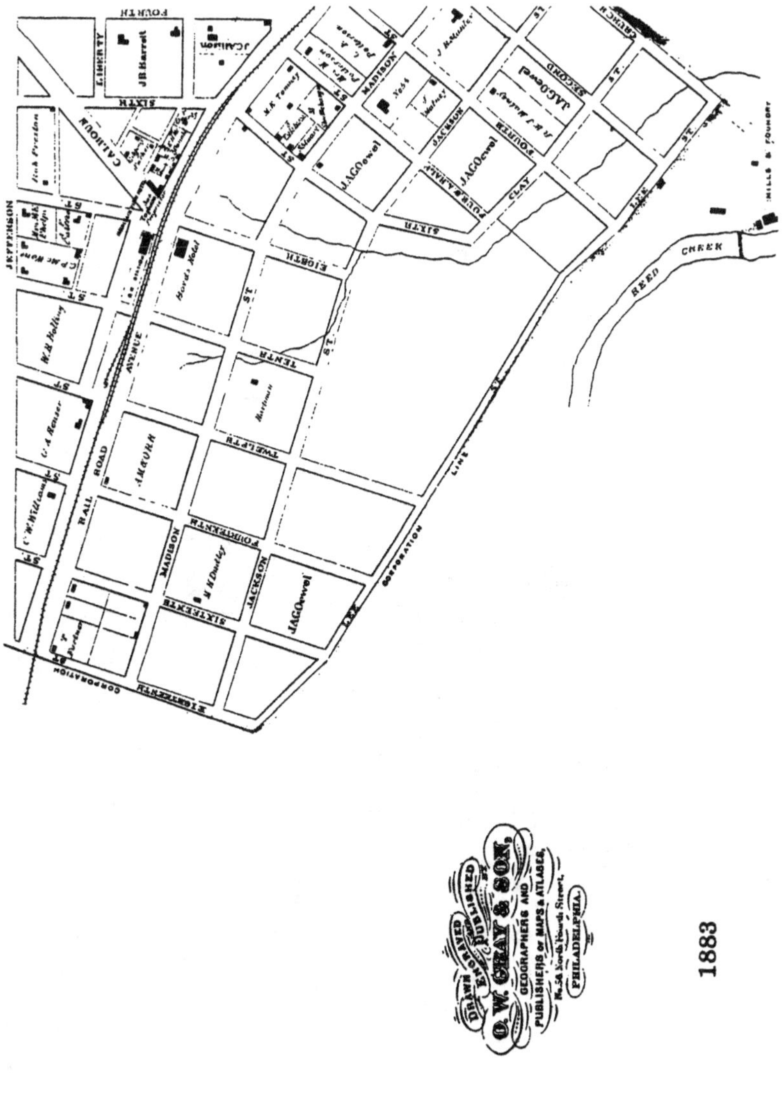
FOURTH
LIBERTY
SIXTH
CALHOUN
JEFFERSON
MADISON
JACKSON
SECOND
CLAY
LEE
EIGHTH
TENTH
TWELFTH
FOURTEENTH
SIXTEENTH
EIGHTEENTH
RAIL ROAD AVENUE
CORPORATION LINE ST.
REED CREEK
MILLS & FOUNDRY
JB Harrett
Hord's Hotel
W.H. Holliday
G A Hauser
M H Dudley
DRAWN, ENGRAVED & PUBLISHED BY
O. W. GRAY & SON,
GEOGRAPHERS AND
PUBLISHERS OF MAPS & ATLASES,
No. 54 North Fourth Street,
PHILADELPHIA.

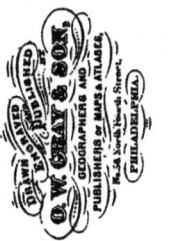

1883

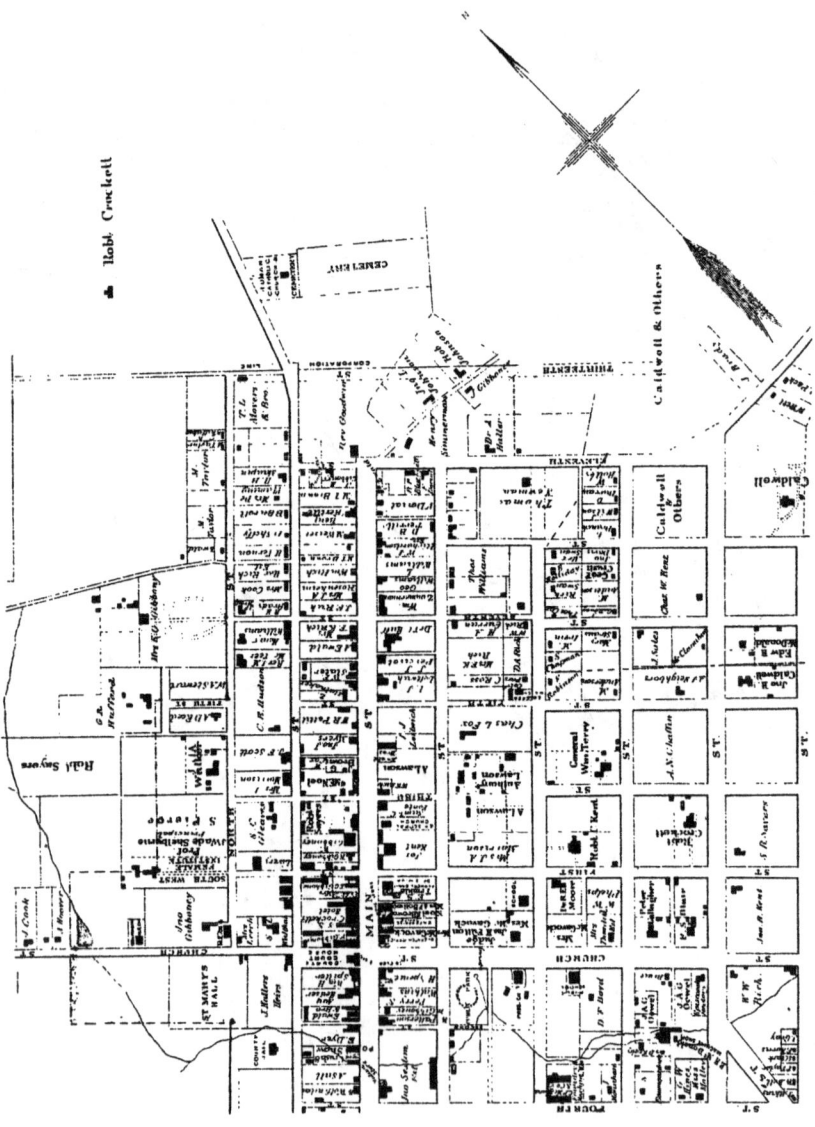

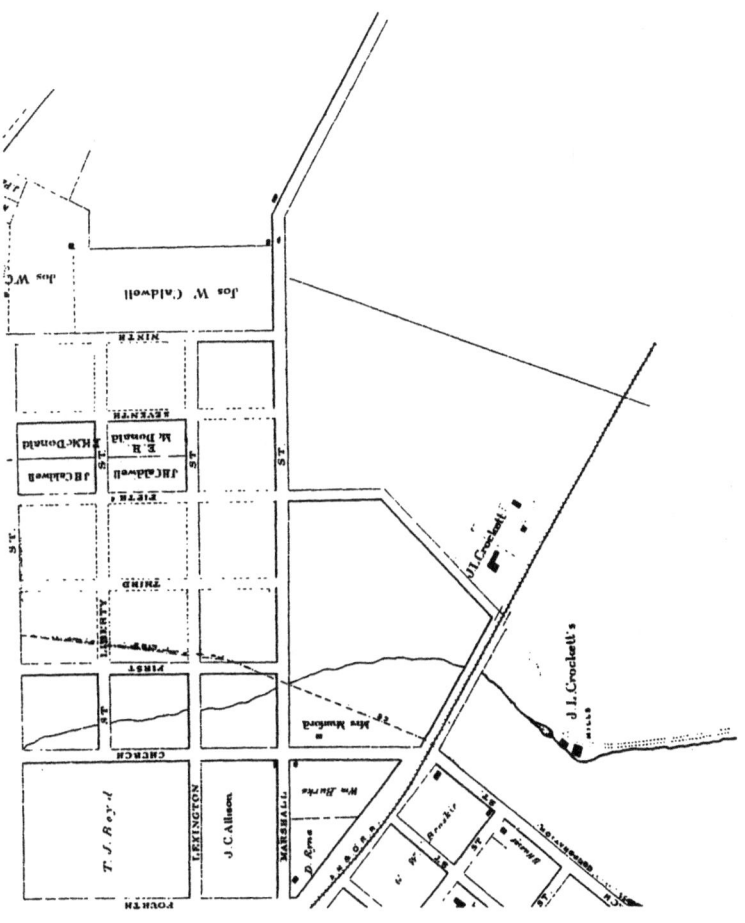

Personal Histories of Wythe County

Taken from *Hardesty's Historical and Geographical Encyclopedia, Special Supplement* by R. A. Brock - New York, 1884. pps. 415-424.

REV. WILLIAM DAVID AKERS—son of Amos and Missouri (Kelley) Akers, of Pulaski county, Virginia, was born in that county, July 31, 1855. He was educated for the work of the ministry, and became an itinerant of the Methodist Episcopal Church (South), when his studies were completed, traveling for some time circuits in North Carolina, and residing for several years in that State. As a liberal Christian, of sterling worth, he has left his impress upon all the people with whom he has been associated. At Asheville, Buncombe county, North Carolina, October 17, 1878, he was united in marriage with Istalena Robeson. She was born in that State and county, June 20, 1856, a daughter of John H. and Harriet (Cumming) Robeson. Her father is still living in Buncombe county, where her mother died September 27, 1874. Lewis Robeson, born August 25, 1881, and Dwight Cumming, born May 6, 1884, are the children of Mr. and Mrs. Akers. In October, 1883, Mr. Akers entered upon his present labors, with the people of Rural Retreat, Wythe county, Virginia.

CHARLES BAUMGARDNER—born in Wythe county, August 30, 1842, at the age of nineteen years became one of Virginia's defenders, enlisting for the impending war in April, 1861, at Rural Retreat, second lieutenant of Company B, 45th Virginia Infantry, which entered the service a part of Floyd's brigade. In April, 1862, he was appointed first lieutenant, at the Narrows of New River, re-enlisting at the same time, and about the close of the year he was elected captain. He was a participant in all the engagements of his regiment until made prisoner at Winchester, September 19, 1864, after which he was held nine months at Fort Delaware. Among these battles were: Cotton Mountain, Sewel Mountain, Carnifax River, Lewisburg, Cloyd Mountain, two heavy battles at Winchester, one at Berryville, Hawks Nest—these in the Virginias, and Jonesboro, Tennessee. John and Malinda (Umbarger) Baumgardner were the parents of Charles, both natives of Wythe county. His father died in August, 1853, and his mother died July 3, 1882. Ellen V., daughter of Hugh and Jane (Ward) Spence, is the wife of Charles Baumgardner. She was born in Wythe county, February 19, 1850, and they were married in Bristol, Tennessee, June 21, 1868. Their children were born: Lulu May, May 5, 1871; Hugh Stuart, March 8, 1873; Mattie Simon, March 28, 1877; Bessie Belle, March 17, 1881. The mother of Mrs. Baumgardner died in this county in 1855, and her father died December 15, 1882.

HENRY G. BOURNE—son of William H. and Carrie (Stone) Bourne, was born in Montgomery county, Kentucky, September 23, 1845. His mother is deceased, his father still living in Montgomery county, Kentucky. His grandfather, Walker Bourne, originally from Culpeper county, Virginia, was a soldier of the 1812 war, and his services are honorably mentioned in the early history of Montgomery county, Kentucky. Henry G. was in the Confederate States service when little more than seventeen years of age, serving in the famous cavalry led by General John Morgan. He participated in that daring raid of 1863, and was among the captured at Cheshire. Ohio, July 26, 1863. He was taken to Camp Chase, Ohio, thence to Camp Douglas, Illinois, near Chicago, thence sent to Richmond on parole, and finally exchanged. In Wythe county, November 15, 1866, he was united in marriage with Lizzie Simmonson, who was born in Wythe county, September 30, 1845, a daughter of John P. and Mary A. Simmonson. Her father died December 4, 1881, her mother is living in Wythe county. In 1867 Mr. Bourne took up his residence in Wythe county, and here his children were born: John S., November 23, 1867; Carrie S., March 17, 1869; Willie A., August 21,   ; Henry G., jr., October 4, 1874; Stephen T., February 9, 1876; M. Lulu, August   ,   ; Jennie E., December 29,   ; Eddie, July 21,   ; B. Mason, June 17, 1884. The families of both Mr. and Mrs. Bourne are of the good old Virginian stock, and have been honorably identified with the annals of the State. Mr. Bourne owns and cultivates an estate of 400 acres, lying east of Wytheville, and receives his mail at Kents Mills, Wythe county, Virginia.

STEPHEN C. BRALLEY—is a son of John S. Bralley, who was a son of James Bralley, an early settler in Wythe county. John S. Bralley married Jane Carter, and until their decease their home was in Wythe county. In this county their son Stephen C. was born, April 2, 1837, and here he was married in 1865. His wife is Austes, daughter of Wilson and Eliza Jones, of Wythe county now, but she was born in Franklin county, this State. Their children are five sons and one daughter: William, Robert Lee, Thomas, Monroe, Jeremiah, and Laura Bell. Stephen C. Bralley is one of five brothers who were in the Confederate States army during the civil war. These brothers were Stephen C., Saul S., Edwin J., Andrew J., and G. W. J. M. Bralley. Stephen C. enlisted in Company D, 45th Virginia Infantry, at the commencement of the war, and when the regiment was disbanded at the. close of that struggle he was the only one present of its original muster. He was twice wounded, at Cloyd Mountain and at Piedmont, during the war, and at Piedmont he was captured, but paroled to care for the wounded Confederates on the field. His brother G. W. J. M. was killed in the Winchester battle of September 19, 1864; he ranked as sergeant, and at his death was leading the company in a charge. Stephen C. Bralley follows the occupation of a blacksmith, with postoffice address at Red Bluff, Wythe county, Virginia.

WILLIAM H. BRAMBLETT, M. D.—is a son of parents born and raised in Bedford county, Virginia, Elkanah Bramblett and Mildred Allen Dearing, who were united in wedlock in Bedford county in 1828. Their firstborn child was named William H., his birth in 1829 in Bedford county. In 1861 he enlisted in Grayson county. Virginia. as captain of the "Grayson Cavalry," attached to the 8th Virginia Cavalry, and assigned to service for the first year of the war in Floyd's brigade. At the re-organization of the army in 1862 he was appointed surgeon, and remained on duty with the 63d Virginia Infantry till November, 1863, when he was assigned to hospital duty, in which branch of the service he remained till the close of the war, at which time he was on duty at Macon, Georgia. Among the battles in which he was an active participant were Guyandotte, Charleston, Kellys Store, in Virginia, Chickamauga, Georgia, and many other smaller affairs. His first marriage was with Eliza Hamil Thomas, of Smyth county, Virginia, who died without issue. At the close of the war he settled in Pulaski county, Virginia, where he was engaged in the practice of his profession until he removed to Wytheville in 1883. In 1871, he married Mary W., daughter of Edwin Watson, M. D., and Malinda F. (Pierce) Watson. Her birth was in Pulaski county. Since 1883, Dr. Bramblett has been settled in practice with the people of Wytheville.

HENRY S. BOWEN—born in Tazewell county, Virginia, August 3, 1820, and is a resident of Wythe county. Henry and Ellen (Tate) Bowen were his parents; his father died in 1850, and his mother in 1832. Rees Bowen, grandfather of Henry S., emigrated from Big Lick, Roanoke county, Virginia, and settled in Tazewell county among its pioneers He served in the Indian war of 1776, and was killed in the battle of Kings Mountain. His son Henry, father of Henry S., was a soldier of the 1812 war. The subject of this sketch, true to the traditions of his family, enrolled himself among Virginia's soldiers when her first call for troops was made, to defend her own soil from aggression. He served first on General Marshall's staff, was then made colonel of the 22d Virginia Cavalry, and joined Early's division, serving through the war. Henry S. Bowen has been twice wedded, his first wife, Eliza, nee Black, died in 1848. They had one son, Henry A., who died at the age of five years, September, 1854. In Wythe county, June 25, 1854, Henry S. Bowen and Mary E. Miller were united in marriage. She was born in this county, October 21, 1828, a daughter of James R. and Emily (Pearce) Miller. Her mother died in 1846, and her father in 1880. Farming is Henry S. Bowen's occupation, and his postoffice address is Wytheville, Wythe county, Virginia.

JAMES A. BROWN—has passed a long and honored life in Wythe county, engaged in the work of the ministry of the Gospel among the people with whom he was born. His birth was in Wythe county, December 21, 1816 the date, and Christopher and Anna Maria (Rader) Brown his parents. They were born in Wythe county, their immediate families honorably identified with the best interests of the county from its earliest settlement. Christopher Brown held a captain's commission in the army during the 1812 war. James A. Brown has been twice wedded, his first wife Eleonora C. Herbst, born August 1, 1819, died July 20, 1879. In Wythe county, September 19, 1880, Alice V. Sharitz became his wife. She was born in Wythe county, May 4, 1856, a daughter of John P. and Clementina (Hudson) Sharitz, who are residents still in this county. For forty-one years Mr. Brown has been engaged in labor with the people of his church. He resides on his estate of 200 acres, near Wytheville, which is his postoffice address.

REV. STEPHEN F. BROWN—is a son of John A. and Sarah (Tartar) Brown, of Wythe county, and was born in this county, January 26,

1854. Here his wedded life began, Eugenia F. Brown becoming his wife on the 30th of September, 1879. Ernest H., their son, was born October 13, 1882. Eugenia F., daughter of Rufus and Margaret (Earheart) Brown, was born in Wythe county, October 14, 1857. Her parents were born in this county, where her father still resides; her mother died on the 30th of October, 1880. Two brothers of Mr. Brown were soldiers of Virginia during the internecine war, Nicholas C. and Robert A., members of Company H, 45th Virginia Infantry. Nicholas served as lieutenant. Neither were wounded in the service, but both were captured toward the close of the struggle, Nicholas taken to Elmira, New York, and Robert to Point Lookout; both were held until paroled after the surrender. Stephen F. Brown is a farmer, living on a farm of 600 acres of beautiful land under direct cultivation, and owning an interest in a tract of 5,000 acres. He is also engaged in the work of the ministry, a faithful and efficient laborer. His postoffice address is Wytheville, Wythe county, Virginia.

JOHN BUCHANAN—son of William and Catherine (Kinder) Buchanan, was born in Wythe county, Virginia, August 19, 1826. His parents were of families long honorably identified with Wythe county history, and his father died March 4, 1853, in this county; his mother died June 12, 1840. His grandfathers (Robert Buchanan and Peter Kinder) were in the Revolutionary war and engaged in the battle of Kings Mountain and others. Robert Buchanan was a captain in that war. In Wythe county, May 6, 1847, John Buchanan and Sophia Brown were united in marriage, and they have three sons and two daughters, born: William Michael, July 8, 1853; Barbara Catharine, October 3, 1855; Hobson Clarke, August 25, 1858; Albert Sydney, July 10, 1861; Laura Jane, June 3, 1866. The wife of Mr. Buchanan was born in Wythe county, June 23, 1824, a daughter of Michael and Barbara (Nippe) Brown, of Wythe county, now both deceased. John Buchanan organized Company B. 45th Virginia Infantry, and was mustered into service as captain of the company, May 29, 1861. He was thrown from a horse, near Princeton, West Virginia, and severely injured. He continued in active service some time after, until compelled by disability to resign. He farms a beautiful estate of about 330 acres, lying one mile south of Rural Retreat, Wythe county, Virginia, which is his postoffice address.

CHARLES H. CALFEE—is a descendant of John Calfee, who was born in 1720, of English ancestry, and lived and died in the Shenandoah valley of Virginia. He held a land patent, now in the possession of the subject of this sketch, from Lord Fairfax, proprietor of the Northern Neck of Virginia (see elsewhere in this work), for 308 acres of land in Augusta county, dated September 23, 1749. John Calfee raised six sons, Henry, John, William, James, Benjamin and Charles, and two daughters, Betsy and Sallie. Charles married Elizabeth Brown of New Jersey, and he and most of his brothers settled on New river, in Wythe county, between 1790 and 1800. He raised two daughters, Betsy and Sally, and one son, John. John, born in 1797, married Margaret, daughter of Ezekiel Howard, son of William Howard of English parentage, and who moved, about the close of the Revolution, from New York to Montgomery county, Virginia. Ezekiel Howard served through the war of the Revolution, was at Brandywine, Germantown, and in Valley Forge camp. After its close he settled in Montgomery county, where as justice of the peace he for a number of years transacted a large share of public business, and promoted peace and order in a community rude and demoralized by war. He married Rebecca Anderson, of Botetourt county, Virginia, and raised two sons, Alexander and Anderson, and five daughters, Sophia, Margaret, Rebecca, Evelina and Juliet. Margaret, born in 1800, married John Calfee, as above noted, and their son, the subject of this sketch, was born in Wythe county, December 28, 1828. His wife died in 1831, and he long survived her, raising a family of three daughters and three sons, and dying in 1873. These daughters were Evelina, Elizabeth and Sophia, and the sons were: R. A., J. A., and C. H. J. A. served through the civil war, in the Western department of the Confederate army, actively engaged in its campaigns. In Montgomery county, Virginia, November 16, 1853, Charles H. Calfee was united in marriage with Sarah J. White. who was born in Montgomery county, August 10, 1829, a daughter of Hezekiah and Sarah (Howerton) White. Mr. Calfee is extensively engaged in business as farmer, merchant and lumber dealer. Postoffice address, Reed Island, Wythe county, Virginia.

M. B. CASSELL—born in Wythe county, Virginia. June 25, 1845, and Mary E. Graham, born in this county February 19, 1851, were here united in marriage on the 16th of February, 1869. Their children were born: Virginia Graham, January 24, 1870; Wythe, December 16, 1872; Lena Jackson, June 16, 1874; Lucy Brown, April 25, 1876; Sallie, April 1, 1878; Mary Susan, June 15, 1880 Colonel Joseph Cassell, who died August 18, 1880, was the father of M. B., and his mother was Susan (Wiseley) Cassell. She died October 14, 1878. Both were residents until death in Wythe county. A. J. and S. O. (Worder) Graham, the parents of Mrs. Cassell, are living in Wythe county. March 1, 1862, Mr. Cassell entered the Confederate States service, a member of Company A, 4th Virginia Infantry, sharing the fortunes in the field of that regiment until captured at Spotsylvania C. H., May 12, 1864. He was taken prisoner to Point Lookout, Maryland, then transferred to Elmira, New York, where he was held until June, 1865. He owns and cultivates a beautiful farm of 300 acres, and is considered one of the substantial men of the county. His postoffice address is Wytheville, Wythe county, Virginia.

MICHAEL CASSELL—son of Joseph and Mary (Foglesong) Cassell, was born near Black Lick, Wythe county, November 26, 1827. His father settled on the farm he now owns many years ago, and it has grown to be one of the most beautiful and productive estates in the county. Michael Cassell, grandfather of the present Michael, was a soldier of the Revolution, serving about eighteen months, and with Washington's army at the surrender at Yorktown. He did not see the surrender, however, being on picket duty at the time it took place. He was born and raised in Pennsylvania, and came to Wythe county, then part of Montgomery, about 1785. The parents of the subject of this sketch were born in Wythe county, and died here. His mother died July 26, 1839, and his father died November 21, 1865. In Wythe county, September 19, 1850, Michael Cassell and Eliza A. Repass were united in marriage. The birth and death record of their children is: George Stuart, born February 19, 1853, died July 1, 1862; Alice Victoria, born July 17, 1855, died June 25, 1862; Emory Hawkins, born January 6, 1858, died May 13, 1862; Ella Jane, born November 1, 1860, died May 7, 1864; Marion Michael, born April 26, 1863, died April 4, 1866; Mary Eva, born February 24, 1866; Stephen Sydney, October 18, 1868; Charles Willis, March 25, 1871. The wife of Mr Cassell was born near Wytheville, January 4, 1830, a daughter of Rufus and Sally (Brown) Repass. Her parents were born in Wythe county, and her father died in this county July 31, 1878. Mr. Cassell served in the Home Guards under Colonel Joseph F. Kent during the late war. He was called out with the militia to repel a raid in 1862, and was two weeks under arms. From July, 1861, until July, 1873, he ably filled the office of justice of the peace. His time is now all given to farming and raising stock. Rural Retreat, Wythe county, Virginia, is his postoffice address.

SAMUEL H. CASSELL—one of the successful farming residents of Wythe county, was born in this county, on the 16th of October, 1846. He is a son of Joseph and Susan (Wiseley) Cassell, and he married Ciddie P., daughter of Albert and Nancy H. (Wiseley) Haller. She was born in Wythe county, June 8, 1852, they were married in this county, May 30, 1876, and of their union have been born three children: Willie H., January 24, 1879; Joseph D., September 18, 1881; and Samuel H., jr., April 27, 1883. Three brothers of Mr. Cassell, Daniel W , Charles H. and M. B , were soldiers of the late war, in the army of Northern Virginia, and participating in its glorious record. The subject of this sketch was not nineteen years of age when the conflict ended, but had seen one year's service with the veterans of that army. Wytheville, Wythe county, Virginia, is his postoffice address.

WILLIAM MARION COLEY—son of Christopher K. and Lydia (Copenhover) Coley, honored residents of Wythe county, was born in this county October 26, 1858. Here he was married, Josephine A. C. Neff becoming his wife on the 27th of December, 1881. Nettie McNair, born November 8, 1882, and Myrtle Neff, born April 18, 1884, are the children of this union. Josephine, wife of Mr. Coley and daughter of Daniel and Amanda Jane (Scott) Neff, was born in Wythe county, February 27, 1863. Her father was born in Wythe county, her mother in Smyth county, Virginia, and they are now residents of Wythe county. William M. Coley is one of the younger generation of the farmers of Wythe county, and during the winter months of the year gives his time to the profession of teaching. Rural Retreat, Wythe county, Virginia, is his postoffice address.

REV. WILLIAM PATON COOPER—on his father's side of Irish descent, and on his mother's side descended from Scotch ancestry, is of one of the oldest families of Southwest Virginia. His grandfather served in the war of the Revolution, with rank of adjutant-general, and lived to the extreme old age of 104 years. His father was a soldier of the 1812 war, Alexander Cooper, who died in February, 1861. The mother of William P., Elizabeth Cooper her maiden name, died in June, 1876. William P. Cooper was born in Russell county, Virginia, September 21, 1826, and was about eight years old when his parents made their home in Wythe county, where he has lived ever since. In this county, July 23, 1856, he married Eliza Jane, daughter of Mathias and Rachel (Umbarger) Tarter, of this county. She was born in Wythe county, September 17, 1833, her father died here January 6, 1865, and her mother died in 1879. Mr. Cooper resides on a fine farm near Rural Retreat, which he owns and operates in connection with local work in the ministry, preaching regularly every week. He receives his mail at Rural Retreat, Wythe county, Virginia.

WILLIAM CRAWFORD—born in Wythe county, March 7, 1819, was a son of William and Elizabeth (Smith) Crawford, of this county, long honored among its residents. His father was for more than thirty years a justice of the peace of the county, previous to the Constitutional amendment of 1852. Before, during and after the war, the subject of this sketch held the same office for about eight years. The family is of Irish descent, the first of the name to settle in Virginia, the great grandfather of the present William, coming from Ireland more than two hundred years ago. In October, 1851, in Wythe county, William Crawford was united in marriage with Elizabeth Jane Alford, who was born in this county, August 1, 1830, a daughter of John and Elizabeth (Baker) Alford. The living children of William Crawford and wife were born: William Shepherd, March 7, 1853; John Thomas, August 9, 1855; Elizabeth Rachel, April 5, 1860; Joseph Stuart, October 23, 1862; Robert I. J., May 22, 1866; Joanna Jane, May 19, 1868; Susan Margaret, October 12, 1870; Wesley Lee, February 9, 1874. Death has taken from them two children, George Washington, born October 15, 1857, died September 2, 1859; Mary Ellen, born September 10, 1864, died June 18, 1865. Mr. Crawford combines the occupations of farming and mining. Postoffice address, Reed Island, Wythe county, Virginia.

HENRY S. CROCKETT—physician and surgeon—is of a family early seated in Southwestern Virginia. His parents were John S. and Margaret B. (Taylor) Crockett, and he was born in Wythe county, which was the home of their married life, his birth on the 22d of September, 1846. In Pulaski county, Virginia, May 28, 1873, he married Minnie, daughter of John D. and Sarah (Shepherd) Howe. She was born in Pulaski county, May 23, 1852, and their children were born at their home in Wythe county: Howe T., March 6, 1874; Henry L., March 17, 1876; Elden Kent, October 10, 1877; Stuart R., September 2, 1879; Argyle Campbell, November 16, 1881. The father of Dr. Crockett died July 4, 1864, and his mother is living in Wythe county. The mother of Mrs. Crockett died in March, 1859; her father, born in Pulaski county, is still living. During the civil war Dr. Crockett was a cadet at the Virginia Military Institute, and was with the battalion called out in 1864, before the New Market battle, serving from that time till the close of the war. He has been two years physician of the Western Lunatic Asylum, but is now settled in practice in Rural Retreat, Wythe county, Virginia.

JOHN S. CROCKETT—is of one of the early and enterprising families of Wythe county, and a son of Allen Taylor Crockett (deceased) and Caroline, his wife, nee Minter, who is now living in Wythe county. In this county John S. was born, and here in August, 1876, he married Elizabeth Boyd. Their children are three sons: Thomas B., Allen T., and David B. The wife of Mr. Crockett was born in Wythe county in 1858. Thomas J. and Minerva (French) Boyd, her parents, made their home in this county in 1828, and are still honored residents here. During the years of the civil war, John S. Crockett was too young for service, but he had two brothers in the field, Samuel Floyd and Eugene. The first named was only sixteen years of age when he gave his promising young life in the defense of the Confederacy. He was killed at the first battle of Manassas by a grape shot wound in the head. The latter joined Morgan's cavalry at the age of sixteen and fought through the balance of the civil war and came out unscathed. John S. Crockett read law at University of Virginia, and in due time qualified and was admitted to practice. From 1875 to 1883 he was commonwealth attorney for Wythe county. He is now engaged in practice at the countyseat, where he has his residence.

HON. THOMPSON S. CROCKETT—farmer and stock raiser of Wythe county, Virginia, is known and honored as one of the substantial men of the county, which has always been his home. John and Agnes (Graham) Crockett, of Wythe county. were his parents, and he was born in this county on the 28th of February, 1821. In Tazewell county, Virginia, he married Rachel L Cecil, born in that county, October 5, 1826, a daughter of Samuel Cecil. They were married November 9, 1847, and their children are two daughters and a son, born: Sarah A., November 11, 1848; Samuel R., June 23, 1850; Mary A., February 19, 1852. Thompson S. Crockett is now the representative of Wythe county in the Virginia legislature. His estate lies in Fort Chiswell district, and his postoffice address is Wytheville, Wythe county, Virginia.

W. G. CROCKETT—is a native of Wythe county, born June 17, 1818. He was a son of John and Nancy (Graham) Crockett, now many years dead, and a relative of Davy Crockett, of frontier fame, who fell in the battle of Alamo, Texas, gallantly fighting by the side of Colonel Bowie. In Wythe county in 1849, W. G. Crockett married Emily, granddaughter of David Pierce, now deceased, and Elizabeth (Chaffin) Pierce. The wife of Mr. Crockett was born in North Carolina, in 1824, and of their union have been born four sons and four daughters: John G., Chaffin C., David P., Alexander G., Elizabeth, Nancy, Mary and Emily. Chaffin C. makes his home in Summers county, West Virginia, and the other children are living in Wythe county. W. G. Crockett has devoted the years of a long and useful life to the pursuits of agriculture, and now lives upon his farm in Fort Cheswell district, with postoffice address at Wytheville, Wythe county, Virginia.

HENRY A. EIFFERT—is a native of Tennessee, born in Bradley county, that State, on the 2d of May, 1843. James and Malinda (Stamper) Eiffert, now living in Kansas, are his parents. He enlisted in July, 1861, in Schuyler county, Missouri, Company B, 10th Missouri Infantry, as a private, and gave four years service to the cause of the Confederacy, receiving discharge in May, 1865, at Jackson, Mississippi. Among the battles in which he was a participant were Prairie Grove, and Helena, Arkansas, Corinth, Mississippi, Mobile, Alabama. He was made prisoner at Helena, July 4, 1863, and was held eight months at Alton, Illinois, twelve months at Fort Delaware. He settled in Wythe county in 1866, and in this county September 5, 1867, he married Susan T. Brown, who was born in Wythe county, March 31, 1851. Her parents, John C. and Margaret Ellen (Sharitz) Brown, are living in Wythe county. Six children were born to Mr and Mrs. Eiffert, of whom death has taken two: John W., born July 20, 1868; Wythe B., born June 5, 1871, died April 3, 1872; Ella May, born May 8, 1873, died August 30, 1882; Alice Virginia, born October 28, 1876; Nannie Brown, January 7, 1880; Nellie Flora, July 15, 1882. Mr. Eiffert is a thrifty market gardener, and cultivates a garden of forty acres. Rural Retreat, Wythe county, Virginia, is his postoffice address.

ROBERT H. AND GEORGE WYTHE GLEAVES—are sons of James T. and Melvina (Crockett) Gleaves, who lived and died in Wythe county. Their mother was closely related to Davy Crockett, of border annals. On their father's side they are of a family represented on the battle-fields of Virginia for three generations. Their grandfather, William Gleaves, was a lieutenant under General Greene in the Revolutionary war, their father was ensign in the 1812 war, and stationed at Norfolk, and five of his sons enrolled their names for the defense of Virginia in the late war. Robert H. enlisted at Wytheville, May 29, 1861, and served one year as Captain of Company D, 45th Virginia Infantry. At Saltville, in July, 1862, he re-enlisted, captain of Company E, 21st Virginia Cavalry, and served until discharged for ill-health at Greenville, in 1864. George Wythe was major in the Wythe Home Guards, and participated in the battles of Saltville, Wytheville, and Crocketts Cave. Robert H. fought at Pearisburg, Rogersville, Blue Springs, Greenville, Henderson Mill, Bluntville, Carter Station and Wytheville. Of the other brothers, Dr. S. C. was surgeon of the 45th Infantry, James T. was sergeant of the Wythe Greys, 4th Infantry, and died at Winchester, December 17, 1861, from exposure, Andrew J. was in the Home Guards, and died in December, 1862, from disease contracted in the line of duty. In Guilford county, North Carolina, January 27, 1876, Robert H. Gleaves married Julia K. Benbow. He was born in Wythe county, January 30, 1836, and she was born in the county where her marriage occurred. July 30, 1852 was the date of her birth, and their children were born: James T., May 8, 1878; Anna M., March 30, 1880; Robert Lee, May 3, 1882; Jessie Lilian, March 12, 1884. Jesse and Anna Clark Benbow, of Guilford county, are the parents of Mrs. R. H. Gleaves. The father of Mr. Gleaves served in the Virginia legislature for several terms, and was a number of years presiding justice of the Wythe county court. George Wythe Gleaves was born in Wythe county, April 17, 1827, and he married Isabella C. Sanders, December 5, 1855, in Wythe county, where she was born July 22, 1827, a daughter of Colonel I. A. and Elizabeth (Oury) Sanders. Since the war he has been four years magistrate of Wythe county. The brothers are engaged in the pursuits of agriculture, with postoffice address at Speedwell, Wythe county, Virginia.

SAMUEL CROCKETT GLEAVES—physician and surgeon, is a son of James Turk Gleaves, who was born in Wythe county, of a family early seated in the county and honorably identified with its history. James T. Gleaves was a soldier of the 1812 war, ranking as captain, until promoted major, commanding troops stationed at Norfolk. He served a number of terms in the Virginia legislature, and was often solicited to run for senate and congress, but declined, preferring the comforts and privacy of home life. He married Melvina Crockett, and both are now deceased, his death occurring in 1862, and hers in 1870. Their son, subject of this sketch, was born at Cripple Creek, Wythe county, October 12, 1823, and his first marriage was with Maria L. Crockett, who died March 23, 1878. They had three sons, now ably filling distinguished positions: James Lucian. A. M., D. L., born November 12, 1852; Charles Wythe, A. M., M. D., born August 13, 1855; Taylor, A. M, Civil Engineer, born May 27, 1860. In Mobile, Alabama, June 6, 1883, Dr. Gleaves wedded Fannie D., daughter of Edmund S. and Roxana (Brock) Dargan. She was born in Mobile in 1845; her mother, born in Georgia, is now living in

Mobile; her father, a native of North Carolina, is deceased. Samuel C. Gleaves was graduated from the Pennsylvania Medical University, April 17, 1848, and has ever since devoted himself to the duties of the profession he had chosen. In 1875 he was president of the State Medical Society, in 1880 was appointed director of the Medical College, in 1883 of the Western Lunatic Asylum. During the years of the war he was surgeon of the 45th Virginia Infantry, and medical director of the Confederate States army. He has his residence and postoffice address at Wytheville, Wythe county, Virginia.

REV. JOSEPH BROWN GREEVER—is a son of Rev. J. J. and Margaret (Peery) Greever, of Tazewell county, Virginia, and was born in that county, June 26, 1845. He became a resident in Wythe county in 1872, and in this county he married Emma, daughter of Joel and Ann (Buck) Cormany. She was born in Wythe county, April 25, 1856, and their children were born: Corsie Ann, October 4, 1873; Bismarck Maurice, September 25, 1875; John Joel, April 25, 1877; Krauth, March 6, 1880, died June 25th following; Margaret May, August 22, 1881; Thomas Mark, February 6, 1884. The parents of Mrs Greever are residents of Wythe county. For three years previous to the abandonment of the system of State militia, Mr. Greever held commission of 1st lieutenant in same. He is ably filling many positions of trust in the county, editor of the *Rural Star*, principal of the M. &. F. Seminary at Rural Retreat, and pastor of the Lutheran Church in the same place.

SAMUEL P. HALL—is a native of Rockbridge county, Virginia, born November 28, 1820, a son of James M. and Sallie (Cunningham) Hall. In 1849 he took up his residence in Wythe county, and in this county, September 16, 1851, he was united in marriage with Mary C. Lewis. They have one daughter, Sarah M., born September 5, 1852. Mary C., wife of Mr. Hall was a daughter of James and Lucy (Holt) Lewis, and was born in Sullivan county, Tennessee. April 14, 1830 was the day of her birth. Mr. Hall has been twice married, his second wife having been Ellen C. Bralley. Samuel P. Hall owns and operates a fine farm of seven hundred acres, has a natural genius for mechanics, and is one of the most practical men of his day, his sound financial standing in the county indicating his good judgment and practical management of business affairs. Max Meadows, Wythe county, Virginia, is his postoffice address.

JOHN M. HICKS—a merchant of Rural Retreat, became a resident of Wythe county in 1883, immediately entering upon the business his integrity and ability is daily extending. He was born in Sullivan county, Tennessee, in 1835, a son of Isaac and Rebecca R. (Hull) Hicks, and he married in Bristol, Tennessee, Cynthia A., daughter of Henry Yost Douthat and Eliza (Baylor) Douthat. She was born in Christiansburg, Montgomery county, Virginia, in 1844, and they were married April 17, 1862. Their children are two daughters, Minnie W., born May 30, 1864, in Marion, Smyth county, Virginia; Mary B., born April 29, 1873, at Bland C. H., countyseat of Bland county, Virginia. Mr. Hicks was four years postmaster at Bland C. H. During the civil war he was a participant in the sufferings undergone by those shut up in the siege of Vicksburg. His father and two brothers were soldiers of the Confederacy during that war. John M. Hicks' postoffice address is Rural Retreat, Wythe county, Virginia.

ELI HILLENBURG—is a grandson of Daniel Hillenburg, who came from Switzerland seeking a home in the New World, and settled in Wythe county, Virginia, at last, entering upon the cultivation of land, in which pursuit his grandson, the subject of this sketch, follows his example. Daniel Hillenburg evinced his love for the land of his adoption by fighting for its independence through all the years of the Revolutionary war His son Daniel married Nancy Ann Repass, and their son Eli was born in Wythe county, May 25, 1829. The mother of Eli died in Wythe county, and his father is living here, now aged seventy-nine years. In Wythe county, April 25, 1852, Eli Hillenburg was united in wedlock with Catharine Hilton, a union from which eight children were born: James Austin, April 7, 1853; Margaret Adaline, May 21, 1855; Crockett Gleaves, October 4, 1857; Mary Ann, February 21, 1860; William Eli, June 11, 1863; Emily Catharine, June 1, 1866; Laura Ellen, December 4, 1868; Sarah Alice, November 26, 1871. James A. died August 10, 1854, Margaret A. is the wife of Thomas J. Groseclose, of Washington county, Virginia, and the other children are all in Wythe county. Jacob Hilton, now deceased, and Polly (Miller) Hilton, living in Wythe county, were the parents of Catharine, wife of Mr Hillenburg. She was born in Wythe county, August 12, 1830. Eli Hillenburg enlisted in the second year of the war between the States at Wytheville, in Company B, 29th Virginia Infantry, the regiment was first in service in Marshall's brigade, then in Corse's brigade, Pickett's division. It took part in all the movements of the Army of Northern Virginia, Mr. Hillenburg sharing its fortunes unharmed until on the Appomattox field, they lay down their arms with the rest of that heroic army. Crocketts Depot, Wythe county, Virginia, is Mr. Hillenburg's postoffice address.

JOHN MILTON HOWARD—is a son of Anderson Howard, who was born in Montgomery county, Virginia, and Sallie (Calfee) Howard, born in Wythe county. He was born in Wythe county, October 11, 1826, and was married in this county, Rhoda Jane Allison becoming his wife on the 8th of December, 1852. His children are six living, two deceased, born: John A , March 4, 1854; Mary E., September 22, 1855; John A. died October 24, 1856, and another son, born June 24, 1857, was named John A.; Susan Jane, born June 12, 1859; Margaret Alice, June 8, 1862; David H., July 19, 1865; Russell, July 31, 1867; Cora Lee, June 3, 1870; Russell died December 18, 1869. The parents of Mrs. Howard were Halbert and Mary B. (Sayers) Allison, of Wythe county, and she was born in this county on the 5th of March, 1830, and died June 22, 1884. Mr. Howard owns and cultivates an estate of 600 acres, lying on New river, and is interested in stock raising. His postoffice address is Grahams Forge, Wythe county, Virginia.

WILLIAM G. HOWE—born in Pulaski county, Virginia, July 21, 1847, is a son of William H. Howe, of Pulaski county. His mother, whose maiden name was Mary M. Fisher, was born in Augusta county, Virginia, and died in 1883. Although too young to be subject to military duty, William G. Howe entered the Confederate States army in 1864, August 1st, and served in the cavalry under Fitz Hugh Lee until the close of the war. In Wythe county, December 30, 1874, he was united in marriage with Alice Virginia Brown, who was born in this county February 3, 1851, a daughter of Granville H. and Jane E. (Snavely) Brown. Daisie Marian, born February 12, 1876, and

Willie Alice, born March 3, 1879, are the children of Mr. and Mrs. Howe. The parents of Mrs. Howe were born in Wythe county, and her father died here in 1878. Her family is one of the oldest of the county, the pioneer settlers of the name coming here when few of the primeval forest trees had been cut down, and the red man alone was sole proprietor of this vast domain. Mr. Howe owns and operates one of the most beautiful stock farms of Virginia, lying on Reed creek, about ten miles from Wytheville, in the richest blue grass region of Virginia. His postoffice address is Rural Retreat, Wythe county, Virginia.

DAVID HUDDLE—was born in Wythe county, December 18, 1824, was married in Mount Airy, North Carolina, April 7, 1857, and died in Wythe county October 20, 1880. He was a son of Henry and Nancy (Elzey) Huddle, who until death resided in Wythe county, and he married Margaret P., daughter of John and Mary (Stanger) Earhart. She was born in Wythe county, October 25, 1831, and her parents are now deceased. The children of Mr. and Mrs. Huddle were born: Mary E. P., January 15, 1858, is now the wife of Mitchel Swecker; Maggie E. D., May 7, 1860, wife of Samuel M. Fulton; Robert E. Lee, October 6, 1862; N. E. Kyle, October 9, 1864; John H., March 8, 1867; Garland E., November 15, 1870; Willie D. S., September 5, 1874. The second daughter has her home in Grayson county, this State; the others are with their mother, or have their homes near her in Wythe county. David Huddle was thirty years a magistrate of Wythe county. From the time the Home Guards were called out during the late war he served with them. Mrs. Huddle had four brothers in the army: George W., John S., A. C. M., and Ely D. Earhart. The first named served from Missouri, the others from Wythe county. Ely D. was supposed to have been killed at the battle of Cloyd Farm, and has never been heard of since. Mrs. Huddle resides on the estate left by her husband, with her postoffice address at Red Bluff, Wythe county, Virginia.

ISAAC NEWTON HUDDLE—one of the substantial farming residents of Wythe county, owns and cultivate a farm of 184 acres of fine land, three miles north of Rural Retreat. He was born in Wythe county, May 7, 1849, and in this county his wedded life began, Sarah Jane Steffey becoming his wife on the 3d of October, 1872. Two daughters are the sunshine of their home: Emma, born October 27, 1879; Minnie, born March 12, 1881. Jonas and Elizabeth (Brown) Huddle, born in Wythe county, were the parents of Isaac N., and his wife is a daughter of Martin and Barbara Steffey, also natives of this county, and still residents here. Jonas Huddle died May 24, 1881. Mr. Huddle has served his township as clerk for three terms, his 're-elections testifying to his ability in the discharge of the duties of the office. He receives his mail at Rural Retreat, Wythe county, Virginia.

JOSEPH F. KENT—is a great grandson of Jacob Kent, who was eminent among the pioneer settlers of this section of Virginia. He is a son of Robert and Elizabeth (Craig) Kent, and was born in Montgomery county, March 20, 1820. In the year of his birth his parents settled in Wythe county, where his father was born. His mother was born in Montgomery county. Both are now deceased. The first wife of Joseph F. Kent, who died June 7, 1860, was Fannie P. Brown. Of their marriage the children born were five:

Bettie M., now the wife of George M. Harrison, of Staunton; John B., married Lucy McGavock, and lives in Wythe county; Jennie L., the wife of Howe P. Cochran, of Richmond; Emma R., the wife of John O. Yates, of Wythe county; Alexander S. B., resides in this county. In Augusta county, Virginia, September 11, 1869, Virginia F. Peyton became the wife of Mr. Kent, and their children are three: Joseph F., born September 16, 1870; Susan P., born September 16, 1876; and Mary P., born March 11, 1881. John Howe Peyton, formerly of Stafford county, Virginia, and now deceased, was the father of Mrs. Kent, and her mother, whose maiden name was Ann Montgomery Lewis, is also now deceased. She was born in what is now Monroe county, West Virginia. The subject of this sketch was one of four brothers who gave their services to Virginia through the years of the civil war. He served from the beginning to the close of the struggle. His brothers in service were George M, Clarence and Edwin D. For five years Mr. Kent was clerk of the Farmers Bank at Wytheville, and he has efficiently filled the office of postmaster at Wytheville, at which place he is now engaged in the manufacture of woolen goods.

ROBERT CRAIG KENT—was born in Wythe county, Virginia, November 28, 1828, a son of Robert and Elizabeth Montgomery (Craig) Kent. He was graduated from the Princeton (New Jersey) College, class of 1849, and read law in the office of the Hon. Andrew S. Fulton, judge of the county court of Wythe county. His practice has been in Wythe and adjacent counties, and he has served Wythe county as prosecuting attorney. In 1861 he was a member of the important State convention passing the ordinance of secession. Mr. Kent has been twice married, his first wife, who was Eliza Ann Woods Patton, dying December 12, 1863, having been the mother of three sons: William, now an attorney of Owensboro, Kentucky; Robert C. and Tyler Gatewood, both at home. In Pulaski county, Virginia, July 21, 1867, he married Anastasia Pleasants Smith, and they have four children: Mary Cloyd, born March 7, 1868; Eliza Ann Woods, Anas P., and Joseph Cloyd. The wife of Mr. Kent was born in Washington county, Virginia, November 5, 1842, a daughter of Pleasants and Mary E. Smith. Her father is no longer living. Robert C Kent has his office and residence in Wytheville.

GEORGE PHILIP KESNER—son of Charles H. and Sarah A. (Byars) Kesner, was born in Washington county, April 26, 1840. In Wythe county, at Wytheville, July 29, 1868, he married Senah M. Oury, who was born in Wythe county, August 9, 1846. She was a daughter of Van Buren and Thursey (Smyth) Oury. Her mother is living in Wythe county, and her father died here. The most of Mr. Kesner's life has been passed in Smyth county, and his father died in that county. His mother died in Illinois. His mother was a daughter of George Byars, who lived in Smyth county, and held a captain's commission in the 1812 war. Mrs. Kesner's grandfather served as a private in that war. John Kesner, paternel grandfather of George P., came from Washington county, Virginia, to Augusta county, and the family have since made their home in Southwestern Virginia. Mr. and Mrs. Kesner have been the parents of seven children: Victoria Virginia, born November 1, 1869; Lacy Dallas, March 29, 1871; Osceola, March 23, 1873; Irey Mintres, May 9, 1875; Manley Henning, April 8, 1877; Lucy Margaret, May 12,

1880; child born and died October 22, 1883. In April, 1861, at Marion, county-seat of Smyth county, George Philip Kesner enlisted in the Smith Dragoons, which became Company A, of the 8th Virginia Cavalry, attached to Jenkins' brigade. He was wounded at Barboursville in 1861, was captured at Sewell Mountain in 1862, and again wounded at Fishers Hill in 1864. He was a participant in the battles of Cross Lanes, Charlestown, Buffalo, Cannelton, Point Pleasant, Barboursville, Guyandotte, Sewell Mountain, Dry Creek, Lewisburg, Meadow Bluff, Princeton, Rogersville, Knoxville, Lynchburg, Fishers Hill, Strasburg, Kernstown, Winchester and Cedar Creek. Since January, 1865, the home of Mr. Kesner has been with the people of Wythe county, and he is carrying on a saddlery business at Crocketts, Wythe county, Virginia.

CALLOHILL M. KITCHENS—son of John W. and Nancy J. Kitchens, was born in Franklin county, Virginia, December 3, 1832, and became a resident of Wythe county in 1848. He is a dealer in mineral properties, with postoffice address at Red Bluff, Wythe county, Virginia.

JOSEPH LAMBERT—was born in Wythe county, February 4, 1814, a son of Michael and Mary (Michaels) Lambert. His father was born in this county, his mother in Germany, and they died in Wythe county. Joseph Lambert married the granddaughter of two pioneer settlers of Smyth county, George Keesling and George Horn. They came to Southwest Virginia from Pennsylvania. She is Catharine, daughter of Catharine (Horn) Keesling, and was born in Smyth county. The marriage of Joseph Lambert and Catharine Keesling was solemnized in Smyth county, October 26, 1843, and the birth and death record of their children is: Mary C., born November 1, 1844; Elizabeth Jane, born September 4, 1846, died March 13, 1862; William C., born October 5, 1850, died January 29, 1854; Peter M., born December 16, 1852, died March 2, 1862; Sarah A., born September 26, 1856, died March 11, 1862; Francis E., born February 28, 1861, died July 4th following; Martha E , born April 9, 1862, died December 14, 1864; George A., born March 12, 1867. The father and mother of Mrs. Lambert died in Smyth county. Joseph Lambert belonged to Ward's Home Guards during the civil war, and was called out for local defence for two months. He is a bricklayer and farmer. Postoffice address Cedar Springs, Wythe county, Virginia.

ROBERT LANDRETH—son of William M. and Nancy (Hendrick) Landreth, was born in Wythe county, September 30, 1847. His parents died in this county. Here, in 1869, he was joined in wedlock with Mary Florence Bralley, who was born in Wythe county, April 29, 1851, a daughter of Samuel and Pauline (Jessup) Bralley. Her father died in this county, and her mother is still living here. Ada Lee, born May 22, 1871, died October 3, 1880, was the first of the children of Mr and Mrs. Landreth. With them are six children, born: Alberti Paulina, January 26, 1873; Samuel Cloyd, October 3, 1874; Robert Edgar, May 5, 1876; Lizzie Gertrude, November 15, 1878; Lena May, June 17, 1881; Flora Pearl, October 29, 1883. Mr. Landreth joined Company G, 22d Virginia Cavalry, in 1863, and was in service till the close of the war. He was a participant in thirteen battles, among them Cloyd Farm, Monocacy Junction, Cumberland' City, Moorefield, Winchester, Fishers Hill, and Gordonsville. His brother Thomas J. was in the Wythe Reserves, and another brother Andrew Jackson, served in Company D, 45th Virginia Infantry. The latter was taken prisoner to Camp Morton, Indianapolis, where he died in 1864. Robert Landreth combines the occupations of farming and millwright, and receives his mail at Speedwell, Wythe county, Virginia.

JAMES PIPER McTEER—born in Wythe county, April 13, 1856, is a son of Rev. John M. McTeer, who was born in Blount county, Tennessee, and is now an eminent divine in the Methodist Church. The mother of James P., whose maiden name was Eliza C. Kelly, was born in Washington county, Tennessee, and died April 23, 1856. At "Locust Grove," Wythe county, December 19, 1877, James P. McTeer was united in marriage with Maggie, daughter of Stephen and Margaret J. (McNutt) Porter. Her father, born in Wythe county, died September 17, 1883; her mother was born in Blount county, Tennessee. Her birth was in Wythe county, February 21, 1857 the date, and Eliza Stuart, born November 15, 1878, and John M., jr., born January 31, 1883, are the children of Mr. and Mrs. McTeer. In 1880, when twenty-three years of age, James P. McTeer was elected judge of the 79th judicial district county courts of Wythe and Pulaski counties, by the general assembly, perhaps the youngest man who ever held that office in Virginia. He discharged its duties with ability and zeal until 1888, when he was elected commonwealth attorney for Wythe county, by about 400 majority, and he is still the efficient incumbent of the office. He resides on his estate, "Oakland," near Wytheville.

JOHN HARRISON MOORE—was born on Cripple creek, in Wythe county, on the 14th of July, 1858, a son of John W. and Elizabeth (Collins) Moore. His father was a son of John Moore, prominent among the residents here early in this century, and his mother was a daughter of David Collins, also of Wythe county. The father of Mr. Moore, now filling the office of deputy sheriff of Wythe county, has several years ably discharged the duties of magistrate. John H. Moore has embarked in a mercantile business which he is prosperously conducting at McTeer, Wythe county, Virginia.

ROBERT EMMETT MOORE—physician and surgeon, is a son of Alfred Cleon Moore, who was born in Patrick county, Virginia, December 12, 1805, and who married Ann Frances Kent, born in Wythe county, January 2, 1805. Alfred C. Moore is still living, but his wife died in April, 1852. Robert Emmett Moore was born in Wythe county, on the 14th of October, 1838, and, with all the other male members of his immediate family, offered his service in defense of the rights of Virginia during the struggle for State sovereignty in 1861-5. His father was colonel of the 29th Virginia Infantry; his elder brother, A. S. Moore, was adjutant of the same regiment, and died from exposure and disease contracted in the line of duty; J. M. Moore, next eldest, was lieutenant of a cavalry company; W. O. Moore was captain of a cavalry company, and Robert E. was surgeon, Confederate States army. In Aberdeen, Mississippi, May 23, 1863, he was united in marriage with Martha S. Glascock, who was born in Fauquier county, Virginia, January 20, 1841. Her father, William O. Glascock, was born in Bardstown, Kentucky, May 18, 1812, and died February 18, 1879, and her mother, Adelaide Eliza (Adams) Glascock, was born May 18, 1818, in Fauquier county, and died February 14, 1869. Dr. Moore is settled in practice among the people of Wytheville and vicinity.

ROBERT ROLEN MOORE—is a Kentuckian by birth, born in Bath county, that State, February 3, 1823. He was a son of John Moore, who died in 1829, and Lillie (Butler) Moore, who died in 1846. His first marriage was with Emeline, daughter of Colonel William Benton, of Irvine Estill, Kentucky. She died in 1849, without issue, and he married, secondly, in Wythe county, Virginia, May 27, 1863, Mary M. Simmerman, who was born in Wythe county in 1842. They have six children, born: Mary K., April 6, 1864; John S., November 3, 1866; Robert R., August 6, 1869; Blanche A., April, 1870; Millie E., April, 1873; William B., April 25, 1874. John P. M. (deceased) and Mary A. Simmerman, now lives in Wythe county, were the parents of Mary M., wife of Mr. Moore. R. R. Moore was a contractor in the Confederate States service during the war between the States, and in 1863 made his home in Wythe county. He is engaged in farming, giving special attention to the raising of fine stock. Wytheville, Wythe county, Virginia, is his postoffice address.

WILLIAM ORVILLE MOORE—was born at Locust Hill, Wythe county, February 17, 1841: His parents were Alfred Cleon Moore, who was born in Patrick county, Virginia, December 5, 1805, came to Wythe county in 1834, and married Ann Frances Kent, who died April 3, 1852. His father, William Moore, served in the 1812 war with rank of major, and at the outbreak of the 1861 war Colonel Alfred C. Moore entered the Confederate States service, at the age of sixty years, and served three years as colonel of the 29th Virginia Infantry. He had four sons in the service, A. S., J. M., R. E., and W. O. All served till the close of the war except Algernon Sidney, who was adjutant of the 29th Virginia Infantry, and died April 23, 1862, from disease contracted in the service. William O. was 3d lieutenant of Company D, 45th Virginia Infantry, for one year, then adjutant with his father's regiment for fifteen months, then captain of Company G, 22d Virginia Cavalry for one year. He was in battle at Carnifax Ferry, Cedar Hill, Winchester, Monocacy, Five Forks, and Appomattox C. H. He was with Early in his valley campaign in 1864, and with Lee around Richmond in 1865. In Wytheville, October 28, 1872, Page Taylor became the wife of William O. Moore. Their children are Helen Taylor, Sidney Page, Page Waller, Addie Kent, Alfred Cleon, Bettie Taylor. The wife of Captain Moore, a daughter of John M. and Bettie (Waller) Taylor, was born in Alabama, in 1848, and came with her parents to Wythe county in 1868. The first wife of Captain Moore was Addie Pearson, daughter of George W. Jones, of Marion, Smyth county. They were married October 29, 1867, their son William Sidney was born August 8, 1868, and another son, George Cleon, was born September 3, 1870, and the mother died on the 11th of September following. The babe died January 21, 1871. Captain Moore is engaged in the pursuits of agriculture, his estate lying in Speedwell district, and Wytheville, Virginia, is his postoffice address.

DANIEL NEFF—son of Abraham and Rebecca Neff, and Amanda J. Scott, daughter of William and Elizabeth Scott, were united in marriage in Smyth county, Virginia, in July, 1843. He was born in Wythe county, in November, 1821, and she was born in Smyth county, in March, 1822. Eleven children were the issue of their union, and all are now living in Wythe county except James T., who lives in Smyth: Elizabeth M. (Copenhaver), born May 19, 1844; Sarah E. (Etter), December 6, 1845; James P., December 22, 1847; Bollard H., February 10, 1850; William S., January 16, 1853; John A., October

27, 1855; Mary V. F. (Hounshell), April 11, 1858; Stephen D., October 28, 1860; Josephine A. C. (Coley), February 27, 1863; Charles M., March 29, 1866; Emma C., June 15, 1867. This sketch is compiled for the fifth child and third son, William S., who is a teacher and farmer, with postoffice address at Rural Retreat, Wythe county, Virginia.

JACOB M. NEFF—born in Wythe county, July 8, 1834, in this county, on the 25th of January, 1866, was united in marriage with Mary E. Snavely. She was born in Smyth county, January 7, 1847, and the children of their marriage were born in Wythe county: Robert C., May 6, 1868; Charles C., April 13, 1870; Elizabeth A., December 15, 1871; Gussie H., May 31, 1873; Edward M., April 10, 1875; Virginia A., July 31, 1877; Lena M., September 7, 1879; George R , April 2, 1881; Ella C., January 23, 1883. Abraham and Elizabeth (Repass) Neff were the parents of Jacob M., and his wife is a daughter of John C. and Ann (Lambert) Snaveley. Her mother lives now in Wythe county; her father died in Smyth county; the father of Mr. Neff, who was a son of Michael Neff, an early and prominent resident in the county, died September 3, 1880. His mother is no longer living. Jacob M. Neff served one year in the civil war in Company B, 45th Virginia Infantry, then one year in Company B, 29th Virginia Infantry. He was severely wounded at Suffolk county bridge, and crippled in the leg, after which he served in Company G, 22d Virginia Cavalry Reserves. Farming is the occupation of Mr. Neff, and his postoffice address is Rural Retreat, Wythe county, Virginia.

MICHAEL NEFF—born in Wythe county, February 9, 1831, son of Abraham and Elizabeth (Repass) Neff, is one of the farming residents of the county. His parents died in this county, his mother's death occurring December 28, 1871, and his father dying September 3, 1880, at the age of eighty-two years. His father was a son of Michael Neff, who came from Pennsylvania to Wythe county, and whose father came from Germany to Pennsylvania. The maternal grandfather of Michael Neff was John Repass, of this county. In Smyth county, June 26, 1856, Rachael H. Scott became the wife of Mr. Neff. They have three living children: Paulina, born February 24, 1860, now the wife of Joseph S. Clark; Maggie E., born August 15, 1862; Callie Frances, March 31, 1868. Their first born, Sarah Ellen, died at birth, May 17, 1857; Wiley Winton, born May 26, 1858, the only son, died September 10, 1859. John Scott, who died in 1863, and Margaret (Porter) Scott, who died in 1871, were the parents of Mrs. Neff. She was born in Smyth county, February 6, 1837. Michael Neff volunteered his services for the defense of Virginia at Wytheville, and was three years a member in active service of the 63d Virginia Infantry, Company H, as sergeant. His regiment fought in Reynold's brigade, Stephenson's division, Buckner's corps, and was in the battles of Stone River, Chickamauga, Resaca, Atlanta, Zions Church, Jonesboro, and many others. He was with Johnston's army in North Carolina at the surrender. He had four brothers in the army, William in his company, Henry in the 45th Infantry, Jacob and Pearson in Company B, 29th Virginia Infantry. Michael Neff's postoffice address is Rural Retreat, Wythe county, Virginia

ALBERT MICAJAH OGLESBY—farmer and raiser of thoroughbred cattle in Lead Mine district, Wythe county, was born in this county,

June 14, 1835. He is a son of Nicholas P. and Jane C. (Sayers) Oglesby, whose record appears in this page, and he married Lizzie A., the daughter of John and Martha P. (Oglesby) Jackson. She was born in Wythe county, February 28, 1837; they were married in this county October 22, 1862, and their children were born: Jennie S., August 12, 1863; Nicholas P., March 21, 1865; Martha I., September 19, 1867; John J., November 2, 1869; Lillian G., November 12, 1873. During the war between the States Albert M. Oglesby was one year a member of the "Wythe Greys," which went into the service as Company A, 4th Virginia Infantry, assigned to the "Stonewall Brigade," and sharing its gallant action in the campaigns of Northern Virginia. Ill health forced him to leave the service. His postoffice address is Jacksons Ferry, Wythe county, Virginia.

HON. NICHOLAS P. OGLESBY—born and raised in Wythe county, was a son of N. P. and Jane C. (Sayers) Oglesby, and a grandson of Thompson Sayers, of Revolutionary fame. June 12, 1867, he married Sallie A., daughter of Thomas S. and Rachel L. (Cecil) Crockett, of this county. Their eight children were born: John T. S., April 4, 1868; Samuel C., April 1, 1870; Jennie L., September 13, 1872; Nicholas P., September 2, 1874; Mary S., April 16, 1876; Albert C., February 25, 1878; Frank S., July 14, 1880; William B., September 12, 1883. Thompson Sayers, grandfather of Nicholas P. Oglesby, served with distinction through the war for Independence, was wounded through the lungs at Guilford C. H., a wound thought to be fatal, but being a man of uncommon constitution he recovered, and lived to be about sixty years old. His brother, Robert Sayers, held a colonel's commission in the same war, and was several times elected to represent his county in the State legislature. Their father was an early and prominent settler of the county. Colonel Robert was a man of great business capacity, owned the Anchor and Hope estate, of Wythe county, and a large estate in Birks Garden, Tazewell county. The subject of this sketch was a Confederate States soldier, as was his brother, Albert M. He served in the Army of Northern Virginia, participating in the battles of Spotsylvania C. H., the Wilderness, around Richmond, Mine Run, etc. In the years 1877 and 1878 he represented Wythe county in the legislature. He resides upon his estate, "Elmwood," in Fort Chiswell district, where he has one of the largest and best herds of thoroughbred short-horns in Virginia. Mr. Oglesby may be addressed at Max Meadows, Wythe county, Virginia.

WILLIAM E. PEERY, Jr.,—is a son of William E. and Kate M. (Cecil) Peery, of Tazewell county, Virginia. His father served in the Army of Northern Virginia from the beginning of the war, sharing in all its campaigns, and holding rank of captain, until the terrible fight at Gettysburg, where the flower of Virginia chivalry was mowed down, he shared the fate of many brave comrades, was wounded, losing an arm, and made prisoner. Thomas R. Peery, uncle of William E. jr., was killed in one of the Winchester battles, at the age of nineteen years. William E. Peery, jr, was born in Tazewell county, May 10, 1861, and was married in Bland county, Virginia, November 16, 1881. His wife is Josie A., daughter of Hermon and Mary A. (McDonald) Newberry, of Bland county. She was born in that county, July 26, 1861, and their son, Edward C., was born May 1, 1883. On the 15th of August, 1883, the subject of this sketch became a resident of Wytheville district, settling on a farm and devoting his attention to grazing and farming. His postoffice address is Kents Mills, Wythe county, Virginia.

DAVID STUART PEIRCE—is a grandson of David Peirce, who settled in Wythe county in 1785. Possessed of great energy, David Peirce built the first iron furnace in this section of Virginia, and after the Revolution he bought the lead mines, which he continued to work with some profit until his death, in 1833. His son James Newell Peirce married Anna Dabney Stuart, and their son, subject of this memoir, was born in Pulaski county, Virginia, September 19, 1846. Not twenty years of age when war between the States was ended, he had seen one year's hard service with the war worn veterans of the Army of Northern Virginia. James N. Peirce died in 1854, and his wife died in 1846. David S. Peirce received instructions of the literary and scientific courses at the Virginia Military Institute, and his professional studies were pursued at the celebrated University of Virginia, whence he was graduated in 1867. He was admitted to the bar in 1868, at Wytheville, and has since been in successful practice in Wythe and adjoining counties. For two years, 1870-1, he was commonwealth attorney, and in 1876 was presidential elector on the Democratic ticket, casting his vote for Samuel J. Tilden. Wytheville, Wythe county, Virginia, is his postoffice address.

JAMES BURTON PEIRCE—was a son of David R. Peirce, who was a son of Alexander Peirce, who was a son of David Peirce, who came from England to Virginia, and settled in Wythe county, where the succeeding sons, as mentioned, were born. David R. Peirce married Sarah N. Wall, and their son, James Burton, was born November 25, 1851. At Barren Springs, Wythe county, April 26, 1876, he married Nancy Jane Porter, and three children are now the sunshine of their home: Mary Ann, born May 31, 1877; Joseph Foster, May 16, 1880; Carrie Jane, September 2, 1882. The wife of Mr. Peirce was born in Carroll county, Virginia, July 17, 1856, a daughter of John A. and Mary E. (Pearman) Porter, now of Pulaski county, Virginia. James B. Peirce is a millwright and merchant of Ivanhoe, Wythe county, Virginia.

J. B. PEIRCE, M. D.—was born near the lead mines, in Wythe county, February 22, 1842, the youngest son of Alexander and Elizabeth (Bell) Peirce. In September, 1853, at the age of eleven years, he was sent to Georgetown College, District of Columbia. Leaving there January, 1856, he afterwards attended parts of two sessions, 1857-58, at Emory and Henry College, Washington county, Virginia. He taught a "field school" in Old Town, Grayson county, in 1859 and 1860, which was closed out about Christmas of that year. April 17, 1861, he was mustered into the service of the State, at Richmond, Virginia, in the Wythe Greys. The incorporation of this regiment in the 4th Virginia Infantry, and the assignment and service of the regiment in the field, are elsewhere given in this work. Because of intermittant fever, Dr. Peirce was not permitted to accompany his regiment into the Maryland campaign, after Chintilly, and was ordered to Winchester. When sufficiently recovered he hastened to resume his place in the ranks, was with his company at the surrender of Harpers Ferry, and joined General Lee at Sharpsburg, on the night of September 17th, too late to take part in the battle. He was slightly wounded in the battles of second Manassas, Chancellorsville, and in the Wilderness, and was severely wounded in the battle of Monocacy Junction, from which wound he did not recover until several years after the cessation of hostilities. In the fall of 1866 Dr. Peirce attended the lectures of the medical department of the University of Virginia, and the next year he was graduated in medicine from the Washington University of Maryland, Baltimore. The day he received his diploma he also received a telegram to hasten to the bedside of his father, who had suffered apoplexy and paralysis of the right side. He remained in attendance on him for twenty-three months, and after his death, which occurred February 2, 1870, undertook to settle the business he had left, and of which the doctor had made a study. It required thirteen years of litigation to accomplish this. During all this time Dr. Peirce had attended regularly and conscientiously upon his extensive practice. He has never married.

CHARLES TAYLOR PEPPER, M. D.—was born December 2, 1830, in Montgomery county, Virginia, a son of John and Mary (Robertson) Pepper, of that county, and of one of the oldest families settled in that part of Virginia. Samuel Pepper, who settled in Pulaski county at the spot named Peppers Ferry in his honor, as early as 1745, was his grandfather. The mother of Dr. Pepper died in 1857 and his father in 1867. Dr. John G. Pepper, brother of Charles T., was surgeon of the 1st Tennessee Cavalry, from the beginning to the close of the civil war. In Pulaski county, Virginia, May 18, 1858, Charles T. Pepper and Isabella McDowell Howe were united in marriage. The bride was a daughter of William Henry and Mary (Fisher) Howe, of Pulaski county, and was born in that county October 10, 1838. Her mother died July 17, 1883. The children of Dr. and Mrs. Pepper were born: William Howe, April 11, 1859; Charles Robertson, November 14, 1862; Mary Margaret, December 10, 1865; Louis Ervin, February 14, 1872; Ruth McDowell, August 20, 1874. Mary Margaret died October 30, 1868. Dr. Pepper served the Confederacy as acting surgeon in charge of hospital at Bristol, Tennessee, nearly two years during the war. Since 1879 he has made his home in Wythe county, and he combines the practice of his profession with the cultivation of his estate of 190 acres. His postoffice address is Rural Retreat, Wythe county, Virginia.

JOHN C. RAPER—son of Robert and Mary Craig (Crockett) Raper, and Sallie S. Crockett, daughter of John Stuart and Margaret Buchanan (Taylor) Crockett, were united in bands of wedlock in Wytheville, on the 4th of December, 1872. He was born in this county, May 31, 1834, her birth was in the county February 17, 1851, and their children were born: Maggie Stuart, October 7, 1874; Robert H. C., January 7, 1878; Virginia L., October 3, 1880. Mr. Raper is one of the most enterprising business men of Wythe county, owning and cultivating a farm, and engaged in the manufacture of shot. Born of lineage distinctly Virginian for many generations on the mother's side, he is a thorough type of the old-time Virginia gentleman. His father was of English birth. Max Meadows, Wythe county, Virginia, is his postoffice address.

NEWTON HERSCHEL REPASS—was born on New Years Day, 1835, in Wythe county, a son of Jesse and Lydia (Brown) Repass. In the spring of 1862 he entered the Confederate States service, Company C, 51st Virginia Infantry, the regiment assigned to Wharton's brigade, Breckinridge's division, Early's corps. While in service in Maryland he was assigned to duty as lieutenant in the brigade sharpshooters. He was a participant in the battles of Princeton, Fayette C. H., and Charleston, in West Virginia, in Mt. Jackson, Kernstown, Winchester and Martinsburg in the valley of Virginia, and with Lee in the fighting from Hanover Junction to Cold Harbor, under Early in his fight with Hunter at Lynchburg, and in his invasion of Maryland, including the battle of Monocacy Bridge. He was captured at Winchester, September 19, 1864, and held in Fort Delaware until after the close of the war, about nine months. In Wythe county, August 14, 1872, Newton H. Repass and Margaret Agnes Brown were united in marriage. They have two sons, Joe Brown, born February 15, 1874, and George Jesse, February 25, 1881. The wife of Mr. Repass is a daughter of Joseph and Sarah (Hudson) Brown, of Wythe county, and was born in this county, on the 13th of February, 1843. George F. and Henry L. Repass, brothers of Newton H., were soldiers of the Army of Northern Virginia. Henry L. was captured at Waynesboro, sent to Fort Morton, Indiana, and died there. Another brother, Joseph W., was in the Southwest Army, under McCullough, and his record is that saddest of all war records, "Missing." He was at Cane Hill, Arkansas, when that post was captured, and is supposed to have been killed, or to have died, as nothing has since been heard from him. Newton H. Repass is a farmer and cattle raiser, postoffice address, Wytheville, Wythe county, Virginia.

WILLIAM GORDON REPASS—is of German descent, grandson of Frederick Repass, sr., who emigrated from Pennsylvania to the then Western borders of civilization in Virginia, and was honorably identified with the settlement of Wythe county. Stephen and Rosanna (Brown) Repass were the parents of William G., whose birth was in Wythe county on the 2d of June, 1838. He married Sarah Jane Fisher, who was born in this county February 22, 1839, a daughter of Joseph and Sarah (Baumgardner) Fisher. Their marriage was solemnized in this county, September 22, 1859, and its issue was three daughters and four sons: Elmira E., Margaret A. and Clarence A. are at home; Joseph M., Stephen W., Mary A. and Edward F. are no longer living. The parents of Mrs. Repass are deceased, her father dying in 1866 and her mother in 1883. The father of Mr. Repass died in 1876, his mother still lives, and has her home with her son in Bland county, Virginia. Mr. Repass entered the service of the Confederate States as a private in Company K, 51st Virginia Infantry. He received merited promotion, to sergeant, then lieutenant, then captain, and later was transferred to the 7th Confederate Battalion of Cavalry as major. He participated in all the engagements of Floyd's brigade, and from his transfer to the close of the war was in cavalry service. He was slightly wounded five times. He had two brothers in the army, James A. and Rufus B. He follows the occupation of farm life, his estate lying in Wythe county, and Wytheville his postoffice address, and since January 1, 1882, he has been county superintendent of schools, an office he still fills efficiently.

WILLIAM ASBURY RICHMOND—was born in Rye Cove, Scott county, Virginia, a son of William F. and Elizabeth Richmond, still of Scott county. At Stickleyville, Lee county, Virginia, June 19, 1879, the marriage vows were recorded of William Asbury Richmond and Alice May Litton, and in the years that have ensued three sons have been given them: Walter Ernest, born August 1, 1880; Jackson Litton, March 23, 1882; Willie Clyde, March 23, 1884. Andrew Jackson Litton and Ada Victoria Litton, of Lee county, are the parents of the wife of Mr. Richmond, and she was born in that county, at Stickneyville, September 6, 1860. B. F. Richmond, brother of William A., was a member of Company C, 27th Virginia Infantry, and served with that company as a part of the Confederate States army during its existence. He was wounded at Fishers Hill. In 1880 William A. Richmond cast his fortunes in with the people of Wythe county, and he is prosperously conducting a mercantile business in Rural Retreat, this county.

JOHN T. SAYERS—born in Wythe county, Virginia, April 27, 1831, is now one of the substantial farming residents of his native county. During the years of the war between the States, he was a soldier of the Confederate States army, enlisting as sergeant and receiving merited promotion to second, then first, lieutenant. He was in service from April, 1861, till the close of the struggle, and was twice wounded, slightly at second Manassas; severely at Gettysburg; he was captured on the field at Gettysburg, and was held during the time of his imprisonment at Johnsons Island, in Lake Erie. In Botetourt county, Virginia, March 31, 1870, John T. Sayers and Martha V. Miller were united in marriage. Robert, their first child, was a Christmas gift, in 1871; Lizzie S. was born November 23, 1873; Senah R., December 16, 1875. Robert Sayers, born in Wythe county, and now deceased, and Senah N. Sayers, born in Pulaski county, Virginia, now living in Wythe county, were the parents of Mr. Sayers. His wife was born May 6, 1841, in Greenbrier county, (now) West Virginia, and was a daughter of Fleming B. and Elizabeth A. (Selden) Miller. Her father, no longer living, was born in Botetourt county, Virginia, in 1791, and her mother was born in 1801, and died in 1857. John T. Sayers' postoffice address is Wytheville, Wythe county, Virginia.

NICHOLAS A. SAYERS—son of William and Isabella H. (Stephens) Sayers, was born at Reed Island, Wythe county, July 10, 1845. He enlisted at Staunton, Augusta county, in July, 1863, but on account of weak lungs was rejected for active field service. He, however, found opportunity to do yeoman's service with the Home Guards, and was a participant in the battle of Cloyd Mountain among other engagements. In Roanoke county, Virginia, January 19, 1871, he married Mary L. Deyerle, daughter of Andrew Jackson Deyerle and Jane Barnette Deyerle. Her father first held office at the age of sixteen years, ably discharging the duties of magistrate, and at the opening of the civil war he held commission of colonel in militia. He raised a company in Salem, which became incorporated in the 42d Infantry. At Cedar Mountain he commanded the regiment, where it was so severely engaged that of his old company going into battle, forty-nine men, only four returned unharmed. He was himself reported mortally wounded, but in time partially recovered. For gallant conduct on this field he received commission of colonel, but unable, from the effects of his wound, to ride on horseback, he was never again able to take the field. He was then elected to the legislature, and served till the close of the war. Although able to move only on crutches his war spirit is still uncrushed, the vigor of his intellect unimpaired, and at his home at Big Spring, Montgomery county, he lives, a gray-haired veteran of the war. His wife is of the old Irish family of Barnettes on her father's side, and through her mother is descended from the Lewis family, famed in Virginia's annals. Colonel Deyerle is of Franco-German descent; his grandfather, Peter Deyerle, who ran away from his father's home on the Rhine, worked his passage to America, became a miller to Mr. Bowman of Eastern Virginia, and married his daughter Rebecca. He became one of the first settlers of Montgomery county, and a wealthy land owner in Montgomery and Roanoke counties. He owned a vast track in what is now Kentucky, including the present site of Louisville, and on one occasion while prospecting his lands there, the Indians attacked the boat in which he was, with a flight of arrows, upon which he called out: "Take care, mit your nonsense, you might preak mine schmoke-pipe!" His wife was equally fearless, and once shot a bear from a large tree which still stands on the banks of the Roanoke. His son Abraham, father of Colonel Deyerle, inherited "Kent Home," his principal estate in Roanoke county. Mary L. (Deyerle) Sayers, is a woman of natural genius and fine literary attainments, the authoress of several poems, the most noted being "Memory," of which it has been said that it "is one of the two gems of American verse." She has been several years an active and able contributor to newspaper and periodical literature. This sketch is compiled for Mary Alberta Deyerle, born October 2, 1881, on Lopez Island, in Puget Sound, an arm of the Pacific ocean off Washington Territory, daughter of J. William Deyerle and Pink Barnett, his wife, both Virginians. They returned to settle in Montgomery county, Virginia, in 1882, and have kindly loaned their third babe to her childless uncle and aunt. Mr. Sayers' business is farming and stock raising, and his postoffice address is Reed Island, Wythe county, Virginia.

GEORGE AUGUSTUS SEAGLE—is one of the eleven children of James and Nancy O. (Rader) Seagle, early and honored residents of Wythe county. James Seagle, born October 14, 1801, died January 16, 1883. His widow still survives him; she was born June 18, 1805. Nicholas L. and Mary J. (Hendricks) Welsh, of Wythe county, are the parents of Bettie E., wife of Mr. Seagle. He was born at Speedwell, Wythe county, April 14, 1850, she was born at Speedwell, August 28, 1855, and they were married at Speedwell, January 29, 1873. Their children are six, born: Jettie K., November 5, 1873; Cora B., July 23, 1875; Blanche C., July 7, 1877; Viola G., August 22, 1879; Curtis B., November 30, 1881; Edna M., February 3, 1884, died April 1, 1884. John S. and J. B. Seagle, brothers of George A., were members of Company D, 45th Virginia Infantry, during the years of the civil war, John S. serving till killed at Cloyd Mountain, May 9, 1864; J. B. enlisting very young and in service through the last two years of the war. George A. Seagle has devoted his attention to the science of pisciculture; and in April, 1882, was appointed superintendent of the United States fish hatchery near Wytheville, which position he still ably fills, with postoffice address at Wytheville, Wythe county, Virginia.

JOSEPH CAMPBELL SEXTON—was born in Wytheville, November 26, 1833, a son of John and Priscilla Sexton. His father, born in 1811, died in 1868; his mother, born in 1805, died in 1843. Three sons of John Sexton were soldiers of Virginia during the war between the States. One gave his life for the Lost Cause. Napoleon B. served in King's Artillery, and survived the war, dying in 1867, in Baltimore, Maryland. John McAllister Sexton was a private of Company A, 4th Virginia Infantry, Stonewall brigade, aged 22 years; he was wounded during Early's invasion of Maryland, at Monocacy

Bridge, a gunshot wound causing compound fracture of right thigh, middle-third, July 9, 1864, and he died at Frederick City, Maryland, August 6th following. Joseph C. enlisted at Wytheville, April 17, 1861, for the war, private in Company A, 4th Virginia Infantry. The regiment was assigned to the 1st brigade, afterward Stonewall Brigade, 1st division, 3d corps. September 11, 1861, he was promoted regimental commissary with rank of captain; April 1, 1862, brigade commissary, with General Garnett, with rank of major. He served through the four years until the surrender at Appomattox, a member of the staff of Generals Jackson, Garnett, Winder, Terry, Walker, and J. B. Gordon. Another veteran of the Army of Northern Virginia is "Charley," Mr. Sexton's war horse, bought of Charles Harris in Winchester, December 23, 1861. Charley traveled not less than 25,000 miles during the war, always ready to switch his tail in defiance of the enemy. He is now thirty-one years old and since the war has been in constant use to the present time (1884). J. C. Sexton conducts a harness and saddlery business at Wytheville, Wythe county, Virginia.

JOHN P. SHARITZ—son of Josephand Beatta (Yonce) Sharitz, was born in Wythe county, April 6, 1826. In this county, November 2, 1854, he was joined in wedlock with Clementina R. Hudson, who was born March 8, 1834, in that part of Wythe county now included in Bland county. Three daughters and three sons were born of their union: Alice V., Janie H., H. Bettie, George Wythe, jr., James B. and John W. George and Hannah (Shannon) Hudson are the parents of Mrs. Sharitz, her father born in what is now Bland county, her mother in Pulaski county, Virginia, and both died in Bland county. The father of John P., Joseph Sharitz, born in Wythe county, February 5, 1803, died October 31, 1879. His mother was born in Wythe county, December 18, 1803, and died March 16, 1845. John P. Sharitz went to serve in the Richmond defenses in 1864, in October of that year, at Camp Lee, near the capital. He joined Company K, 1st Virginia Infantry, Terry's brigade, Pickett's division, Longstreet's corps, as private, and served until made prisoner, April 6, 1865, three days before the surrender, then held at Point Lookout until June 20, 1865. He is a farmer and surveyor, and has ably filled the office of justice of the peace for twenty years. His postoffice address is Wytheville, Wythe county, Virginia.

JOSEPH SHARITZ—born February 5, 1803, and Beatta Yonce, born December 18, 1803, both of Wythe county, were married April 1, 1824, and were the parents of the following children: Amos K., born January 30, 1825, died November 5, 1864; John P., born April 6, 1826; Frances E., February 11, 1828; Daniel M., October 23, 1829; Thomas R., December 5, 1831, died June 10, 1834; David McA., February 25, 1834, died in the Confederate service, at Bowling Green, Kentucky, January 17, 1862; Catharine A., born February 5, 1836; Hiram A., born October 12, 1840, and died at Meadow Bluff, Greenbrier county, West Virginia, October 12, 1861, in the service; Canaro J., born September 20, 1844; these, and two infants who died unnamed, were the children of Beatta, wife of Mr. Sharitz. She died March 16, 1845. He married secondly Patsy Baker, who was born June 26, 1819, and their children were born: Emory A., November 26, 1846; Robeson M., October 8, 1848, died October 12, 1854; Mary E., born March 28, 1850; Charles W., April 6, 1852; Elmira C., March 11, 1854; Henry L., September 3, 1855; Guy H., July 8, 1858; Lillie C., February

8, 1862. The two sons of the first marriage who died in the army were members of Company E, 51st Virginia Infantry. The father of these children departed this life in the full assurance of the Christian faith, October 29, 1879, leaving an aged widow and twelve children to mourn their irreparable loss.. His father, Daniel Sharitz, was born in Pennsylvania, February 24, 1776, and died October 12, 1840. He married Polly Ann Sluss, who was born in Virginia about 1775, and who died September 18, 1859. Douglas Baker, father of Patsy Baker Sharitz, was born in Wythe county, November, 1776, married Mary Hoge, May 14, 1812, and died in September, 1847. His wife was born in Montgomery county, Virginia, April 24, 1789, and died in December, 1852. Their childred were seven, Perlina H., Elizabeth, Patsy, Catharine, James H., Harosneth, Montgomery, of whom only three survive. Mis. Patsy Sharitz is' passing her old age on the family farm in Wytheville district, and the family postoffice address is Wytheville, Wythe county, Virginia.

DANIEL WINTON SHEFFEY—born in Wythe county, Virginia, March 10, 1848, was a son of Robert S. Sheffey, now of Giles county, Virginia, who was a son of Henry Sheffey, of Wythe county. The mother of Daniel W. was Elizabeth F., daughter of Wendall Swecker, who came from Pennsylvania to make his home in Wythe county. Mary A., daughter of William P. and Elizabeth (Saul) Allison, was born in Wythe county, November 6, 1845, and in North Carolina on the 3d of January, 1866, she became the wife of Daniel W. Sheffey. Their six children were born: William R., May 17, 1868; Margaret E., March 28, 1872; Sarah Ann Louisa, 1877; Nellie Preston, September 10, 1882; James Price and High Price, February 25, 1884 The parents of Mrs. Sheffey were residents until death in Wythe county. Two brothers of Mr. Sheffey, James W. and Hugh Trigg, were soldiers of Virginia during the war between the States. James W. was a member of the 63d Infantry, and Hugh was in the cavalry service. D. W. Sheffey served in Company B, 51st Virginia Infantry, for three weeks just preceding the surrender of the army of Northern Virginia. Farming is his occupation, his location in Speedwell district, and his postoffice address is Red Bluff, Wythe county, Virginia.

JOHN P. M. SIMMERMAN—son of Thomas H. and Mary (Sanders) Simmerman, of Wythe county, was born in this county November 18, 1821. He was a grandson of the man who donated the land on which Wytheville, the present countyseat, was laid out. In Wythe county, March 18, 1841, he married Mary A. G., daughter of John A. and Mary (Wiserman) Simmerman. Her father was born in Wythe county, her mother in Augusta county, and she was born in Wythe county, July 29, 1825. The birth and death record of the children of Mr. and Mrs. John P. M. Simmerman is: Mary M., born December 28, 1841, died March 14, 1878; Letitia, born October 16, 1843, lives in Pulaski county; Lizzie, born September 13, 1845, lives in Wythe county; W. A., born March 30, 1848, died March 31, 1875; Thomas H., born January 28, 1851; S. S., November 18, 1854; J. P. M. ,March 11, 1857; Virginia, December 22, 1860; George W., August 19, 1863; R. L., August 22, 1866—these six living in Wythe county. John P. M. Simmerman was a man of remarkable business capacity, and more than ordinary mental endowments. He lived a life which endeared him to all in his community, accumulated a fortune, and died on the 4th of December, 1880, mourned and loved by all who knew him.

This sketch is compiled for his son Stephen S., who is a farmer and stock raiser of Lead Mine district, with postoffice address at Ivanhoe Furnace, Wythe county, Virginia.

JAMES MADISON SNAVELY—a native of Smyth county, Virginia, born October 8, 1838, is a son of Peter B. and Mahala (Leedy) Snavely. He entered the Confederate States army May 12, 1861, and served in Company B, 45th Virginia Infantry, first as private, then first sergeant, then second lieutenant. He was wounded in action in the Piedmont valley, was taken prisoner a few days later and sent to Johnsons Island, in Lake Erie, where he was held nearly thirteen months, and released only to reach home July, 1865, after the surrender. January 16, 1866, in Wythe county, he married Sallie Kyle Shores, who was born in this county January 3, 1845. She was a daughter of Francis H. and Eliza J. (Mercer) Shores, both now deceased. Her father was born in Wythe county, and died in June, 1876; her mother was born in Smyth county, and died May 21, 1871. The father of Mr. Snavely was born in Smyth county, and died in 1863; his mother, born in Wythe county, is still living here. The family of Mrs. Snavely are descendants of General Brown, of Revolutionary fame, and are highly connected with the first families of Virginia. Mr. Snavely settled in Wythe county in the year of his marriage. He is proprietor of the Snavely House, at Rural Retreat, and to some extent engaged in farming

JAMES S. STEPHENS—son of Joseph and Isabella (Longacre) Stephens, was born March 23, 1830, in the house which is now his childrens' home, in Wythe county, and which was built by his grandfather, Lawrence Stephens, about the year 1790. Lawrence Stephens was one of the pioneers in the settlement of this county, honorably identified with its development. In Smyth county, Virginia, October 11, 1853, James S Stephens was united in marriage with India S. Rogers, who was born in Smyth county, October 28, 1836, a daughter of Samuel and Clarinda P. (Campbell) Rogers. The children of Mr. and Mrs. Stephens are recorded: Joseph R., born July 31, 1854; James C., August 4, 1856, died September 6, 1880; Mary A., September 16, 1858; Charles G., October 19, 1860, died August 26, 1863; Maggie F., October 9, 1862; Anna B , May 6, 1865; John M., April 4, 1867, died November 28, 1870; Albert C., November 15, 1869. James S. Stephens died October 21, 1873, and his wife preceded him to the land of rest, her death occurring on the 20th of September, 1870. September 19, 1871, he married Lenah A. Saunders, a daughter of Stephen Saunders, by whom he had one child, Stephen S., born August 26, 1873. His widow is now living in this county. Joseph B., for whom this sketch is compiled, has the management of the estate left by his father, which contains some 800 acres. His postoffice address is Reed Island, Wythe county, Virginia.

ROBERT E. SWECKER—is a son of Jacob and Nancy (Jackson) Swecker, who were born in Wythe county, and are still residents here. He was born in this county September 5, 1842, and entered the Confederate States army at the beginning of the civil war and served with honor till its close. His brother B. F. was a soldier of Virginia, also. May 3, 1866, in Wythe county, Robert E Swecker was united in marriage with Margaret R. Alford, and to them have been given a daughter and two sons: Nancy E. J., born

May 28, 1867; Robert Lee, May 20, 1870; John H. W., May 26, 1883. The wife of Mr. Swecker, a daughter of John and Elizabeth (Baker) Alford, was born in Wythe county, July 5, 1842. Robert E. Swecker is the efficient manager of the Bertha Zenk mines, in Lead Mine district, with postoffice address at Reed Island, Wythe county, Virginia.

JAMES E. TARTER—physician and surgeon—son of Elijah and Catharine (Baker) Tarter, was born in Wythe county, Virginia, March 14, 1857. Letitia V. Gose, daughter of Stephen and Mary J. (Kegley) Gose, was born in this county, July 2, 1861. She became the wife of Dr. Tarter in Wythe county, December 28, 1882, and their daughter, Mary Edith, was born October 18, 1883. The parents of both Dr. and Mrs. Tarter were born in Wythe county. His father departed this life November 11, 1863. Her father was in the Confederate army, and his death occurred in April, 1863. Dr. Tarter owns and cultivates a fine farm of 300 acres, and is also engaged in the practice of his profession, a physician of unquestioned ability and with large practice. His postoffice address is Wytheville, Wythe county, Virginia.

REBECCA C. TATE—was born in Augusta county, Virginia, September 30, 1839, a daughter of John A. and Margaret M. A. (Randolph) Tate. Her father died in Augusta county. Her mother is still a resident in the county of her birth. July 25, 1867, she became the wife of John M. Tate, who was born July 15, 1833, a son of Charles C. and Elizabeth F. (Graham) Tate. He was born in Wythe county, which became her home after marriage. Their children were born: Anna Randolph, March 3, 1871; Lizzie Graham, August 22, 1872; J. M. Friel, April 6, 1874. Mrs. Tate resides upon a farm, to the cultivation of which she gives her supervision. Her postoffice address is Max Meadows, Wythe county, Virginia.

HON. WILLIAM TERRY—is a son of Thomas W. and Catharine (Robinson) Terry, both born in Amherst county, Virginia, in which county he was born on the 14th of August, 1824. His father was born in 1793, and died in 1873, and his mother was born in 1795, and died in 1867. William Terry made his home in Wythe county in 1851, and was married in Bedford county, Virginia, in 1852, October 26th, to Emma, daughter of Benjamin and Harriet B. (Scott) Wigginton. She was born in Bedford county, November 10, 1828, and their children were born: Benjamin W., October 23, 1853; William, jr., August 21, 1855; John Young, March 23, 1858; Frank Hanson, September 21, 1860; Lizzie Emma, October 26, 1863; Beverly Lacy, September 14, 1866; Kate Waller, June 9, 1870. The father of Mrs. Terry was born in Culpeper county, Virginia, in 1781, and died July 10, 1864, in Bedford county. Her mother was born in Bedford county February 24, 1791. At Wytheville, April 17, 1861, William Terry entered the Confederate States service as first lieutenant of Company A, 4th Virginia Infantry, the regiment assigned to the famous "Stonewall Brigade," and partaking of its fortunes. At Harpers Ferry he was elected captain; in April, 1862, at Swift Run Gap, he was elected major; was appointed colonel in February, 1864, and brigadier-general in May, 1864, at Spotsylvania C. H. He was five times wounded in the service, and participated in all the actions of the Army of Northern Virginia except Kernstown and Cedar Mountain battles, which occurred when he was sick and wounded, and Sharpsburg battle, when he was on leave of absence, wounded. For two years, commencing in 1869, he was Grand Master of Masons of the

State of Virginia. In the 42d and 44th Congresses he represented the Ninth Virginia District, the only political office he has held. In Wytheville he is now engaged in the practice of law.

COLONEL ABRAHAM UMBERGER—was born in Wythe county, Virginia, October 5, 1816. In Pulaski county, November 16, 1840, he was united in marriage with Maria Miller, who was born in that county, July 2, 1815. Their children are recorded: Sarah Elizabeth, born February 15, 1842, died September 8, 1861; Charles Wiley, born June 3, 1843, Edward Harlow, March 18, 1845, live in Wythe county; Margaret Sophia, born May 4, 1847. died September 24, 1864; Crittenden L. G., born December 6, 1849, Everett W., January 2, 1853, live in Wythe county; Stephen Buchanan, born December 26, 1856, died September 3, 1864; Robert Shannon, born twin of Stephen B., lives in Wythe county. By a second marriage seven children were born to Colonel Umberger: Anna Maria, Lula May, Netta Jane, David B. L., Heber S M , John Lattie, Abraham M. Two sons of the first marriage, Charles and Edward H., served with honor through the civil war, members of Company C, 51st Virginia Infantry. This family sketch is compiled for Everett W. Umberger, who is a dentist of Wytheville, Wythe county, Virginia.

CHARLES WILEY UMBERGER—is a son of Colonel Abraham Umberger and Maria, his wife, whose record has just been given, and is one of the representative men of Wythe county, and owner of an estate of 1,300 acres within its limits. He was born in Wythe county, June 3, 1843, and his marriage was solemnized in Montgomery county, Virginia, January 4, 1870, when Sarah Eliza Martin became his wife. In the home their marriage established are now seven children, who were born: Mary Maria, October, 1870; Minnie Bess, August 12, 1872; John C. A., May 8, 1874; Sallie Allena, September 7, 1875; Oliver T. H., December 23, 1879; Brook Morton, September 3, 1881; Maggie Everett, April 1, 1884. The wife of Mr. Umberger was born in Montgomery county, September 27, 1844, and her parents are still living in that county, John and Mary Ann (Holmes) Martin. Her father was born in Montgomery county, and her mother in Franklin county, Virginia. From the outbreak of the war between the States till the last battle in the Valley of Virginia, Charles Wiley Umberger was a soldier in active service, Company C, 51st Virginia Infantry. He was captured at Waynesboro, taken to Fort Delaware, and there held until released on parole, June 21, 1865. His postoffice address is Wytheville, Wythe county, Virginia.

MICHAEL UMBERGER—deceased, was born in Wythe county, July 2, 1810, and died on his estate in Wytheville district, June 11, 1870. He was first married to Nancy Cassell, born in 1809, died in 1841, by whom five children were born: Ephraim S., January 28, 1835; Joseph H., November 13, 1836, died July 1, 1863; Mary F., October 12, 1838; Margaret E. and Maria A., August 15, 1841. In Smyth county, Virginia. February 3, 1822, was born Mary Kusling, who, on the 8th of December, 1842, in Smyth county, became the wife of Michael Umberger. Their children are recorded: Isaac M., born May 16, 1844; Catherine K , March 6, 1847; Jane L., June 27, 1849, died in 1857; Nannie M., August 31, 1851, died in 1882; Rachel C., July 11, 1853, died in 1857; Rosanna E., August 11, 1855; Lucy E., September 7, 1857; George W., August 21, 1859; Emery P., August 25, 1862, died same year; Orpha R., August 20, 1864. Mr.

Umberger had one son in the Confederate army, who served from 1862 till the close of the war, in Company C, 57th Virginia Infantry, and another son who was in the Federal army, enlisting in Iowa. Michael Umberger was three years a magistrate in Wythe county, and was a member of that body of statesmen who amended the State constitution in 1866. He left his family the comfortable home and estate upon which the best years of his life had been passed, and this sketch is prepared for two of his sons who are engaged in its cultivation. The family postoffice address is Wytheville, Wythe county, Virginia.

WILLIAM ALBERT UMBERGER—born in Wythe county, Virginia, September 21, 1841, and Catherine K. Umberger, born in this county, March 6, 1847, were here united in marriage on the 22d day of August, 1866. Their children are nine, born: Walter L., September 28, 1867; Elsie Florence, December 16, 1868; Maria Letetia, September 3, 1870; Claudius Neal, May 10, 1872; Mary Cordelia, June 29, 1874; Clara Virginia, September 22, 1875; Morris Price, July 14, 1877; Mather Marvin, March 16, 1881, Emeline, February 28, 1883. Levi and Mahala Umberger were the parents William A., and his wife was a daughter of Michael and Mary (Kusling) Umberger. Her further family record, with her father's death, will be found preceding this sketch. The father of William A. was born in Wythe county, and died January 6, 1884. His mother was born in Campbell county, Virginia. Mr. Umberger served as corporal in Company C, 51st Virginia Infantry, from the beginning for one year, and as orderly sergeant of brigade sharpshooters to the close of the civil war. He was taken prisoner at Waynesboro and sent to Fort McHenry, where he remained until paroled after the close of the war, June 20, 1865. Farming is his occupation, and Wytheville, Wythe county, Virginia, is his postoffice address.

NOAH T. VAUGHT—was born in Wythe county, December 3, 1839, a son of Abraham and Mary (Swecker) Vaught. His parents were born in this county, and until death were residents here; his father's death occurred in 1864. His father was a son of George Vaught, who came from Pennsylvania to make his home here, and whose father was of German birth. The mother of Mr. Vaught was a daughter of Wendell Swecker, who came from Spotsylvania county to make his home in Wythe. At Rural Retreat, August 4, 1861, Noah T. Vaught enlisted in Company B, 29th Virginia Infantry, and the regiment went into service as part of Corse's brigade, Pickett's division, Longstreet's army corps. At Camp Cumbo, in April, 1862, he re-enlisted to serve through the war. He served first as second sergeant, and received merited promotion through the rank of first sergeant, to third lieutenant, then second lieutenant. He took part in the battles of Middle Creek, Princeton, Suffolk, New Berne, Drewrys Bluff, Highters Gap, Blue Ridge, Cold Harbor, Hatchers Run and Appomattox. His brother, Jefferson M., served in the company with him, and was made prisoner and held four months. In Grayson county, Virginia, April 30, 1862, Noah T. Vaught married Minerva Jane Atkins. She was born in Grayson county, January 15, 1840, and their children were born: Mary Emma, July 28, 1863; Elbert Lee, March 24, 1866; Sidney Bays, February 16, 1868; James Edward, October 16, 1870; Edgar Sullins, January 7, 1873; Susan Ida, September 30; 1875; Herbert Brown, June 25, 1878; William Cameron, January 2, 1881; Ernest, September 1, 1883. Elbert Lee died December 5, 1880. The parents of Mrs. Vaught, David and Elizabeth (Moore) Atkins, were residents until their decease in Grayson county. The farm which Mr. Vaught cultivates and owns lies in Speedwell district, Wythe county, but his postoffice address is Cedar Springs, Smyth county, Virginia.

PETER VAUGHT—is a grandson of George Vaught, who came from Pennsylvania among the pioneer settlers of what is now Wythe county, and who started to join the Continental army for service in the war for Independence, but was detailed to return home, being a miller, and run his mill at the head of Cripple creek for the good of the cause. Peter and Molly (Wampler) Vaught, long honored residents of Wythe county, and now deceased, were the parents of Peter, the subject of this sketch. He was born in Wythe county, March 22, 1824, and he married in Smyth county, October 22, 1851, Elizabeth Burkett. She was born in Smyth county in June, 1823, daughter of George and Polly (Vaught) Burkett, who died in Smyth county. The children of Peter Vaught and wife are four, three daughters living in Wythe county, married, and one son, whose home is also in Wythe county. These children were born: Polly Jane, now Mrs. Austin Wampler, April 24, 1854; John M., September 6, 1856; Sarah A., now the wife of J. Wampler, August 20, 1859; Nancy C., now Mrs. Emory Blackard, October 23, 1861. Peter Vaught, the elder, was a sergeant in the 1812 war, and until his death drew a pension for services rendered. Peter, the younger, enlisted in Company B, 45th Virginia Infantry, in 1862, was badly wounded at Cloyd Farm, and still suffers from its effects, but remained in service till the close of the struggle. His occupation is farming, and his postoffice address is Rural Retreat, Wythe county, Virginia.

JAMES ALEXANDER WALKER—born in Augusta county, Virginia, August 27, 1832, was graduated from the Virginia Military Institute in 1852; studied law at the University of Virginia, 1854-5; practiced in Pulaski county from 1855 to 1879, and has since been engaged in practice in Wythe and adjoining counties, with residence in Wytheville. He served ably as commonwealth attorney for Pulaski county, from 1859 to 1862; represented the same county in the House of Delegates, sessions of 1871-2 and 1872-3, and for four years from January 1, 1878, was lieutenant-governor of Virginia. He was a son of Alexander and Hannah (Hinton) Walker, his father of Augusta county and his mother born in Rockingham county. The former died in Augusta county in 1865, and the latter died in the same county in February, 1880. In November, 1858, in Augusta county, James A. Walker and Sarah A. Poage were united in marriage. The bride was a daughter of Major William and Margaret (Allen) Poage, both of Augusta county, where her father died in 1854; her mother died in 1864.

JAMES E. WARD—born in Wythe county, Virginia, March 6, 1839, and Letitia S. Stoner, born in Roanoke county, Virginia, December 19, 1839, were in Wythe county united in marriage on the 20th of March, 1867. Lilbourn R. and Anna G. (Grossclose) Ward were his parents, his father still a resident in Wythe county, his mother no longer living, her death having occurred on the 25th of April, 1870. Daniel and Matilda (Campbell) Stoner, of Roanoke county, are the parents of Mrs. Ward. From May, 1861, until made prisoner at Piedmont, June 5, 1864, James E. Ward was a soldier of the Confederacy, in active service in Company D, 45th Virginia Infantry. Upon his capture he was carried to Camp Morton, Indianapolis, and held there until March, 1865, and never returned to service. He is a merchant of Crocketts Depot, Wythe county, Virginia,

LILBOURN RUTLEDGE WARD—born on the 2d day of July 1816, in Wythe county, was a son of William and Polly (Young) Ward, and a grandson of William Ward, an early settler here, who was a son of William Ward, of Augusta county. William, grandfather of Lilbourn R., was many years a magistrate of Wythe county, and a number of years colonel in the State militia. His son James was several years sheriff of Wythe county. From the time he was twenty-two years of age Lilbourn R. Ward was captain of a militia company for seven years. He raised a company of guards for home defense in the late war, and was made its captain, the company assigned to Colonel Joseph Kent's regiment, and called out twice, but never in action. The marriage of Lilbourn R. Ward was solemnized in Wythe county, March 8, 1838, when Anna, daughter of Peter and Elizabeth (Gose) Grossclose, became his wife. Her parents have been now many years dead, living until their decease in Wythe county. She was born in this county, June 10, 1816, and the children of Mr. and Mrs. Ward were born: James Ephraim, March 6, 1839; Mary Elizabeth, March 16, 1841; Emily Catharine, February 22, 1843; Everet Rush, March 24, 1845; Ballard Preston, June 5, 1847; John Albert, April 25, 1851; Emmet Brown, March 12, 1854. Mary Elizabeth died January 28, 1846; Emily Catharine died January 27, 1846, and the two little daughters were laid to rest in one grave. Mrs. Ward died on the 23d of April, 1871. The living children are all residents in Wythe county. James E. is married to Letitia Buford; Everett married Mary A. Lambert; John A. married Margaret Knuckles; Emmett B. married Elizabeth Wilson. L. R. Ward is one of the substantial farming residents of Wythe county. He served as magistrate, 1863-6; and before the war for about ten years as overseer of the poor. His postoffice address is McTeer, Wythe county, Virginia.

JOHN McINTIRE WILSON—owns and cultivates a beautiful farm of 500 acres, lying along the waters of Pine run, lying about eight miles from Wytheville, and near Brush mountain. He took up his residence in Wythe county in 1870, and was born in Smyth county, Virginia, December 11, 1836. His parents, who came to Wythe county with him, were William Anderson Wilson, died June 23, 1873, and Margaret (Williams) Wilson, still living in the county. In Wythe county, April 18, 1861, John McIntire Wilson and Eliza J. Litz were united in marriage, and three children have been given them: William Henry, born August 16, 1862; Albert Basil, April 21, 1867; Laura Ellen, April 8, 1870. Eliza J., daughter of John Henry and Barbara (King) Litz, was born in Wythe county, March 1, 1838. Her parents were born in this county, and her father died here in 1869. For the eight months preceding Lee's surrender the subject of this sketch was in the Confederate States service as hospital steward. For over seven years he rode as sheriff of Wythe county, and he is now deputy county treasurer. His fine farm is largely devoted to grazing purposes, and his stock is fine. Wytheville, Wythe county, Virginia, is his postoffice address.

WILLIAM LOCKHART YOST—was born in Wytheville, Wythe county, February 29, 1848. He was a son of James Lockhart Yost, who was born in Wythe county, March 7, 1811, and who married Nancy Ellen Wygal, born in Pulaski county, February 14, 1813. They were married October 27, 1840, and he died on the 23d of February, 1868; she died on the 20th of February, 1856. Captain Henry A. Yost, who fought through the civil war, commanding a company in the 45th Virginia Infantry, Confederate States Army, was a brother of James Lockhart Yost. The grandfather of W. L. Yost was Rev. Casper Yost, of Staunton, Augusta county, born May 7, 1785, and married Euphemia Bickle, of Staunton, February 17, 1806. He removed to Wythe county at an early day, and was the first Methodist Episcopal minister who settled in the county. He founded the church of that denomination here, and filled the pulpits of the church until his death, a zealous and popular worker in the ministry. His death occurred January 4, 1850. He was many years a magistrate of Wythe county, and sheriff many years, was a leading Mason, and a man of wide social and Christian influence. He was father of a large family, now scattered over the Union. His wife, Euphemia, died April 18, 1862. James Lockhart Yost was a distinguished member of the Wythe county bar. William Lockhart Yost taught school three years, was clerk of the Sharon township, Bland county, elected in May, 1870, and re elected 1871-2-3; deputy sheriff of that county 1871-2; supervisor of Sharon township, elected May 28, 1874, and resigned December 7, 1874; began practice of law October 23, 1874; was elected mayor of Seddon, Virginia, July 8, 1876, and re-elected in 1877; resigned and came back to Wythe county, entering upon the practice of law here, and in July, 1882, was nominated on the Democratic ticket for commonwealth attorney, but the Readjuster party carried all the county offices and he lost the place. He is now settled in practice in Wytheville, the countyseat.

Jack Jouett and Paul Revere in Petticoats

The Heroine of the Battle of Wytheville

by J. R. V. Daniel

Virginia Cavalcade, Vol. I, Number 1, 1951, pps. 33-36.

HER name was Molly (Mary Elizabeth) Tynes, and her age was twenty-six. She had lived in Shawsville and in Lynchburg, Virginia, and had attended Hollins College, then known as the Female Seminary at Botetourt Springs. Thus—and surely it makes her feat the more remarkable—she was really a "city" girl, not a country-raised lass. She has been described as "fair of form and face . . . as graceful as she was fair, as resolute as she was graceful."

At the time of this story Molly was helping her father, Samuel Tynes, care for her invalid mother at his place known as "Rocky Dell," located about three miles east of Jeffersonville (now Tazewell), Virginia. They were helped by two faithful servants, not improbably slaves, who shared their constant anxiety for the welfare as well of Molly's lover, the Honorable W. B. Davidson, as of her only brother, Captain Achilles J. Tynes, both of whom were away in the army.

Molly had not witnessed much of the horror of war, but she knew what it was to do without enough proper food and clothing and in other ways to contribute to "the cause." She and her father knew well, too, how greatly the Confederacy depended on the lead mines near Wytheville and the salt mines in the next county. But little did she know, as she went about her home duties, that she was soon to play a daring and heroic part in the saving of those precious, basic supplies and that, in today's language, her exploit would carry the terse but meaningful summation, "Mission accomplished."

A difficult but vitally important surprise raid was conceived by the Federal command. Colonel J. T. Toland of the 34th Ohio Infantry, mounted for the venture, and Colonel William Henry Powell of the 2nd Virginia (Union) Cavalry, with 1,000 men, were given a multiple objective: to capture Wytheville and make it into a Federal fortress verily in the heart of southwestern Virginia; to cut the Virginia and Tennessee (now the Norfolk and Western) Railroad at Wytheville; to take over the Saltville salt mines and the lead mines near Wytheville. Obviously the plan, if successful, would shut off the chief sources of supply of salt and lead for Lee's army and for a considerable portion of the entire Confederacy. The expedition was formed at Brownsville (now Huntington), West Virginia, on July 13, 1863, and set out with determination.

On July 17, perhaps around noon, word reached Samuel Tynes at "Rocky Dell" that Toland's army that morning had camped temporarily on the farm of Captain William E. Peery about a mile west. The messenger did not see Molly, but she heard his news. As quickly as possible Tynes sent the livestock and other valuables off into the mountains with old Tom, the Negro man, but for possible emergency Molly's mare, "Fashion," was left in the stable. This accomplished, Tynes was in process of hiding some hams under the house when two or three Union soldiers rode up. Despite his consternation at being caught thus redhanded, the old gentleman kept his wits about him and launched into conversation with the soldiers, as a result of which he learned from these stragglers or pickets the size of their force and their objectives. Their divulging this information has two possible explanations: either they were utterly irresponsible or they and their officers, realizing that the Wytheville area was little, if at all, defended—practically all men of fighting fitness being away at the front—considered it unnecessary to make any secret of their mission.

Samuel Tynes was instantly conscious of the vital importance of warning Wytheville and the people along the route. But how? Even had his advanced years permitted it, he dare not leave his invalid wife and his daughter unprotected in the path of approaching enemy troops. On the other hand, to find quickly a reliable messenger seemed impossible; it was now late afternoon, and every hour, perhaps every minute, counted. If there be a co-hero of this story, then such is Tynes himself, for it took heroism to make his fateful decision—the decision to yield to Molly's urging that she be permitted to go.

At twenty-six, Molly was not an over-impulsive girl and was emotionally controlled. She was not unaware of the danger and hardship of the long and lonely ride. Doubtless her father's realization of the perilous nature of the undertaking was even more acute than hers. But the die was cast. Molly's courage rose to the occasion. Possibly with a thought of how she was serving her brother and her lover, as well as the cause in general, she saddled her mare and was off.

Molly soon left the road and took to the bridle path that wound up Rich

Mountain, the first of four mountains she must cross. Youth and stamina were on her side, valuable aids to her resolve. Fortunately, too, "Fashion" had been unridden that day and the preceding, and thus was fresh for the ordeal. On and on, up and up, Molly urged the mare at a lively rate, though not at the utmost so soon, lest her four-footed friend give out ere the distant goal was reached. At any cabin she passed she slowed up or paused just long enough to give the surprised mountaineers the warning, "The Yankees are coming at dawn."

The sun was getting low as Molly ascended Garden Mountain, and it was dusk when she called at a home in Burke's Garden. As the door opened she shouted her news and was gone, leaving the lad who opened the door wondering if he had seen and heard an apparition. That lad was to become Dr. Caleb Thompson of Tazewell, who often told of the incident—a nightmare indeed, but not a dream, for *night* was upon them and the *mare* was "Fashion."

And now Molly realized that the journey onward from Burke's Garden would pass through the wildest and most hazardous country in the darkest hours. The dangers again paraded themselves before her—the dense forests were known to harbor wild animals such as bear, panther, wolf, and wildcat; for long stretches the route was hardly more than a bridle path, certainly not a road; in those times one encountered now and then desperate stragglers or even deserters from the armed forces, more fearfully dangerous to her than any wild beast. If the perfectly natural thought of turning back flashed across her mind, Molly forthwith dismissed it and rode on, stopping only occasionally for the twofold purpose of breathing her mount and listening for possible pursuers.

The descent of Garden Mountain was much more difficult than the ascent. There and on Brushy Mountain the frequent tangle of trees and thick underbrush tore her clothes and scratched her from head to foot. Low, entwining vines caught at her horse's feet, and slippery rocks, holes, and fallen timbers made life increasingly miserable for horse and rider. In the blackest, pre-dawn period Molly labored up and over Walker Mountain, and by the first streaks of daylight she galloped across the open fields and into the streets of Wytheville.

Weary and sore, her hair a mass of tangles, and her clothes shredded, Molly shouted her warning at every door and waved her bonnet to an astounded, sleepy populace which couldn't believe what it saw and didn't want to believe what it heard. Alone and unarmed, this slip of a girl had ridden the forty-one miles over those utterly wild and rugged ranges from Tazewell? The people rubbed their sleep-laden eyes and jarred their heads in an effort to take in the seemingly impossible.

Recovering from the stupor and the near-panic caused by Molly and her news, the old men, the youngsters, the wounded, and the women caught the spirit of the girl and set about feverishly to defend their homes. The blow, long feared, had come at last, but the enemy had advanced, not up the valley, as anticipated, but over the mountains. Let the famous editor, Horace Greeley, tell what happened: "They swooped down on Wytheville, a village . . . of considerable importance. . . . They had passed over a . . . region having very few inhabitants and no elements of resistance; but charging into Wytheville, they were fired on from the houses. Colonel Toland was soon killed and Colonel Powell . . . severely wounded. After firing some of the buildings whence they were assailed, our men, abandoning their dead and wounded, fell back two miles and encamped, starting for home . . . early next morning. . . . They rode 400 miles, lost 83 men and at least 300 horses and endured as much misery as could well be crowded into a profitless raid of eight days."

Of course neither Greeley, nor Colonels Toland and Powell, nor any of the 1,000 defeated men knew that they had been thwarted (and those vital supplies saved for the Confederacy) by a lone young girl whose amazing ride rivaled, if indeed it did not exceed, in importance and daring those of Jack Jouett and Paul Revere of Revolutionary fame.

The Wytheville campaign was lost sight of in the larger issues then and since, but it is believed that the pages of history do not reveal a like accomplishment by which a lone and unarmed girl saved her country from a thousand-man menace. Well deserved is the prophetic tribute paid by William Henry Tappey Squires in his *Land of Decision*—"Molly Tynes, slender, graceful, bruised and bleeding, will not be forgotten while Tazewell's mountains stand." ✓ ✓ ✓

Showers of Shot

Molten Lead Rained Down the Shaft of Wythe County's Old Shot Tower

By Elizabeth D. Coleman

Virginia Cavalcade, Vol. V, Number 2, 1955, pps. 33-35

ON A TREE-RIMMED BLUFF above the New River in Wythe County a seventy-five-foot-high tower rises with age-defying rigidity. Its gray, stone walls are as much as three feet thick. Its base is about twenty or twenty-five feet square. Its sides slope slightly toward its pyramidal roof.

Some local historians assert that construction of the tower began in 1807. Others say that it was started in 1820. With equally glaring lack of proof, still others have mentioned other dates. These contradictory reports are typical of everything that has been written about the tower. Very little is known of it with certainty. An article like this must mix some traditions and possibilities with the few known facts, differentiating between the proved and the unproved.

We do not even know positively who was responsible for erecting the mysterious structure that seems to stand like an unneeded sentinel above a quiet stretch of the New River in a pastoral valley. The builder may have been a certain Thomas Jackson who was not, we hasten to remark, that other Virginian of the same names, with Jonathan between them, who was to become better known as "Stonewall." The Jackson who owned for some years the land on which the old shot tower was built was a native Briton. According to an inscription on his tombstone at Austinville, Virginia, he was born at Appleby in England's Westmoreland County in 1762.

While Thomas Jackson was a relatively young man, he crossed the Atlantic, but we do not know just when. By 1796 he probably made his home in Wythe County; we know, at least, that he then began to acquire lands there. Possibly he had been persuaded to become an immigrant by **Moses and Stephen Austin, the brothers who were interested in various mining projects and settled down for about eight years in the 1790's to operate the lead mines beside the New**

River in the southeastern part of Wythe County. One of their descendants has claimed that they brought English miners into Virginia.

Enterprising businessman that he was, Jackson himself acquired partial ownership of the Austinville lead mines in 1806. He and his two partners paid £9,550 for them—a high figure, but one that is a matter of official record. Jackson lived about three miles downstream from the mines. There he operated a ferry across the river. Today its site is that of Jackson's Ferry Bridge, about sixteen miles southeast of Wytheville, which carries traffic using U. S. Route 52 across the river. And above the bridge stands the tower that may be a relic of a third business with which miner and ferryman Jackson was associated.

Ordinarily, it would seem to have been economical for the mining partners to have manufactured shot at the Austinville mines, the source of their raw material. And it is said that a shaft was located there for the making of shot, but nobody has ascertained just when the production of shot at Austinville began or ended. Tradition asserts that Jackson and his partners quarreled and explains on that ground his alleged construction of the shot tower on his own land a few miles away. Hearsay has it that the building was not completed until the year of Jackson's death, 1824, and that his nephew, Robert Raper, leased the property and poured in that same year the first shot made there.

The process by which shot was made in such towers was essentially simple, but it was not easy. Lead was melted in kettles or small furnaces in the tops of the towers. When the metal had been made liquid, it was poured through some kind of sieve or drop pan. Drops of the molten lead were rounded into globular shape as they plunged down the towers' shafts, and at the bottom they were chilled and hardened when they fell into tanks of cool water.

In the old shot tower at Jackson's Ferry the fall is supposed to have aggregated 150 feet. Half of that distance is said to have been below ground level. In order to make easier the tasks of providing cool water and of getting the product started on its way to the consumer, a tunnel is reported to have been dug from the bottom of the shaft toward the river.

The shot manufactured in such facilities were unlike molded bullets. They were tiny pellets to be packed, after the powder charge, into muzzle-loading shotguns. So small were such shot that thirty to 2,000 or more of these pellets, depending upon their size, might weigh only one ounce, although lead is a heavy metal. The largest shot might be as much as a fifth of an inch in diameter; pellets of the BB size might run about sixty to the ounce. Ammunition of this type was used chiefly by hunters for small game. Thus, when the shotguns were fired, the shot would scatter over a wide area surrounding the target.

Some investigators of the history of the old shot tower beside the New River have concluded that its usefulness as a producer ended in 1839, which would mean that its service spanned perhaps no more than fifteen years. A descendant of Thomas Jackson presented the abandoned tower in 1929 to a local patriotic society, the Stuart Chapter of the Daughters of the American Revolution. More than $1,185 was spent in restoring the weathered structure, and a historian of the D. A. R.'s restorations used a picture and historical sketch of the tower in his book. Since the facility apparently postdated the Revolution, however, the Daughters lost interest in it. The United Daughters of the Confederacy considered acquiring it but decided not to do so when no evidence that it aided the South's cause in the war of the 1860's could be located. The Association for the Preservation of Virginia Antiquities has also been unwilling to maintain it. It has remained for the Ruritan Club of Austinville to perform the public service of caring for that relic of a short-lived but useful local industry. It may have made possible no victory on glorious fields of battle, but it probably enabled thousands of hunters to experience a thrilling sense of triumph. ✦ ✦ ✦

THAT DARING YOUNG MAN

By Curtis C. Davis

James Hays Piper led six lives—as educator, engineer, politician, clergyman, Federal official and militia officer—but he has been remembered only for the one adventure he wanted to forget.

Virginia Cavalcade, Vol. IX, Number 1, 1959, pps. 11-15.

In the meandering wake of her history Virginia has produced a whole pride of adventurers. Their claims to fame have taken some of them to distant places of the earth. John Colter, of Augusta County, went to the Far West and discovered the Yellowstone. Alexander Macaulay, of the Yorktown family, went south to Colombia and stirred up enough attention to be executed by a firing squad. Lewis Littlepage, of Hanover County, went east and did a variety of things, such as becoming the first American to be formally presented to a Russian sovereign. Some

Virginians even went north, but we won't talk about them. But there was one who achieved his brief and peculiar fame by staying right in his home county of Rockbridge and going in a different direction. He went up.

He was James Hays Piper (1800-1854). His life span, which almost bracketed the unspecialized antebellum era, gave him time to pursue half a dozen careers. He gained distinction in every one of them, but today his name is unknown. No likeness of him has ever been located. Yet his reputation—the lingering memory of what he symbolized—has never died since his eighteenth year. This is because he decided, one day that summer, to stroll south from Washington College in Lexington (now Washington and Lee University), where he was studying for the Presbyterian ministry, and have a look at Mr. Jefferson's Natural Bridge. When he got there, almost as an afterthought, he climbed it.

That might have been an end to the matter if one of the three fellow students who also went along had not resolved to write the whole thing down, on the spot, as proof of an incredible tale. He testified that Piper had climbed straight up the rock overhang of the Bridge and emerged fresh enough to meet the rest of them coming down the mountain side. Then he left his manuscript with the caretaker of the Bridge, a free Negro called Patrick Henry. The annalist was a Lexington boy, two years younger than Piper, named William A. Caruthers. In later years Caruthers combined the successful practice of medicine with a writing bent that established him as one of the earliest significant novelists Virginia produced and his first recorded writing has had a career of its own. As much as anything else he wrote, even *The Cavaliers of Virginia* or *The Knights of the Golden Horse-Shoe*, this teen-age screed was responsible for adding his name to such monumental compilations as *The Cambridge History of American Literature* and the University of Chicago's *A Dictionary of Americanisms*. For Caruthers had recorded a fantastic feat by a daring young man and the nation at large has always admired daring. He had recorded, as it were, another American epic and within ten years James Hays Piper was a legend.

In July, 1828, a new Philadelphia weekly called the *Natural Souvenir* printed a brief article entitled "The Natural Bridge, or a Scene in Virginia." Its author was anony-

307

ginning three tendrils of distortion commenced to twine outwards from the story's central stem, in places as remote as London, England, or Bradford, Vermont. This stripling had climbed the Bridge because, when halfway up, he'd been afraid to come down. . . . At the final stage he'd been hauled to safety and success by a rope (or a pole). . . . Once on top, "in a state of perfect exhaustion and violent nervous agitation" (to take the English traveller Henry Tudor's 1834 interpretation) he'd fainted dead away.

As the decades rolled by, the tendrils sent out small extra shoots. Take the climber's first name, for example. Burritt had called him William. In the 1880s, Charles Dudley Warner claimed it was Henry. Take his last name. The English economist, Harriet Martineau, gave it as Blacklock in her *Retrospect of Western Travel* (1838). The New York *Hearth and Home* magazine (1862) gave it as Pepper. Two well-known figures, David Hunter Strother, or "Porte Crayon," in 1857 and John Esten Cooke in 1871, denied the youth had climbed the Bridge at all. He had really slunk up the adjoining mountainside. Even The Father of His Country got into the act by proxy. When that one-man paper mill from Philadelphia,

mous, which may be why he felt so free to describe just how that daring young man felt as he inched his way to the crest of the awesome structure. The humble *Souvenir* went out of business two years later, but by that time this little item had been reprinted at least twice. In 1837 it attained regional prominence down in Tennessee when a collector of "elegant extracts," William Fields, Jr., included it in the second edition of his *Literary and Miscellaneous Scrap Book.* In 1846 Elihu Burritt, the "Learned Blacksmith," also tried his hand at recording the climber's exact sensations. He did so in an eye-misting essay called "The Natural Bridge; or, One Niche the Highest," for his volume, *Sparks from the Anvil.* When this was reprinted as "The Ambitious Youth" in McGuffey's *Fifth Reader* (1853), James Piper, still anonymous, had reached the big time. There were two points of view as to how he had.

The *Souvenir* author, whose account was reprinted as recently as 1946, saw in this feat nothing but "a monument of hardihood, of rashness, and of folly." Elihu Burritt saw just the opposite. Here was a personification of undaunted youth. Since neither gentleman had bothered about accuracy, from the very be-

ing the Natural Bridge," for the July issue of the *Knickerbocker Magazine* in New York City. Here at last were the facts, by someone who wished neither to denigrate nor to glorify, but to attest. They have been quoted with gusto, if not so frequently as the fantasies, at least by a few of the more careful chroniclers, such as Henry Howe in his *Historical Collections of Virginia* (1845) and Colonel William Couper in his *History of the Shenandoah Valley* (1952). Now over the decades, each of these commentators —opponent, admirer, or neutralist—was actually engaged in creating one impression: somebody's fame for derring-do. By the 1870s Moses White could assert that Tennessee youngsters were reading the story of that daring young man with as much fascination as they did Mrs. Radcliffe's *Mysteries of Udolpho* or Mrs. Roche's *Children of the Abbey*. In other words the deed, not the doer, was the thing. How did the doer feel about all this?

He didn't like it.

When Samuel Kercheval, historian of the Valley of Virginia, tried to interview Piper on the subject in 1836, he got nowhere. For by now James H. Piper, having burned his bridges behind him, was a person

George Lippard, published *Washington and His Generals* (1850), he of course repeated the long-bearded legend about Washington's having carved his initials on the Bridge. Then he added that, having done so, the great one proceeded to climb the Bridge as well. The Bridge's height shot up to five hundred feet (it is two hundred and fifteen). In 1879, when Moses White was orating about the early history of the University of Tennessee to some of its alumni, he gravely assured them that "a peculiar pallid appearance was wont, by [Piper's] acquaintance, to be attributed to the fright which he received on that occasion." When Piper's wife died in 1882, almost thirty years after her husband, the Woodstock *Shenandoah Herald* granted her a prominent obituary. But it wasn't really about her. Captioned "A Thrilling Incident Recalled," it was actually a rehash of all the old errors about Piper's ascent of Natural Bridge.

Meanwhile William A. Caruthers' first-hand report of the incident remained available at the Bridge. Relatively few people saw it, of course, and about 1845 the manuscript was destroyed by fire. By 1838 Dr. Caruthers had had his fill of the fantasies going around the nation and released his eyewitness account. "Climb-

of substance. After taking his A.B. degree at Washington College in 1819, he had taught school in Rockbridge, then in 1824 made a very good marriage. It was to Frances Smyth, a daughter of Alexander Smyth of Wythe County, former Inspector General in the War of 1812, now United States Congressman, and the man for whom Smyth County is named. Shortly thereafter Piper journeyed southwest to Columbia, Tennessee, where he opened another school. Though he was probably a Presbyterian minister by this time, he now changed to the Episcopal church, helping establish a congregation in Columbia, attending the first Episcopal convention in the State at Nashville, in 1829, and according to church annalist Arthur H. Noll becoming the "providential instrument" whereby the future father of Episcopalianism in Tennessee, and a founder of the University of the South, Bishop James H. Otey, entered the fold. He also became friendly with the local lawyer and United States Congressman, James K. Polk, and his attractive wife, Sarah. In 1830 Piper earned his M.A. degree from East Tennessee College at Knoxville and assumed the chair of mathematics on that campus. In 1833 he became its President.

For some reason he wasn't happy in the post, resigned the next year, and tried to get an appointment through Congressman Polk as a Visitor to West Point. When this didn't work out, he went back to Wythe County, Virginia.

From there on April 19th, 1836, as a good Jacksonian Democrat he wrote Polk, now Speaker of the House, recommending his brother-in-law, Colonel Harold Smyth, for the office of Governor of the new Wisconsin Territory. Polk had done Piper a good turn some time back so a week later he wrote again, asking that he himself be named Surveyor General for the Territory as he needed the income badly. When he didn't get it, he turned to the field of civil engineering. As assistant to State Engineer, Claudius Crozet, for the southwestern part of the Commonwealth, Piper located the road from Grayson Court House across the Blue Ridge to Mount Airy, North Carolina. He was also active in politics, and for the five sessions from 1840 to 1846 was State Senator at Richmond for that vast mountain barony occupied by the counties of Carroll, Grayson, Pulaski, Smyth, Tazewell, and Wythe. People began calling him Colonel. When Polk was nominated for the Presidency, Piper informed a mutual friend, Dr. John B. Hays, back at Columbia on September 23rd, 1844, that this "appears, indeed, to have been the dictate of a kind and all-wise Providence" and that Democratic success in Virginia "will dissolve, *inevitably* and *forever*, the villainous combination of the Whig party." From his Richmond vantage point he kept the new Chief Executive informed of local political maneuvers. By February, 1845, providence—a word beginning with the same initial as Polk—rewarded the Colonel with a slot in the Administration.

On April 13th, 1846, Piper and General Jacobs of Knoxville sat down to a family dinner with the Polks at Washington. That same night the President informed Senator Pennypacker of Virginia that next day he was going to nominate Piper for the post of Chief Clerk in the General Land Office (now the Bureau of Land Management), Department of the Interior. Despite a tiff with Secretary of State Buchanan over a lazy underling he wanted to fire, and Buchanan wanted retained, Piper had Polk's confidence and rose to be Acting Commissioner of the Land Office. After a year and a half, however, and despite a salary of $1,800 annually, he had had enough. On November 6th, 1847, he wrote the President, in his typically copper-plate hand, a one-sentence letter of resignation to take effect ten days later. Then he went back to southwest Virginia.

Since the '40s Piper and his wife Frances—there were no children—had had a big brick home in Wythe County about a mile and a half west of Speedwell on the north side of Cripple Creek. Here they settled down, and the Colonel proceeded to resume his status of prominent local citizen. He became president of the Southwest Turnpike Company. He drew up the first town plan of Wytheville, was active in Fraternal Lodge #5 A.F. and A.M., and conducted the leading academy.

In March, 1852, the *Southern Literary Messenger* at Richmond reported that this living legend still adamantly refused to discuss the romantic feat of his youth: climbing the Natural Bridge. When the legend died on September 8th, 1854, at the Sulphur Springs in Grayson County, it was nothing romantic that killed him. He had been at work locating the Wytheville-Raleigh turnpike through Wythe and Grayson when taken ill with dysentery.

Here was a man who had, you might say, led six

lives: educator, engineer, politician, clergyman, Federal official, militia officer. Yet the most intense search has never turned up a single obituary notice. Perhaps Piper wanted it that way. If so then that vixen, Fate, in spinsterly vexation has willed otherwise, decreeing that he be remembered for the one thing he did that he most wished forgotten. Why had he done it? Because as the moutain climbers say, it was *there*. It issued a challenge. He answered that challenge. He did it deliberately, and he did it first. True, he never got as high toward Heaven as the Himalayas, as did Sir Edmund Hillary, and there was no Queen to knight him. But is he not in the authentic ancestral line? Does he not make one with all those explorers royal who scale the crests, plumb the deeps, burrow through the bowels of old Mother Earth in their endless attempt to assay her unutterable mysteries?

THE SMALL BANG AT BANGS

The Wise family had such a penchant for duelling that it was poetic justice when one of them helped put an end to the practice.

by Curtis Carroll Davis

Virginia Cavalcade, Vol. XI, Number 2, 1961, pps. 4-9.

It was the next-to-last duel in Virginia. It led to the end of all duelling in Virginia and in the nation at large. Since the *code duello* is the most theatrical single aspect of human intercourse and since, in the popular imagination, Southerners personify that code, this affair of honor becomes by definition, an event of some significance.

It occured in July, 1882, back in the bitter post-Reconstruction period. Yet its story has never been fully told. Now that the private papers of one of the participants have been explored, for the first time in seventy-nine years it can be. No one should be surprised that the participants were lawyers and opposite-camp politicians. They were also of different denominations and hailed from opposite ends of the Old Dominion. Who were they?

The westerner was John Stuart Crockett, a Presbyterian, born in 1852 at Crockett's Cove, Wythe County, being the fourth generation from immigrant Samuel Crockett, whose son John first settled the Cove area. Crockett attended the University of Virginia in 1871, earning a Certificate of Distinction for his studies in constitutional and international law. Returning to Wythe County to practice, he married the former Elizabeth Boyd, by whom he had three sons, all of whom became officers in the United States Army. Crockett developed into a successful lawyer, a leader of the local Democratic Party, and Commonwealth's Attorney for Wythe. He was six feet tall, of slender build, prompt to resent an insult.

The easterner was John Sergeant Wise, an Episcopalian, born in 1846 at the American Legation, Rio de Janerio, where his father, Henry Alexander Wise, was Minister Plenipotentiary to Brazil. Reared in Accomack County, young Wise entered the Virginia Military Institute, where he was soon caught up by the war and served all through it. Afterwards he took bachelor and law degrees at the University (1865-1867), married Evelyn Douglas of Nashville—by whom he was in process of having what he termed his "baseball team" of seven sons and two daughters—and hung out his shingle at Richmond. Only three months before the duel he had been appointed by President Arthur to the post of U. S. District Attorney for the Eastern District of Virginia and currently was campaigning for election to Congress on the Readjuster, later Republican, Party platform. He stood five feet, eight inches and already was inclining to that portliness which would mark him throughout his career.

Both men knew that, since one of them was a State official, their affair of honor was indictable under Article 3, Chapter 69, of the General Assembly's *Act To Suppress Duelling in the Commonwealth of Virginia*, effective May 1st this very year. Both chose to dismiss the fact as a niggling detail. Crockett was noted for a high temper and articulate tongue. So was Wise. And since it is Wise's papers which make our story possible, that story, while an inside one, will also be one-sided.

The first Wise had settled on the Eastern Shore in 1635, and down the line his successors had acted out their role of being to the manor born. Our District Attorney did more than passively inherit a tradition. An avid genealogist, he danced 'round his family tree with all the single-minded enthusiasm of those New England Anglicans jigging 'round their Maypole His maternal great-grandfather, John Cropper, who commanded the 11th Virginia Regiment during the Revolution, had once gone after an acquaintance with a knife because the churl had spoken too lightheartedly of General Washington. In 1798 the fifth John Wise had challenged Thomas Jefferson to a duel. Our D. A.'s father had fought a duel, served as second in another, and issued challenges for two more. His older brother Jennings, diplomat, editor of the Richmond *Enquirer*, though seemingly demure as a vicar, had sailed blithely through eight duels in less than two years.

From his ripe Continental experience Jennings taught his little brother to become adept with the foils. Johnny taught himself how to shoot by drawing the outline of a man on the family garden wall, then wheeling and firing at it by the hour with a trusty horse pistol. At age twelve he abruptly discovered he was a better shot than Jennings. He had another advantage: he was ambidextrous. He could shoot well with either hand but better with his left. In an article he wrote for the *Saturday Evening Post* in June, 1906, entitled "The Fire-Eaters: 'Gentlemen's Battles' under the Code of Honor," Wise would admit that, as a young man, he had always been "rampant on duels. They could not come fast enough to satisfy me. I simply devoured every book I could lay hands on containing accounts of dueling."

When just a few months out of the University, he and a cousin had taken the cars to Baltimore and there as a joint enterprise shot the Virginia journalist Edward A. Pollard for what they deemed his overly acerb vocabulary with regard to their pa (by now *ex*-Governor Wise). The affair originated in the recent appearance of Pollard's book, *Lee and His Lieutenants* and the resultant "recontre" became front page news in the Richmond *Daily Whig* on November 16th, 18th, and 21st, 1867. Bail for the boys was a thumping $3,000 apiece.

Five thousand was the amount of bond he and George Ben Johnston, M.D., were each put under at Richmond after the lawyer had challenged the physician. Wise, proposed for membership in the new Westmoreland Club, presently learned through the grapevine that fifteen members had blackballed him on the score of his Readjuster politics. Thereupon he denounced all fifteen on the stump and in the press. He individually insulted two, with special attention to Dr. Johnston, great-nephew to the General. Before he finally surrendered at the Third District police station, Wise had seen fit to go into hiding disguised so skillfully as a Jewish peddler, complete with dark goggles and linen duster, that even his eight-year-old son Hugh failed to recognize him. His lieutenant in the Light Infantry Blues (of which Wise was captain), Thomas Nelson Page, served as his attorney.

Two years passed. The *code duello* was once again to make news.

The affair began—as Wise recalled it, years later—in early June, 1882. In Wytheville on business, he was chatting genially at the hotel there with John S. Crockett and some other acquaintances of the opposition, Democratic Party. A saying attributed to the late Frank Blair (by whom Wise probably meant Francis P. Blair, Jr., Republican Senator from Missouri) was being made much of by the Democrats: "Honor will not buy a breakfast." Wise opined there was too much sentimentality going around on the subject of debts and indebtedness. Telling a man, "I'd rather *owe* you, all my life, than *cheat* you out of a cent" seemed to him, said Wise, a poor way of regularizing a debt. There was no special dissent and shortly the gathering broke up.

A few weeks later, as he was preparing to strike out for southwest Virginia to inaugurate his campaign for Congressman at Large, an old friend, Colonel W. W. Gordon, dropped by his Richmond home with a piece of news. He'd just returned from a session of the Court of Appeals at Wytheville, said the Colonel. There he had been tipped by Robert Crockett to inform Wise that John S. Crockett was spreading the report that the Richmonder, during their conversation of some time back, had in substance certified the low concept of honor reflected in the Blair maxim.

About July 10th Wise was orating in Newbern, Pulaski County, and by the succeeding Saturday had worked his way down to Marion in Smythe County. After unloading his local speech quota he was walking along the street the following Monday, July 17th, when he spotted John S. Crockett taking it easy on the hotel porch. Striding up to the other lawyer, Wise repeated what had been told him, and inquired if this fairly represented his utterances?

Crockett retorted that it did not. He went into detail as to what he *had* said. After a minute or two Wise interrupted him. "Well, sir, I've heard enough to satisfy me that whatever you said, you lied." With which he gave the younger man the back of his hand across the face so eloquently it nearly knocked Crockett out of his chair. (A Richmond *Whig* dispatch telegraphed from Marion on July 19th elaborated the single blow, as recalled by Wise, into a revelation "that Captain Wise gave him three Sullivanian licks direct from the shoulder, and came out of the difficulty without a scratch.") Struggling from his seat, Crockett went for Wise. Persons nearby intervened. Both battlers were arrested, haled before a Justice of the Peace, and fined $2.50 apiece for scuffling on a tavern porch. That same night Wise departed for Bristol.

From Bristol he made speeches through Scott, Lee, and the "back Counties" and wound up a week later at the Colonnade Hotel, Abingdon. There at 9:15 A.M., Monday, July 24th, just as he was ready to go forth and orate, he was handed a missive from J. Stuart Crockett, cousin to his adversary. The two-sentence note advised that Mr. Crockett, having reached town last night from Wytheville with a "communication. . .of a private nature" for him, respectfully requested an interview "at such early time and place as you may designate." At 9:35 A.M. Wise was perusing the following epistle. Dated Wytheville, July 23rd, it came in a shouting-yellow envelope and was just one sentence lengthier than its predecessor:

Sir

In view of your conduct at Marion on Monday last I demand at your hands the satisfaction due from one gentleman to another.

You will therefore please designate the time & place where we may meet.

This will be handed you by my friend Mr. Jno Stuart Crockett who is authorized to act for me.

Respectfully
Jno. S. Crockett

At once the machinery of the *code duello* began to whir. For his second Wise brought in a fellow cadet from the V.M.I., a chap who had fought alongside him at New Market and attended the University the same years as he—George William Ward, Jr., attorney, judge, editor of the Abingdon *Virginian*. For his physican he reached all the way to Richmond for Lewis Wheat. He borrowed pistols from Alex Holladay, a professor at the Abingdon school. Crockett's second was his cousin; his physician was R. E. Moore of Wytheville. Shortly after dawn July 25th, 1882, four counties northeast, the duel took place.

"Was staged" might be apter. For this latest *rencontre* of two human beings bent on demolishing one another as punctiliously as possible emerged a very human parody on humankind. We have a primary source in George Ward's three-page "Memo," jotted down on the spot at 6 A.M. the same day. Wise inserted his own interpretation into Chapter XVIII of his romance about the Reconstruction in Virginia, *The Lion's Skin: An Historical Novel and a Novel History* (1905). Therein the author—whose duelling hero, "Powhatan Carrington," is Wise himself—employs the word, "farce."

At 4:20 A.M. Wise, Ward, and

Dr. Wheat stepped down from the east-bound train at Christiansburg, Montgomery County, and took the road northwest toward Yellow Sulphur Springs. After proceeding three-quarters of a mile, they clambered over a fence on the right-hand side and walked to a high point of ground. Here they were met by Stuart Crockett.

The other principal was nearby. Also present to relish the action were —according to the Richmond *State's* issues for July 25th and 26th—a good half dozen cohorts of either party including Governor Cameron's secretary, J. M. Browning, and Major Ballard of the *Whig*. A special dispatch from Christiansburg to the Baltimore *Sun* pointed out that Wise "is regarded as a splendid marksman, both with pistol and fowling piece."

Stuart Crockett and Ward now proceeded to select the site. They picked a spot two hundred yards farther on, at the edge of a woods on a natural plateau in a tiny vale. The two physicians took their place on the slope of the hill, twenty or thirty feet away. The general area was perhaps a quarer of a mile from a depot stop on the A.M. & O. Railroad known as Bangs.

Ward won the toss, and accordingly chose the point where his man should stand. The distance to be stepped off was fixed at ten paces. Stuart Crockett won the word, *i.e.*, the right to call the commands. Both seconds now retreated. Both principals, in position, elevated their weapon arms.

At that instant Stuart Crockett noted that Wise had raised his *left* arm. He strode over to Ward, and whispered. Ward, if he had ever known, had forgotten that his man was a better left-hand shot, and had signed the terms of the cartel on the more customary right-hand basis. Moreover a left-hand stance exposed his principal's heart. Horrified, Ward scurried into the fire area and explained the situation.

"Damn the cartel!" Wise fumed. "I never heard of it before. Don't you know I am very left-handed?"

Ward murmured that the entire set-up might be a trick. Why not let him formally withdraw them?

"Not much!" hissed Wise. "I'll chance him this way."

Ward withdrew. Wise shifted his pistol to his right hand. Stuart Crockett commenced the count.

"One!" "Tw—!" Before the command left his lips, just as the sun was rising, Crockett and Wise fired almost simultaneously.

Both missed.

Promptly the seconds moved toward their principals to reload for them. Across the serene early-morning air carried the voice of John S. Crockett, muttering to his cousin. The voice said: "This is all damn foolishness."

Reloading the weapons, Ward and Stuart Crockett gave them back. Just as John S. Crockett accepted his, it went off in his hand, right across the line of fire. Fortunately the shot was high. Turning toward Wise, his opponent bowed slightly and said, "Mr. Wise, you must excuse me."

"Certainly, gentlemen," the other replied—to both Crocketts. Wise "was hopping mad by this time" for having missed. He now determined to let his adversary open the second exchange and miss, then take him down at leisure. Laying his pistol on the ground, Wise waited.

With Crockett's weapon reloaded, the principals resumed position. Just as Stuart Crockett was about to give the word, Wise turned to both seconds and remarked, "Gentlemen, don't you think you had better stand back a little? You are very near the line of fire." The pair acquiesced.

Down the hill Dr. Moore, who had never served at an affair of honor, was fidgeting. At last he turned to Wheat and exclaimed, "Doctor, for God's sake is there nothing *we* can do to stop this thing?" But Dr. Wheat, who had attended several such sessions, was enjoying himself.

"One!" intoned Stuart Crockett. John S. Crockett fired. He missed.

Wise, confident he'd failed the first exchange only because of right-hand awkwardness, was resolved not to fail again. He took dead aim.

"Two!" Wise pulled the trigger. The hammer clicked tonelessly. Praying it would still go off within the time limit, he held his aim. Nothing happened.

In disgust Wise slowly pointed his weapon upwards. Looking at Ward he said, "My pistol has failed to discharge."

At once Stuart Crockett moved toward the other principal to reload his weapon. As he did so, John S. Crockett left his position—in violation of cartel, which decreed that seconds must advise principals when to leave—and took a step or two toward his cousin. He whispered something to him.

Thereupon Stuart Crockett turned to Ward and announced, "Gentlemen, we are satisfied." Ward looked toward his principal.

Wise, still in position, was surprised and chagrined. As he explained his feelings in *The Lion's Skin*: "It was contrary to every rule of the duello, by which, when a man who has received a blow challenges, he must continue to fire until he or his adversary is disabled."

Masking his contempt, the Richmonder addressed Stuart Crockett. Raising his hand to his hat, he bowed and said, "Very well, Sir, if your principal is satisfied, I bid *you* good morning." Turning on his heel, he stalked away. No arrests were made (no "evidence"), and Wise campaigned that night as usual. The small bang at Bangs was over.

This is how it led to the end of duelling in Virginia...

Shortly after the gubernatorial campaign of 1885 Crockett, who was having marital troubles and drinking too much, left his family and headed West. Settling at Seattle, he practiced law there until January, 1904, when failing health necessitated his being brought home. In March he died of throat cancer at Wytheville and was buried in the family graveyard at Crockett's Cove. His brick home still stands.

"He was"—as Frank H. Terry informed Wise from Wytheville on March 19th, 1904—"a bright fellow; a strong man mentally, but exceedingly weak in many other respects..." Terry, editor of the *Wytheville Dispatch* in the 1880s and '90s and son to the Confederate brigadier, had written Wise first on March 12th. He stated that Crockett's recent death had prompted him to work up an article on the duel and he hoped for Wise's version. From his Manhattan law offices Wise replied in detail two days later, forwarding George Ward's "Memo" along with his own recollections.

"I believe this was," Wise told Terry, "as you say, about the end of dueling in Virginia, and if I had any instrumentality in breaking it up, may be the good Lord will credit me with it against the long column on the other side. I never saw Mr. Crockett again; long ago forgave him any injustice he may have done me and charged it to the folly of politics, which besets us all at times, and hope that his life was happy, his death peaceful and that his future is assured."

By the spring of 1883 Wise had decided, reluctantly, at the urging of friends—especially his old V.M.I. roommate "Duck" Colonna, now a civil engineer with the Coast and Geodetic Survey—never to answer a challenge to combat again. He was vastly relieved his pistol had failed to fire against Crockett, for he was certain he'd have killed the man. When, therefore, the smoke-snorting Captain Page McCarty, editor of the Lynchburg *Campaign*, reviled him choicely in that organ for his Readjuster/Republican beliefs, Wise took cognizance by a "card," *i.e.*, an open letter, to the Richmond papers. The *code duello* was, he affirmed flatly, uncivilized. It was also illegal. He himself had a wife, a houseful of children, a paying profession, and too much sense by now to risk any of them. He herewith renunciated the principle and practice of the code.

Since everybody knew of Wise's impeccable War record, plus his reputation as a marksman, and could scarcely assign him to the no'count class, his integrity went unchallenged. Hence this sprightly pronunciamento, which earned widespread comment, may be said to have established a small landmark in the social history of the Commonwealth. The Richmond *Whig* and *State* published it in their respective issues of March 5th and 6th, 1884. Patterson reprinted it in his *The Code Duello* in 1927. "It was probably," said Patterson, who himself knew Wise, "the bravest act of his life, and most fruitful in its results."

As Wise had declared, in his *Saturday Evening Post* article of 1906, "I believe many people were waiting for somebody to take that stand."

He himself, after a distinguishd career, was buried amid pomp and circumstance on New Market Day, May 15th, 1913 in Hollywood Cemetery, Richmond. The news was carried in papers from Boston to San Francisco.

And there were no more duels in Virginia.

[NOTE: P. 315. Frank Blair was probably the Wythe County Blair and not the Senator from Missouri, Ed.]

INDEX

A

Abrams, Rev. W. E., 162
Abingdon Presbytery, 123
Adams, George, 119
  John, 169
  Robert, 106
Adkins, Freal, 11
  R. A., 7
Ager, H.M., 183
Agriculture, 57, 58, 78
Agricultural Implements, 174
Akers, Amos, 267
  Andrew, 128
  Dwight Cumming, 267
  Istalena Robeson, 267
  John, 153
  Joseph, 11
  Lewis Robeson, 267
  Margaret J., 153
  Missouri Kelly, 267
  Phillipp, 128
  Robert, 154
  Vachael, 9
  Rev. Wm. David, 267
Alexandria, Rev. J. H., 181
Alford, 17
  Elizabeth Baker, 273, 293
  John, 273, 293
  R. J., 179
Allen, Carr, 15
  Samuel, 15
  William, 15
Allison (Alison)
  C. C., 183
  David, 11
  David S., 6
  Elizabeth Saul, 291
  Halbert, 277
  J. C., 256, 257
  James, 11
  Leander S., 15
  Mary B. Sayers, 277
  William R., 291
Alsey, Edmond Gannaway, 145
Anchor of Hope Church, 120, 121, 123
Anders, Henry, 7
Anderson, 17
  G. W., 15
  John, 17
Andis Mines, 109
Andrews, E. A., 182
Annals of Southwest Va., 105
Ant Hills, 193
Archer, Robert C., 6
  Thomas, 11
Armbrister (Armpriester)
  A. J., 157
  George, 128, 130, 131

George W., 18, 151, 183
  Henry, 131
  Philip, 131
Arnburn, John, 11
Arney (Arny)
  John, 7
  J. W., 154
Arnold, A., 153
  George, 18, 153
  Sam, 183
  William, 17
Asbury, Bishop, 143
Ashburg (Asbury) Academy, 181
Asbury Camp Ground, 138, 139, 140, 143
Asbury Camp Meeting Promoters, (List) 138
Asbury Methodist Church, 142, 143, 145
Asbury Town, 139
Atkins, Elizabeth Moore, 296
  David, 296
  Rev. K. C., 248
Atlantic, Mississippi & Ohio Railroad, 30, 32, 61, 62, 63
Attorneys, 174, 246, 247
Auctioneers, 174
Auman & Co., 176
Aumann (Auman), James, 227
  William C., 86
  Drug Store, 227
Austin, Moses, 303
  Stephen, 303
Austinville, 50, 51, 73, 81, 146, 147, 156, 188, 191
Austinville Pentecostal Holiness Church, 164
Austinville Post Office, 173
Averell, Col. William Woods, 165
Avery, Franklin, 17
  John, 17

B

Bach, Michael, 128
Bailey, D. C., 175
  E. H., 237
  G. W., 10
  Dr. John M., 254
  Robert K., 5
Baker, Catharine, 291
  Douglas, 122, 291
  Elizabeth, 291
  George W., 149
  Haros Neth, 291
  J.J., 149, 182
  Rev. J. T., 164
  James, H., 291
  Joseph McC., 156
  Mary Hoge, 291

INDEX

Baker, Montgomery, 291
  Patsy, 291
  Perlina H., 291
  R. G., 86
  R. P., 18
Bakers (commercial), 174
Bakers Chapel Pentecostal Holiness Church, 164
Baldwin, William G., 5
Baldwin & Co., 177
Bane, Rev. T.M., 163
Banks (commercial), 174, 238, 239
Bank of Wytheville, 239
Baptist Churches, 162
Barbers, 174
Barnitz, J. A., 177
  John A., 259
Barometric Averages, 68
Barren Springs, 147, 191
Barren Springs Furnace, 68, 94, 147
Barren Springs Mines, 109
Barrow (Barren) Springs P.O., 173
Barrett, Mrs. J.B., 259
  John B., 109
  Nelson, 10
Barrett's Foundry, 109
Barrett, J. B. Co., 111, 232
Barrett's Mills, 109
Barytes, 56
Bateman, Daniel, 5
  John J., 159
Baughman, C. D., 179
Baumgardner (Baumgartner) (Bumgardner)
  Bessie Belle, 267
  Charles, 9, 267
  Charles L., 125
  Ellen V., 267
  Ephraim, 9
  Hugh Stuart, 267
  Jacob, 17
  John, 131, 267
  L. K., 125
  Lulu May, 267
  Malinda U., 267
  Mattie Simon, 267
  M. L., 9
  Silvester, 17
Baylor, Harrison, 146, 156
Beaver's Branch, 157
Beaver Creek Church, 123
Beckett, M. D., 181
Bell's Forge, 90, 102, 189
Bell's Furnace, 90
Bell, Joseph, 89, 90
  Sarah, 89
  Wm., 102
Bellefield, 87, 105, 106
Benbow, Anna Clark, 275
  Jesse, 275

Benington, John, 183
  Madison, 7
Benton, Col. William, 282
Berea Christian Church, 159
Bergman, S., 175
Bermington, M., 182
Berry, William J., 10
W.O., 165
Bertha Mineral Co., 81
Bertha Mine (s), 63, 109
Bertha P. O., 173
Bertha Zinc Mine, 51, 180
Bethany Lutheran Church, 135
Bethany Methodist Church, 156
Bethel Methodist Church, 146
Bethesda Church, 123
Bethpage Christian Church, 159
Beuchler, G.T., 174, 175, 215, 236
Beverly Furnace, 41, 69, 82, 99, 154
Beverly Mill, 154
Beverly Post Office, 154
Beville, James A., 5
  J. M., 181
Big Spring Congregation, 119
Big Walker's Mountain, 30, 45, 46, 48, 49
Billiards and Pool, 174, 245
Birch, Rev. Thomas Erskine, 120
Bird, Rev. John, 154
Bishop, N.W. & Son Mills, 179
Black, James A., 5
Blackard, Austin, 7
  Emory, 296
  Nancy C. Vaught, 296
Black Lick, 56, 119, 134, 148, 150
Black Lick Church, 123
Black Lick Presbyterian Church, 125
Blackwell, R.P., 174, 258
  William P., 10
  R. P. & Co., 228
Blair, Andrew, 11
  F. S., 247
  Capt. F. S., 254
  Frank, 315
  H. E., 173
  Jas., 183
  Jerome, 97, 180, 183
  Robert, 158
  Thomas, 11, 89, 183
  W. F., 183
  & Blair, 174
  C. D. & Co., 176
  Ore Bank, 47
  & Sampson, 175
Blessing, Anthony, 131
  Granville, 10
  Peter F., 10
Boarding Houses, 173, 204, 215, 218, 219, 220

INDEX

Bobbett, Caleb, 88
Bohanon, Thomas, 156
Boiling Springs, 193
Boiling Spring Congregation, 120
Bok (See also Buck), Christian, 128
Bolling, David, 11
  & Stanley, 174
Bolt, Rev. A. J., 248
Booksellers & Stationers, 174
Boom Furnace, 38
Boot Manufacturers & Dealers, 174
Boothe, William, 11
Booze, Rev. Raymond L., 134
Bottimore, W. G., 110
Bourn (Bourne), A.P., 6
  B. Mason, 268
  Carrie Stone, 268
  Eddie, 268
  Henry, 183
  H. G., 18, 157
  Henry G., 268
  Henry G., Jr., 268
  J. A., 6, 151
  Jennie E., 268
  Jno, A., 183
  John S., 268
  Lizzie Simmonson, 268
  M. Lulu, 268
  Stephen T., 268
  Walker, 268
  Wm. H., 268
Bovell, Rev. Stephen, 122
Bowen, Eliza Black, 269
  Ellen Tate, 269
  Henry, 269
  Henry A., 269
  Henry S., 269
  H. S., 18
  Mary E. Miller, 269
  Rees, 269
Bowles, George W., 5
  William A., 5
Bowman, Mr., 288
Boyd, Andrew, 169
  Capt. C.R., 90
  Minerva French, 273
  T. J., 215
  Thomas J., 136, 216, 273
Boyd's Hill view from, 205
Boyd's Hotel, 216
Boyd's Map, 91
Boyd's Mine, 31
Boyer, C. Q., 176
Brady, J., 174
  J. C., 181
  Mrs. Josephus, 163
Brally (Bralley), Mrs., 155
  A.J., 259
  Andrew J., 268
  Austes Jones, 268

Brally Edwin, J., 268
  G. F., 179
  G. S., 15, 183
  G.W.J.M., 11, 268
  James, 268
  Jane Carter, 268
  Jeff, 11
  Jeremiah, 268
  John S., 268
  Laura Bell, 268
  Mitchell, 11
  Monroe, 268
  Pauline Jessup, 280
  Robert Lee, 268
  S. C., 173, 183
  Samuel, 11, 280
  Saul S., 268
  S. S., 180, 183
  Stephen C., 11, 268
  Thomas, 268
  William, 268
  A. J. & Son, 177
  W. H. & Co. 175
Bramblett, Eliza Hamil Thomas, 269
  Elkanah, 268
  Mary Watson, 269
  Mildred Allen Dearing, 268
  William H., 268
  W.H., M.D., 18
Bray, Lewis, 5
Breckenridge, George, 120
Brick Church Black Lick, 124
Brick Church Cove, 125, 165
Brick Manufacturers, 174
Bridges, C.S., 173
  J.B., 158
Bridle, Rev. D. A., 159
Brien, Henrich, 129
Brinkley, Rev. J. I., 163
Bristol First Church, 123
Brock, Richard S., 75
Brophy, P., 258
Brown (Braun)
  Alice V. Sharitz, 269
  Anna Maria Rader, 269
  Andreas, 129
  Andrew, Sr., 131
  Andy, 10
  Asa, 31
  Barbara Nippe, 270
  B. F., 150
  Christopher, 131, 269
  Christopher, Jr., 131
  Coal Bank, 31
  Cornelius, 145
  D. S., 157
  Eleanora C. Herbst, 269
  Ernest H., 270
  Eugenia F., 270
  Granville H., 277

INDEX

Brown, George Michael, 129
  Rev. J. A., 135
  J. B., 9
  J. C., 15, 183
  J. E., 173, 182
  J.G., 174, 178
  J. W., 154, 155
  Jacob, 131
  James A., 269
  James E., 92
  Jane E. Snavely, 277
  John, 131
  John A., 129, 269
  John C., 148, 158, 274
  Jno. G., 239
  John W., 5
  Josiah, 183, 287
  Joseph, 129
  Rev. Lee C., 125
  Margaret Earheart, 270
  Margaret Ellen Sharitz, 274
  Mrs. Maria M., 122
  M.D., 10
  Michael, 131, 270
  Michael Jr, 131
  Michael, Sr., 131
  Montgomery P., 18
  Nicholas C., 13, 270
  Perlina H., 125
  Polly, 125
  Robert, 180
  Robert A., 13, 270
  Robert C., 6
  Rufus, 183, 270
  Sarah Hudson, 287
  Sarah Tartar, 269
  Rev. Stephen F., 269
  W. E., 176
  Hill Furnace, 40, 42 (drawing), 69, 97, 98 (photo)
  Hill Iron Co., 97
  Hill Post Office, 56, 69
  Iron Ore, 32
  J. H. (Hotel), 177
Browning, S. P., 183
Brownlow, William Gannaway (Parson), 86
Bruce, G.S., 144, 230, 239
  G. S. & Co., 176
Bruner (Brunner) (Prooner) (Pruner)
  Frederick, 131
  George, 131
  G. Michael, 131
  Jacob, 128, 129, 131
  Michael, 131
Bryant, J.E., 162
Buchanan, Albert Sydney, 270
  Alex, 7
  Barbara Catharine, 270
  Catherine Kinder, 270

Buchanan, Harvey, 10
  Hobson Clarke, 270
  James, 9
  John, 9, 119, 120, 270
  Laura Jane, 270
  Mary C., 125
  Robert, 9, 119, 270
  Sophia Brown, 270
  W. A., 183
  William A., 7
  Wm. B., 139
  W.M., 179
  William, 270
  William Michael, 270
  William N., 7
Buck (see also Bok) Ephraim, 17
  Felix, 10
  Franklin, 9
  Isaac P., 154
  J.H., 183
  James H., 10
  Lafayette, 17
  Sal, 183
  W.W., 176
  W.W., Dr., 180
Buckingham, P.S., 136
Buckley, Joel S., 10
  John, 9
  H.D.C., 174, 183
  R.J., 10
  Wm. A., 10
Buford, Mrs. Lucy, 124
  N.W., 173, 183
  Stuart & Co., 68
Buhn, Henry, 131
Bullard, Rev. F.F., 248
Bunckly, Peter, 131
Bunts, John M., 151, 173
Burch, J.T., 257
Burgiss, John, 150
Burkett, George, 7, 296
  Mitchell, 7
  Polly Vaught, 296
Burns, Allen C., 11
Burress, James, 10
Burris, Rev. L. M., 155
Burton, E.C., 183
Businesses Wythe Co., 174-182
Butchers, 175
Butner, Alexander H., 6
Byars, George, 279
Byrne, James, 84

C

Cahl, John, 131
Caldwell, Mrs. Ellen C., 219
  J.W., 174, 215
  M.M., 246
  William, 11

324

INDEX

Calfee, Benjamin, 270
  Betsy, 270
  C.H., 113, 271
  Charles, 270
  Charles H., 270, 271
  Elizabeth, 271
  Elizabeth Brown, 270
  Evelina, 271
  Henry, 270
  J.A., 271
  James, 270
  John, 270, 271
  L.D., 175
  Margaret Howard, 270, 271
  R.A., 183, 271
  Sallie, 270
  Sarah J. White, 271
  Sophia, 271
  T. K., 173
  William, 270
  William B., 18
  Robinson & Co., 176
Calhoun, William, 120
Callaghan & Yates, 175, 248
Callaghan & Yates Mill, 179
Callaghan's Mills, 179
Calvary Church, 151, 157
Calvin, Pelter J., 5
Campbell, 5
  A.A., 77, 173, 174, 175, 219
  Dr. C.C., 18
  Patrick, 119
  William, 119
Candler, Mrs. Emma, 177
  R.D., 175, 176, 178
  R.D. & Co., 176
Cannaday, Daniel, 91
Carlin, Daniel, 102
Carnahan, J.E., 180
  John W., 178
Carriage, Coach & Wagon Co., 175
Carriage Material, 175
Carriages & Wagons, 242
Carrico & Bourne, 175
Carpenter, Rev. Mr., 130
Carpenters & Builders, 175
Carrington, Mrs. Jane, 124
Carter, Frank, 182
  Franklin, 18, 113
  George L., 105
  R.M., 15
  Coal & Iron Co., 86, 91, 95, 99
Carter's Ferry, 68
Carter Mines, 109
Cassell (Cassel) (Kapel)
  Alice Victoria, 271
  Andrew, 131
  Charles, 11

Cassell, Charles H., 272
  Charles W., 13
  Charles Willis, 271
  Ciddie P. Haller, 272
  Daniel, 173
  Daniel W., 272
  David, 131
  Elize A. Repass, 271
  Ella Jane, 271
  Emory Hawkins, 271
  Franklin, 10
  James L., 133
  George Stuart, 271
  John, 146
  Joseph Col., 271
  Joseph, 272, 271
  Joseph D., 272
  Lena Jackson, 271
  Lucy Brown, 271
  M., 183
  M.B., 6, 183, 271, 272
  Marion Michael, 271
  Mary Eva, 271
  Mary Foglesong, 271
  Mary E. Graham, 271
  Mary Susan, 271
  Michael, 131, 134, 166, 271
  Nicolaus, 131
  Sallie, 271
  S. H., 18
  S.S., 166
  Samuel, 183
  Samuel H., 272
  Samuel H. Jr., 272
  Stephen Sydney, 271
  Susan Wiseley, 272, 271
  Thos., 183
  Virginia Graham, 271
  Willie H., 272
Caterson, E.D., 18
Catholic Churches, 160
Catron (Ketring)
  Andrew, 149
  C.D., 82
  Ephraim, 17, 82
  John, 8
  John, 128
  Joseph, 8
  Peter, 7
  P. O., 173
  William, 149
Catlett, Dabney, 11
Catterson, John, 13
  William, 13
Cave Hill Furnace, 82, 100
Cecil, Samuel, 274
Cedar Run, 92
Cedar Run Furnace, 68, 82, 91, 92
  95 (picture), 189
Cedar Hill Church, 156
Cedar Springs Farmers, 182

INDEX

Cedar Springs P.O., 173
Chadwell (Chatwell)
  Henry, 10
  Jacob, 6
  Jacob S., 5
  Jane Eller, 107
  Strolter, 7
  Thomas, 5
  Wm. S., 10
  William, 107, 108
  William N., 152
  Forge, 107, 108, 189
Chaffin, Alexander, 89
  A.M., 182
  Elizabeth, 156
  Frank, 182
  George P., 149
  Mrs., 183
  W.W., 182
Chapman, George W., 87
Chalybeate Springs, 251
Chapman, John 87
Charcoal, 57
Chatman, Jno., 183
Chauvenet, S.E., 60, 75, 193
Chimney Rocks, 60, 193, 211
Chiswell, Col., 188
Christian Churches, 159
Churches, 77, 193, 248
Cigar Manufacturers, 175
Clark, B.T., 257
  Clarence M., 75
  David G., 15
  George, 183
  H.C., 7
  Joseph S, 283
  J.S., 154
  Paulina Neff, 283
  R.E.L., 183
  Blessing & Co., 236
  Post Office, 173
  Summit, 28, 31, 32, 45
  Summit Mine, 109
Clayton, J.P., 174
Clemens (Clemmons), Henry, 131
  John I., 5
  Joseph, 11
Clift, Alfred, 256
Climate of County, 63, 76, 192, 203
Cline, Ephraim, 10
  Jackson, 10
  James, 177, 179
Clothing Stores, 175
Clyne, Joseph, 183
Coal, 2, 30, 31, 32, 189
Coal Analysis - Stonyfork, 32
Coal & Wood Dealers, 175
Cochran, Howe P., 279
  Jennie L. Kent, 279
Coldicott, C.R., 178

Cold Spring Church, 123
Coleman, John, 145
Coley, Christopher K., 272
  C.K., 8, 183
  Isaac, 8
  J.N., 183
  James N., 7
  Jeff, 8
  Joseph, 183
  Josephine A.C. Neff, 272, 283
  Lydia Copenhaver, 272
  Myrtle Neff, 272
  Nettie McNair, 272
  William M., 272
  William Marion, 272
  W.M., 176
Colfre, R.A., 18
Collins, Adam, 158
  A.M., 179
  David, 281
  E.J., 75
  W.D., 10
  Weyman, 17
  William, 17
  William P., 18
Collops Church, 130
Commercial House, 177
Commission Merchants, 175
Commissioners in Chancery, 175
Company A, 4th Va. Inf.- organized, 4
Company B, 29th Va. Inf. Roll, 7
Co. B, 45th Va. Inf. Roll, 9-14
Co. D, 45th Va. Inf. Roll, 11
Co. H, 63rd Va. Inf, 17
Conerly, B.F., 165
Confectioners, 175
Confree, Godfree, 127
Consolidated Mining Co., 176, 180
Convent, 197
Cook, Jacob C., 5
  Jno. A., 258
Cooley, Felix, 11
  J. M., 10
Cooper, Alexander, 272, 145
  Elizabeth, 272, 145
  Eliza Jane Tarter, 272
  R. P., 173, 182
  William P., 272
  Rev. Wm. Paton, 272
Copenhaver, Daniel, 7
  D.F., 183
  Ephraim, 148, 182
  Elizabeth M. Neff, 282
  Issac, 7
  J. L., 182
  J. P., 182
  Pierson, 7
  W.P., 182
Copper, 2, 54, 55, 189

INDEX

Corinth Lutheran Church, 134
Corinth Sunday School, 166
Cormany, Ann Buck, 276
    Joel, 276, 183
Cornett, W.H., 18
Corvin (see Covin), Stephen, 18
The Cove, 60, 134, 165
Cove Church, 126
Cove Churches, 121
Cove Lithia Springs, 178, 208, 224
Cove Mountain, 30, 45
Coveton Methodist Church, 164
Covin (Corvin), Charles, 183
Cox, James A., 175
Crabill, A.B., 175
Craig, Rev. John, 119, 120
Craighill, Rev. F. H., 137
Crawford, Elizabeth Jane Alford, 273
    Elizabeth Rachel, 273
    Elizabeth Smith, 273
    George Washington, 273
    Joanna Jane, 273
    John Thomas, 273
    Joseph Stuart, 273
    Mary Ellen, 273
    Robert I.J., 273
    Susan Margaret, 273
    Wesley Lee, 273
    William, 273
    William Shepherd, 273
    William, Sr., 156
Crawford Mines, 109, 191
Crigger (Creger, Creager, Krieger, Kregger)
    Amandreth, 10
    Austin, 10
    Eli, 7
    Ephraim, 11, 17, 183
    Franklin, 7
    H. A., 10
    J. M., 18
    James, 7, 17
    John, 11, 17
    Kent, 183
    Mary, 125
    Michael, 131
    Mrs., 126
    Sons, 175
    William R., 10
Creger & Clift, 237
Crescent Horseshoe & Iron Works, 100
Cripple Creek, 26, 34, 40, 55, 73, 80, 90, 94, 97, 99, 102, 151, 152, 154
Cripple Creek Camp Ground, 38
Cripple Creek Church, 121, 124
Cripple Creek Mines, 191
    Post Office, 173

Cripple Creek Village, 133
Crockett, 133
    A.G., 158
    A. G., Dr., 180
    Mrs. Agnes, 125
    Agnes (Nancy) Graham, 274
    Alexander G., 274
    Allen Taylor, 273
    Andrew, 91, 104
    Argyle Campbell, 273
    Byron, 183
    Caroline Minter, 273
    Chaffin C., 274
    Charles L., 123
    David B, 273
    David P., 274
    Davy, 274, 275
    Easter, 120
    Edward L., 5
    Elden Kent, 273
    Elizabeth, 274
    Elizabeth Boyd, 273, 313
    Emily, 274
    Eugene, 273
    Henry L., 273
    Dr. Henry S., 273
    Howe T., 273
    J. G., 183
    J. Gratt, 173
    James, 11, 91, 92, 104
    James S., 90, 155
    James T., 6
    Mrs. Jane L., 122
    John, 11, 92, 274
    John F., 13
    John G., 121, 274
    John S., 274, 273
    John Stuart, 286, 313-319
    Joseph, 5, 31, 120
    Joseph M., 6
    Joseph N., 121
    Margaret Buchanan Taylor, 273, 286
    Mary, 274
    Mary Ann, 121
    Mrs. Mary Anne, 126
    Mary H., 121
    Minnie Howe, 273
    Nancy, 274
    Rachel L., 274
    Rachel L. Cecil, 284
    Robert, 174
    Robert J., 5, 106
    Sallie F., 121
    Samuel, 92, 120, 313
    Samuel F., 6
    Samuel Floyd, 273
    Samuel R., 121, 274
    Samuel R., Sr., 122, 125
    Mrs. Sarah, 126

INDEX

Crockett, Sarah A., 274
  S.R., 183
  Mrs. S.S., 174, 220
  Stephen, 106
  Stephen S., 106
  Stuart R., 273, 317, 318
  Thomas B., 273
  Thomas S., 284
  Hon. Thompson S., 274
  W.G., 125, 274
  Wm., 183
  Wm. G., 121, 224
  William R., 155
  W.R., 105
Crockett & Co., 69, 86, 90, 92, 94, 95, 99, 155
Crockett Depot, 62
Crockett Depot Farmers, 182
Crockett Industry, 59
Crockett Iron Works, 91, 104
Crockett & Thomas, 224
Crockett, Town of, 78, 135, 149
Crockett, Sanders & Co., 90
Crocketts, 105
Crockett's Chapel, 154, 155
Crockett's Cove, 45, 164
Crockett's Depot P. O., 2, 69, 173
Crockett's Falls Photo, 225
Crockett's Forge, 91, 92, 103, 104
Crockett's Mills, 106
Crone, Mr. (Stone Cutter), 130
Cropper, John, 314
Crowder & Rider, 178
Crowder's Tailor Shop, 105
Crowe, Rev. John Moore, 155
Crowgey, H.J., 150, 183
  R.H., 113, 183
Crusenberry & Kitchen Mine, 52
Cummings, Rev. Charles, 119

D

Dake, N.S., 176
Dallihide, Andrew, 12
Danner, J.A., 180
  John H., 255
Darter, See Tarter
Dargan, Edmund S., 275
  Roxana Brock, 276
Daugherty, James H., 160
Davidson, Erastus G., 5
  Honorable W.B., 299
Davis (Davies)
  Abraham, 156
  Andrew, 11
  Andrew J., 159
  Eliza, 148

Davis, E.M., 178
  F.H., 157
  George, 7
  Henry, 8, 11, 120
  H.H., 10
  Jacob, 131, 156, 157
  James, 8, 12, 120
  Jane, 120
  J.M., 183
  John, 131
  John C., 12
  Joseph, 131
  Joseph S., 15
  J.W., 173
  Lewis, 5
  Margaret, 148
  Marion, 12
  Melville, 12
  M.R., 56
  S.C., 164
  Thomas, 120
  W.C., 151
  Widow, 131
  William, 8, 11, 169
Dean, H., 151
  W.H., 156
DeBord, 152
Deckerd, George, 8
  Peter, 8
Deep Well Ore Bank, 180
Delham, Robt., 86
Densham, Robert, 86
Denting, Jas., 182
Dentists, 175, 246
Derting, David, 8
  J.F., 8
  John S., 17
  Thomas, 8
  Thomas E., 8
Denel, E.C., 215
Dew, Mrs. T.R., 77, 182, 223
Deyerle, Abraham, 289
  Andrew Jackson, 288
  Charles, 10
  Col., 289
  Jane Barnette, 288
  John B., 10
  J. William, 289
  Mary Alberta, 289
  Peter, 288
  Pink Barnett, 289
Dickens, Mrs. Fannie, 163
Dilman, Christopher, 131
Distillers, 175
Dix, Henry M., 5
  T.F., 182
Doak, C.D., 183
  Canara D., 148
  David, 120
  Edley, 148
  Family, 119

INDEX

Doak, H.T., 10
  James, 148
  K.D., 18
  N.S., 18
  Rebecca, 125
  Robert, 120
  William, 148
Dora Furnace, 92
Dotson's Hollow, 146
Dottinger (see Dutton), Adam, 128
Douthat, Elize Baylor, 276
  Henry Yost, 276
Draper's Mountain, 27, 45, 49, 189
Draper's Mountain Ores, 44
Drug Stores, 226, 227
Druggists, 176
Dry Goods Stores, 176
Dunford, George W., 15
  G.W., 151, 183
  T.R., 153
  William, 12
Dunn, Geo, R., 215, 239
Dutton, Adam, 133
  Jonas, 18
Dyers, 176
Dyer, E., 144, 246
  Elijah, 146
  J.A., 173
  Jas, A., 149
  J.D., 149
  Nathan, 147

E

Eagle Furnace, 41, 68
Earhart, A.C.M., 10
  Alfred, 12
  Ely D., 278
  David, 10
  Frances, 125
  George W., 278
  Henry, 125
  John, 278
  John S., 278
  Mary Stanger, 278
  Polly, 125
Early, J.J., 176
  J.T., 183
  James T., 146
  Robert M., 182
Education & Religion, 192, 193
Edwards, W.J., 179
Effort (Eiffert)
  Alice Virginia, 274
  Ella May, 274
  Henry A., 158, 274
  James, 274
  John W., 274
  Malinda Stamper, 274

Effort (Eiffert)
  Nannie Brown, 274
  Nellie Flora, 274
  Susan T. Brown, 274
  Wythe B., 274
Eller, Henry, 107
  Jane, 107
Enterprise Publishing, 181
Episcopal Churches, 136, 137
Etter, Daniel, 130, 131
  Ephraim, 8, 10
  James A., 10
  John, 131
  John J., 10
  Mrs. J. Stuart, 135
  Mary, 130
  S.S., 13, 182, 183
  Sarah E. Neff, 282
Etter Post Office, 173
Evans, James, 5
  Jesse, Sr., 89
  John, 8, 103
Evans Creek, 120
Evansham, 143
Evergreen Methodist Church, 150
Eversole, E.C., 6, 175
  Dr. E. C., 125
  E., 13
  Isaac, 6
  Leander, 5
Evis, Rev., 138
Ewald, Anthony, 129
  A.R., 257
  Chas. A., 215
  J.H. & Bro., 178, 181, 182, 238
  Joseph, 234
  S.F., 178, 229, 257
Ewing, John, 107

F

Fairview Methodist Church, 150
Fairview Church, 135
Fairview Church, Rural Retreat, 154
Falls Mining & Mfg. Co., 182
Farmer, Dr. Wm., 246
Farmers Bank of Southwest Va., 174, 238
Farmer, Haller & Ewald, 175
Farmers Hotel, 177
Farmers Listed, 182-183
Favonia Post Office, 173
Felts, John W., 19
  Raleigh, 15
Felty (Filty), Jacob, 16, 131, 158
  John, 131
  Nicolaus, 131
Fertilizer Mfg. & Agents, 176

INDEX

Festic, Lewis, 138
Fifty-first Va. Infantry, 14-17
Findly, George D., 15
Fink, David V., 149
Fish Hatchery, 63, 78, 172, 193, 197 (photo), 221 (photo)
Fisher, Absolom, 157, 159
  Andrew, 140
  David, 157
  Harvey J., 17
  H. J., 18, 157
  Jacob, 131, 146, 183
  James, 147, 156, 183
  Rev. James, 146
  James W., 18
  Jason L., 12
  Joseph, 12, 183, 287
  Joseph S., 13
  Lewis, 12
  Melville, 12
  Nellie Virginia, 166
  Reuben, 157
  S.O., 182
  Sarah Baumgardner, 287
  Thomas, 15, 159
  Thomas W., 150
  William H., 142
Fishers Mill, 179
  S.O. & Bro., 176
Fisher, S.O. & Bros. Mill, 179
Flannagin, A.C., 8
  Madison, 8
  William, 8
Fleming, David, 153
Fleming Methodist Church, 105, 152, 153, 156
Flohr, Rev. George D., (Father), 129, 130, 131, 133, 168
Florists, 176
Foglesong - See Vogelsong
  Crockett, 8
  Thomas, 8
Fontaine, Charles H., 144
Foote & Johnson, 174, 175, 176, 181, 242
Forest Methodist Church, 121, 146
Forges, 68, 69, 80, 189
Forge, Bell, 102, 189
  Bell - Herbert, 102
  Bells (Joseph), 90
  Chatwell, 107, 108, 189
  Crockett, 103
  Graham, 103, 104, 105, 189
  at Gray Eagle, 95
  Herbert's, 103
  High Rock, 103
  Huddle's, 41, 108, 189
  Lockett's, 41, 108
  Alex Peirce, 41
  Peirce, 97, 102
  Poplar Camp, 102
  Porter's, 43, 109, 189
  Products, 81
  Toncray's, 105, 106
  Forney's Mine, 51
  Rich Hill, 38
Fort Chiswell, 3, 118, 136, 188, 194
  Stock Farm, 74
Forty-fifty Va. Inf. Formed, 9
Fourth Virginia Infantry, 4
Foster, John, 12
  William, 141, 142
  William B., 12, 173, 215
  William H., 143, 144, 146, 156
Fosters Falls, 94, 109, 191
Fosters Falls Church, 149
Foster Falls Furnace, 82, 95, 96
Fosters' Falls Hotel, 177
  Mfg. Co., 176, 177, 180
  Mills, 179
  Saw Mills, 179
  Mining & Mfg. Co., 95, 178
  P.O., 173
Foundry, McDonald, 110
  McWane, 110, 112
  of Wytheville, 109
  Wytheville, 110
Fountain, C.R., 183
Fourth Avenue (photo), 241
Fourth Avenue Hotel, 177, 217
Fox, Charles, L., 124
  Rev. D.S., 134
  Rev. Father Edward, 160
  Mrs. Jane, 218
Frances, Maria, 121
Francis Mill Creek, 33, 41, 94, 99
Frank, I., 215
  Jacob, 257
  & Co., 175, 232
Fredeking, C.A., 124
Friel, Manassas, 85
Freeman, George, 8
  George W., 159
  James, 147
Fruit, 191
Frye, Abram, 159
Frye's Hill, 56
  Marble Quarry, 56
Fry, W.F., 153
  W.H., 150
Fuchs, Henry, 131
  Peter, 128
Fulhon, John H., 6
Fuller, Daniel, 16
  James, 15
  J.W., 8
  William, 163
Fulton, A.K., 90
  A.S., 123, 136
  Hon. A.S., 136, 137, 279
  Andrew S., 90

INDEX

Fulton, Benjamin D., 5
  C. McG., 144
  Cynthia McG., 144
  J.H., 144, 174
  John H., 5
  Maggie E.D. Huddle, 278
  Samuel M., 278
  W.E., 162, 173, 174
  Wm. B., 173
Funk, E.M., 182
Furgerson, Samuel H., 5
Furnaces, 68, 69, 73, 80, 82
Furnace Products, 81
Furnace, Barren Springs, 94
  Bell, 90
  Beverly, 41, 99, 154
  Boom, 38
  Brown Hill, 40, 42, 97, 98
  Cove Hill, 100
  Cedar Run, 91, 189
  Dora, 92
  Eagle, 41
  Fosters Falls, 95, 96 (photo)
  Graham's New, 39
  David Graham's, 34
  Gray Eagle, 94
  Irondale, 99, 101(Photo)
  Ivanhoe, 99
  Little Wythe, 94, 189
  Max Meadows, 100, 191
  Noble, 33, 41
  Parry Mount, 91
  Poplar Camp, 88, 188
  Ravenscliff (Raven Cliff), (Raven Clift), 41, 69, 82, 89, 189
  Roaring Falls, 95
  Rock (Panic), 45
  Sayers & Oglesby, 33, 41
  Speedwell, 43, 84-88
  Walton, 40, 97
  White Rock, 100
Furniture Dealers, 176

G

Gaines, Rev. D.S., 138
  Rev. W.A., 157
Galena Church, 121, 123
Galena Mills, 179
Galilee Christian Church, 159
Gallagher, P., 144
  Pelton, 5
  Peter, 100
Gallimore, Miner, 54
Galleys, Benj, 95
Gammon, A.A., 125
Gammon, A.A. & Son, 176, 178
Gannaway, John, 138, 143
  John Sr., 155
  Mines, 109
  Rev. Robertson, 87

Gannaway, Sallie, 87
  Seymore W., 155
  Thomas, 155
  Thomas M., 11
General Merchants, 176, 177
Geology of Wythe Co., 26, 187-188
German Club, 78, 208
Gibboney, Albert H., 123
  D.K., 178, 206
  D.K. & Co., 176, 177
  J. Hal & Co., 245
  Mrs. Jane, 174
  Miss Janie K., 215
  Jas. M., 173
  Mrs. Margaret, 122
  Robert, 86
  Thomas, 143
Gibson, P.R., 174
Gilman, Michael, 6
  Richard, 10
Glade Church, 153
Glade Ore Bank, 44
Glade Mountain, 49
Glade Mountains, 45
Glade Spring Church, 123
Gleaner, J.L., 173
Glascock, Adelaide Eliza Adams, 281
  William O., 281
Gleaves, Andrew J., 275
  Anna M., 275
  C.W., Dr., 180
  Charles W., 246
  Charles Wythe, 275
  Fannie D. Dargan, 275
  Dr., G.W., 253
  George W., 151
  George Wythe, 275
  Isabella C., 151
  Isabella C. Sanders, 275
  J.L., 174
  James Lucian, 275
  James T., 6, 90, 275
  J.T., 89
  James T. Sr., 90
  James Turk, 275
  Jessie Lilian, 275
  Julia K. Benbow, 275
  Maria L. Crockett, 275
  Melvina Crockett, 275
  Peggy, 89
  Robert H., 11, 13, 275
  Robert Lee, 275
  S.C. Dr., 275
  Samuel C., 276
  Samuel C. (Surgeon), 19
  Samuel Crockett, 275
  Taylor A.M., 275
  William, 89, 275
  William, Jr., 89

INDEX

Glenbrook, 218
Glenwood Methodist Church, 147
Gold, C.A., 10
  R.D., 10
Goodson, Elijah, 12
Goodman, J.E., 10, 183
  N.W., 10
  Rev. F.D., 137
Gose, David, 145
  Jonathan, 145
  Mary J. Kegley, 293
  Stephen, 12, 293
  Susan, 145
  William G., 5
Graber, Rev. Henry, 126
Grace Lutheran Church, 135
Grahams, 91
Graham, A.J., 271
  Charles T., 149
  Crockett, 122
  David, 34, 39, 68, 69, 92, 94, 104, 105, 123, 124, 147, 149, 189
  David P., 16, 90
  Major David Peirce, 92
  D.P. (residence), 39
  James, 156
  James M., 149
  J.T., Dr., 180
  Jane, 121
  John, 121
  John G., 121
  Joseph T., 139
  Mary, 121
  Miss Mary G., 121
  Mrs. Nannie M., 124
  Nannie W., 149
  Robert C., 149
  Rev. Robert, 122, 124
  Rev. R.C., 125
  S.O. Worder, 271
  Wirt B., 19
  W.B., 183
  Mr. & Mrs. Wythe B., 121, 158
  W.W., 255
  William T., 149
  Zeb V., 121
Graham's Forge, 39, 68, 91, 103, 105, 149, 189
  Church, 149
  Post Office, 2, 123
Graham Memorial Bldg., 121
Graham's Nail Works, 39, 69
  Rolling Mill, 39, 69
Graham & Robinson, 68, 92, 94, 149, 176
  Mill, 179
  Saw Mill, 179
Graham's Stoves, 105
Grain, 63
Grant, R.E., 124

Graph, Rock Formations, 29
Gravel Hill School, 150
Gray, David, 17
  E.C., 8
  G.W., 17
  Mines, 109
  Eagle Forge, 95
  Eagle Furnace, 68, 82, 94
Grayson Sulphur Springs, 85, 155, 208
Grayson & Raleigh Turnpike, 55, 164, 165
Green, 138
  Castle Church, 148
  & Gibboney, 230
  John W., 90
  Dr., P.B., 253
Greenbrier Road, 147
Green Spring Church, 123
Greenwalt, T.B. & Co, 178
Greever, Bismarck Maurice, 276
  Corsie Ann, 276
  Emma Cormany, 276
  Rev. J.J., 276
  John Joel, 276
  Rev. Joseph Brown, 276
  Krauth, 276
  Margaret May, 276
  Margaret Peery, 276
  Thomas Mark, 276
Gregory Homestead, 146
  Mines, 109
  T.J., 182
Grocers, 177
Groseclose, Alex, 10
  Andrew, 10
  Elizabeth Gose, 297
  H.B., 7
  J.C., 182
  J.E., 151
  J.H., 152
  John, 8
  Margaret A., 277
  Peter, 297
  Simon, 10
  Solomon, 6
  William, 16
  Stephen, 8
  Thomas J., 277
Groseclose Chapel, 152
  Mill, 149
Grove, F.A., 173
Grubb, A.J., 159
  Curtis, A., 12
  Elbert, 175
  E.L., 180
  Emory, 8
  Harvey, 8
  Jackson, 17
  Jacob, 159
  John W., 151

INDEX

Grubb, Joseph, 145
  Mary, 145
  Wesley, 8
Gruchs, Davidson, 5
Gunners, A. P., 180
Gutman, John, 128
Guy, Rev. J.T., 147
Gwathmey, Rev. D.L., 137
Gypsum, 2, 55

H

Hagan, J.H., 174
Hager's Spring, 120
Hall, Alexander, 17
  Ellen C. Bralley, 276
  James, 122
  James M., 276
  Mary C. Lewis, 276
  Samuel P., 151
  Sallie Cunningham, 276
  Samuel P., 276
  Sarah M., 276
Haller, Albert, 272
  Cathrine, 143
  Charles A., 123
  Edwin C., 5
  John, 131, 143
  J.P., Dr., 180
  Nancy H. Wiseley, 272
  Mrs. Malinda, 124
  Dr. W.P., 252
Halsey, James, 126
  James C., 108
Hamatite Ore Bank, 180
Hammer Ore Bank, 180
Hammet, Mrs. Marceem, 124
Hancock, J.A., 19
  J.M., 19
  L.D., 220
  William, 12
Hancock House, 177, 220
Hanover Presbytery, 118, 119
Hanson, Mrs. C.A., 124
  George M., 5
Harden, Andrew, 10
Hardware Stores, 177
Harkrader (Harkrider, Herkerother, Hercherother, Herrcherother, Hukrader)
  B.D., 10
  David, 131
  Isaac, 131
  I.R., 19
  Jacob, 131
  John, 10, 131, 169
  J.R., 173
  Hohannes, 129
  Sol, 131, 141, 142, 148
  T.K., 150
  & White, 178

Harmon, J.B., 10
Harmony (Draper's Valley) Church, 123
Harper, J.A., 174
Harrigan, Michael, 161
Harris, James, 120
Harrison, Bettie M. Kent, 278
  George M., 278
  L.D., 174
  Luther D., 176, 233
  M. L., 162
  William H., 5
Harsh, J.B., 13
  J.F. 10
  John C., 10
Harvey, E. P., 179, 183
Hatcher, A.D., 178, 245
Hat Factory, 107
Hatton, W.G., 10
Hawke & Rider, 175
Hawkins, Betty, 158
  Chapel, 135
  Rufus, 158
Head, John J., 142
Hearn, Alex, 163
  Mrs. Alex, 163
  H.J., 163
  Mrs. H. J., 163
  Joseph, 163
  Mary, 163
  Virginia, 163
  William, 163
"Hedgefield", 160
Hedrick (Headrick)
  Eveline, 145
  Joseph, 17, 158, 173
  William, 145
  W.W., 182
Heldreth (see Hildreth)
Helton (see Hilton)
Hemetite Iron Co, 176
Hematite Mines, 109, 191
Heiser, H.J., 174
Heilig, A.M., 182
Hendrick Bros., 99
Hendricks' Bros. Furnace, 69
Hendrick's, 51
Henkel, Rev. Paul, 126
Henly, James, 6
  Lewis, 6
  Nathan, 149
  Robert, 6
  School House, 135
  William, 19
Herbert's Forge, 103
  Thomas, 89, 103
  William, 89, 102, 103, 120
Henser (Heuser), H. M., 173, 174
  Bros, 174, 228
  H.J. & Co., 226
Hickman, William, 122

INDEX

Hicks, J.M., 125, 176
  John M., 276
  Mary B., 276
  Minnie W., 276
  Cynthia A. Douthat, 276
Hicks, Isaac, 276
  John M., 276
  Rebecca R. Hull, 276
Higgins, Richard, 119
High Rock Methodist Church, 147
High Rock Forge, 103
  Post Office, 103
  Roller Mills, 103
Highley (Hiley), William, 12, 102
Hildreth, James T., 10
  John J., 10
Hildenberger, Daniel, 128
Hill, John, 16
Hillenburg, A.W., 10
  Austin, 13
  Austin G., 8
  Catharine Hilton, 277
  Catherine Miller, 277
  Crockett Gleaves, 277
  Daniel, 277
  Eli G., 19, 148, 277
  Emily Catharine, 277
  James Austin, 277
  Laura Ellen, 277
  Margaret Adaline, 277
  Mary Ann, 277
  Nancy Ann Repass, 277
  Sarah Alice, 277
  William Eli, 277
Hillsville Church, 123
Hilton (Helton), A.J., 182
  J.R., 173
  Jacob, 277
  Joseph, 12, 145
  Polly Miller, 277
  Turley, 145
Hines, Abner, 154, 155
  James, 175
  William, 12
Hoback, Clifton, 12
  Mrs. Frank, 163
  Joseph, 175
Hobbes, Richard, 89
Hoffman, E.H., 10
  George W., 10
Hoge, Rev. Daniel, 122
Hoilman, Archie, 159
Holbrook G.J., 6, 177
  Garland S., 5
  & Thomas, 174
Holiday, Wiley, 6
Holland Iron Works, 115
Hollandsworth, G.O., 183
  Joseph W., 151
Holliday, Robert, 12

Hollis, James, 120
Holston, Christopher S., 146
Harvey, 10
Holy Advent Lutheran Church, 134
Holy Trinity Lutheran Church, 134
Honaker, J.R., 176
  Mary J., 173
Hoppes, Henry, 128
Horn, David, 138, 143
  D.J., 152, 159
  George, 280
  Isaac, 8, 17
  John (Jno), 8, 182
  W.R.B., 7
Hotel Boyd, 177
Hotels, 177, 204, 216, 217, 220
Houdashall, Andrew, 8
Hounshell (Haunschel)
  Jacob, 131, 142
  Jeff, 10
  Pearson, 12
  Mary V.F. Neff, 283
  P.W., 183
  Robert, 10
Houseman, Samuel, 150
Howard, Alexander, 271
  Anderson, 124, 271, 277
  Cora Lee, 277
  David H., 277
  Evelina, 271
  Ezekiel, 270
  John A., 277
  John Milton, 277
  Juliet, 271
  Margaret, 271
  Margaret Alice, 277
  Mary E., 277
  Milton, 97
  Rebecca, 271
  Rebecca Anderson, 271
  Rhoda Jane Allison, 277
  Russell, 277
  Sallie Calfee, 277
  Sophia, 271
  Susan Jane, 277
  William, 270
  & Saunders, 69
Howe, Alice Virginia Brown, 277
  Dasie Marian, 277
  John D., 273
  Mary M. Fisher, 277
  Mary Fisher, 286
  Sarah Shepherd, 273
  W.G., 19, 183
  William H., 277
  William Henry, 286
  William G., 277
Hoytman, Charles, 12
Hubble, James, 10

INDEX

Huddle, B.J., 19
  David, 95, 108, 278
  Eli, 10
  Elizabeth Brown, 278
  Emma, 278
  Emory, 8
  Eva, 133
  Forge, 41, 108, 189
  Garland E., 278
  Henry, 278
  James, 10
  J.H., 183
  J.P.M., 173
  John H., 278
  Jonas, 278
  Isaac Newton, 278
  Margaret P. Earhart, 278
  Minnie, 278
  N.E. Kyle, 278
  Nancy Elzey, 278
  R.E.L., 183
  Robert E.L., 151
  Robert E. Lee, 278
  Sarah Jane Steffey, 278
  William D.S., 151, 278
  William L., 17
Huddle Memorial Church, 151
Hudson, George, 290
  George W., 150, 151
  G.W., 180, 183
  Hannah Shannon, 290
  Jane, 150
  John, 16, 151
  Robert, 12
  William, 10, 151
  W.R., 183
Huff, V.C. (Dr.), 174, 253
Hufford, A.J., 257
  D.C., 258
  George R., 113, 173
  G.W., 183
  James, 12
  Dr. R.D., 253
  S.R., 174
  William, 156
    & Brown, 174, 177
Hughes, John, 8
Humphreys - Davidson Hardware, Co, 113
Hurley, D.P., 147
Hurst, A., 10
Hurst Mines, 109
Hurt, John B., 113
  Mrs. Mary, 174
Hushour, W. H., 178
Hutchinson, H.H., 10
Hutzel, John, 131
  Louis, 131

I

Ice Companies, 178

Indian Camp Mines, 109
Indian Camp Mining Co, 176
Industries, 191
Ingle, E.H., 144
Inman, Jesse, 16
  John, 16
  William P., 5
Insurance Agents, 178
Insurance Co's. - Fire, 178
Irondale Furnace, 69, 82, 99, 101
Iron Fencing, 178
Iron Founders & Machinists, 178
Iron Mountain, 27, 32, 33, 41, 44, 47, 48, 49, 189
Iron Ores, 26, 32-48, 80, 81, 188-189
Iron Ore Analysis, 33, 40, 43-47
Iron Ore Mines listed, 109
Iron Works, Crocketts, 91, 104
  Holland, 115
Irvin, Annie, 145
  Jacob, 12
  James A., 7
  John, 145, 159
  L.S. & Co., 237
Ivanhoe, 102, 121, 146, 189
  Furnace, 99
  Furnace Post Office, 2
  Inn, 177
  Mines, 109, 191
  Mining & Smelting Corp, 100
  Mission Church, 137
  Mountain Mission, 155
  News, 180
  Pentecostal Holiness Church, 164
  Post Office, 173

J

Jackson, Andrew, 143
  Burton, 12
  Calhoun, 12
  Charles A., 182
  John, 149, 183, 284
  George, 146
  J.W., 162
  John B., 146
  M., 176
  Maggie, 156
  Marion F., 183
  M.H., 87, 149, 156
  M.J., 156
  Martha P. Oglesby, 284
  Richard, 183
  Robert, 12
  Rufus, 183
  Rush, 147

INDEX

Jackson, Thomas, 12, 303, 305
   Thomas M., 13, 182
   Mrs. T.W., 147
   William, 12, 183
   William J., 147
   W.J., 156
   Wm. J., 13
Jackson's Ferry, 59, 87, 95, 120, 162
   Ferry Post Office, 2, 69
   Park Hotel, 77
   William (Mine), 109
James, D.C., 51
   D.E., 183
   D.E. & Sons, 69
   David E., 86
   J.C., 183
   J.M., 173
   J.M. & Co., 176
   J.R., 152
   R.L., 152
Jandler, George, 131
Jantz - See Younce
Johnson (Jonsohn)
   Augustus, 8
   Balzer (see Paulser), 128, 145
   John David, 128
   Elizabeth, 145
   George D., 5
   Gustavus, 16
   J.A., 182
   James K., 109
   J.H., 10
   Joel, 145
   John S., 151
   Larkin, 156
   R.P., 107
   Thomas, 8
   Wesley, 165
Jeffersonville Church, 123
Jenkins, Father Edward, 161
Jeweler, 223

Johnston, James A., 148
   John, 131
   W.A., 227, 244
   William J., 151
Jonas, Peter, 8
Jones, B.F., 19
   Calvin, 12
   Eliza, 268
   George W. Sr., 106
   George W., 282
   Henderson, 12
   Jacob, 10
   John, 10
   William, 175
   Wilson, 268
Judge, Rev. Raymond J., 160

K

Kane (Kain), Bishop John J., 161, 162
Kaolin (mineral), 56, 190
Keen, Rev. James, 122
Kessling (Keasling, Kisling)
   Mrs. A. V., 163
   Catherine Horn, 280
   E., 16
   E.S., 182
   Elbert S., 154
   G.M.P., 16, 173, 182
   G.W., 17
   George, 280
   Harry, 16
   J.G., 139, 152
   Joseph, 16
   M.L., 256
   P.P., 182
   Peter, 138, 143, 155
   Peter P., 159
   Robert T., 149
   & Son Mill, 179
Kessler, Gordon, 17
Kegley (Keckly, Geckly)
   Alexander, 17
   Christian, 131
   Doctor C., 159
   George W, 159
   James, 17
   John, 131
   J.G., 183
   John G., 159
   Joseph, 145
   Lee, 17
   Louis, 131
   Martin, 131, 143, 159
   Mary, 145
   S.A., 150
   Susan, 159
   W.B., 174
Keller, W.J., 110
Kelley, Rev. Charles, 164
   James, 12
   John, 12
Kennedy, John H., 147
   Rev. J.H., 155
Kennerly, Samuel, 138
Kent, Alexander S.B., 279
   Anas P., 279
   Anastasia Pleasants Smith, 279
   Ann Frances, 282
   Clarence, 279
   David, 106
   Edwin D., 279
   Eliza Ann Woods, 279
   Eliza Ann Woods Patton, 279
   Elizabeth Craig, 278

INDEX

Kent, Elizabeth Montgomery Craig, 279
  Fannie P. Brown, 279
  George M., 5, 279
  Jacob, 278
  John B., 279
  Joseph, 131
  Joseph Cloyd, 279
  Joseph F., 6, 123, 272, 278
  Joseph G., 136, 183
  Lucy McGavock, 279
  Mary Cloyd, 279
  Mary P., 279
  R.C., 183
  Robert, 106, 278, 279
  Robert C., 279
  Robert Craig, 279
  Robert Emmett, 106
  Susan P., 279
  Tyler Gatewood, 279
  Virginia F. Peyton, 279
  William, 279
Kent's Mills, 59, 105, 107
  Post Office, 2
Kesler, Rev. D.K., 163
Kesner, Charles H., 279
  George P., 19
  George Philip, 279
  Irey Mintres, 279
  John, 279
  Lacy Dallas, 279
  Lucy Margaret, 279
  Manley Henning, 279
  Osceola, 279
  Sarah A. Byars, 279
  Senah M. Oury, 279
  Victoria Virginia, 279
Killinger, J.C., 182
Kimberling Lutheran Church, 123, 128, 133, 166
Kimberling, Martin, 126, 133
Kincannon, Andrew, 89
  F.E., 90
  Frances E., 90
  James E., 90
  James N., 90
Kinder, John G., 10
  Isaac, 10
  Joseph M., 10
  Peter, 270
  Phillipp, 128
Kincer (Kinser, Kinzer)
  D.C., 182
  George, 128
  Jacob, 128
  J.T., 182
King, Cathrine, 133
  George M., 5
  H.W., 182
  Isaac
  Jefferson, 133
  J.J., 10, 182

King, John S., 10
  John, 148, 182
  Morgan Co., 85
  "Kingsville" Furnace, 85
King, Rufus, 183
  Sampson, 102
  Victor, 168
  Kings' Grove Methodist Church 148
  Stephen R., 12
  Trigg Morgan, 87
  William, 87, 102, 104
  Wm. of Washington Co., 85
  William R., 13
Kirby, Rev. R.J., 162
Kitchens, B.F., 19, 183
  Callohill M., 280
  John W., 280
  Nancy J., 280
  & Painter's, 51
Kitts, N.G., 180
Knitting Mills, 179
Knopp, Philip, 131
  Peter, 131
  Werner, 131
Kuhners, George, 5
Kyle, James, 152
  James Mill, 179
  Julia, 152

L

Lackey, Mrs. Julia, 174, 215
Lacy, Judge B.W., 254
  Rev. Wm. Sterling, 121
LaHue, S.C., 6, 215
LaRue, Rev. James E., 162
Lambert Catharine Keesling, 280
  Elizabeth Jane, 280
  Francis E., 280
  George A., 183, 280
  Henry, 127
  Joseph, 280
  Martha E., 280
  Mary C., 280
  Mary Michaels, 280
  Michael, 280
  Peter M.,
  Robert, 180
  Riley, 8
  Sarah A.,
  T.S., 183
  William, 182
  William C., 280
Lampkin, Henry S., 5
Land Agents, 178
Landreth, Ada Lee, 280
  Alberti Paulina, 280
  Andrew Jackson, 280
  Flora Pearl, 280
  Lena May, 280
  Lizzie Gertrude, 280

INDEX

Landreth, Mary Florence Brally, 280
  Nancy Hendrick, 280
  Robert, 19, 280
  Robert Edgar, 280
  Samuel Cloyd, 280
  Thomas J., 280
  William M., 280
Lanter, D.M., 183
  James, 149
Laundries, 178
Laurel Creek, 32
Lawson, Mrs. A.B., 183
  Anthony, 123
  Joseph, 16
L.C.W. Co., 176
Lead Mine Company, 146, 147
Lead Mines, 2, 34, 63
Lead Mine's Hill, 40
Lead & Zinc, 49-52, 188
Lead & Zine Mines, 40
Lead & Zinc Ores, 26
Leather & Findings Co, 178
Leather, Saddles & Harness, 238
Lebanon Lutheran Church, 123, 133
Leedy, J.T., 182
  Josiah, 183
  Martin, 12, 14
Leftwich, Isaac J., 123, 141, 142
  Isaac T., 90
  Rev. J.T., 124
Leggon, Samuel, 10
Lenhart, Frederick, 131
Lenart, George, 131
Leslie, H.W., 14
  J.W., 10, 176
  James M., 12
  James W., 14
Lewis, Rev. F.N., 125
  James, 276
  Mrs. Jane, 174
  Rev. J.W., 126
  Lucy Holt, 276
Liberty Grove Baptist Church, 162
Liberty Hill Pentecostal Holiness Church, 164
Lick Mountain, 27, 45, 49, 55, 56, 115, 189
  Ores, 44
Liddle, William, 12
Limestone, 190
Lindamood (Lindemuth)
  Andrew, 133
  John J., 131
  Joseph, 157, 158
  Joseph L, 14, 183
  L.A., 175
  Robert A., 19
  Stephen, 19
  W.M. & Bros, 177
Lindebarger, John, 131

Lindsay, Calvin, 17
  William, 8
Lindsey, C.S. & Son, 182
Ling, S.K., 182
Lithia Springs (Waters), 178, 249-260
Little Walker's Mountain, 30
Little Reed Island Creek, 38, 51, 103
Little Walker's Creek, 32
Little Walker's Mountain, 28, 45
Little Wythe Furnace, 82, 94, 189
Little Wythe Mines, 109
Littreal, George, 179
Litz (Lits, Littz)
  America F., 154
  Barbara King, 297
  Catherine, 133
  James P., 154
  John, 8
  John Henry, 297
  John J., 8
  M.F., 154
  Polly, 154
Litton, Ada Victoria, 287
  Andrew Jackson, 287
Livery Stables, 178, 245
Livesay, Rev. C.B., 159
Lloyd, Samuel Y., 148
  W.F., 183
  William F., 16, 148, 158
Lobdell Car Wheel Company, 63, 69, 97, 100, 177, 178, 180
Lockett, David, 12
  H.H., 11
Lockett's Forge, 41, 108
  James, W., 108
  Samuel D., 5
Locust Hill Mine, 109, 191
Logan, Rev. Mercer P., 137, 248
Look & Lincoln Wagon Mfg., 111
Long, Daniel, 161
  Ellen Murphy, 161
Losser, Nicholaus, 131
Louthien, John, 12
Love, William, 84, 85
Loyal Company, 89
Lucas, Chas. S., 173
Lutheran Churches, 126-135
Lyons, Charles W., 147

M

McBride, Rev. John, 248
McCabe, Rev. James D., 136
McCall's, 105
McCaw, Mrs. E.J., 258
McClintock, Charles, 5
  George L., 5
McConnell, David, 95
  Rev. James, 121

INDEX

McCormick, Cyrus, 111
McDaniel, Rev. Charles, 164
McDonald Brothers, 110
  E.H., 110, 178, 181
  Foundry, 110
  Institute, 181
  Mangus, 84
  Professor, 63
McFaden, Rev. T.F., 125
McGavock, Mrs. Abbie J., 144
  A.J., 144
  Mrs. A.J., 136
  David, 91, 127
  E., 136
  Emily M., 147
  Hugh, 91
  J. Cloyd, 144
  Jacob C, 91
  James, 91, 136, 169
  James H., 5, 6
  J.C., 183
  J.H., 144, 183
  J.R., 183
  J.W., 147
  J. Williamson, 94
  Mrs. J. Williamson, 94
  Lysander, 92
  Maggie M., 144
  Margaret M., 144
  Randall, 144
  Sarah J., 144
McGee, J.P, 16
McGuire, Elijah, 12
McInery, Rev. Michael, 160
McKinsie, Greenburg G., 88
McMillian, Samuel B., 16
  William, 16
McNutt, Rev. Samuel H., 120
McPheeters, Rev. Wm. M., 125
McPherson, S.T.M., 147
McTeer, Eliza C. Kelly, 281
  Eliza Stuart, 281
  Frances Smyth Piper, 155
  James Piper, 281
  J.M., 144
  John M., 86, 145, 155, 281
  John M., Jr., 281
  Maggie Porter, 281
  Post Office, 2
McWane, Arthur T., 113
  Cast Iron Pipe Co., 113
  Charles, 111
  Charles P., 110, 113, 114(photo)
  C.P. & Co., 111, 234
  Foundry, 110, 111
  Henry E., 113
  H.E. & Co, 111
  James, 110, 111
  J.R., 113
  Robert C., 113
  William, 113

M. & F., Seminary, 276
Mabry, J.C., 162
Mabybe, Pleasant, 16
Macedonia Church, 148
Madison, James, 91
  Thomas, 136
Magnetic Iron Ore, 48
Mahady, J.S., 177
Main St. Christian Church, 159
Main Street, Photo, 231
Main Street Wytheville, 207
Mallet, Sir Robert, 35-38
Malory (Mallory), Thomas, 19
  Robert, 12
  Thomas, 12
Manganese Ores, 26, 49, 189
Manuel, Sampson, 12
Manufactures, 58
Maple Cascade, Photo, 243
Marble, 55, 56, 189
Marble Works, 178
Marshall, C.M., 175
  Lewis S., 138, 143
  T.A., 183
  W.C., 150, 183
Martin, D.T., 125
  John, 294
  Mary Ann Holmes, 294
Martin's Station, 52
Marvin Church, 148
Massie, Thos., 259
Masters, F.W., 177
Mathews, Capt. John P., 160
  H.J., 149
  Malvina, 160
Marion, 12
  Mrs. M., 124
  Richard, 131
  R.T., 136
Matting, Henry, 17
Matuny, William H., 19
Matthews, Harold I., 5
  Harold J., 6
  Joseph, 10
Maupin, H.B., 215
  & Bruce, 234
Mayberry, Rev. L.D., 158
Mayer, George, 131
Max Meadows, 28, 31, 62, 73, 74, 75, 120, 122
  Depot, 30, 31, 49, 54
  Furnace, 73, 100, 191
  Iron Co, 73, 74
  Land & Improvement Co., 74, 158
  Methodist Church, 158
  Post Office, 2, 173
Mead, Bishop, 136
Meadows, John, 10
Meirs, Stephen, 128
Mercer, Albert, 8

INDEX

Mercer, George W., 7
   Madison, 8
   Sanders, 8
   W.W., 8, 19
   Walter, 8
Merchant Tailors, 178
Messerschmitt, Bernhart, 131
Methodist Church, 138
Meyers, Thomas I., 5
Mies, John, 131
Mill, J.H., 181
Miller, Austin, 148
   D.K., 10
   Elizabeth A. Selden, 288
   Emily Pearce, 269
   Felix, 8
   Fleming B., 288
   Hiram, 151
   Jacob, 150
   James B., 5
   James R., 269
   John, 8
   Joseph M., 10
   Michael, 8
   Thos. C., 218
   T.K., 19
   Winton, 8
   W.H., 177
Millinery Shops, 179, 223
Mills, 179, 248
Mills at Peirce Forge, 102
Mills, Saw & Planing, 179
Millwrights, 179-180
Minerals, 188, 210-213
Mineral Springs, 60, 192, 208
Mines, Coal, 180
   Iron, 180
   Zinc, 180
Mitchell, George D., 8, 19
   Rev. J.D., 124
   Rev. John W., 162
   William, 147
   W.L., 182
   Zachariah, 138, 143
   Z., 139
Mize, E.C., 10
   J.M., 19
Mohler, Joseph, 131
Monks Corner Church, 122
Montgomery, Hugh, 102
   James, 120
   John, 120
   Joseph, 120
   Robert, 120
   Samuel, 120
   William, 120
Montgomery County, 2, 3, 172
Montgomery Presbytery, 123
Moore, A.S., 281, 282
   Addie Kent, 282

Moore, Addie Pearson Jones, 282
   Col. Alfred C., 282
   Alfred Cleon, 281, 282
   Algernon Sidney, 282
   Ann Frances Kent, 281
   Bettie Taylor, 282
   Blanche A., 282
   Elizabeth Collins, 281
   Emeline Benton, 282
   George Cleon, 282
   Helen Taylor, 282
   J.M., 281, 282
   John, 281, 282
   John H., Dr., 181
   John Harrison, 281
   John S., 282
   John W., 281
   J.W., 177
   Lillie Butler, 282
   Martha S. Glascock, 281
   Mary K., 282
   Mary M. Simmerman, 282
   Millie E., 282
   Page Taylor, 282
   Page Waller, 282
   Dr. Robert Emmett, 253, 254, 281, 282, 316-318
   Robert R., 282
   R.R., 157, 183, 282
   Robert Rolen, 282
   Mrs. S. E., 259
   Sidney Page, 282
   William, 282
   William B., 282
   William O., 11, 282
   William Orville, 282
   William Sidney, 282
   W.O., 183, 281, 282
Morehead, Barbara Catherine Yonce, 166
   G.B., 168
   James, 166
   James W., 14
   John Alfred, 166-168
   John C., 14
   J.W., 259
Morgans, 87
   King Trigg, 85
   Mary Trigg King, 88
Morlick James M., 19
Morphy, Edward, 131
Morrell, Rev. W.M., 147
Morris, 138
   Rev. J.W., 154
   William, 12, 16
   Mines, 109
Morrison, Mrs. J.A., 124
Moser, John, 128
Mosser, Jacob, 131

INDEX

Mount, Mt., and Mountain
  Airy, 48, 55
  Airy Presbyterian Church, 125
  Carmel Church, 123, 152
  Ephraim Methodist Church, 145
  Mitchell Church, 157
  Pleasant Methodist Church, 142, 150
  Tabor Presbyterian Church, 122, 123
  View Methodist Church, 164
  Zion Methodist Church, 150, 153
Mozer, Adam, 128
  George, 128
  Michael, 143
Muirhead, 166
Mullen, Joseph, 162
Muller, Martin, 128
Murry, Ransom, 16
  Ranson, 159
Musser, Franklin, 10
  F.H., 175
  J.J., 10
  Michael, 17
Myers, David, 12
  Frank, 258
  Michael, 146
  W.A., 19, 175

N

Naylor, Rev. James, 122
Neel, Rev. Henry C., 147
Neese, G.J., 19, 157
Neff, Abraham, 282, 283
  Amanda Jane Scott, 272, 282
  B.H. Mill, 179
  Bollard H., 282
  Callie Frances, 283
  Charles C., 283
  Charles M., 283
  Daniel, 272, 282
  Edward M., 283
  Elizabeth A. 283
  Elizabeth Repass, 283
  Ella C., 283
  Emma C., 283
  George R., 283
  Gussie H., 283
  Henry, 10, 154, 283
  Jacob, 8, 283
  Jacob M., 14, 283
  James P., 282
  James T., 282
  John A., 282
  Lena M., 283
  Maggie E., 283
  Mary E. Snavely, 283
  Michael, 17, 19, 283
  N.W., 176
  Pearson, 8, 283

Neff, Rachel H. Scott, 283
  Rebecca, 282
  Robert C., 283
  Sarah Ellen, 283
  Stephen D., 283
  Virginia A., 283
  Wiley Winton, 283
  William, 17, 283
  William S., 282
  W.S., 183
  Z.M., 183
Nelson, Isham, 17
  Jasper, 159
Neighbors, A.B., 6
  Charles W., 5
  H.W., 6
  W.H., 182
  William H., 5, 233
Neilly, Alexander, 119
Neusang, Martin, 128
Newberry, A.B., 87, 105, 106
  Hermon, 284
  Mary A. McDonald, 284
Newberry City, 249, 256, 259
  Mills, 179
  Mills P.O., 173
New Bethel Church, 149
New Dublin Church, 123
Newell, James, 104, 169
New Hope Methodist Church, 149
Newland, James, 138, 142
  John, 138, 142
  Joseph, 142
  M.F., 182
  Mary, 148
  William, 141, 142
Newman, Alex, 8
  David, 8
  Thomas I., 5
  T.J., 6
New River, 2, 26, 34, 39, 52, 73, 92, 95
New River Iron Co. Furnace, 69
  Mineral Co., 69, 99, 100, 177, 178, 180
  Presbytery, 123
  Railroad proposed, 63
Newspapers, 61, 180
Norma Mines, 109
Nuckolls, Charles, 102
  John, 145
Nye (Ney), A.B., 10, 183
  Dr. George L., 252-255
  G.W., 178
  John F., 131
  W.H., 10, 173

INDEX

Nye Lithia Springs, 249-260.
Nicewander, Rev. David, 163
Nichols, William C., 12
Nixon, Robert P., 16
Noble, Mrs., 82
  Allen & Co, 69, 82, 99
  Furnace, 33, 41
  P.O., 173
Noel, C.J., 144
  Mrs. M.E., 174, 218,
  Walter, 180, 236
Norfolk & Western R.R., 75, 78, 100, 172, 187, 249

O

O'Connor, James, 161
  John, 183
O'Donnell, Michael, 161
Obenchain, Mrs. E.A., 219
  T.J., 173
Odell, D.H., 175
"Old Brick Church", 134
Oglesby, Albert C., 284
  Albert M., 5, 7
  Albert Micajah, 283
  Frank S., 284
  Jane C. Sayers, 284
  Jennie L., 284
  Jennie S., 284
  John J., 284
  John T.S., 284
  Lizzie A. Jackson, 284
  Lillian G., 284
  Martha I., 284
  Mary S., 284
  N.P., 156, 182
  Nicholas P., 7, 284
  Sallie A. Crockett, 284
  Samuel C., 284
  William B., 284
Olive Branch Methodist Church, 145
Omnibus Line, 245
Osteman, Eugene, 5
Otey, C.N., 245
  C.U., 181
Oury, Alfred S., 5
  Christopher, 131
  George, 131
  Henry C., 5
  James, 10
  Stephen, 10
  Van Buren, 279
  Thursey Smyth, 279
Owens, R.A., 147

P

Pack School House, 154
Pack, William, 154

Painter, Abraham, 40, 54, 97, 121
  Branch, 69
  Ezra, 8
  George (Rev.), 12, 122
  Gus, 18
  J.D., 149
  James, 8, 97
  James F., 17
  James P., 124
  L.E., 182
  Leicester, 12
  Leicester E., 14
  Rev. George, 121
  Sidney, 8
  Stewart, 10
  Thomas, 8
  William, 16
  William A., 155
  William M., 97, 146
  W.M., 183
  Abraham & Sons, 69
  & Carson, 181
  J.D. & Bro., 177
  Mines, 109
Painter's Store, 56
Painter, Wm.M. & Son, 177
Palison, G. H., 182
Palmer, Rev. David C., 125
  David P., 125
Panic Furnace, 45
Paperville Church, 123
Parks, Whelan, 18
Parmer, James, 12
Parry Mount Furnace, 91
Patriot & Herald, 180
Patterson, 191
Patterson, C.E., 182
  Mrs. E.O, 163
  James, 12
  Mines, 109
  Post Office, 103, 173
Pattison, Charles E., 5
  J.H., 183
  Thomas W., 5
  William, 143, 159
Patton, John, 18
  Russel, 18
  William, 120
  William E., 120
Paulett, Weslie S., 5
Pauley, J.B., 10
Paxton Glade, 127
Pearman, Thomas, 183
Pechin, Edmund C, 75
Peck, John A., 16
  William, 155
Peery, Edward C., 284
  Josie A. Newberry, 284
  Kate M. Cecil, 284
  Thomas R., 284
  Capt. William, 300

INDEX

Peery, William E., Jr., 284
  William E., Sr., 284
Peirce (Pearce, Pierce)
  Alexander, 285
  Anna Dabney Stuart, 285
  Carrie Jane, 285
  David, 89, 94, 102, 103, 188, 189, 285
  David P., 274
  David R., 285
  D.S., 174
  David S., 20, 100, 285
  David Stuart, 285
  Elizabeth Bell, 285
  Elizabeth Chaffin, 274
  J.B., 7, 181, 285, 286
  James B., 285
  James Burton, 285
  James N., 156
  James Newell, 285
  Joseph B., 5
  Joseph Foster, 285
  Mary Ann, 285
  Nancy Jane Porter, 285
  Sarah N. Wall, 285
  William Dr., 181
  W.R., 182
Peirce, Alexander (Forge), 41
  Bros., 175
  Bros., & Van Doren, 182
  Falls, 26, 39, 59, 69
  Forge, 97, 102, 189
  Mill, 102
  Ore Bank, 39
Pendleton, Mann, 183
  M.M., 19
  R.N., 183
  Rev. W.H.K., 137
Penna, Zinc & Iron Co., 180
Pentecostal Holiness Churches, 163
Pepper, Charles Robertson, 286
  Dr. Charles Taylor, 286
  Isabella McDowell Howe, 286
  John, 286
  Dr. John G., 286
  Louis Ervin, 286
  Mary Margaret, 286
  Mary Robertson, 286
  Ruth McDowell, 286
  Samuel, 286
  Dr. T.C., 125, 176, 181
  William Howe, 286
Pepper's Ferry Road, 134, 146
Percival, Joshua, 145
  Mrs. Sarah, 174
  S.E., 177
Percival Mines, 109
Perkins, J.E., 257
  John E., 5, 7
  J.R. Mill, 179
Perry, Charles, 181

Petersburg Savings & Ins. Co. 178
Pettit, Mrs. M.A., 181
Petunia Christian Church, 160
  Hotel, 177
  Mill, 179
  Post Office, 173
  School, 181
Peyton, Ann Montgomery Lewis, 279
  Rev. C.J., 163
  John Howe, 279
Phelps, E. McG., 177, 233
  George, 8
Phillippe, Alex, 7
  Rev. Alexander, 134, 152, 181, 248
  Andrew, 8
  B.F., 17
  Christ., 8
  Daniel, 8
  E.W., 8
  E.M., 8
  George, 138, 143
  John, 126, 138, 143
  John M., 20
  J.M., 159
  L.K., 8
  Sylvester, 17
  William H., 8
Phipps, J.M. Dr., 181
Phlegar, Archer A., 149
Photographers, 180, 227, 236, 244
Physicians, 180-181, 246
Pig Iron, 63
Pilot Mountain, 32, 33, 44
Pine Grove Chapel, 152
Pine Ridge, 28, 48, 60
Pinkley (Binkley) Catherine, 85
Piper, Col, James H., 85, 86, 90, 136, 155, 306-312
  Frances Smyth, 310
  Widow, 86
Pipe Works, 81
Pleasant Grove (Rich Valley) Church, 123
Pleasant Hill Church, 128
Plumbers & Gas Fitters, 181
Plummer Memorial Female College, 77, 181, 222
Plumer, W.S., (photo), 222
Poage, Margaret Allen, 296
  R.L., 176, 258
  R.L. & Co., 226
  Major William, 296
  W.R., 174
  W. S., 174
Poff, (Pfoff)
  Carl, 131
  Charles, 145, 148
  Harvey S., 19

INDEX

Poff, John, 131
  Mary, 145
Pope, Lafayette, 12
Poplar Camp, 102, 156, 162
  Forge, 39, 89, 102
  Furnace, 88, 89, 188
  Mines, 109
Poplar Grove Lutheran Church, 134, 158
Porks, W.M., 16
Porter, A.L., 183
  Andrew, 89
  Andrew L., 109
  A.S., 19
  B.F., 151
  Calvin, 13
  Daniel, 94
  David H., 14, 148
  David, 12
  D.H., 182
  Frances, 125
  George, 145
  John, 11
  John A., 285
  John M., 14, 148
  J.M., 182
  Kenney, 12
  Mary E. Pearman, 285
  M.F., 183
  Margaret, 145
  Margaret J. McNutt, 281
  Samuel E., 94
  S.L, 183
  S.S., 14
  Stephen, 109, 152, 155, 281
  Stephen S., 12
  T.J., 183
  Wm., 175
  William B., 146
Porter's Cross Roads, 145
  Forge, 43, 109, 189
  Mines, 109
Posey Mines, 109
Powell, J.J.A., 174, 175
Presbyterian Churches, 119-126
Preston, Col. James F., 4
  John, 127
  J.P., 259
  Mrs., 95
  Rev. S.R., 77, 222
  W.B., 177
Price, C.L, 177
  Rev. Richard N., 147
Printers, 181
Prichett & Bro., 177
Production statistics, 63
Prim, David, 18
Providence Iron Co, 86
Provision Dealers, 181
Pruner (Prooner, see Bruner)
Puck, William M., 16

Puckett, John H., 176
Pucket & Hudle, 176
Pulaski Development Co., 86, 90, 95, 99
Pulaski Iron Co., 94, 103
Purgatory Branch, 103
Pyott, Rev. W.W., 155
Pyrus, William, 86

Q

Quaker Church, 152
Queen's Knob, 28, 45, 55
Quirk, 120
Quisenbury, James G., 20
  William, 20

R

Rader (Rother, Roder, Rather)
  Casper, 128-130
  Casper, Sr., 131
  Casper, Jr., 131
  Jacob, 131
  John, 131
Radick, John, 131
Rain Fall Averages, 66, 192, 204
Raper, Capt., 121
  J.C., 182
  John C., 123, 173, 286
  Maggie Stuart, 286
  Mary, 122, 124
  Miss Mary Anne, 126
  Mary Ann, 121
  Mary C., 121
  Mary Craig Crockett, 286
  Capt. Robert, 122, 123, 124
  Robert, 121, 124, 125, 286, 304
  Robert H.C., 286
  Sallie S. Crockett, 286
  Sally, 123
  Sally V., 123
  Virginia L, 286
  W.J., 182
  Wm. J., 123
  William J., 7
  William I., 5
  Wm. & Co. Mill, 179
Ratcliff, Joseph, 13
Raven Cliff Mills, 91
Raven Cliff property, 90
Ravenscliff Furnace (Raven Cliff), (Raven Clift), 41, 69, 82, 89, 189
Real Estate Agents, 181
Rector, William, 174
Red Bluff Farms, 183
  Post Office, 2, 173
Red Hill, 191
Red Iron Ores, 47

INDEX

Reed Creek, 26, 92
Reed Island Country, 49
Reed Island Creek, 34, 147
  Post Office, 3
Reese, J.N., 10
Repass (Raypass, Raybass)
  A., 157
  Alfred, 10
  Clarence A., 287
  Rev. Daniel, 133
  Edward F., 287
  Elmira A., 287
  Frederick Sr., 287
  G.B., 183
  George F., 287
  George Jesse, 287
  Henry L, 287
  Rev. Jacob, 168, 169
  Jacob, Jr., 131
  James A., 287
  Jesse, 286
  John, 131, 283
  John Jacob Sr., 131
  Joe Brown, 287
  Joseph M., 287
  Joseph W., 287
  J.W., 173
  Lydia Brown, 286
  Margaret A., 287
  Margaret Agnes Brown, 287
  Mary A., 287
  N.H., 183
  Newlon H., 16
  Newton Herschel, 286
  Rosanna Brown, 287
  Rufus, 129, 272
  Rufus B., 287
  Sally Brown, 272
  Sarah Jane Fisher, 287
  Stephen, 287
  Stephen W., 287
  S.W., 183
  Walter, 10
  William, 131
  William G., 16
  William Gordon, 287
  W.R., 173
  Crosby & Davis, 244
Restaurants, 181
Rhother, William, 13
Ribble, Dr. W.H., 124, 181, 253
  Dr. W.H. Jr., 253
Rice, 138
Rich, David A., 259
  Mary T., 218
  W.W., 136, 144, 176, 182, 255
Rich Hill, 38, 189, 191
Rich Valley, 49
Rich, W.W. & Son, 179, 242
Richmond, Alice May Litton, 287
  B.F., 287

Richmond, Elizabeth, 287
  Jackson Litton, 287
  Walter Ernest, 287
  William Asbury, 287
  William F., 287
  Willie Clyde, 287
Richardson, Mrs. C., 176, 179, 229
  Mrs. Charlotte, 174
Rider, Albert C., 5
  Christina, 143
  James A., 5
  James F., 7
  James H., 5
  William, 143
Rider & Crowder, 182
Riggle (Riegal), George, 156
  Henry, 131
  Simon, 131
Right, Dr. Richard, 131
Roanoke College, 166
Roaring Falls Furnace, 95
  Mountain, 39
Robertson, E.H., 183
  Thomas, 11
Robeson, Harriett Cumming, 267
  John H. 267
Robinson, Mrs. Andy, 163
  B.G., 149
  C.R., Dr., 181
  E.H., 183
  E.H., Dr., 181
  J.M., 20
  John W., 90, 149
  W.J.H., 159
  & Blair, 177
  E.H., Mill, 179
Rock Furnace, 45
Rock Spring Church, 123
Rogers, Clarinda P. Campbell, 292
  John, 183
  Samuel, 292
  Thomas H., 20
  John D., 5
Rolling Mill, 81
Rosenbaum, A.J., 20, 182, 183
  Frank, 13
  Peter, 13, 14
  Stephen, 13, 135
Rosenbaum's Chapel, 135
Rosenheim, R.D., 256
  Mrs. R.D., 229
  & Finkle, 174
Ross, J.W., 183
Ross Mill, 89
  William, Mill, 88
Rowe, Benjamin, 97, 146
  W.H., 125
  & Walters, 177
Rowen, H.S., 20
Royal Oak Church, 123

INDEX

Runion, Jason L, 149
Rural Retreat, 62, 78, 135, 173
   Depot, 31
   Methodist Church, 158
   Post Office, 3
   Times, 180
Ruth, John, 131
Ryan, Permelia, 110
   W.B., 173
Rusling, E.S. Mill, 179

S

St. Andrews Church, 152
St. Andrews Mission, 137
St. Clair, D.A., 181
   James, 143
   James H., 5
St. John's Episcopal Church, 136
St. John's Lutheran Church, 92, 128-129, 130, 164, 168
St. Luke Lutheran Church, 134
St. Mark's Church, 128
St. Mark's Lutheran Church, 134
St. Mark's Methodist Church, 151
St. Mary's Catholic Church, 130, 160, 161, 235
St. Patrick's Catholic Church, 161, 162
St. Paul's Church, 126, 129, 130
St. Paul Pentecostal Holiness Church, 164
St. Peters Lutheran Church, 130, 133, 156
Saddlers & Harness Makers, 181
Sailor, Alfred, 13
Salem Camp Ground, 141
   Camp Grounds School, 142
   Church (Reed Creek), 119
Saloons, 181
Saunder (Sanders)
   Adam, 124
   Elizabeth, 152
   Elizabeth Oury, 275
   G. Burton, 149
   George, 13, 140, 157
   George A., 152
   Hannah, 124
   Col. I.A., 275
   J.A., 89, 183
   John A., 152
   J.P.M., 90, 182
   John, 124
   John P.M., 90, 123
   Richard W., 90
   Dr. Richard Walton, 97, 181, 183
   Robert, 102
   S., 84
   S.D., 158, 182
   Samuel C., 5
   Stephen, 11, 90, 104
   Steven C., 5
   Stephen S., 292
   W.D., 149
   William C., 11
   C.F. & Bro., 180, 183
   Mines, 109, 191
Sandstone & Sand, 190
Sarett, James H., 13
Sash, Doors & Blinds Co., 181
Saufley (Saftly, Seftly)
   Adam, 143
Saufley's Tavern, 143
Saul, Edmund, 16
Saw Mills, 236
Sayers, 51
   David, 120
   David H., 16
   Isabella H. Stephens, 288
   James A., 5, 16
   John G, 5
   John T., 169, 288
   Mrs. John T., 258
   Mrs. Kate, 124
   Lizzie S., 288
   Martha V. Miller, 288
   Mary L. Deyerle, 288, 289
   Nicholas A., 288
   R., 180
   Col. R., 259
   Rebecca Bowman, 289
   Robert, 124, 169, 174, 284, 288
   Col. Robert, 94, 100
   Dr. S.R., 254
   Senah N., 288
   Senah R., 288
   Thomas, 17
   Thompson, 284
   William, 120, 147, 288
Sayers, Oglesby & Co, 69, 94
Sayers & Oglesby Furnace, 33, 41
Scherer, Rev. Daniel, 126
   Rev. Jacob, 126, 133
Schools, 77, 181, 192
Schumacher, John, 131
Schneberly (see Snaveley)
Scott, A.P., 8, 182
   C.L., 255
   Elizabeth, 282
   J.A.B., 175, 182
   J.F., 237
   James R., 13
   John, 283
   Margaret Porter, 283
   William, 138, 143, 282
Seagle, Blanche C., 289
   Bettie E. Welsh, 289
   Cora B., 289
   Curtis B., 289
   Edna M., 289
   George Augustus, 289
   J.B., 14, 289

INDEX

Seagle, James, 289
  Jas. F., 215
  Jettie K., 289
  John, 13
  John A., 14
  John S., 289
  Nancy O. Rader, 289
  Viola G., 289
  J.F. & Son, 176, 182
Second Horizon Brown Ores, 34
Seftly (See Saftly)
Sehorn, Marion, 107
Sells & Gormany, 175
Seventh Day Adventist Church, 165
Seven Springs Pentecostal Holiness Church, 164
Sewing Machines, 181
Sexton (Saxton)
  Charles Harris, 290
  David, 159
  G.S., 179
  J.C., 181, 244
  John, 110, 289
  John M., 5
  Joseph Campbell, 7, 289
  John McAllister, 289
  Napoleon B., 289
  Priscella, 289
Sexton, G.S. & Co., 174, 176, 177
Sexton, George & Co., 240
Shaffer (Schaffer, Shafer)
  Cloyd, 17
  Jacob, 5
  Jas., 183
  John, 131
  Joseph, 151, 173
Shank, Rev. Oliver, 162
Sharitz (Shuretze, Schoritz, Sharetz)
  Amos K., 290
  Alice V., 290
  Beatta Yonce, 290
  Canard J., 290
  Catharine A., 290
  Charles W., 290
  Clementina Hudson, 269
  Clementina R. Hudson, 290
  Daniel, 291
  D.M., 150
  Daniel M., 291
  David McA., 290
  David, 131, 141, 150
  Elmira C., 290
  Emory A., 290
  Frances E., 290
  George Wythe, Jr., 290
  Guy, 150
  Henry L., 290
  Hiram A., 290
  James B., 290
  Janie H., 290
  John, 131
  John P., 20, 269, 290
  John T., 183
  John W., 290
  Joseph, 142, 150, 290
  Lillie C., 290
  Mary E., 290
  Patsy Baker, 290
  Polly Ann, 291
  Robeson M., 290
  Thomas R., 290
Sharon Alum Springs, 208
Sharon Church, 123
Sheffey, D.W., 17, 291
  Daniel, 131
  Daniel Winton, 291
  Elizabeth F. Swecker, 291
  Henry, 291
  Hugh Price, 291
  Hugh Trigg, 291
  J.P., 183
  James Price, 291
  James W., 291
  Margaret E., 291
  Mary A. Allison, 291
  Nellie Preston, 291
  Sarah Ann Louisa, 291
  Robert S., 291
  Rev. Robert Sayers, 141
  William R., 291
Shelton, Mrs. John, 163
Shenall, Calvin, 16
Shenandoah Furnace, 177, 180
Shepherd, James H., 5
  R.F., 7
Shores, A.H., 160, 173
  Elize J. Mercer, 292
  Frances H., 292
  Mrs. L.F., 160
  R.K., 160, 176, 177, 183, 220
  R.K. Mill, 179
Short, Mrs. B.B., 223
  J.R., 163
  Mrs. T.B., 179
Shot Tower, 54, 87, 193, 196, 303-305,
Shrader, Archibald, 13
  William, 13
Shriver, Howard, 63, 66-68
Shupe, John, 13, 147
Silcox, R.J., 11
Siloam Methodist Church, 150, 151
Silver, 2
Simmerman (Zimmerman)
  Andrew, 18
  Christopher (Stophel), 18, 131, 1(
  Erhart, 131
  Erhart Sr., 131
  Mrs. E.V., 183
  Geo., 131

INDEX

Simmerman, George W., 291
  John A., 291
  J.P.M., 183, 282
  John P.M., 108, 182, 291
  J.P.M., Jr., 292
  Letitia, 291
  Lizzie, 291
  Mary A.G., 291
  Mary M., 291
  Mary Sanders, 291
  Mary Wiserman, 291
  R.E.L., 183
  R.L., 183, 291
  S.S., 183, 291
  Thos., 131
  Thomas H., 291
  W.A., 291
  W.H., 150
  William, 123, 156
  Mines. 109, 195
Simmerman, R.L. Mill, 179
Simmonson, John P., 268
  Mary A., 268
Singer Manufacturing Co, 181
Sinking Spring Church, 123
Sisk, James, 183
Sisk Mines, 109
Sittle, W.R., 10
Six, Samuel, 183
Sixty-Third Va. Inf., 17
Slagle, George, 13
  George W., 14
  T.G., 20
Slate Springs Methodist Church, 157
Slater, Frank Mill, 179
Sluss family, 126
Smart, David, 16
  William P., 16
Smeltzer, Ferrell, 13
Smith (Smyth), Alexander, 85, 104, 194, 310
  Rev. Adam, 136
  Calvin, 13
  D.A., 164
  Elijah, 164
  E.M., 177
  Frances, 85
  Francis, 89, 155
  George G., 164
  John, 20
  John W., 5, 10
  Rev. J.W., 144
  Larkin, 143
  Margaret, 164
  Mary, 85
  Mary E., 279
  Pleasants, 279
  Richard, 7
  S.R., 177
  William, 5, 13
Smyth Co., 34, 43
Smyth Co. Furnace, 81
Snaveley (Schneberly)
  Ann Lambert, 283
  J.M., 176, 177
  James M., 9
  James Madison, 292
  John C., 283
  Mahala Leedy, 292
  Peter B., 292
  Phillip T.C., 159
  Sallie Kyle Shores, 292
  John, 128
  Thomas S., 11
Snodgrass, Henderson, 5
Snow, Rev. D.A., 159
Soultien, J.W., 18
South Fork Church, 123
South, James F., 20
Southwest Virginia Enterprise, 180
Spanglor (Spangler), Peter, 84, 133
  William H., 20
Spantzler, Daniel, 131
Speedwell, 87, 100, 109, 152, 164
  Furnace, 43, 69, 82, 83 (photo) 84-88, 155
  Iron Works, 87, 88
  Methodist Church, 155
  Mines, 191
  Post Office, 3, 173
  Tract, 86
Spence, (Spense), Hugh, 267
  Jane Ward, 267
  Henry, 13
  J.W., 177
  John W., 158
  Wiley, 13
Spiller, Francis S., 5
  Mrs. Susan, 124, 137
  W.H., 176, 177, 232
Spottswood, Alexander, 1
Spraker (Sprecker), B.F., 164
  Christopher, 133
  Jacob, 8
  Alexander, 13
  Jonas, 7
  Stephen, 13
Spring Creek Church, 123
Springs, Yellow Sulphur, 317
Staley, Alex, 7
  E.P., 182
  Mrs. James, 125
  William R., 20
  E. H. Mill, 179
Stanger, Jacob, 148
  Rev. John, 133, 168, 169
Steel Making, 108

INDEX

Steffey (Stiffy)
  A.M., 154
  Barbara, 278
  E.J., 7
  Emory W., 159
  Franklin, 18
  Henry, 128
  I.J., 10
  John, 128
  L., 7
  Martin, 278
  Michael, 126
  Peter, 8, 128
Stephens, Albert C., 292
  Anna B., 292
  Bethiah, 85
  Catherine, 85
  Charles G., 292
  Henry, 85
  India S. Rogers, 292
  Isabella Longacre, 292
  James, 103, 156
  James C., 292
  James S., 147, 292
  John, 84, 85, 94, 169
  John M., 292
  Joseph, 292
  Joseph B., 292
  Joseph R., 292
  Lawrence, 292
  Lenah A. Saunders, 292
  Maggie F., 292
  Mary A., 292
  William, 85
Stiffey (see Steffey), W.A., 10
Steptoe, John L., 5
  R.D.L., 9
Stern Brothers, 228
  Nathan, 175
Stone, G.B., 182
  Riley, 16
  Samuel, 16
Stoner, Daniel, 296
  Matilda Campbell, 296
Stoner's, 55
Stony Fork, 31
Stony Fork Baptist Church, 163
Stoots, Henry, 147
Stove Factory, 81
Stoves & T.nware, 182
Straw (Stroh) (Stran)
  Leonard, 90, 128
  Mrs. N.M., 183
  W.R. Dr., 181
Street, W.A., 178
Stroup's Branch, 56
Stuart, Mrs. Ellen, 124
  James W., 124
  John D., Dr., 125
  Mrs. Nannie, 124

Stuart, Dr. Walter, 246
  William, 5
  Farm, 120
  & Tuttle, 94
Sudduth, J.M., 162
  & Hershberger, 177
Sullivan, Miss Jennie, 179
  Rev. J.O., 125
Sulphureted Iron Ores, 48
Sult, John, 183
  M.M., 174, 177
  William H., 144
  & Co., 175
  Shrader & Co., 242
Summers, L.P., 105
  Rev. G.W., 256
Summit Baptist Church, 163
Supreme Court of Appeals, 61, 62, 76
Sutherland, John, 20
Sutphin, Elkanet, 8
Swecker, B.F, 292
  Isaac N., 18
  Jacob, 147, 292
  John H.W., 293
  Margaret R. Alford, 292
  Mary E.P. Huddle, 278
  M.P., 177
  Mitchel, 278
  Nancy E.J., 292
  Nancy Jackson, 292
  Robert E., 16, 292, 293
  Robert Lee, 293
  Wendell, 145, 291, 295
Swint, Most Rev. John J., 160
Syfer, Andrew, 131

T

Tailors, 182, 246
Tanners & Curriers, 182
Tany, George, 128
Tarter, Catherine Baker, 293
  Elijah, 157, 293
  James, 18
  Dr. James E., 293
  James H., 20
  J.W., 157
  Lettie V. Gose, 293
  Mary Edith, 293
  Mathias, 141, 149, 272
  Rachel Umbarger, 272
  Susan M., 157
Tate, Anna Randolph, 293
  Charles C., 293
  Elizabeth F. Graham, 293
  James G., 5, 7
  John A., 293
  J.M. Friel, 293
  John M., 293

INDEX

Tate, Lizzie Graham, 293
    Margaret Ma. Randolph, 293
    M.B., 90
    Rebecca C., 293
    Robert C., 17
    William H., 17
    William, 5
Taylor, Bettie Waller, 282
    John M., 282
    Jonathan, 20
    Mrs. Mollie, 256
    Rev., 138
    Robert M., 5
    W.H., 157
Tazewell Street Methodist Church, 143
Tazewell Turnpike, 46
Tazewell & Fancy Gap Turnpike, 158
Telegraph Companies, 182
Temperature Averages, 67, 192, 204
Terry Ben W., 247, 293
    B.W., 215
    Beverly Lacy, 293
    Catharine Robinson, 293
    Emma Wigginton, 293
    Frank Hanson, 239, 293, 318
    John Young, 293
    Kate Waller, 293
    Lizzie Emma, 294
    Thomas W., 293
    William (General), 5, 20, 200, 247, 293
    William Jr., 293
Thomas, C.B., 90
    E.A., Dr., 181
    Jacob, 18
    Rev. J.D., 125
    Lucinda, 145
    Margaret, 145
    & Co., 178
Thompson, Andrew, 158
    Dr. Caleb, 301
    Frances, 142
    James, 17
    William, 169
Thompson Valley Church, 123
Thorn, William S., 7
    Mrs. William S., 121
    W.S., 183
Thornburg, W.J., 11
Tiffert, H.A., 180
Timber, 57, 190
Tipton, R.M., 182
    Mines, 109, 191
Tivis, John, 138
Tobler, Stephen, 8
Toland's Raid, 300
Toncray, Anthony, 105, 106
    James, 106

Toncray, Mary, 106
Toncrays Forge, 105, 106
    Mills, 106
Topham Bros, 177, 240
Town Officers, 215
Trigg, 87
    Daniel, 87
    G.F.S., 136
    John J., 102
    Mary, 87
    E.& Son, 181
    & Johnson, 245
    & King, 102
Trinity Church, 129
Trinity Hall School, 181
Trinkle, Mrs. E.S., 183
Troster, William B., 14
Tucker, 13
Tungry, James, 131
Turner, Marshall, 8
Twenty-Ninth Va. Inf., 7
Tynes, Achilles J., 299
    Molly (Mary Elizabeth), 299-302
    Samuel, 299, 300

U

Umbarger (Umberger)
    A., 150
    Abraham (Col.), 55, 141, 142, 150, 294
    Abraham M., 294
    Alex, 183
    Andrew, 183
    Anna Maria, 294
    Austin, 183
    Brook Morton, 294
    Catherine K., 294, 295
    Charles W., 17
    Charles Wiley, 294
    Clara Virginia, 295
    Caludius Neal, 295
    Crittenden L. G., 294
    Daniel, 183
    David, 141, 142
    David B.L., 294
    Edley, 13
    Edward Harlow, 294
    E.H., 17
    Elizabeth, 150
    Elsie Florence, 295
    Emeline, 295
    Emery P., 294
    Ephriam S., 294
    Everett W., 294
    E.W., 175
    F.T., 150
    George W., 294
    Harvey 11
    Herber S.M., 294
    Henry, 131

INDEX

Umberger, Henry, Jr., 131
 Henry Sr., 131
 Isaac M., 17, 294
 James L., 5
 James, 11, 13
 Jane L, 294
 Rev. J. H., 158
 Johiel F., 150
 John Jr., 131, 141
 John, 131, 142
 John C.A., 294
 John Lattie, 294
 Joseph, 158
 Joseph H., 294
 Rev. K.Y., 135
 Leonard, 129, 131, 141, 145
 Levi, 150, 295
 Lucy E., 294
 Lula May, 294
 Maggie Everett, 294
 Mahala, 295
 Malinda, 145
 Margaret, 294
 Margaret Sophia, 294
 Maria A., 294
 Maria Letitia, 295
 Maria Miller, 294
 Mary, 141
 Mary Cordelia, 295
 Mary F., 294
 Mary Keesling, 294, 295
 Mary Maria, 294
 Mather Marvin, 295
 Michael, 13, 141, 142, 159, 294, 295
 Minnie Bess, 294
 M.L., 183
 Morris Price, 295
 Nancy Cassell, 294
 Nannie M., 294
 Neta Jane, 294
 Olive T.H., 295
 Orpha R., 294
 Philip, 131
 Pucket, 183
 Rachel C., 294
 Robert Shannon, 294
 Rosanna E., 294
 Sallie Allena, 294
 Sarah Elizabeth, 294
 Sarah Eliza Martin, 294
 Simon, 145, 183
 Stephen, 183
 Stephen A., 148
 Stephen B., 294
 Stephen Buchanan, 294
 W.A., 17
 Walter L, 295
 William Albert, 295
 Wm, 11

Undertakers, 182
Union Meeting House, 124
Unity Church, 120
Utt, John, 142

V

Vance, Rev. J.I., 248
Vancourt, R.E., 257
Vaughn, Daniel, 13
 Rev. T.C., 154
 William A., 13, 14
Vaught, A., 139
 Abraham, 295
 Andrew, 138
 D.B., 8, 154
 E., 182
 Edgar Sullins, 295
 Elbert Lee, 295
 Ernest, 295
 Elizabeth Burkett, 296
 Ephraim, 8
 Franklin, 9
 George, 295, 296
 George W., 9
 G.W., 140
 Henry., 133
 Herbert Brown, 295
 H.T., 182
 Jas., 175
 James Edward, 295
 Jefferson M., 295
 J.M., 8
 John M., 296
 John W., 11
 J.Z., 7
 Mary Emma, 295
 Mary Swecker, 295
 Minerva Jane Atkins, 296
 Molly Wampler, 296
 Noah T., 295
 N.T., 7, 20
 Miss Ordelia, 176
 Peter, 14, 296
 Sidney Bays, 295
 Stephen, 9
 Stephen D., 11
 Susan Ida, 295
 William Cameron, 295
 William F., 9
Vermillion, Mrs., 125
Virginia Development Co, 74, 75
Virginia Fire & Marine, 178
Virginia Iron, Coal & Coke Co., 86, 91, 94, 95, 100, 149
Virginia State Ins., 178
Virginia & Statesville Railroad, 63
Virginia Steel Co., 74
Virginia House(Hotel), 177

INDEX

Vogelsong (See Foglesong)
  Carl, 131
  Christian, 131
  Susanna, 131
Volcanic Energy - Treatise by
  Malley, 36-38

W

Wadley, H.G., 215
Waddle, K., 180
Walker, Alexander, 296
  Allen P., 176
  Edward, 123
  Hannah Hinton, 296
  James Alexander, 20, 156, 157, 254, 296
  Sarah A. Poage, 296
Walker's Branch, 151
Walker & Caldwell, 174
Walker's Mountain, 172, 189
Wall, Burrell, 145
Wallace, James, 13
Waller, Mrs. Owens, 163
Waller, W.M., 163
Walls, E.W., 175
Walters, Rev. George I., 160
  James, 18
  J.Y., 183
  John, 97, 146
  John B., 18
  John P., 180
  Michael, 183
  Posy, 183
  William, 20
Walters' Bridge, 209
Walton, Ellen C., 173
  George, 97
  Furnace, 40, 69, 82, 97
  Furnace P.O., 173
  Mines, 109
Wampler (Waumpler) A.A., 11, 182
  Austin, 14, 296
  Christopher, 128
  George, 18, 128
  Isaac A., 11
  J.T., 182
  J., 296
  Joseph, 128
  L.P., 148, 181, 182
  Magdelene, 168
  Michael, 126, 128
  M.M., 182
  Peter, 128
  Polly Jane Vaught, 296
  Rufus M., 148
  Sarah A. Vaught, 296
Wappett, Thomas P., 244
  T.P., 177
Ward Anna G. Groseclose, 296

Ward, Anna Groseclose, 297
  Ballard Preston, 297
  B.E., 140
  Chester, 21
  D.J., 21
  Elizabeth Wilson, 297
  Emily Catharine, 297
  Emmet Brown, 297
  Everet Rush, 13, 183, 297
  George, 316-317, 319
  J.A., 183
  James, 297
  James E., 13, 14, 296
  James Ephraim, 297
  J.E., 175-178
  John, 183
  John Albert, 297
  John D., 13
  Letita Buford, 297
  Letitia Stoner, 296
  Lilbourn Rutledge, 183, 296, 297
  Margaret Knuckles, 297
  Mary, 155
  Mary A. Lambert, 297
  Mary Elizabeth, 297
  Polly Young, 297
  Robt., 183
  Robert N., 148, 149
  S.R., 21
  William, 139, 155, 169, 297
Warden, Thomas, 180
Washington County Formed, 2
Wassum, Joseph, 17
Watchmakers & Jewelers, 182
Waterhouse, Bishop, 145
Watson, Ed., 124
  Dr. Edwin, 269
  Malinda F. Pierce, 269
  S.F., Jr., 183
Wanhop, Polly, 125
Weaver (Weber), George, 133, 128
  Joseph, 18
Welcher, Nathaniel, 120
Welsh, Mary J. Hendricks, 289
  Nicholas L, 289
  Nicholas S., 20
Wenrich, Michael, 128
Western Hotel, 220
Western Union, 182
Wetherly Hosea, 9
Wetzel, George, 131
  N., 131
  Peter, 131
Wharey, Rev. J.M., 122
Wheeler, Samuel B., 17
  Samuel, 103
  Samuel V., 147
  William R., 17, 147
Wheeler's Mills, 103
Whelan, Rt. Rev. Bishop R.V., 160
White, Hezekiah, 271

INDEX

White, Sarah Howerton, 271
White Rock Furnace, 82, 100
    Mountains, 45
White Top Church, 146
Whitlock, Thomas, 103, 104
Whittman (Whitman), Andrew, 131
    A.C., 13
    David, 155
    James W., 13
    Henry, 131, 141, 142, 143
Wigginton, Benjamin, 293
    Harriett B. Scott, 293
Wilderness Road, 194
Wilkerson, Samuel, 9
Wilkinson, James, 90, 102
    S.J., 215
    William, 90
Williams, Andy F., 21
    Burgess, 145
    C.A., 182
    Charles, 18, 145
    "Doc", 154
    Emmett, 163
    Mrs. Frances H., 136
    George H., 215
    Henry, 5
    Jacob, 11
    James E., 5
    James M., 11
    Jane, 145
    John, 9, 11, 113, 183
    Robert P., 102 151, 173
    Samuel B., 5
    Judge Samuel W., 173
    S.J., 146
Willy, Rev., Berned, 128
    Rev. Leonard, 133
Wilson, Albert Basil, 297
    A.S., 11
    Eliza J. Litz, 297
    Rev. G. A., 123
    George W., 11
    J.J.M..20
    J.H., 173
    J.M., 183
    John McIntire, 297
    Laura Ellen, 297
    Margaret Williams, 297
    Mrs. M.S., 256
    Wm.A., 125
    William Anderson, 297
    William Henry, 297
    William S., 125
    William V., 125
    & Kincer, 177
Windle, D.P., 140
Winn, Henry H., 9
    Nicholas W., 148
Winskell, John, 13
Wise, Evelyn Douglas, 314
    Jennings, 314

Wise, John, 314
    John Sergeant, 313
    Henry Alexander, 313
Wiseley, (Weisly, Wisley)
    Albert, 20
    Barbara Anne, 151
    Daniel, 131
    Isaac, 151
    Isaac N., 11
    James P., 11
    Michael, 11
    Michael, Jr., 151
    Michael, Sr., 151
Wissler, J.H, 182
Withers Col, R.E., 252
    R.E. & Co., 178, 181
Wolf, John, 128
Wolfenden, W.C., 175, 177
    Brothers, 240
Wolford (Wholford, Wohlfahrt, Wholford)
    Charles, 13
    G.M., 182
    George M., 21
    Henry, 13
    Jacob, 131
    Louis, 131
Woodson, Rev. C.J., 162
Woolen Mills, 179
Wright, Jno., 183
    Sam'l. F., 175
Wood, James, 9
    Rev. Philip, 125
    R. Raper, 21
Wyatt, Henry, 11
Wyrick (Wayerick, Wairick)
    E.R, 182
    Joseph, 149
    Leonard, 142
    Martin, 131, 142
    Martin Jr., 131
    Nicolas, 131
    Rufus, 134
    William, 18
Wythe County Area, 2, 187
    Boundaries, 2, 25, 172
    Businesses, 174-182
    Constables, 173
    Forges, 8
    Furnaces, 81
    Geological, 26-28, 30, 50-52, 187-188
    Magistrates, 173
    Mining & Manufacturing Co., 39
    Ore Fields, 24
    Officers, 173
    Population, 2, 187
    Post Offices, 2, 3, 173
    Supervisors, 173
    Taxation, 2, 187
    Topography, 187

INDEX

Wythe Furnace, 69
  George, 2
  "Greys", Co. A 4th Va. Inf., 4
  "Greys" - Muster Roll, 5
  Lead & Zinc Mines, 50-54
  Lead & Zinc Co, 177, 180
  Lead Mines, 69
  Mining Co, 180
  Parish (Episcopal), 136
  Speedwell Mining and Manufacturing Co., 86, 90, 95
Wytheville, 2, 60-62, 75, 77, 173, 187, 198(Photo), 201-203
  Baptist Churches, 162
  Dispatch, 239
  Female Seminary, 181
  Foundry, 110
  Foundrys, 109
  German Club, 208
  Ice Factory, 92
  Ice & Dairy Co., 178
  Ins., & Banking Co., 174, 178
  Lithia Springs, 178
  Main Street, 207
  Main Street, 231 (photo)
  Male Academy, 77, 219
  Male College, 182
  Manufactured Goods, 61
  Manufacturing Co., 181
  Marble Works, 244
  Masonic Lodge, 137, 162
  Methodist Church, 143-145
  Population, 2, 78
  Post Office 3, 173
  Presbyterian Churches, 123
  Schools & Churches, 61
  Seminary, 77, 223
  Summer Resort, 200-202
  Watering Co., 94
  Water System, 92
  Woolen & Knitting Mills Co, 178, 179

Y

Yates, Emma R. Kent, 279
  J.A., 21
  John O., 279
Yonce (Yantz, Jantz)
  Catherine, 131
  James A., 11
  John Peter, 128
  Peter, 129, 130
Yost, Casper (Rev.), 139-145, 168, 169, 298
  Euphemia Bickle, 169, 298
  Captain Henry A., 298
  James L., 141-143
  James Lockhart, 298
  L.M., 150
  Nancy Ellen Wygal, 298
  William Lockhart, 298
  W.L., 174
Yost Gun Factory, 169
  Ore Bank, 47

Z

Ziegel, Jacob, 131
Zion, 132
Zion Luth. Ch., 133
Zinc, 63

Special Thanks for Valued Assistance
In Compilation of this Index to
Mesdames Mary B. Kegley,
               Mary O. Osborne, and
               Ruth Otey.

Old Shot Tower at Jackson's Ferry in Wythe County.
From a linoleum block by Conway Smith, 1931.

MAP OF WYTHEVILLE

According to a survey made in pursuance to an Act of the General Assembly of Virginia passed March 6th 1839, and within six months after the passage of said act; and in conformity with ordinances of the Trustees of said Town of 3rd May and 15th July 1839 except with regard to Tenth, Twelfth and North Streets, and 314½ feet of the Southwestern extremity of Monroe Street and the alleys marked c, d, e, f; which streets and alleys, and the intervening lots, numbered 41, 43, 45, 47, 49, 22, 23, 24, 25, & 26, were surveyed and laid off at the same time and have been established as surveyed and marked by an ordinance of said Trustees of the 4th October 1839.

James H. Piper, Surveyor.

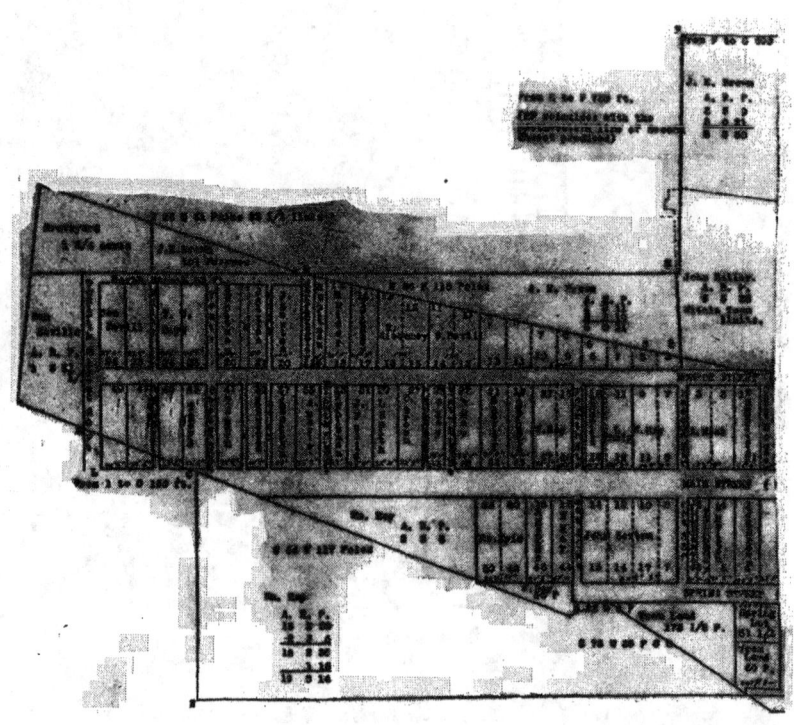

Virginia:

In the Clerks Office of Wythe County Court the 18th day of December 1839.

This map of Wytheville with the certificate annexed was returned to said office and admitted to be recorded.

Teste:
J. P. Matthews, C.C.

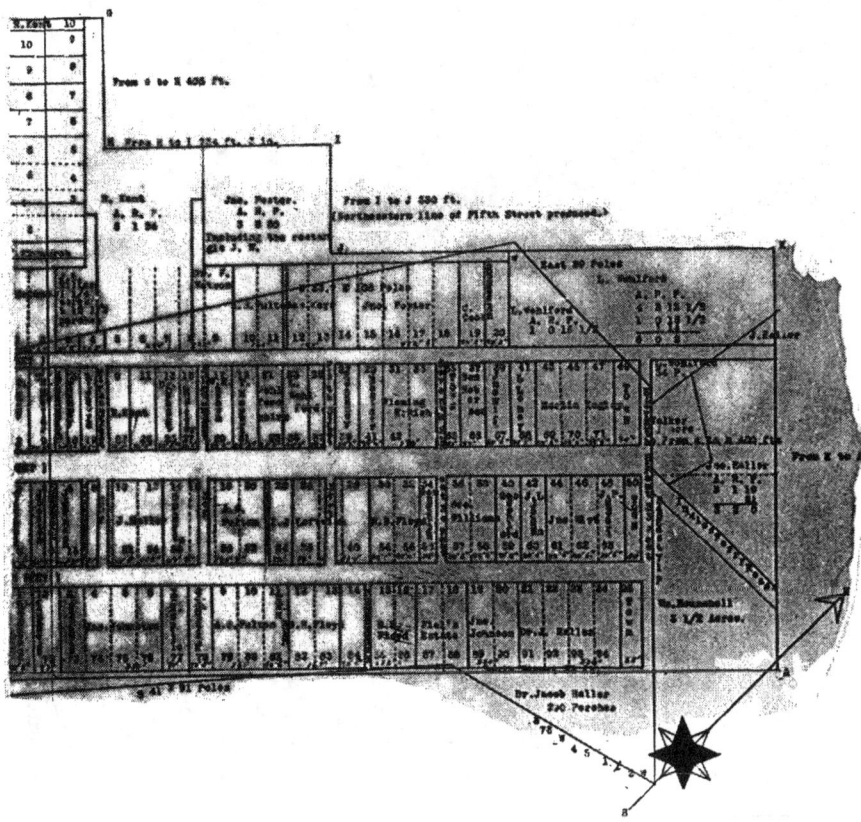

Roanoke Citizens Visit Rural Retreat Cabbage Festival, Ca. - 1910 — The welcome sign is spelled out of cabbages. Notice also the early truck in upper left corner.

www.ingramcontent.com/pod-product-compliance
Lightning Source LLC
Chambersburg PA
CBHW072132220426
43664CB00013B/2223